GAETANO SALVEMINI

Photo courtesy of Instituto Storico della Resistenza in Toscana, Florence, Italy.

GAETANO SALVEMINI

A Biography

Charles Killinger

Italian and Italian American Studies
Spencer M. Di Scala, Series Adviser

Westport, Connecticut
London

Library of Congress Cataloging-in-Publication Data

Killinger, Charles.
    Gaetano Salvemini : a biography / Charles Killinger.
       p.   cm.—(Italian and Italian American studies, ISSN 1530–7263)
    Includes bibliographical references (p.   ).
    ISBN 0–275–96873–1 (alk. paper)
    1. Salvemini, Gaetano, 1873–1957.   2. Anti-fascist movements—Italy.   3. Anti-fascist
movements—United States.   4. Italy—Politics and government—1922–1945.
5. Fascism—Italy—History.   6. Exiles—United States—Biography.   7. Historians—
Italy—Biography.   8. Socialists—Italy—Biography.   I. Title.   II. Series.
DG575.S29K55   2002
945.09′092—dc21   2001036698
[B]

British Library Cataloguing in Publication Data is available.

Library of Congress Catalog Card Number: 2001036698
ISBN: 0–275–96873–1
ISSN: 1530–7263

First published in 2002

Praeger Publishers, 88 Post Road West, Westport, CT 06881
An imprint of Greenwood Publishing Group, Inc.
www.praeger.com

Printed in the United States of America

The paper used in this book complies with the
Permanent Paper Standard issued by the National
Information Standards Organization (Z39.48–1984).

10 9 8 7 6 5 4 3 2 1

To Philip Cannistraro
without whose inspiration, encouragement, and bountiful patience
this story would remain untold

Contents

Foreword

By all accounts, Gaetano Salvemini had an irritating personality. He seemed to go out of his way to be "countercurrent," to cite the title of a Boston journal to which he contributed. Yet time has proved that his positions were frequently correct. As a member of the Italian Socialist Party in the early twentieth century, he championed the cause of universal suffrage, including the vote for women; when World War I broke out, he was a pre-Wilson Wilsonian; and he was one of the first anti-Fascist exiles. When he came to the United States to teach at Harvard University, he created an international controversy that swirled around that venerable institution. In the United States, his prestige made him the natural leader of other exiled Italian professors teaching in the country's top schools—but his activities got him into hot water with the Italian-American community. When Fascism fell, he severely criticized American policy toward Italy, getting into trouble with the government.

Charles Killinger's biography fully explains Salvemini's thinking and his actions and finally does Salvemini justice. This is a considerable accomplishment because the ideologies that Salvemini criticized during his lifetime took their revenge in the historical literature. The biographies of this important figure are rare, not well informed, and frequently biased. Killinger has based his conclusions on a thorough analysis of the historical literature and of original documents that other biographers have not utilized. His biography has the great merit not only of considering Salvemini's role in Italy but also of illuminating the American phase of his career. At the same time, Killinger examines Salvemini's impact without political preconceptions. By judging the persistent gadfly in a serene manner, he has given Salvemini his proper place in the historiography of the twentieth century.

Spencer M. Di Scala
Series Adviser

Acknowledgments

Many people have assisted and encouraged me over the two decades it took to bring this work to life. To them I owe much more than the recognition I give here. Among them, several made indispensable contributions. Philip Cannistraro guided the scholarship and writing and gave unselfishly of his time, effort, and expertise. Spencer Di Scala and Peter Kracht selected the manuscript for the Praeger series on Italian and Italian American Studies and graciously lent advice. Michele and Helen Cantarella provided inspiration and insight, extensive documentation, and poignant memories and welcomed my wife and me as members of their family. H. James Burgwyn furnished expert advice on a number of chapters, as did Alexander De Grand. Glenn Hayden accomplished the tedious job of editing with commitment, precision, and levity, while Judith Antonelli saved numerous errors by her expert copyediting. Luciana Capaccioli generously and doggedly acquired a photograph under difficult conditions, while Daniela and Gabriele Giuffrida and Antonio Cervone provided invaluable advice in translating. Pam Killinger, through her love and support, made this work possible.

A number of scholars have contributed their collective wisdom to this work as well. Among them are Earl Beck, Neal Betten, Thomas Campbell, William Rogers, Lawrence Cunningham, John P. Diggins, H. Stuart Hughes, Norman Kogan, Jerre Mangione, Joel Blatt, A. William Salomone, Arthur Schlesinger, Jr., and Max Salvadori. James E. Miller and Louis J. Nigro provided scholarship, friendship, shelter, and timely advice. Support from the National Endowment for the Humanities, Valencia Community College, Florida State

University (Florence), and the Patricia Havill Whalen Endowed Chair proved indispensable.

Of the many accommodating librarians, researchers, and archivists who assisted me, several deserve special mention. Barbara Meloni and William Whalen of the Harvard University Archives and Jessica Owaroff of the Houghton Reading Room generously placed the Harvard Salvemini resources at my disposal. Sally Marks at the National Archives was extremely helpful, as were Ronald Bulatoff at the Hoover Institution Archives and Rudolph J. Vecoli, Director of the Immigration History Research Center at the University of Minnesota. Judi DeLisle, Paulette Smith, and Donna Carver of the Raymer Maguire Learning Resources Center at Valencia Community College contributed untiring expertise in locating and acquiring bibliographical resources. Special thanks are also in order to the staffs of the Archivio Centrale dello Stato in Rome, the Istituto Storico della Resistenza in Toscana, and the Biblioteca Nazionale in Florence, Italy, the Biblioteca Comunale in Molfetta, Italy, the Library of Congress, the Franklin D. Roosevelt Library, the University of Virginia, the Vassar College Library, the New York Public Library, the Tamiment Collection at the New York University, the International Ladies' Garment Workers Union Archives, and the Hoover Institution on War, Revolution, and Peace (Stanford University). Extremely important were the contributions of Stephen Tanner, who provided valuable documentary materials from World War II, and Carmine and Gabriella Spadavecchia and Giovanni De Gennaro, longtime Salvemini loyalists from Molfetta, who provided hospitality and negotiated graciously on my behalf in Bari province. Special thanks go to the former Mayor of Molfetta for honoring this work.

Friends and colleagues in Florida have encouraged me from the beginning of the project. Especially supportive through the years were Monte Finkelstein, Mark Goldman, Dick Crepeau, Ivan Applebaum, Jared Graber, Nancy Jay, Tom Byrnes, Ron Nelson, David Skinner, David Smith, Paul Gianini, and James Gollatscheck. In addition to moral support, expert proofreading services were cheerfully furnished by David Fear, Michael Germaine, William Prentiss, Don Tighe, Chauncey Parker, and Nicole Cournoyer of Praeger. Thanks are due, as well, to Cindy Dupree, Cheryl Williams, and the Word Processing Staff at Valencia; Pam Oliver, who provided timely word processing assistance in the early stages; and Bob Browning, Bela Horvath and Valerie Conlan, Bill and Terry Osborne, Dick and Carol Endicott, and Walter and Gertrude Lemann, dear friends all. Natasha, Katrina, and Isabella were, as always, occasional typists and indispensable companions. In spite of the assistance of all, I am solely responsible for the interpretations and for any errors contained herein.

Abbreviations

Abbreviations are used in note sections throughout.

ACS	Archivio Centrale dello Stato (Rome)
AG	Aldo Garosci
AG, *Sdf*	Aldo Garosci, *Storia dei fuorusciti* (Bari, 1953)
AG, *VCR*	Aldo Garosci, *Vita di Carlo Rosselli* (Florence, 1973)
AGG	Alessandro Galante Garrone
AGh	Archangelo Ghisleri
AGL	*Archivio Giustizia e Libertà*, ISRT
AGS	*Archivio Gaetano Salvemini*, ISRT
AHR	*American Historical Review*
AK	Anna Kuliscioff
AnC	*Luigi Antonini Collection*, ILGWU
APID	Atti del Parlamento Italiano. Discussioni (Rome)
ASMAE, *SAP*	Archivio Storico del Ministero degli Affari Esteri (Rome), *Serie Affari Politici*
AsP	*Max Ascoli Papers*, Manuscript Collections, Boston University
AsP"M"	*Max Ascoli Papers*, "Mazzini Society" file
AsP"S"	*Max Ascoli Papers*, "Salvemini" file
AsP"T"	Max Ascoli Papers, "Tarchiani" file
AT	Alberto Tarchiani
AWS	A. William Salomone

AWS, *IGE*	A. William Salomone, *Italy in the Giolittian Era* (Philadelphia, 1960)
b.	busta (box)
BB	Bernard Berenson
BCM	Biblioteca Comunale, Molfetta
BF, *L'U*	Beniamino Finocchiaro, ed., *L'Unità di Gaetano Salvemini* (Venice, 1958)
BM	Benito Mussolini
BM, *OO*	*Opere Omnia di Benito Mussolini*, Edoardo and Duilio Susmel, eds., 37 volumes (Florence, 1951–1963)
BoP	*Roberto Bolaffio Papers* (ISRT, Florence)
BP	*Ray Stannard Baker Papers*, Library of Congress
CaP	*Anthony Capraro Papers*, IHRC
Cart 1912	Gaetano Salvemini, *Carteggio 1912–1914*, Enzo Tagliacozzo, ed. (Rome, 1984)
Cart 1914	Gaetano Salvemini, *Carteggio, 1914–1920*, Enzo Tagliacozzo, ed. (Rome, 1984)
Cart 1921	Gaetano Salvemini, *Carteggio, 1921–1926*, Enzo Tagliacozzo, ed. (Rome, 1985)
CD, *ME*	Charles F. Delzell, *Mussolini's Enemies* (New York, 1974)
CdS	Il Corriere della Sera (Milan)
CG	Consul General of Italy
CK	Charles Killinger
ClP	*Edigio Clemente Papers*, IHRC
CoP	*James B. Conant Papers*, HA
CP	*Michele Cantarella Papers* (Leeds, Massachusetts)
CPa	Constantine Panunzio
CPC	Casellario politico centrale
CPC	MI, DPGS, *Casellario politico centrale*, ACS
CPC"S"	*CPC*, "Salvemini" file
CR	Carlo Rosselli
CS	*Critica Sociale* (Milan)
DDI	*I documenti diplomatici Italiani*, Ministèro degli affari esteri (Rome)
DeBC	*Lauro de Bosis Collection*, Houghton
DeC, *Sal*	Gaspare De Caro, *Gaetano Salvemini* (Turin, 1970)
DeF	Renzo De Felice
DeF, *il fas* I	Renzo De Felice, *Mussolini il fascista*, Vol. I (*La conquista del potere, 1921–1925*) (Turin, 1966)

DeF, *il fas* II	Renzo De Felice, *Mussolini il fascista*, Vol. II (*L'organizzazione dello stato fascista, 1925–1929*) (Turin, 1968)
DeF, *il riv*	Renzo De Felice, *Mussolini il rivoluzionario, 1883–1920* (Turin, 1965)
DeG	Alexander De Grand
DeG, *IL*	Alexander De Grand, *The Italian Left in the Twentieth Century* (Bloomington, 1989)
DeV	Antonio De Viti De Marco
DGPS	Direzione Generale Pubblica Sicurezza
DiS	Spencer Di Scala
DiS, *DIS*	Spencer Di Scala, *Dilemmas of Italian Socialism* (Amherst, Massachusetts, 1980)
EBB	Ernesta Bittanti Battisti
ED	Elsa Dallolio
EG	Eugenio Garin
EG, *Sal*	Eugenio Garin et al., *Gaetano Salvemini* (Bari, 1959)
ER	Ernesto Rossi
ES	Ernesto Sestan
ES, *ACGS*	Ernesto Sestan, ed., *Atti del Convegno sul Gaetano Salvemini*, Florence, November 8–10, 1975 (Milan, 1977)
ET	Enzo Tagliacozzo
ET, *Sal*	Enzo Tagliacozzo, *Gaetano Salvemini nel cinquantennio liberale* (Florence, 1959)
f., sf.	*fascicolo, sottofascicolo* (file, subfile)
FBI"S"	Federal Bureau of Investigation, U.S. Department of Justice (Washington), "Salvemini" file
FDR	Franklin Delano Roosevelt
FDRL	FDR Library, National Archives and Records Service (Hyde Park, New York)
FeF	Guido Ferrando file, VL
FlP	*Henry P. Fletcher Papers*, LC
FNB	*Papers of the Foreign Nationalities Branch*, OSS
FrP	*Felix Frankfurter Papers*, General Correspondence, Box 101, Manuscript Division, LC
FRUS	*Foreign Relations of the United States*
FS	Fernande Salvemini
FT	Filippo Turati
GA	Gaetano Arfé

GA, *SSI*	Gaetano Arfé, *Storia del socialismo italiano (1892–1926)* (Turin, 1965)
GC, *Sal*	Gaetano Cingari, ed., *Gaetano Salvemini tra politica e storia* (Bari, 1986)
GD	Giuseppe Donati
GF	Giustino Fortunato
GG	Giovanni Gentile
GGM	Gian Giacomo Migone
GiS	Gino Speranza
GLR	Giuseppe Lombardo Radice
GP	Giuseppe Prezzolini
GS	Gaetano Salvemini
GS, *FDI*	Gaetano Salvemini, *The Fascist Dictatorship in Italy* (New York, 1967, reprinted from the 1927 edition)
GS, *IFAUS*	Gaetano Salvemini, *Italian Fascist Activities in the United States*, P. V. Cannistraro, ed. (Staten Island, 1977)
GS, *Ld'A 44*	Gaetano Salvemini, *Lettere dall'America 1944/1946*, Alberto Merola, ed. (Bari, 1967)
GS, *Ld'A 47*	Gaetano Salvemini, *Lettere dall'America 1947/1949*, Alberto Merola, ed. (Bari, 1968)
GS, *Mem*	Gaetano Salvemini, *Memorie di un fuoruscito*, Gaetano Arfé, ed. (Milan, 1973)
GS, *MD*	Gaetano Salvemini, *Mussolini Diplomatico* (Paris, 1932)
GS, "MeS"	Gaetano Salvemini, "Memorie e soliloqui" in *Opere* VI, 2
GS, "NM"	Gaetano Salvemini, "Non Mollare," in Gaetano Salvemini, Ernesto Rossi, and Piero Calamandrei, *Non Mollare* (Florence, 1955)
GS, *Opere*	*Opere di Gaetano Salvemini* 19 vols. (Milan, 1961–1974)
GSL	Salvemini letters, HoL
GSP	Salvemini publications, WL
GSS	Salvemini Scrapbooks, HoL
GS, *SSQM*	Gaetano Salvemini, *Scritti sulla questione meridionale (1896–1955)* (Turin, 1958)
GuP	*Humbert Gualtieri Papers*, IHRC
HA	Harvard University Archives, Harvard University (Cambridge, Massachusetts)
HC	Hélène Cantarella
HM	Harriet Marple
HoL	Houghton Library, Harvard University (Cambridge, Massachusetts)

HSH	H. Stuart Hughes
IHRC	Immigration History Research Center, University of Minnesota (St. Paul, Minnesota)
ILGWU	International Ladies' Garment Workers' Union Archives (Cornell University, Ithaca, New York)
IP	*Harold L. Ickes Papers*, Manuscript Division, LC
ISML, *a Prato*	Istituto Nazionale per la Storia del Movimento di Liberazione in Italia (Milan), *Fondo Carlo a Prato*, b. 4, f. 1
ISRT	Istituto Storico della Resistenza in Toscana (Florence)
JB, *IFP*	H. James Burgwyn, *Italian Foreign Policy in the Interwar Period, 1918–1940* (Westport, Connecticut, 1997)
JB, *LMV*	H. James Burgwyn, *The Legend of the Mutilated Victory* (Westport, Connecticut, 1993)
JD, *MFas*	John P. Diggins, *Mussolini and Fascism* (Princeton, New Jersey, 1972)
JM	James E. Miller
JM, *EMP*	James E. Miller, *From Elite to Mass Politics* (Kent, Ohio, 1990)
JM, *USI*	James E. Miller, *The United States and Italy, 1940–1950* (Chapel Hill, North Carolina, 1986)
L&M, *IFP*	C. J. Lowe and F. Marzari, *Italian Foreign Policy, 1870–1940* (London, 1975)
LA	Luigi Albertini
LaGP	*Papers of Fiorello LaGuardia*, Municipal Archives (New York)
LAn	Luigi Antonini
LaP	Giorgio La Piana
LaPP	*Giorgio La Piana Papers*, Andover-Harvard Theological Library (Cambridge, Massachusetts)
LB, *Sal*	Lelio Basso, *Gaetano Salvemini, socialista e meridionalista* (Manduria, 1959)
LBi	Leonida Bissolati
LC	Library of Congress (Washington, DC)
LeP	*Herbert H. Lehman Papers*, School of International Affairs, Columbia University (New York)
LongP	*Breckinridge Long Papers*, Manuscript Division, LC
LS	Luigi Salvatorelli
L'U	*L'Unità* (Florence)
MA	Max Ascoli
MacP	*Papers of Archibald MacLeish*, Manuscript Division, LC
MAE	Ministero degli Affari Esteri, ACS

MB	Mary Berenson
MC	Michele Cantarella
MCP	Ministero della Cultura Popolare, Rome
MCP	*Papers, Ministero della Cultura Popolare*, ACS
MG	*Manchester Guardian*
MI	Ministero dall'Interno, Rome
MI, "Mazzini"	MI, DGPS, categoria G-1, f. 948, "Società Mazzini"
MLS, *Sal*	Massimo L. Salvadori, *Gaetano Salvemini* (Turin, 1973)
MoP	*Papers of Henry Morgenthau, Jr.*, FDRL
MP	ISRT, AGL, Fondo "Mazzini Society"
MS	Max Salvadori
n.	number
NA	National Archives of the United States (Washington, DC)
NK	Norman Kogan
NR	Nello Rosselli
NRep	*New Republic*
NT	Nicola Tranfaglia
NYHT	*New York Herald Tribune*
NYPL	New York Public Library
NYT	*The New York Times*
OFF	Office of Facts and Figures, OWI
ONI	Office of Naval Intelligence
OSS	Office of Strategic Services, Washington, DC
OWI	Office of War Information
PaP	*Constantine Panunzio Papers*, Hoover Institution on War, Revolution and Peace (Stanford, California)
PC	Philip V. Cannistraro
Pd'I	*Il Popolo d'Italia* (Milan)
PG	Piero Gobetti
PoP	*Charles Poletti Papers*, LeP
PPF	President's Personal File, FDRL
PRO, FO	Public Record Office, Foreign Office, Great Britain, Group 371 (London)
PiC	Piero Calamandrei
PiC, "IlM"	Piero Calamandrei, "Il Manganello, la cultura e la giustizia," in Gaetano Salvemini, Ernesto Rossi, and Piero Calamandrei, *Non Mollare* (Florence, 1955)
PS	Pietro Silva

PSaF	President's Safe File, FDRL
PSeF	President's Secretary's File, FDRL
Pusey	Nathan Pusey Library, Harvard University (Cambridge, Massachusetts)
PV	Pasquale Villari
PWB	Psychological Warfare Branch (RG 59, NA)
QGL	*Quaderni di Giustizia e Libertà* (Paris)
QP	*George Quilici Papers*, IHRC
RB	Roberto Bolaffio
RC	Rafaele Colapietra
RF	Bruno Roselli file, VL
RG 44	Record Group 44, Records of the Bureau of Intelligence, OWI, NA
RG 59	Record Group 59, General Records, U.S. Department of State, NA
RG 84	Record Group 84, Records of the State Department Foreign Service Posts, NA
RG 165	Records of the War Department General and Special Staffs, NA
RG 208	Record Group 208, Records of the OWI, NA.
RG 218	Records of the Combined Chiefs of Staff, Records of the U.S. Joint Chiefs of Staff, NA
RG 226	Records of the OSS, NA
RG 331	Records of the Allied Control Commission (Italy), NA
RP	Randolfo Pacciardi
RV	Roberto Vivarelli
SAC	Special (FBI) Agent in Charge
SI	Interview with Arthur M. Schlesinger, Jr., December 1, 1994, New York City
SPD	*Segretaria Particolare del Duce*, ACS
SPD, CR"S"	*Segretaria Particolare del Duce, carteggio Riservato*, b. 45, "Salvemini," ACS
STDS	Special Tribunal for the Defense of the State
S-W, *ILF*	Christopher Seton-Watson, *Italy from Liberalism to Fascism, 1870–1925* (London, 1967)
TP	*Alberto Tarchiani Papers*, ISRT, AGL
UGM	Ugo Guido Mondolfo
UO	Ugo Ojetti
USOC	U.S. Office of Censorship
VaP	*Girolamo Valenti Papers*, Tamiment Collection, New York University Libraries

VL	Manuscript Section, Vassar College Library (Poughkeepsie, New York)
WaP	*Edwin Watson Papers*, Manuscript Department, University Archives, University of Virginia (Charlottesville, Virginia)
WL	Widener Library, Harvard University (Cambridge, Massachusetts)
WLA	Robert F. Wagner Labor Archives, Tamiment Collection, New York University Libraries
WWP	*Woodrow Wilson Papers*, Library of Congress
Z-B	Umberto Zanotti-Bianco

GAETANO
SALVEMINI

Introduction

The voyage from Paris on the steamer *France* afforded Gaetano Salvemini an opportunity to reflect on his fifty-three years as historian and political activist. When he arrived in New York harbor in January 1927, somehow the New World represented hope. It was not the same hope shared by millions of his southern Italian countrymen who had fled poverty and arrived in steerage class via Ellis Island; his was the hope of political freedom and the chance to resume his profession. It was also the hope that he would find support in his struggle against Fascism and those who had driven him out of his native Italy.

Nonetheless, he could not erase the awful memory of Blackshirt thugs abruptly terminating his academic career at the University of Florence. Nor could he forget his arrest, his trial and imprisonment, and, worse, the revocation of his citizenship. Benito Mussolini had deprived him of the royalties from his books, his only remaining source of income. Seventeen months before, he had escaped into exile and managed to live hand-to-mouth among friends in England and France. Now he looked forward to an extended lecture tour in the United States that would produce some income and provide professional contacts. More important to him still, he hoped to build an anti-Fascist political organization that would enlist the American public and the great power of the U.S. government in the campaign to topple the Fascist dictatorship in Italy. This ambition is what someone later would refer to as "the campaign of one man against a regime."

Little had come easily to him in those fifty-three years, yet he drew strength from his past triumphs. He had overcome the confines of poverty and provincialism to become a respected and influential professor. He had endured bouts of depression and unspeakable personal tragedy, although not without scars. He had survived numerous political battles with nationalists, liberals, and socialists. He had fought and lived through the war on the Austrian front and had survived life as a political prisoner. And he knew in his more confident moments that he would, somehow, outlast Fascism.

A *New York Times* reporter met him and took notes for a story that would appear the next day. Salvemini was a short, bespectacled, paunchy man whose rather large head rested atop broad shoulders. His sudden, widening smile revealed a prominent set of teeth in the midst of his black mustache and pointed beard. His broad, bald forehead seemed to make his dark eyes smaller. Their glimmer conveyed kindness, intelligence, and a purposeful intensity.

At the first inquiry, the professor launched a bitter attack of the Fascist regime with disarming animation. The March on Rome had been a "military coup d'état against democratic institutions. . . . The Fascist Party was *not* the Italian nation, but only an unscrupulous armed minority." With Salvemini there was no such thing as a routine interview.[1]

Also waiting for his arrival was an agent who had arranged a lecture tour of the United States.[2] Almost everyone the agent had consulted described Salvemini in superlatives, and many conveyed a sense of almost apostolic admiration. Salvemini was known for his magnetism, his humanism, his integrity, and his instinctive enthusiasm. His students idealized him as a Socrates; among them he had shaped a new generation of Italian scholars and political activists.

Salvemini had a reputation as one of the most courageous political figures of his age. He had championed social and political reform as a party activist, a political commentator, and a public officeholder. He never separated scholarship from political activity, either by instinct or by choice. The archetypal intellectual in politics, he believed that actions should conform to ideas. As a result, his life became something of a prism through which were refracted all the major themes of modern Italian history.

Still, there was another dimension. In spite of the mythical imagery that often enveloped him, he was quintessentially human, a man whose flaws and strengths were so manifest as to be readily apparent to all but the most biased. He was by reputation combative and sternly moralistic, a heretic against all orthodoxy. With little patience for political compromise, his social and political analysis was always irreverent, often indignant and caustic. Such audacity had produced scores of adversaries. In addressing the political issues of the day, he spared neither leaders nor groups and inevitably clashed with most of them. One of his best friends described him as essentially a nonconformist. Another saw him as an anti-Machiavellian figure. Others saw him as a malcontent.

However, neither the agent nor anyone else would truly know Salvemini until they comprehended his anti-Fascism. Mussolini's seizure of power in 1922 had radically reoriented Salvemini's life. It was said that the Fascists were anti-Salvemini before he became an anti-Fascist. His vehement protests against the infamous 1924 murder of socialist deputy Giacomo Matteotti had sealed his fate. Fascist authorities considered public remonstrations from a man of Salvemini's stature incompatible with the solidification of the Fascist state, so they silenced him. As a result, Salvemini became to Fascists and anti-Fascists alike a symbol of the early Italian resistance. Now his name was synonymous with the growing resistance movement in exile. By the time he arrived in New York harbor, anti-Fascism had consumed him.

Hence, Salvemini introduced to America the first significant campaign against Fascism, and it would soon be said that he was "one man against a regime." He did not yet know the American people, but he had an instinctive reliance on their democratic values. He was scheduled to address several prestigious groups, and thus he hoped to make some contact that would give him an entree into the government, at least someone at the Department of State whose support he could enlist. His greatest optimism, however, was reserved for the Italian-American clubs, where he was certain that he could rally support for the cause of liberty.

He did not know that each appearance would eventually be shadowed by Fascist agents and that some would provoke near riots, giving testimony to the growing polarization within Italian-American communities. Nor did he know that friends would arrange for him to teach at a prestigious American university, where he would renew his career and remain for nearly fifteen years, from 1933 to 1947. Not even his most ardent admirers anticipated that he would eventually be known as the conscience of the anti-Fascist movement in exile, that this role would attract the scrutiny of American intelligence agents—making him the simultaneous target of two governments—or that his one-man campaign against Fascism would become legendary. His many partisan skirmishes assured that few who knew him would remain neutral, for he was, in virtually every instance, a man who aroused a passionate response. Few would be surprised that his life, the history he wrote, and his political campaigns have provided a rich and contentious source of debate that has long outlived him.

NOTES

1. *NYT*, January 6, 1927; *L'Italia del Popolo*, January 7, 1927. Emphasis added.
2. GS, *Mem*, 59.

Photograph from *A Need to Testify*, copyright ©1984 by Iris Origo, reproduced by permission of Harcourt, Inc.

Chapter 1

The Making of an Intellectual

This extraordinary *élan vital* that everyone who had the good fortune of knowing Salvemini saw in his gestures, in his works, in his eyes, this lust for life, this explosion of vitality, of protest, of revolt—all this he wanted and knew how to transform into lucid reason. How extremely difficult, particularly for a temperament as violent and rebellious as his.

Franco Venturi, 1957[1]

As Gaetano Salvemini faced the panel of three examiners on an afternoon in early September 1890, he knew that his future was in peril. The examiners held the power to award twenty academic scholarships to the Istituto di Studi Superiori of Florence. He had scored well enough on his senior examinations to qualify, and the scholarship offered, among other things, an alternative to the priesthood, a career that he might be expected to choose as a bright youngster of his impoverished background.

As soon as the examiners began their questioning, the cultural contrast materialized. Steeped in the Renaissance, they predicated questions on broad classical assumptions. His answers revealed the limitations of a Jesuit seminary education in a town without even a library. As the inquiry progressed, a professor of Italian literature probed: "What is the core of the legend of Aeneas?"

Salvemini froze.

"I do not understand the question. If you would like a summary of the *Aeneid* I can do that; if you would like me to translate the *Aeneid* from the original, I believe that I can do that. But where I come from, nobody taught me that legends have cores."

One laughed. They then dismissed him. Fortunately, he had prepared a good essay, and the candor of his response had helped. That afternoon, he was awarded the last of twenty scholarships. Years later, he mused that the committee that day had saved him from a religious vocation and at the same time had saved the bishop many headaches.[2]

The scholarship interview revealed a great deal about Salvemini. While his answers betrayed a lack of academic preparation, they also reflected a form of pragmatism, skepticism, and directness not unknown in the South even among boys his age. He had learned early lessons from the fishermen and agricultural laborers of his hometown, "a repugnance for abstraction and a respect for concrete reality." This outlook never changed.

Later, as a mature historian and political observer, he would retain the candor evident in the interview as well as a distrust of theory and abstraction. His skepticism in part explains his later rejection of ideology and his many campaigns to expose the overblown political rhetoric of Italian leaders. Moreover, in spite of a long and cosmopolitan career, he would claim to remain all his life essentially a villager from Apulia.

Gaetano Salvemini was born on September 8, 1873, in the southern Italian town of Molfetta, the oldest child of debt-ridden smallholders in an extended family of peasants and fishermen. It was, in his own words, a family "rich in children and poor in money."[3] Influences of family—but, more important, of southern, provincial poverty—would mark him indelibly and shape his enduring values.

His mother, Emanuela Turtur, descended from a family of maritime traders who, he suspected, had somehow been involved in smuggling. She was a woman of intelligence, vitality, and strong character whose influence on her first son was manifest. She had read to him extensively, building to the *Divine Comedy* by the time he was five. She maintained an active interest in politics and was a staunch supporter of the Italian Left, although, like other Italian women, she was ineligible to vote.[4]

His father, Ilarione Salvemini, was a *carabiniere* (national policeman) of moderate education who earned an extra twenty-five lire per month as a part-time teacher. More significant, Ilarione had volunteered for battle with Giuseppe Garibaldi's Red Shirts in their military campaign that liberated southern Italy from the oppression of the Spanish Bourbons. The elder Salvemini revered his former guerrilla commander, who, together with the republican patriot Giuseppe Mazzini and others, represented the radical democratic tradition of the Risorgimento, the unification movement. The Italian state was barely a decade old at Gaetano's birth, and so the radical heritage was embedded in his psyche from infancy.

The mystique of Garibaldi's rebellion still lived in southern memory. Southerners remained convinced that the Risorgimento had been stolen from them by alien northern forces and by a monarch to whom they felt little loyalty. By the time Gaetano enrolled in the *liceo* (high school), that sense of betrayal had been perpetuated by several decades of misgovernment in which corrupt bargains had solidified the power of northern business interests in tandem with southern landholders. As a result, the young man was nurtured in the tradition of southern radicalism.

At the same time, Salvemini was subjected to the counterbalancing forces of southern conservatism. His uncle, Mauro Giovanni Salvemini, was a priest with strong Bourbon loyalties, an obstinate man whose personality outshone his intelligence. Don Mauro held a genuine affection for Gaetano that the boy reciprocated. He taught the youngster the rudiments of Latin, took him to the seminary school, and tried to influence him toward the priesthood. Although Mauro's religious influence had little lasting effect, Gaetano claimed to have inherited his uncle's obstinacy.

Don Mauro also engaged him in his earliest political-historical discussions. One evening, when he was nine years old, he was vividly recounting to his family his history teacher's enthusiastic description of Garibaldi's expedition against the Bourbons. Growing more and more agitated, his uncle exploded in invective, labeling King Victor Emmanuel an "usurper" and furiously denouncing both teacher and pupil as "Epicureans" surely bound for hell.[5] Thus, from childhood Gaetano "breathed the air of politics," caught between Bourbonist and Garibaldino, the Right and the Left, expressing under one roof the major political groupings of the day. Gaetano soon found his place as a partisan of the radical republican tradition.

The other family member to whom he became most strongly attached was his oldest sister, Camilla. He remembered her as beautiful, energetic, and quite intelligent. Like her mother, however, Camilla's opportunities would be severely limited. Italian girls from poor families, particularly those in the South, rarely acquired formal education in that era, and she had been forced to drop out of school after the second grade to take care of her younger brothers. Whenever he thought of the unrecognized heroism of millions of Italian women he remembered Camilla.

Ilarione and Emanuela Salvemini lived in the town of Molfetta, in the tradition of southern peasant families who for centuries had chosen an urban setting for protection from roving bands of brigands. Gaetano was born in a modest, multistory, attached house, one room wide, built of heavy stones quarried nearby. As a child, he could gaze through the back window across the small Piazza Mazzini to the Adriatic Sea. Across the same piazza stood the arched gate affording entrance through the walls of the ancient city, its narrow, regular streets revealing a pattern of early medieval urban design. Above the stone

walls, he saw the Romanesque Duomo of the Church of San Corrado, its cupo-
las and towers defining the northern skyline. A left turn out his front door took
him toward the town's center, to the Piazza Garibaldi and the seminary he
would later attend. A turn to the right led him to the wharf, a mere 100 yards
from his doorstep. Molfetta was a town of only 25,000 inhabitants, but it
opened to a wider world that intrigued Salvemini even as a boy of seven.

Molfetta lay on the railroad between Foggia and Brindisi, on the level shore-
line bounded on the inland side by the red soil of the plain of Apulia and then the
first foothills of the Apennine range. The plain and the sea had shaped the
town's character. The land was covered with just enough natural vegetation to
graze herds of sheep in the winter months. Even so, the summers were so hot
and dry that farmers desperately depended on the irrigation provided by the
great Apulian aqueduct that distributed water from the Apennine watershed.
The region's wheat crop had long fed the population. Romanesque cathedrals
dominated many of its towns, and the surrounding countryside had more than
its share of castles, both town and country revealing the earlier dominance of
Norman and Hohenstaufen dynasties.

In the late 1870s, Molfetta enjoyed sudden prosperity when the infestation
of French vineyards forced the French to import Italian wine. The new prosperity enabled the Salvemini family to acquire a modest plot of land and a small
house in town. Molfetta's farmers rededicated extensive acreage to vineyards,
and the export of wine attracted so many new industries that the chamber of
commerce began to refer to Molfetta, hyperbolically, as "the Manchester of
Apulia." In 1887, however, the Italian government touched off a trade war with
France, thrusting the region into an economic crisis that ruined many farmers
and businessmen and permanently altered the town's class structure. Salvemini
would remember that his family suffered and was often hungry. Indeed, the
poverty the fourteen-year-old boy experienced would shape his values.

Some owners of the large estates—the *latifondisti*—had actually prospered,
but even they were routinely victimized by the whims of the agricultural market. For smallholders like the Salvemini family, as for the many agricultural laborers, farming had always been a struggle. Methods remained archaic, as
evidenced by the continuing use of the donkey-powered *bindolo*, a device derived from the Egyptian system of wheels, gears, and buckets that raised water
from wells to cisterns. This primitive irrigation technique mirrored a culture
that had changed as little as its agricultural technology.

The Adriatic Sea afforded a livelihood for about one-third of Molfetta's
adult males, who fished its waters using methods similarly unchanged for five
centuries. The sea also furnished a link to the outside world, and thus in a way
Molfetta, unlike many inland villages, was as much a Mediterranean as an Italian town. It also had produced a small, fluid, and modest middle class that expanded and contracted with the fortunes of the town and added a degree of

diversity to an otherwise homogeneous population. This maritime commercial activity provided the sole cosmopolitan influence on the young Salvemini, whose life was otherwise insulated in a near-medieval provincialism.

The other source of interest in Molfetta was religious, particularly because the cathedrals had generated clerical activity when Molfetta had been made an episcopal see. The domes of the old Cathedral of San Corrado dominated the harbor and remained a source of local pride. Others considered the "new" cathedral of Santa Maria Assunta far more elegant; thus, growing up in Molfetta meant listening to trivial provincial arguments, as locals endlessly quarreled over whose church had the most beautiful bell tower.

Petty aesthetic arguments aside, reality for Molfetta's fishermen and farmers was its suffocating poverty. Trade and political interests had drawn Molfetta toward the larger provincial capital of Bari, sixteen miles down the coast. Just as Bari had overshadowed it, Molfetta had always been obscured within the broader history of southern Italy. Most often that had meant exploitation by a long list of foreigners, the latest of whom were the Piedmontese. It was difficult for Apulian peasants to escape the weight of 2,500 years of subjugation.

For a poor young man, even of intelligence and energy, opportunities in Molfetta were limited. Social rigidity meant that Gaetano could aspire, at best, to become a shopkeeper or to pursue a career in the army or the priesthood. If he failed, he could farm or fish, as his ancestors had done. Even at an early age he sensed the hopelessness that had forced thousands like him to flee Apulia in desperation for the more promising shores of North America.[6]

Because his parents could not afford to pay to educate their children, they enrolled Gaetano in a seminary grammar school and *liceo,* where he completed his secondary education. It was a culturally restrictive environment in which he had to dress like a priest, a "horrible" place where he remembered having lost eight precious years. Fond memories were few: his Greek tutor; Euclidean geometry, with its miraculous clarity and order; and a liberal priest whose eloquent lectures on the French Revolution aroused his interest. Although he recalled learning little of lasting value at the *liceo*, he could not forget developing a "desperate hunger for reading," more or less to fill the void. Without a library in Molfetta, and too poor to buy books, he read what friends would lend him. Among Don Mauro's books he discovered a Latin translation of the Bible, where he found inspiration in the "moral power and poetic beauty" of the Psalms, Lamentations, and Prophets. He also managed to read a copy of Alessandro Manzoni's *I Promessi Sposi*, the most inspirational work of the early Italian nationalist movement. This reading, sporadic as it was, would have to pass for an education.

Most ardently he consumed the romantic novels of Jules Verne, who provided for many young Italians a fictional escape from drudgery, and whom Salvemini remembered as the "*maestro* of good moral education for me and many of my generation." What particularly drew him to Verne's novels was the dramatic confrontation between the lone protagonist, equipped only with intelligence and character, and the hostile elements. He was, even as an adolescent, already developing a fundamental sense of moral combativeness.

In his last year at the *liceo*, the priest who taught him history helped him to understand the need to generalize from discrete facts and to interpret causal relationships. At times this seemed simplistic to Gaetano, as in the instance when the priest taught, "Jesus Christ was born and the Roman Empire fell." The point was made, however. The same priest introduced him to the writings of the literary historian Francesco De Sanctis, from whom Salvemini began to learn to hypothesize and to construct logical arguments. Although he would remain ever cautious of excessive generalization, he had begun to develop his critical thinking skills and to cultivate some degree of scholarly perspective. This inclination toward simple, clear, linear thought would dominate his intellectual processes all his life.[7]

While still in the *liceo*, Salvemini encountered local Italian politics for the first time in the person of Molfetta opposition deputy Matteo Imbriani, who was in town campaigning against the policies of Prime Minister Francesco Crispi. In these first stormy years of the Crispi era, Imbriani blamed the trade war and subsequent economic crisis on Crispi's protectionism. To Salvemini, whose family was suffering from the depression of 1887, the relationship between national economic policy and his own life began to take on a sense of reality.

He soon became an ardent supporter of Imbriani, attending campaign rallies and supporting his positions: social-economic reform for the South; irredentism, the quest for "unredeemed" territory still in Austrian hands, a movement that Imbriani had initiated; and opposition to Italy's commitment to the Triple Alliance with Austria and Germany. Although Salvemini would later rethink his position on irredentism, he remained a critic of the Triple Alliance and a strong advocate of tariff reform and other policies designed to stimulate progress in the South. It is not surprising that Salvemini's first political consciousness was parochial in focus; what would lend this advocacy of southern interests broader significance was the growing attention it soon won in the context of Italian national politics.[8]

Salvemini left Molfetta and everything familiar in the fall of 1890 to travel to Florence for the scholarship interview. He had never ventured so far. As he bade his family good-bye, he could not have known how much his life would change. When he reached his destination, weary from the train ride but buoyed by nervous expectation of the interview, excitement built. Florence, with its imposing tradition, opened a new world that would become Salvemini's second home. The broad, new Piazza Vittorio Emanuele symbolized a dynamism that would carry the city beyond its heritage as a museum of Renaissance art. However, as large as Florence appeared, it did not overwhelm. Its gaslights and horse-drawn carriages lent an aura of fin de siècle charm, and its narrow cobblestone streets beckoned to him from one spacious piazza to the next. Florence promised unlimited opportunity. Its maze of streets assaulted his curiosity, and its colorful past lured his intellect.

Nevertheless, in spite of its gentle allure, Florence exposed this poor, southern, Catholic boy of seventeen to cultural forces and personal challenges profoundly different from anything he had ever known. Florence would test his limits and would provide him both his greatest success and his first real failure.

The first evidence of culture shock struck Salvemini in Professor Bartolomeo Malfatti's geography class. After a few introductory remarks, Malfatti began to lecture on the theory of evolution. Diligently taking notes, Salvemini became more and more incredulous. Finally, his parochial sensitivities could bear no more. Fully intending to be heard, he murmured, "Therefore we are descended from worms."

The kind old professor stopped, turned, and responded quietly, "What would be wrong with that?"

A profound disquiet settled inside Gaetano. "Good-bye, Adam and Eve speaking Latin in the Garden of Eden!"

Moving to Latin literature class, dwelling on his exchange with Malfatti, Salvemini was startled by the entrance of Professor Gaetano Trezza, the very examiner who had asked him about the "core" of the *Aeneid*! He quickly found himself transfixed by the surprisingly human stories of Caesar, Cicero, and Horace. Through the classics, Professor Trezza would expose him to a range of emotional experiences he had never known.

As the intensity of the first day's classes subsided, Salvemini began to realize the degree of academic adjustment he faced. With the exception of the assistance of several teachers at the *liceo*, he was a self-made student. He soon discovered that the "intellectual baggage" he carried with him to Florence was "full of gaps" and that most of his classmates seemed better prepared than he, but the self-doubts, magnified by the experiences on the first day of classes, would soon be forgotten. He found the professors of the Istituto a fascinating lot who would not only challenge all of his assumptions but would immerse him in a wondrous new world as well.

Reeling from his sudden introduction to the rational and secular environment of higher education, he occupied himself in those first days in Florence with the practical matters of survival in this strange place. He would mull over the theory of evolution another day; for the moment he needed to find a restaurant he could afford.

Being among the poorest students at the Istituto, he had to live on his sixty-lire-per-month scholarship. While most of his classmates were receiving financial support from their parents, he was sending fifteen lire each month to his family. Out of the balance, he had to pay rent and buy books, supplies, and meals. He could have a glass of milk and a piece of bread for breakfast for three pennies, and a lunch of beans, bread, and salami at a tavern for six pennies. Most of the rest he spent on dinners, usually with new friends at a small trattoria. He remembered thinking, "It may be easy for someone who is well fed to say 'Man does not live by bread alone'; but in reality, without bread, man does not live." To supplement the scholarship, he took a job tutoring a boy in Latin at about one lira per hour, the price of a dinner.[9]

Salvemini began to regard his professors as *galantuomini*, men of honor and courage, inside the classroom and out. The peculiarly Italian concept of the *galantuomo* was one that the priests had forced him to recite since his first day in primary school at the seminary but that had been largely devoid of meaning. Now, for the first time, the concept took human form. His professors were men of strong convictions, committed to the pursuit and expression of truth. They taught a very simple but reliable rule: "Think clearly, then speak just as clearly."[10]

Salvemini's prose style, first developed at the Istituto, would always reflect this simple directness that reinforced his Apulian pragmatism. Later, he recalled fondly that these professors had taught him to be a man. All through his life, he would apply this standard of the *galantuomo* to those he met. Close friends remembered that Salvemini could pay no higher compliment than to say, "That is an honest man."[11]

The memories of this first, "marvelous year" were blemished only by the lingering recollection of his class in theoretical philosophy. The professor, Augusto Conti, reinforced Salvemini's fundamental aversion to abstract discussion. He also found that the professor's arrogance clashed with his own awakening ego.[12]

Among all the faculty of the Istituto, Pasquale Villari exerted the greatest influence on Salvemini's life. He remembered Villari as a witty and lively little man who spoke behind a green lectern that revealed only his prominent forehead. He "set fire—and what a fire! . . . Officially he taught medieval and modern history. In reality he taught us not to be mummies."

It was Villari who exposed Salvemini to the works of the great thinkers: Dante, Machiavelli, Hegel, Montesquieu, and others. Under Villari's tutelage, Salvemini developed a strong affinity for the principles of the Enlightenment, particularly those related to individual rights and the social contract. It was through Villari that Salvemini's political values broadened from the provincialism of their Apulian base to encompass a more secular and universal perspective, and through Villari his political views—to this point largely instinctive—became more rational. These values would remain solid political guideposts for him through the vicissitudes of the new century.[13]

Villari was a classical, nineteenth-century liberal, historian, political activist, and, like Imbriani, a champion of the Mezzogiorno (South). He was a unique blend of iconoclast and traditionalist in a nation and a profession that were changing. His pedagogical technique was fresh. In contrast to the more conventional approach of many of the other faculty, Villari attacked his subject, testing the assumptions of the traditional culture and hurling his students into "the open, threatening, beguiling sea of historical interpretation."[14]

Villari's emphasis on historical interpretation proved invaluable. The 1890s were an era in which the field of history was infused with a new scientific objectivism and positivism, primarily from the German universities, meaning that historians were consciously rejecting any tendency to make moral or political judgments.

Accordingly, in Italy historians were forswearing the heroic interpretation of the Risorgimento in favor of detached criticism. Objecting to this "drying out of historical studies and the impoverishment of political thought," Villari demanded that moral interpretation not be abandoned. Yet he did not ignore the new methodology, teaching that careful reliance on documentation and reasoned logic could lead ultimately to great moral truths. Most notably, he taught that the historian should be actively engaged in political and social causes. Long after he had forgotten the specific content of his courses, it was the model of Pasquale Villari that shaped Salvemini's own self-image of the role of professor as political militant.[15]

Gradually Villari became a mentor to the young Salvemini. They would take long walks, during which they would discuss academic as well as personal issues. The student did not always agree with his tutor, arguing, for instance, that a desire for private property is not an innate human characteristic, an indication that Salvemini was developing views that would depart from nineteenth-century liberalism. Although the professor had once told him that he was "hardheaded," Salvemini nonetheless seemed to enjoy advocating an opposing view. Years later, a teacher himself, Salvemini would encounter similar students: "The harder the heads, the more they pleased me."[16]

In his 1949 tributes to his professors, Salvemini reserved his warmest praise for Cesare Paoli, professor of paleography. Every time Salvemini thought of him, his eyes misted. He believed Paoli was among the best at his craft in all of Europe, albeit undiscovered. Paoli led the class, line by line, through the most beautiful of passages, from Carolingian minuscule through manuscripts of the eleventh century. As the course progressed, Salvemini would go to Paoli's house in the evening, and by the light of a kerosene lamp would read aloud his assignments to the professor as the Paoli children romped in the adjoining room. Thus did the young man, far from his family, bond to the older: "Cesare Paoli was for me a father."[17]

Many of Salvemini's classmates at the Istituto came from more prosperous urban areas in central and northern Italy. Their affluent families had provided them with a cosmopolitan cultural experience and more polished manners. They seemed serious, calm, and reserved to Salvemini. Laughter always came easily to him; as a result, they thought him excessively boisterous. Moreover, his excited gestures and rough-hewn ways confirmed their stereotype of the southern *contadino* (peasant) and subjected him to ridicule. Several who befriended him actually made a project of "breaking him in," and gradually his manners became more acceptable. One of them, intending it as a compliment, said to Salvemini, "It seems impossible that you are a southerner."[18]

Under the stress of adjustment to university life, his southern culture and his self-image under assault, Salvemini found refuge in the small Apulian neighborhood in Florence. His uncle had given him a letter of introduction to an acquaintance, a civil engineer named Minervini. It was through the Minervini family that he met most of the neighbors who welcomed him, fed him, and treated him as a *paesano* and a young scholar, a fellow Apulian who was on the road to success. Soon he began to retreat each Sunday to "Little Apulia" to visit his new friends.

After only a few visits he found that he was drawn to Signor Minervini's oldest daughter. Maria Minervini, four years younger than he, was a small peasant girl, with raven hair and ruddy complexion, remembered more for her good will and strong spirit than for either culture or natural beauty. Gaetano read the sweetness in her "splendid deep black eyes," and as she blossomed into womanhood, he found her captivating.[19] Though not formally educated, Maria was sensible, devoted, and willing to make sacrifices for her family. She reminded him of his sister, who had so selflessly devoted much of her attention to his younger brothers. Within months, he came to terms with the romantic attraction he felt and asked her family to approve their betrothal. It would be a long engagement, particularly because of her youth and his inability to provide an income.

The relationship with Maria also represented a reaffirmation of his Apulian identity and of the traditional values he had absorbed in Molfetta. He would not aspire to being something he was not, and certainly he had chosen a partner in Maria who would provide him with what he expected from marriage.

At the end of this first, difficult year at the Istituto, the financial pressure eased because the faculty voted unanimously to increase his scholarship to ninety lire. That afforded him enough to balance his budget without tutoring and still have money left to buy a few books, purchase several round-trip train tickets to Molfetta, and occasionally attend the theater.

Although Salvemini was not aware of it, Professor Paoli had in this first year discovered his enormous potential and had begun to prepare him for the history profession. At the end of classes, Paoli handed him a lengthy book on medieval

French episcopal elections and asked him to write a review of it. Gaetano, of course, knew nothing of the subject, but he accepted the challenge. Upon returning to Florence in the fall of his second year, he consulted the French history collection at the Biblioteca Nazionale to broaden his understanding. When he submitted the completed review, Paoli published it in his journal, *Archivio Storico*, and paid Salvemini eighteen lire. Gaetano was ecstatic. "In those days of formidable appetites, our currency was not the lira but the beefsteak. Eighteen lire, thirty-six beefsteaks. Not to mention the honor!" Of all the reviews, articles, and books he would later publish, none pleased him more than the first.[20]

Salvemini's second year at the Istituto proved much happier as he began to develop some real friendships, including the Mondolfo brothers and Cesare Battisti. They gathered in the evenings to discuss the new scientific ideas of positivism and socialism, and the discussions led to a kind of bonding that they would maintain through many difficult years. The friend who influenced him most was Ernesta Bittanti.

He met Bittanti while studying for examinations in his second year. He remembered her large brown eyes, her beautiful complexion, and her sweet voice. His relationship with "Ernestina" deepened, but it never became amorous. Many years later, he considered this fortunate: "If a friendship between a boy and a girl remains nonphysical, it is lifted by a feeling of tenderness. It may suddenly become love; but if it doesn't, it remains in the soul, a source of poetry for life. This is better."[21]

Ernesta Bittanti became a mentor. He thought her much better educated than he, and the respect he felt for her explains both their personal relationship and her intellectual influence. She introduced Salvemini to important new ideas and to Russian romanticism and other literary genres. More important, she gave him copies of the *Rivista di filosofia scientifica*, the major Italian positivist journal.

Positivism was attracting a growing audience among the intellectuals of the 1890s. The positivists' rejection of metaphysical interpretations appealed to Salvemini's pragmatic instincts, as did their emphasis on thorough documentation. Partly under Ernesta's influence, he "devoured" the writings of the positivists who published regularly in the *Rivista*. The idealist philosophers dismissed positivism as something other than philosophy, and Salvemini tended to agree, since this was the first "philosophical" reading he appreciated. Although Salvemini did not become a positivist, he did draw upon the methodology of focusing on observable phenomena, that is to say, "facts," in preference to abstract argument.[22]

The intellectual and political turbulence that stirred Florence in the 1890s reflected equivalent disturbances throughout Italian society. This decade, marked by intense political activity, was at the same time critical in shaping Salvemini's ideas. Italy was governed in turn by Francesco Crispi, Antonio di Rudinì, Gen-

eral Luigi Pelloux, and, in a first brief taste of power, Giovanni Giolitti. These
governments not only continued the tradition of *trasformismo* (a system of
building coalitions by trading political influence), they also developed a reputation for scandal, economic failure, repression, and foreign adventurism.

The crises that emerged on a variety of fronts aroused Salvemini's passion
for politics. Italian nationalists clamored for the "unredeemed land" in the
Trentino, Trieste, the Istrian peninsula, and the Dalmatian coast, and they advocated the colonization of North Africa, a quest that culminated in Italy's disastrous and humiliating defeat in Ethiopia. Crispi's tariff increases intensified
rural suffering, produced violent protest, and undermined relations with
France. An extended bank scandal implicated members of Parliament as well
as Crispi and Giolitti themselves. In Sicily, starving, landless peasants lashed
out at symbols of authority in a massive uprising. These dramatic developments
polarized the Italian population, creating greater popular distrust and thus a fertile climate for socialist organizers. The young Salvemini would struggle to
find a place amid the turbulence.

Socialists had won sporadic support in diverse sectors of Italian society in
the 1880s: some industrial crafts guilds, the Milanese Workers' Party, a handful
of deputies, and sympathizers among republicans, radical priests, and rural in-
surrectionists. Although anarchism had passed its apogee, it remained a powerful force. The formation of the Italian Socialist Party (PSI) in 1892 and the
spread of domestic protest and violence prompted the governments of Crispi
and Pelloux to impose a system of political repression. The socialists actually
gained strength in response to the pressure, the PSI claiming fifteen seats in the
Chamber of Deputies by 1895.

The PSI had recruited a strong student contingent, including many of
Salvemini's friends, among them Ernesta and the group that met regularly in
the evenings at her house. Devotees of Karl Marx and the Italian Marxist Antonio Labriola, they read and discussed articles from Filippo Turati's *Critica
Sociale*, the leading socialist review of the day. Salvemini remembered the enthusiasm of their sessions. "At this time in Italy, everyone was becoming a socialist.... And in the evenings we would solve all social problems with so much
zeal that the landlord threatened to evict 'Karl Marx and his congregation' if we
did not lower our voices."[23] The ardor of these sessions inspired Salvemini to
read more sociology and economics and more Marxist interpretations. In the
spring of 1893, two of Marx's books awakened him from his "dogmatic slum-
ber" and converted him to historical materialism and to the theory of the class
movement.[24]

On Sundays, instead of going to "Little Apulia," he now went with his
friends to the suburbs to speak to local union meetings, explaining the ideas of
Marx and Labriola to the workers themselves. Soon he began teaching a class
on the history of Florence at the People's University. "The Socialist Party,"

Salvemini recalled, "was the tree in the shade of which we dreamed the purest dreams of our youth."[25]

The political activism of Salvemini and his young socialist friends led them to several public demonstrations against the Crispi government, which had become anathema to the Italian Left. Because of the Sicilian unrest, the police watched demonstrations closely even in Florence. An anti-Crispi rally in the Piazza Vittorio Emanuele brought him into his first confrontation with authority. He joined a crowd, chanting in unison with them to the point that he became hoarse. Then in the winter of 1895, as the campaign against Crispi gained momentum, he and his friends demonstrated at the National Arena, shouting, "Viva la libertà!" and "Down with the Crispi!"[26]

This initiation into socialist activism was the beginning of Salvemini's long commitment to radical reform. However, given the stubbornness of intellect that Villari had observed, it was unlikely that the young man would adopt Marxist ideology. What had drawn him to socialism, apart from the enthusiasm of his friends, was not its ideology but its promise to solve social problems. "Marxist doctrine is a marvelous potion to awaken sleeping souls," he observed ruefully as he looked back on his introduction to socialism. "But if you abuse it, it will dull your mind."[27]

Though rejecting doctrinaire Marxism, Salvemini remained a socialist, like many others. In the process he started to develop his own form of historical analysis that included elements of materialism, positivism, and socialism. He also tried to shape the PSI by maintaining active membership, though on his own terms, until differences on fundamental issues eventually drove him out. It would prove to be a stormy relationship, particularly because he was determined to force the party to address the suffrage issue and the "problem" of the South.[28]

The "scientific" approach of Salvemini's friends contrasted dramatically with the university faculty's perspective. Villari and the others—none of whom were socialists—knew quite well that these students were actively involved in the socialist movement. For once, Villari was not altogether pleased with his protégé. He used to say about Salvemini, with a sense of paternal irony, "We sowed the seeds of a beautiful plant and weeds came up."[29] However, neither Villari nor any of the other faculty attempted to discourage the students' political activities. Villari maintained his affection for Salvemini and continued to work closely with him. His assistance would soon be needed more than ever.

In January 1894, Salvemini encountered a setback. Three years of academic and personal stress had subjected the twenty-year-old to a greater burden than he could carry. As he moved toward completion of his university work, he suffered what was described as a "nervous breakdown." Although information is sketchy, it appears that he was overcome by severe depression to the point that he even contemplated suicide. Villari intervened, lending him money and prescribing complete rest among friends, including Carlo Placci, who lived in the Tuscan countryside.[30] It was the first indication of a depression that would recur with some regularity over the next decade, undermining Salvemini's political and intellectual activities.

Placci's influence proved helpful. A wealthy aristocrat in his early thirties, he had many influential friends, including the American art critic Bernard Berenson and a group of British intellectuals. Although Placci's circle of sophisticates observed Salvemini's peasant mannerisms with curiosity, they took a sincere interest in helping him. Eventually he would learn to move comfortably among the English radicals, such as John Maynard Keynes, Bertrand Russell, and other Fabian socialists and Labour Party activists.[31]

After his respite with Placci, Salvemini had recovered sufficiently to complete his academic work. Moreover, his scholarly achievements were beginning to win attention within the university. To complete his degree, he finished his graduate thesis on social conflict in thirteenth-century Florence. After a summer at the monastery at Verna, overlooking the chalky Tuscan hills north of Arezzo, Salvemini returned to Florence in the fall of 1895 to begin graduate studies, concentrating in medieval history.

On the strength of his superb examination results and promising manuscript, his professors encouraged him to pursue an academic career. However, as promising a future as he might have, his immediate employment prospects looked bleak. The only certainty was that he would have to leave the security of the university environment, and possibly his fiancée as well, in search of a job, probably in a provincial secondary school. Then, in the summer of 1895, Salvemini learned of an opportunity to teach in a *ginnasio* (junior high school) in Palermo, Sicily. Without other solid offers, he accepted a position teaching Latin to eleven-year-olds. It was a dismal situation. He earned a paltry 116 lire per month, a mere 25 percent raise from his scholarship stipend at the university. In frustration, he complained to Placci: "This teacher, who is supposed to educate our children . . . , how will he buy some books and not appear in the streets dressed as a ragamuffin?"[32]

Not only did the academic setting prove uninspiring, but Salvemini found Palermo devoid of research materials of the sort that Florence had provided. Teaching out of his field also frustrated him, but he compensated by writing and engaging his colleagues in political discussions, proposing socialism as a remedy for their lowly status. This experience with the struggles of secondary education in turn-of-the-century Italy convinced him of the need for an organized movement among teachers.

Meanwhile, in late October, Salvemini went home to Molfetta for a visit, sensing family problems that needed the attention of the eldest son. What he found upset him beyond his expectations. His father had fallen so deeply into debt that he faced the loss of the family home. Shaken by the sense of failure, he had become completely noncommunicative. Gaetano's mother, in a desperate attempt to fend off bankruptcy and foreclosure, had concocted a scheme to defraud the family's creditors. It involved shifting assets and liabilities to Gaetano, which of course required his consent. The plan not only offended the son's sense of right and wrong but threatened to make him "a proletarian for the rest of my sweet life."[33]

A violent argument ensued, and four days after his arrival, Gaetano left home, frustrated and let down. He felt alienated from the world of his childhood and yet guilty because of his inability to save his family from debt. This internal conflict once again brought on depression, "a profound moral prostration such as I have never suffered." From Palermo, he wrote to Placci, "The solution, as I see it, ... demonstrates ... the ingenuity of my mother. But is it moral? ... Am I to become a thief? ... and what would my Maria say?"[34]

This episode dramatically revealed the contrast between the two worlds in which the young Salvemini lived. As he tried to reconcile one with the other, this personal crisis forced the issue. The process was painful. He had now become a man of education and of middle-class standards. Some have questioned the sincerity of his subsequent claims to have remained essentially an Apulian peasant, but they confuse personal development and politics.[35] Personally, he had begun to accept a more cosmopolitan outlook engendered by his years in Florence. This said, however, he would never turn his back on the political needs of the land of his birth.

His experience in Florence reinforced his own predilection toward moralism that had been evident even in adolescence. Just as he had escaped with Jules Verne into the world of the lone hero doing battle against ominous forces, so he would now find himself in that same forsaken position. He had learned from Villari, Paoli, and the other *galantuomini* at the university that life was a struggle between good and evil. Now that he was leaving the security of their world, emerging from adolescence, he found life threatening. Villari perhaps had the strongest sense of the troubles Salvemini would face. Expressing his misgivings at his student's volatile temperament, Villari remarked, "That young man is good and honest, but he will end up badly."[36]

The year Salvemini spent in Sicily provided him with an important laboratory for the development of his political views, particularly the role of the Socialist Party in the South. This became his most original contribution to Italian political thought. He learned valuable lessons from contemporary Sicilian life and developed an appreciation for the island's unique political culture: profound antigovernment attitudes, the tradition of peasant insurrection, and the agitation of workers' groups, all of which had intensified since the violence and repression of 1892–1893. In that confrontation, government troops had killed ninety-two peasants, and Prime Minister Crispi, a Sicilian, had declared martial law and dispatched 50,000 troops to Sicily. Crispi had believed that he was combating an organized socialist revolution when, in fact, it had been a largely spontaneous protest against economic conditions. As a result, Crispi, with the support of Parliament, dissolved the Socialist Party.

Although martial law had ended before Salvemini arrived in Sicily, he found lingering hostility toward the national government. While teaching Latin in Palermo, he discovered surprising support for socialism. The founding of a new Marxist historical review in Palermo excited him, and he was impressed by the depth of Sicilian resentment over the duty on grain, which kept wholesale prices high at the expense of the poor. Many of his students had begun to accept socialist ideas, a phenomenon he indirectly encouraged by criticizing the mistakes of conservative leaders and explaining socialist theory. He had spoken at length to a well-informed young socialist activist connected to the *fasci siciliani*, the peasant leagues, and he had heard of a boy of eleven who had been arrested and jailed as a "dangerous anarchist." Salvemini found this youthful activism as promising as the repercussions were threatening.

He was particularly interested in the Sicilian Separatists and was surprised to find that the strongest potential for revolutionary activity actually came from this middle-class group, which supported the separation of Sicily from the Italian kingdom. He soon began to blend Sicilian influences and his experiences in Molfetta into his emerging concept of southern socialism.[37]

In spite of his interest in these signs of political awakening in Sicily, Salvemini was quite anxious to leave the dismal situation at the *ginnasio*. Isolated in Palermo, he hoped to find a job teaching history in Florence. In the fall of 1896, he transferred to a *liceo* in Faenza, a town in the Emilia Romagna region, about 120 miles northeast of Florence, convenient enough to allow regular visits to his friends at the university.[38]

Curiously, the move north to Faenza only intensified Salvemini's interest in southern politics, and he recalled that he "in truth remained always in southern Italy."[39] As an active member of the Socialist Party, he began to express his disappointment in the party's direction, particularly the tendency of the PSI leadership to ignore southern peasant issues while favoring northern urban workers. It was in this context that Salvemini joined the socialist debate, thereby launching his career of more than sixty years as a political polemicist. He began by writing Marxist interpretations of Italian society, published primarily in Turati's *Critica Sociale* and in the PSI's official newspaper, *Avanti!* Enthusiastic about the new socialist party in Molfetta, he offered to write propaganda pamphlets in dialect for use in recruiting workers and peasants. At the same time, he insisted that the Molfetta group maintain its socialist principles and warned them of a "raid" on their party by radicals and anarchists. This was a reflection of the contests that raged within the European socialist parties, but it also foreshadowed the moralism and rigidity Salvemini would always apply to politics. He employed the same detailed, meticulous approach he had used in Molfetta to analyze the growing socialist movement in Sicily.[40]

In the last months of 1896, when he was newly situated in Faenza, the young history teacher continued his Marxist awakening. Influenced by the works of Marx and Labriola, he composed a Marxist analysis of his hometown that would catapult him into national politics. He sent the article to Turati, who welcomed it enthusiastically: "We are still lacking intelligent and discerning positivist studies, and your work is a true model of such quality." Turati apologized that he had removed an intemperate phrase (describing southern socialist students as "rogues"), perhaps the earliest expression of a dilemma with which Salvemini would learn to cope—that is, the need to rectify political polemic with history.[41]

When Salvemini received his March 1 issue of *Critica*, he found the first of three installments of "Un commune dell'Italia meridionale: Molfetta," attributed to "Un travet" (a penpusher), a pseudonym he used to protect his teaching job. The series was an extended description of the town's population, designed to provide the kind of practical analysis a socialist organizer would find useful. As such, it was an open rejection of the "theoretical discussions" found in journals and at party congresses, consistent with his method and fresh to the readers of *Critica*.

Molfetta did not fit neatly into a Marxist scheme, because its class structure lacked the classic urban workforce. In a sense Molfetta would become a model for his concept of southern communal socialism. He was convinced that the *braccianti*, the day laborers who harvested grapes, olives, and almonds for 1.25 lire per day, constituted the "authentic proletariat." The southern agricultural proletariat, uniquely concentrated in urban centers, would provide the Socialist Party with "the lever to lift the future." He was convinced that the inevitable concentration of wealth would destroy the small landholders and artisans, thus hastening the ultimate collapse of capitalism.[42] Salvemini's attempt to apply Marxist analysis to this semirural town environment, however, left him vulnerable to criticism from orthodox Marxists, who would accuse him of failing to understand the differences between traditional crafts and modern industry.[43]

Salvemini's use of a pseudonym did not prevent socialists from finding out about this forceful, candid new voice. Vilfredo Pareto, influential professor of political economy at the University of Lausanne, wrote to Placci: "Your friend certainly seems to me to have a fixation on the class movement! If it rains, it will be because of the class movement!"[44] Pareto understood his enthusiasm for Italian socialism. "It was a happy time," Salvemini remembered, "when the communist society was preparing for its automatic arrival in the lap of capitalist society, thanks to the concentration of wealth and the political rise of the industrial proletariat." He sensed a historical destiny, "just as the Christians of the first generation were certain of arriving soon in the Kingdom of God."[45]

In the midst of socialist rhapsody, Salvemini put the finishing touches on his first book, *La dignità cavalleresca nel Commune di Firenze*, developed from his graduate thesis. In the first scholarly study of the institutions of Florentine knighthood, Salvemini explained the erosion of the once important codes of chivalry to "meaningless . . . decoration, devoid of any significance whatsoever." The book marked a transition in his thought as well. The detailed study of medieval law reflected the training of Paoli and Villari; the social-economic interpretation revealed the new influence of positivism and socialism.[46]

When Salvemini moved to Faenza, he received a letter from Ernesta Bittanti explaining her plans to marry Cesare Battisti, another of his friends from Florence. If he was stunned, as he might have been, his letter of congratulations showed not a hint of jealousy, only excitement. He had now been engaged to Maria for six years. Yet there is an undertone of regret, as if he felt that the old circle of friends had now been broken and their youth was slipping away.

While he taught at Faenza, Salvemini's historical writing won national recognition when the prestigious Lincei Academy awarded him a prize of 1,500 lire for *La dignità cavalleresca*. Although he considered using the money to support postgraduate study in Germany, he decided instead that he could finally afford to marry Maria.[47]

Salvemini's students would remember his enthusiasm; he, in turn, observed that his teaching was going "full sail" and that his students "adored" him. He counseled and befriended them as they toiled in the library, and on Sundays they walked together in the country. When he challenged them, generating "fermentation in the minds of all," they reciprocated. He felt that most had begun to think independently, to challenge the status quo. "If the marquis Alfieri (Senator) knew how I am preparing the destruction of the status quo that he holds so dear, he would have me imprisoned." Salvemini believed, perhaps naively, that if the Ministry of Public Instruction tried to fire him for his views, all of his students would rebel on his behalf. Reflecting on his influence, he boasted playfully: "If I stay in Faenza another two years, all of the Romagna will be socialist."[48]

At the close of the spring academic term in Faenza, Salvemini traveled to Molfetta to see his family for the last time before his wedding to Maria. It was a bittersweet reunion. His Uncle Mauro had died, depriving his family of his meager financial contribution and his distraught father of needed moral support. He found his family in even more desperate financial condition than when he had last seen them. The creditors were like vultures, "nibbling at the guts." The bankers were preparing to auction the last of the family's ancestral fields. Somehow this face-to-face confrontation with the terrible reality of bankruptcy intensified his sense of personal struggle and his preoccupation with monetary problems, so evident in his correspondence in this period.[49]

The more he thought about the obligation of family life, particularly in light of his financial struggles, the more he began to worry. This anxiety provoked yet another episode of depression, as he told Placci: "I spent the last days of my bachelorhood in a deplorable state: I cried, I didn't eat, didn't sleep, in short, it was awful. I don't know how many times I repeated to myself the same long word: responsibility."[50] In retrospect, his psychological frailty makes more remarkable his ability to endure the perilous challenges that awaited him.

In the midst of this anguish, Salvemini immersed himself in political activities, a foreshadowing of a pattern that would repeat itself in time of even greater stress. Unable to afford the expenses of travel, he declined Turati's invitation to attend the PSI Congress in Bologna and satisfied himself with the politics of Molfetta. "At the congress," he wrote Turati, dramatizing his plight, "take comfort in the thought that at that very moment one more of the lower middle class is disappearing from the face of the earth; in fact, nine more of the lower middle class, because . . . there are nine [Salvemini] children."[51] At no point is there a more dramatic link between his private life and his politics.

He described to Turati the movement he found among the town's radical petite bourgeoisie and socialist peasantry, and the great potential for revolution. He pled with Turati to send a PSI representative to assist him, preferably Andrea Costa, the former anarchist who had in 1882 been the first socialist elected to the Chamber of Deputies. Salvemini tried to convince Costa to address the local socialist organization in Molfetta, at one point admitting to his pseudonym after Costa disagreed with the analysis of Molfetta published in *Critica Sociale* by "Un Travet." However, Costa, who had used his influence to link the socialist movement to the urban workforce rather than to the peasantry, remained unconvinced.[52]

In Molfetta in August 1897, Salvemini married Maria Minervini. He was twenty-four, she twenty-one. The prenuptial anxiety behind him, he found a personal serenity that he had not known. "I am so happy," he proclaimed upon returning to Faenza with his new bride, "that I have not found a minute to write my friends. . . . Maria is so good and she loves me so much that it is impossible that things will not go well for me."[53]

In these days of greatest contentment, Salvemini pursued both politics and profession with renewed intensity. Aware of the need to establish a reputation through historical publications in order to pursue a university career, he worked relentlessly on his manuscript. In part this was the fixation of a driven scholar, but it was predominantly the product of practical consideration. A university teaching position still provided the only realistic escape from lifelong poverty, an even greater consideration now that Maria was pregnant with their first child.[54]

In the spring of 1898, a new political crisis led Salvemini to his most extreme ideological radicalism. The events of the decade had contributed to a spiraling

confrontation between protesters and the Italian government as economic conditions worsened. In January, violence erupted in Rome, leading the government to call on the military to restore civil order. Then demonstrators swept
through Parma, destroying telegraph wires and the newly installed electric
streetlights. In Florence, insurgents broke into the Strozzi Palace and generally
terrorized the city. Anticipating the spread of insurrection, the government expanded surveillance and arrest of suspected conspirators, especially socialists.
Believing that pseudonyms protected his identity from the authorities,
Salvemini remained in obscurity in Faenza. However, he had reason to believe
that his letters had been read by government officials, who regularly intercepted
the mail of Turati and Costa.

In May, the worst violence of the decade erupted in Milan. In the "Fatti di
Maggio," the deaths of two policemen in a riot provoked a military counterattack in which General Bava-Beccaris ordered his troops to fire into an unarmed
mob. After four days of street fighting, the death toll reached eighty. The government of Prime Minister Antonio di Rudinì blamed the socialists and tight-
ened repressive measures by increasing arrests, closing universities, dissolving
clubs and organizations, and suspending more than 100 newspapers. The noose
of political repression was tightening dangerously close to Salvemini and his
socialist friends.

In the midst of the Fatti di Maggio, Salvemini urged the socialists to seize the
opportunity for revolution, an extreme position that attracted a great deal of attention. He told Turati that when a rise in bread prices caused an upheaval, "we
should prepare to intervene to transform it into revolution." The more moderate
Turati, who shunned violence, took the comment as a joke, arguing that his
"seething friend" was exaggerating and that little possibility of upheaval existed.[55]

At the same time, Salvemini anonymously published several articles in
Critica Sociale criticizing Turati's "reformist" policies and condemning the
government, particularly the army. On the basis of Salvemini's denunciation of
the army in the issues of April 16 and May 1, the government stopped the publication of *Critica Sociale*. Still, he believed that he had avoided detection.[56]

Salvemini urged Turati to use his influence as leader of the PSI to push the
party toward a revolutionary stance. Turati's reluctance, Salvemini believed,
represented a missed opportunity to overthrow the monarchy. Nevertheless,
Salvemini's Marxist critics point out that—at this, his most radical point—he
failed to come to terms with a proletarian revolution. In fact, he hardly men-
tioned class warfare, instead focusing on political objectives: overthrowing the
Savoy monarchy, establishing a democratic republic, and then withdrawing
from Africa, restoring commercial relations with France, reducing the military,
ending parliamentary and bureaucratic corruption, and abolishing the dominance of the great landlords. Whether Marxist or not, the advocacy of forceful

means to bring down the monarchy was clearly an extreme and illegal position about which he held no illusions. "If my letters to Turati are seized," he cautioned, "I will go directly to jail." Fortunately for Salvemini, Turati destroyed the letters just before being arrested, charged with inciting rebellion, and sentenced by a military tribunal to twelve years in prison.[57]

In the fall of 1898, Salvemini had to uproot his family anew when he was transferred to a *liceo* in Lodi, a small town in Lombardy near Milan.[58] In November, Maria delivered their first son, named Filipetto. The new father proudly explained each stage of the infant's development to friends: "My tiny boy," he observed, "has not demonstrated any political ideas; he thinks that he wants to remain independent of all parties, for the moment."

Several months later, Salvemini's professional prospects improved. He learned that the Lincei Academy had awarded his manuscript the grand prize of 1,700 lire, the equivalent of ten months of his paltry pay. More important, with continued recognition of his historical writings, the scholarly community would eventually have to take notice of him. At about the same time, he learned of a job opening in modern history at the University of Pavia, a distinguished old institution twenty-five miles southwest of Milan. The position paid reasonably well and offered an entree into the university system. Just as important to Salvemini, it was "quasi-secure," meaning that he would enjoy a much greater degree of academic freedom and thus the prospect of political participation with little threat of reprisal. To compete seriously for a job such as the one at Pavia, he would surely have to find a publisher for his award-winning manuscript.[59]

Throughout the summer and fall he labored to revise the manuscript on thirteenth-century Florence, which now exceeded 400 pages. Afraid that it would prove "too ancient" for publication, he completed a monograph on the political parties of nineteenth-century Milan, adding a final chapter that surveyed recent developments. Before the end of the year, both books appeared in print.[60]

The publications came too late for the appointment at Pavia. "They declared me ineligible," he wrote, "naturally granting eligibility to many people stupider than I." He became convinced that he was turned down not for political reasons but for personal ones. "They rejected me in order to favor the protégés of [Carlo] Cipolla," a well-known historian at the University of Turin. This was a lesson in reality for Salvemini, a kind of initiation into the professional marketplace. Intellect and merit alone, he quickly discerned, would not ensure success. He now understood that university chairs were awarded on the basis of influence and political decisions made on recommendation of parliamentary deputies, a high-stakes game that he was not prepared to play.

The Pavia incident also revealed Salvemini's tendency to personalize events at the expense of more subtle and balanced assessment. Eventually, this tendency would alienate him, even from friends, and embitter him. Furthermore, his penchant for uncovering behind-the-scenes political manipulation would sometimes lead him to blame individuals more than they deserved. In part this was the product of a stern moralism, born of the extremes of life in the South, where powerful forces—landlords and northern businessmen—were regarded as the malevolent causes of poverty and suffering. In this instance, at age twenty-six, rebuffed in his first serious job application, his fragile psyche wounded, he briefly considered giving up the teaching profession. He thought of being a journalist, but he could not think of a newspaper that would be suitable except the Socialist Party's *Avanti!*, and its positions were filled. He decided to allow himself several years to locate a university job. Almost immediately, he returned to the hunt, applying for a position at the University of Padua: "I want to see if I can open the door by pounding on it."[61]

While pursuing professional goals, he published an average of two or three articles each month in *Avanti!*, *Critica Sociale*, and other journals, and his work was constantly solicited by editors. "Your articles are always the most lively and the most quoted," Turati wrote to him.[62] Salvemini maintained a regular exchange of ideas with Italy's leading political voices while addressing the most urgent issues of the era: Italian expansionism, the Triple Alliance, and domestic political repression.[63] At the same time, he scrutinized the political parties and advocated his own favorite cause, pushing the "southern question" onto the national agenda.[64]

Salvemini continued to use pseudonyms to protect his job and avoid arrest. He worried that he would drop his guard, sign an article, enjoy a few months of fame, and suffer a lifetime of destitution as a result. Such caution exacted a further psychological toll. He expressed frustration to Placci, who had urged him to use the pseudonyms: "If I could sign my articles with my name, I would now have an enviable position in Italian journalism. . . . Everyone knows *Travet*, *Tre Stelle*, *pessimista*, *rerum scriptor*; and nobody knows me."[65]

Salvemini's regular commentary in the periodical press both contributed to the political dialogue, albeit anonymously, and served as an outlet for his views in a time of continuing turbulence. After the Fatti di Maggio of 1898, King Umberto I had asked Luigi Pelloux to form a new government, hoping that the general's ties with the moderate Left would defuse the emergency. After an initial period of moderation and restraint, Pelloux imposed a system of unprecedented Constitutional repression. He sponsored legislation to restrict the press and political activity, and on June 22, 1899, issued the infamous *decreto legge* (legal decree) by which he would govern directly under the king's authority, without Parliament.

Salvemini gave the readers of *Critica Sociale* a historical interpretation grounded in the radical democratic tradition of Garibaldi and Mazzini. In placing Pelloux's extraordinary measures in the context of the Italian political tradition, Salvemini underscored his own fundamental beliefs and tried to create a link between the socialists and the radical tradition of the Risorgimento. "When did [Pelloux's] reaction begin?" he asked rhetorically. "It began the day the [democratic] revolution began. It began the day [King] Carlo Alberto, battered by republican and democratic storms, felt the need to save [his] dynasty." Pelloux's *decreto legge* was simply an extension of the conservative, monarchist policies implemented by Prime Minister Camillo di Cavour and his successors to protect the northern bourgeoisie and the House of Savoy from radical democracy.[66]

Pelloux's measures so threatened the Constitution that the fragmented Left pulled together to obstruct business in the Chamber of Deputies and force the premier to revoke the *decreto legge*. They overturned voting urns, filibustered, and employed other parliamentary tactics to interfere with proceedings. Salvemini gave his guarded endorsement to the Left's obstructionist tactics, in full realization of the gamble that could, he feared, destroy the *estrema sinistra* (extreme Left) with whom he had some sympathy. The *estrema*, a loose grouping of small parties of students, professors, positivists, and other intellectuals with about sixty-five deputies and 25 percent popular support, led the parliamentary boycott of Pelloux and as a result won the broad support of the moderate Left.[67]

Throughout the crisis, Salvemini criticized Turati and the PSI for their tendency to compromise at all costs in order to maintain party unity. Even the PSI's support of the parliamentary boycott was a temporary expediency, too much in the Italian tradition of *trasformismo*. What the PSI needed to do, he wrote, was to quit "playing games" with the other parties and commit itself to a solid reform program. Only by making such a commitment could the party overcome the Constitutional crisis the correct way—by electing a socialist government and governing by the principal of cabinet responsibility.[68]

Salvemini was becoming increasingly exasperated with Italian political parties in general as they appeared to forsake principle in their desperate opposition to Pelloux. At one point he told his Republican (PRI) friend Archangelo Ghisleri, editor of the journal *Educazione politica*, that if the PSI refused to accept his ideas he would consider swiching to the PRI. Later, he wrote that he felt like becoming an anarchist. His sense of political isolation was growing.

Salvemini was not uncomfortable in the role of outsider-polemicist, however. In fact, it was a role that he would learn to accept, and at times to relish, throughout life. He urged Ghisleri not to become discouraged: "It is necessary to row against the current" and to express oneself "against all hypocrisy."[69]

At this time of national crisis, as much as he enjoyed the role of political outsider, he looked forward to the next PSI Congress and to the opportunity for direct participation. His experience as a political commentator had both given him a forum and inhibited him: "I wish *to do*, *to organize*, not merely to give words, support, and encouragement," he wrote. The passion to participate in political life already pulled at this otherwise alienated young intellectual, creating a tension between thought and political action that he would never entirely resolve.

In the first half of 1900, Italian politics riveted the public's attention. The persistence of the *estrema* opposition intensified pressure on Pelloux. In February, the high court of appeal ruled the *decreto legge* unconstitutional. In March, the *estrema* walked out of the Chamber, protesting Pelloux's attempt to pass similar repressive measures in legislative form. In April, the moderate Left, led by Giovanni Giolitti and Giuseppe Zanardelli, joined the boycott of Parliament with the support of some conservatives.

Momentum built. The Left's courageous political stance became a cause célèbre among a growing number of writers and intellectuals. The young poet and right-wing deputy Gabrielle D'Annunzio, with a typical flourish that was more gesture than substance, melodramatically crossed the floor of the Chamber, proclaiming his support for the leftist opposition: "I give my congratulations to the *estrema sinistra* for the fervor and tenacity with which they defend their idea. . . . As a man of intellect, I move toward life."[70]

More important, the moderate press, led by the influential Milanese daily *Il Corriere della Sera*, endorsed the *estrema* boycott. In June, Pelloux dissolved the Chamber and called for new elections, hoping to strengthen his hand. The risk backfired as the voters increased the size of the opposition. Pelloux, realizing he maintained only the barest majority, resigned in favor of a transitional government.

In the midst of the political crisis, his wife eight months pregnant, Salvemini was transferred to his third secondary school in four years. The Ministry of Public Instruction notified him of the new position at the Liceo Galileo in Florence.[71] By now, however, Florence had lost some of its appeal. As a student, he had come to accept it as an intimate and secure home. The year after graduation, he had desperately hoped that Villari could find him a teaching position at the Liceo Galileo so he could remain in the city and continue to do research in medieval history. In 1900, an official in the Ministry, impressed by *Magnati e Popolani* and assuming that he was doing Salvemini a favor, used his influence to accomplish the transfer, but as a twenty-six-year-old teacher and journalist intensely attuned to the politics of this turbulent era, Salvemini found the city frustratingly removed from the political mainstream. The "milieu of moderate Tuscans" was now strikingly less stimulating than the political setting in the northern regions of Emilia Romagna and Lombardy, where he had spent the previous four years. It took him a month in Florence to regain his equilibrium from a devastating move. In May, his second son was born.[72]

It now became apparent that the turmoil of the first year of the twentieth century would not soon subside. King Umberto, already blamed for the selection of Pelloux, involved himself further in the controversy by selecting a prime minister from the upper chamber, Senator Giuseppe Saracco. On June 29, in the Lombard town of Monza, an emigrant anarchist named Gaetano Bresci, who had sailed back to Italy to retaliate for the deaths in the "Fatti di Maggio," assassinated the king. Salvemini sensed that the crisis in Rome gave the Socialist Party an unprecedented opportunity to make its influence felt.[73]

Earlier, he had written to Ghisleri that a secure university position would allow him finally to dedicate himself to politics "with greatest vigor." Since graduating from the University of Florence, he had placed his hopes for overcoming poverty and achieving happiness in the prospect of a university teaching career. By November 1901, after six often frustrating years of teaching in secondary schools, scrambling to publish his manuscripts in order to establish a professional reputation, concealing his political views in pseudonyms so as to avoid wrecking his future, Salvemini reached his long-anticipated goal. The Ministry of Public Instruction appointed him professor of medieval and modern history at the University of Messina.

The appointment would take him back to Sicily, far from the pulse of Italian politics but nearer his birthplace. He had always thought of himself as a southerner, and his homecoming, in a heightened state of political self-awareness, promised to reaffirm this identity. It would be one of his goals, once cloaked in the security of the university system, to force Italian political leaders—and socialists in particular—to cease ignoring the South. If he could not take himself to the political hub of Italy, perhaps this son of the South could direct the focus of Italian politics to his native Mezzogiorno.[74]

NOTES

1. Franco Venturi, "Salvemini storico," *Il Ponte* XIII (1957), 1794–1795.

2. GS, "Una pagina," *Opere* VIII, 45.

3. Norberto Bobbio, "Perché Salvemini," in Bobbio et al., *Salvemini: Una vita per la libertà* (Rome, 1971), 3.

4. ET, *Salvemini*, 5.

5. GS, "Una pagina," *Opere* VIII, 41.

6. GS, Preface, xiii–xiv, and "Un commune dell'italia meridionale," *SSQM*, 3–22.

7. GS, "Una pagina," *Opere* VIII, 32–45.

8. ET, *Sal*, 1–20; MLS, *Sal*, 16–17; Ettore Rota, "Una pagina di storia contemporanea," *Nuova Rivista Storica*, III (May–August 1919), 327.

9. GS, "Una pagina," *Opere* VIII, 45–46; ET, *Salvemini*, 11ff.

10. Alessandro Galante Garrone, Preface to GS, *Opere* VIII, 10.

11. Interview with Michele and Hélène Cantarella, Leeds, Massachusetts, 1979 (hereafter Cantarella interview).

12. GS, "Una pagina," *Opere* VIII, 51–54.

13. Armando Saitta, "L'ideologia e la politica," in EG, *Sal*, 42–43. See also HSH, *The Sea Change* (New York, 1975), 86.

14. GS, "I miei maestri," *Scritti vari*, 47–48.

15. GS, "Pasquale Villari," *Opere* VIII, 58–66. See also EG, *La cultura italiana tra '800 e '900* (Bari, 1963), 106–109.

16. GS, "Una pagina," *Opere* VIII, 54.

17. GS, "Una pagina," *Opere* VIII, 53.

18. GS, "Una pagina," *Opere* VIII, 55.

19. Lidia Minervini, "Ricordi di Salvemini: Amico e Maestro," *Il Mondo* (Rome), October 22, 1957, 11–12.

20. GS, "Una pagina," *Opere* VIII, 53.

21. GS, "Una pagina," *Opere* VIII, 55–56; *Salvemini e i Battisti: Carteggio, 1894–1957*, Vincenzo Calì, ed. (1987), 7.

22. GS, "Una pagina," *Opere* VIII, 56.

23. GS, "Una pagina," *Opere* VIII, 56.

24. ET, *Sal*, 16.

25. GS, "Socialismo e tripolismo," *L'U*, December 30, 1911, *Opere* IV (2), 508.

26. ET, *Sal*, 18–19.

27. GS, "Una pagina," *Opere* VIII, 56–57.

28. GS, "Maestri e Compagni," *Opere* VIII, 41–104; EG, *La cultura italiana*, 103–154; Leo Valiani, "Salvemini e il socialismo" in Alberto Aquarone et al., *Gaetano Salvemini nella cultura e nella politica italiana* (Rome, 1967), 11–12.

29. ET, *Sal*, 21; GS, "Una pagina," *Opere* VIII, 56.

30. GS, "Pasquale Villari," *Opere* VIII, 67; ET, *Sal*, 19.

31. DeC, *Sal*, 18–19.

32. GS to Carlo Placci, November 27, 1895, *Opere* IX (1), 10–11.

33. GS to Placci, November 1, 1895, *Opere* IX (1), 7.

34. GS to Placci, November 1, 1895, in *Opere* IX (1), 7–8; Iris Origo, *A Need to Testify* (New York, 1984), 140–141.

35. DeC, *Sal*, 3.

36. ET, *Sal*, 21.

37. GS to Placci, January 6, 1896, *Opere* IX (1), 13–16.

38. GS to PV, February 10, 1896, 18; to Placci, April 30 and June 30, 1896, 25, 52, *Opere* IX (1).

39. GS, preface to *SSQM*, xv.

40. GS to Placci, November 1, 1895, 8–9; Elvira Gencarelli, preface to GS, *Opere* IX (1), xxiv.

41. GS, Preface to *SSQM*, xiii; to FT, February 24, 1897, 51–52; FT to GS, February 22, 1897, 50, *Opere* IX, (1).

42. GS, "Un commune dell'Italia meridionale: Molfetta," *SSQM*, 3–22; preface to *SSQM*, xiii-xiv. DeC, *Sal*, 29.

43. DeC, *Sal*, 26–58.

44. Placci to GS, February 9, 1897, *Opere* IX (1), 44.

45. GS, preface to *SSQM*, xiii; to Placci, June 30, 1896, *Opere* IX (1), 29–33.

46. GS to Cesare Paoli, January 28, 1896, *Opere* IX (1), 17; *La dignità cavalleresca nel Commune di Firenze* (Florence, 1896); ET, "Nota biografica" in EG, *Sal*, 25.

47. ET, *Sal*, 25.

48. GS to Placci, January 29 and February 9, 1897, *Opere* IX (1), 43; ET, *Sal*, 26–28.

49. GS to FT, August 19, 1897, *Opere* IX (1), 61.

50. GS to Placci, November 30, 1897, *Opere* IX (1), 67.

51. GS to FT, August 19, 1897, *Opere* IX (1), 61.

52. GS to FT, August 15, 1897, *Opere* IX (1), 58–59; FT to Andrea Costa, August 18, 1897, quoted in *Opere* IX (1), 59, n. 1; Costa to GS, August 24, September 9, and October 14, 1897; GS to Costa, September 1, October 9 and 14, 1897, *Opere* IX (1), 62–66; DeG, *IL*, 8.

53. GS to Placci, November 30, 1897, *Opere* IX (1), 66–67.

54. GS to Placci, August 28, 1898; to AGh, November 1898, *Opere* IX (1), 76–79.

55. GS to Placci, May 27, 1898, 71–73; FT to GS, May 4, 1898, 71, *Opere* IX (1).

56. GS, "Contributo alla riforma programma minimo," *Opere* IV (2), 52–64.

57. FT to GS, May 4, 1898; GS to Placci, May 27, June 15, and August 28, 1898, *Opere* IX (1), 70–77; ET, "Nota biografica," 218; DeC, *Sal*, 35–64.

58. GS to Placci, August 28, 1898, *Opere* IX (1), 76–77; ET, *Sal*, 25.

59. GS to Placci, June 5, 1899, 92–93; to Cesare Paoli, October 28, 1899, 115; to AGh, June 25, 1899, 96, *Opere* IX (1).

60. GS, *I Partiti Politici Milanesi nel secolo XIX* (Milan, 1899); *Magnati e Popolani in Firenze dal 1280 al 1295* (Florence, 1899); to Francisco Papafava, December 20, 1899, *Opere* IX (1), 121.

61. GS to AGh, December 13, 1899, *Opere* IX (1), 116; to Papafava, December 13, 1899, *Opere* IX (1), 118.

62. FT to GS, October 14, 1900, *Opere* IX (1), 168.

63. For example, GS, "Sempre dritto!", *Avanti!*, February 10 and 15, 1899; "Le origini della reazione," *CS*, July 1 and August 1, 1899; "L'irredentismo," *CS*, January 1, 1900.

64. For example, "Il partito neo-repubblicano," *Opere* IV (2),121–126; "Per la riforma del programma minimo" and "La questione meridionale e il federalismo," *Opere* IV (2), 148–162.

65. GS to Placci, February 25, 1899, *Opere* IX (1), 83.

66. GS, "Le origini della reazione," *Opere* II (2), 13–26.

67. GS to AGh, June 25, 1899, *Opere* IX (1), 95–97; "Il dovere dell'Estrema," *Avanti!*, January 3, 1899.

68. GS, "Ahime, sempre la Sinistra," *Opere* IV (1), 25–31.

69. GS to AGh, February, June 25, August 4 and December 13, 1899, *Opere* IX (1), 80, 97, 101, and 117.

70. *Storia del Parlamento Italiano*, X, Francesco Brancato, ed. (Palermo, 1973), 354.

71. GS to AGh, March 10, 1900, 146; to Papafava, March 11, 1900, 147, *Opere* IX (1).

72. GS to Placci, April 30, 1896, 25; to AGh, March 25 and May 1900, 151, 153, *Opere* IX (1). See also ET, *Sal*, 26–27.

73. GS, "La caduta del Regno Italico e l'assassinio del Prina," *Educazione Politica*, October 31, 1899, 459–462; to Papafava, June 23, 1900, *Opere* IX (1), 159.

74. GS to AGh, June 25, 1899, *Opere* IX (1), 96.

Chapter 2

"So Happy That I Am Frightened"

This state of mind, in which I found myself at fourteen years, was and is the state of mind in 99 out of 100 cases in the South: a quiet rancor toward those of the North, a vague and profound sense of being victims of their greed and arrogance, a bitter antipathy.

Gaetano Salvemini, 1900[1]

Regional differences and hostilities have shaped Italian culture throughout the modern era. Gaetano Salvemini vividly recalled an incident at age fourteen that reflected those same hostile attitudes and helped to solidify his own awareness as a southerner. As he accompanied his mother on a train along the Apulian coast from Molfetta to Bari, they shared their compartment with two young northern men, one the son of a Piedmontese stationmaster. It was the Apulian boy's earliest impression of northern cultural attitudes.

"Bad places," said the young Piedmontese. "Believe me, no one can live here; lucky are those who are returning to the North. Here the air is bad, the water wretched, the dialect incomprehensible except to Turks, the population ignorant, superstitious, barbaric."

"But we are not the least bit barbaric," the young Salvemini interrupted. "When you stole our mon . . ."

A painful pinch from his mother reprimanded him.

Thirteen years later, reflecting on that incident, Salvemini wrote about regional prejudice in a lengthy article called "The Southern Question and Federalism." It is revealing both as an account of the intellectual development of his southern identity and as a broader analysis of North-South stereotyping:

I was fully convinced that this Piedmontese man who had called us "barbaric" had stolen our money. Why did I have this conviction? . . . I cannot say with certainty. I am sure that one contributing factor was the lamentation of my Bourbon uncle who would repeat . . . : "The Piedmontese left us only our eyes for crying." Another factor was my observation from the map of Italy that the railroads were more numerous in the North than in the South; and [my recollection of] the confused and faded stories of arrogance that the Piedmontese officials had exhibited in our region in 1860.

If [my mother's] pinch had not forbidden the discussion, and if this young Piedmontese man had asked me the reason for my accusation, I would not have known what to say; but I would have remained equally resolute in my conviction that Northerners bleed us, make us sweat like animals, and in the bargain call us barbarians. . . .

One fraternal greeting that I have heard many times given by northerners to southerners is: May the water of the sea cover everything from Rome south.

As they say, northerners despise southerners; and, with all their souls, southerners detest northerners. This is the product of forty years of unity.[2]

In January 1902, Gaetano Salvemini moved his family nearly 500 miles south from Florence to Messina. In some respects, the journey was even longer. Sicily's second city, built at the foot of the Peloritani Mountains around the deep natural harbor of the Straits of Messina, was a bustling port at the turn of the century. Like the rest of the big island that had played such a prominent role in the Mediterranean economy since the classical age, the port and the city of Messina were in a state of decline, in spite of the general Italian economic boom. European and northern Italian interests systematically exported its natural resources—even grapes—for processing and sale elsewhere. Messina remained in the modern era what it had been to ancient Greeks, a kind of economic colony.

For Salvemini the move was, in a sense, a step backward. If he had regarded Florence as provincial and apolitical, Messina was virtually insulated and feudal. To cross the Straits was, for most Italians, to regress into a mysterious past, with strong traces of Muslim, Norman, and Bourbon culture, frozen in time, largely bypassed by the industrial age.

For an intellectual, the move could be devastating. More than half the Sicilian population was illiterate, the educational system dismal. The University of Messina, Salvemini's new employer, had a long but uneven history. The Spanish Bourbon dynasty had chartered it in 1591, abolished it before 1700, then reestablished it in 1838. The university had always struggled in a hostile environment, as isolated from modern thought as the island was from modern industry. Professors appointed to the University of Messina often regarded the assignment as penance to be paid to the Ministry of Public Instruction.[3]

For Salvemini, the assignment was a triumph, the culmination of his tenacious campaign to find a university teaching position. If he faced a few years' internship before progressing to a better university, he certainly did not fret about it in 1902. He would be largely immune from the culture shock experienced by Giovanni Pascoli and other northern intellectuals. For Salvemini, the trip across the Straits of Messina was a short one, indeed, from his birthplace. He welcomed the opportunity, for not only the career door but also the political door it opened.

Salvemini remained in Messina for seven years, longer than he had hoped. In these years, in spite of difficulties, he matured intellectually and politically. The militant Marxism of 1898 would soon merge with positivist, reformist, federalist and republican influences to form an original Salveminian view. His professional work would broaden beyond the monographic stage to utilize broader synthesis and interpretation. In politics, he would participate more readily in organizations, hoping to apply his ideas more effectively. Nonetheless, the shrill tone of his criticism and his impatience with the political process would provoke countercharges that he was a quixotic figure, destined to remain politically ineffectual.

Having secured his long-sought university appointment, Salvemini accelerated his political activity. He expected that his newly found academic freedom would enable him to participate more directly in the affairs of the PSI without jeopardizing his job, in spite of warnings to the contrary. Still, he treaded cautiously through the thicket of politics, continuing at Messina to follow the self-imposed ban against participation in the political life of the city where he taught. Instead he confined his active political life to summer vacations in Molfetta and the national campaigns of the teachers' union and the PSI.[4]

It was generally within the context of socialist politics that he would carve out a political career, often frustrating and seldom in agreement with party leadership as he championed various minority positions. As a socialist, he would develop a new constituent group, attempt to capture control of the party from its northern leadership, and eventually enter active politics as a candidate for office.

Like most European socialist parties, the PSI was split. As the European industrial work force grew, the labor movement strengthened and developed a stronger political consciousness. Consequently, where workers were qualified to vote, as in Germany, they joined left-of-center intellectuals and other reformers, swelling the ranks of the socialist party and electing its delegates to parliamentary seats.

This heady success changed the socialist parties. Since many of these delegates had strong ties to labor unions and commitments to reform legislation, they moved the socialist parties away from the revolutionary doctrines of Marx toward a position of parliamentary gradualism bent on achieving material improvements for workers. In spite of the fact that some remained officially Marxist, the European socialist parties became more pragmatic. Led by "revisionists," as the Marxists called the reformists, these parties reshaped European politics in a fundamental sense, muscling their way onto the political stage and carrying with them a social welfare agenda. Italian socialists, late in organizing, were impressed by the parliamentary successes of such socialist parties as the German Social Democrats.[5]

The PSI, only nine years old when Salvemini moved to Messina, was divided along ideological lines. Italian Marxists adapted their patron saint's revolutionary dogma to Italian society, accepting Marx's tenets of irreconcilable conflict between bourgeoisie and proletariat and the inevitability of revolution. In contrast, Italian revisionist socialists called for the integration of the masses into the political system and the pursuit of political and economic reforms. Salvemini regularly expressed his frustration with these debates over ideological tendencies. As a man who rejected ideology, he found himself favoring a case-by-case approach, espousing either peaceful or confrontational methods in response to specific circumstances. Because his political agenda was a unique product of his own experience and values, he never fully agreed with the goals of either faction. In this respect, he was emerging as a highly independent, pragmatic socialist.[6]

In 1900, the reformists had achieved the adoption of Turati's "Minimal" program, designed as a "temporary" expedient while cooperating with the "progressive elements" of the middle class. It was a blueprint for reform by parliamentary means, which allowed the PSI to maintain its theoretical commitment to Marxist revolutionary doctrine. In this regard, it resembled other European socialist parties: Marxist in theory, reformist socialist in practice. Viewing this revisionist approach as hypocritical, Salvemini chided Turati for the absurdity of maintaining two contradictory programs.[7]

In other ways, the PSI was unique. A party that articulated an agenda for the masses, the PSI ironically remained small, never exceeding 50,000 members until 1919. In part its size reflected the Italian franchise laws that severely limited the right to vote, a legacy of Cavour's leadership. The PSI's failure to emerge as a mass party greatly inhibited its parliamentary clout and obligated it to the tactics of cooperation with the middle class. The middle class, however, lacked a strong democratic commitment. Conversely, Turati was never able to convince the party congresses to adopt his tactic of interclass cooperation.[8]

In addition, the party suffered from organizational problems. The major spokesmen were the editors of the party papers, *Critica Sociale* and *Avanti!*, the parliamentary deputies, and the delegates to party congresses. None spoke for the largely autonomous local party groups and socialist cooperatives; consequently, the PSI lacked effective central organization. Furthermore, the party often competed with its largest potential constituent group, the labor movement, which itself succeeded in organizing no more than 5 percent of the workers before World War I.[9]

At best, the PSI could hope to attract only a portion of the ideological Left. It traditionally shared this political terrain with Mazzinian republicans, Garibaldini, anarchists, the Social Revolutionary Party (PSRI) of Andrea

Costa, the Workers' Party (POI) of Costantino Lazzari, and the various workers' organizations, including the mutual aid societies.

In spite of these limitations, the PSI enjoyed growing success, improving from twelve seats in 1895 to thirty-three seats in 1900 out of a 500-member Chamber of Deputies. The party managed to play a role in national politics primarily because of the leadership of a dedicated group of middle-class, educated northerners who coalesced around Filippo Turati and his journal, *Critica Sociale*. Turati, his companion Anna Kuliscioff, Leonida Bissolati, and the *Critica* group had won the right to lead the PSI for several reasons. They had founded the party and its journal in 1891–1892 and had provided strong intellectual leadership throughout the stormy 1890s in the face of criticism from various factions, primarily the party's revolutionary wing.

A classic case study in elitist leadership, the *Critica* group had only the most tenuous ties with the proletariat, whom they mistrusted. The cautious Turati had led his dedicated cadre in virtually abandoning Marxist orthodoxy in pursuit of democratic parliamentary reform. As a result, the PSI gave little more than lip service to revolution. In addition, the PSI leadership was strengthened by virtue of its location in Milan, the center of the Italian "triangle" of industrial and commercial activity and of political power since the days of Cavour. Lawyers from Lombardy, Piedmont, and Emilia-Romagna dominated the leadership group, most of them under age forty. The only southerner in the group was Salvemini.[10]

Salvemini's role in Italian socialist politics was to direct the attention of the PSI toward a unique set of demands that sided with neither the revolutionary nor the revisionist wing. With these demands, he established himself as an independent and original voice, spelling out his proposals in a series of articles, letters, and speeches. The ideas were not entirely integrated, and, as his Marxist critics were quick to point out, did not derive from an ideological base. Rather, they were grounded in a unique composite of Salvemini's experience: the ideas of Mazzini, Carlo Cattaneo, Marx, and the positivists; the culture of the Italian South; and the tempestuous politics of turn-of-the-century Milan. If the elements were familiar, the product seems original. Together, they represent a radical vision of a decentralized, democratic Italian republic.

Salvemini's political democracy found its inspiration in the Risorgimento. During the winter of 1898–1899, he had discovered the works of the nineteenth-century Lombard economist Carlo Cattaneo, whom he came to appreciate as a true Italian genius. In Salvemini's controversial interpretation of Italian unification, Cattaneo—like Mazzini, Garibaldi, and many others—represented the radical traditions of the Risorgimento that had been overcome by Cavour and the House of Savoy. Cattaneo had written during the unification campaign that Italy could achieve either national unity or liberty, but not both, because in unifying under the Piedmontese monarchy to defeat Austria, Italians would inevitably sacrifice their liberty.[11] Salvemini was convinced that Italy's "central-ized, devouring, destructive" government had proven Cattaneo prophetic by oppressing its citizens for forty years.[12]

Salvemini's discovery of Cattaneo led him away from Marxism to federal-ism, which became his primary political axiom in his years at Messina. He be-came convinced that Italy's future lay in a decentralized Italian federation of democratic republics and that republicanism, rather than socialism, repre-sented the real Italian revolution. Although Salvemini acknowledged the im-portance of national unity in diplomacy, foreign trade, monetary policy, and law, he favored as much regional and communal autonomy as possible.[13]

In early 1900, Salvemini hoped to set the stage for a discussion of federalism at the PSI Congress in Rome. He drafted an article for *Critica Sociale* refuting the nationalist arguments of *North and South*, recently published by economist and future Prime Minister F. S. Nitti. In a style for which he would become well known, Salvemini refuted Nitti's statistics with his own, comparing revenue paid to public services received, sector by sector, demonstrating in each in-stance the burden under which the South had traditionally labored. He pointed out that Nitti repeated the mistakes of those who spoke of "an abstract South" and who treated southerners as a "homogeneous block." While methodically rebutting the economist's arguments, Salvemini labeled Nitti a "fanatical uni-tarian," thereby employing the style of rhetorical flourish that would soon be called "Salveminian." It was an intriguing combination of reason and emotion, more revealing of the man than many readers realized.[14]

By 1900 Salvemini was so discouraged by the failures of the central govern-ment and the political parties to solve the nation's problems that he became con-vinced that the system was unworkable. He believed that the Italian government, rather than implementing reforms to benefit the poor, moved so slowly and was so uninterested that it actually impeded such progress. In con-trast, he admired Italy's "thousand democratic communes" (municipal govern-ments) as proof of a better system. For examples of federalist government, he turned to Cattaneo's defense of administrative decentralization in Switzerland and the United States. He implored socialists to heed the words of Pierre-Joseph Proudhon: "Liberty is federalism, federalism is liberty."[15]

Such a fundamental change in structure would require a change in the Con-stitution. He had therefore become convinced of the necessity of convening a Constitutional assembly to transform Italy into a federalist state. "[Local] au-tonomy presents inconvenience and danger," he acknowledged of his proposal, "but liberty is always preferable to tyranny."[16]

Another axiom of Salvemini's program, closely related to federalism, was universal suffrage. The central government had continued to abuse power, he argued, precisely because so few Italians held the right to vote. By 1902, he be-gan to call directly for universal suffrage, extended to women as well. His persistent advocacy of this principle proved quite controversial, and his voice remained a rather lonely one, even within his own party.[17]

Salvemini saw his campaign for universal suffrage as one of simple justice. The restrictive electoral law of 1882, with its literacy requirements, disenfranchised virtually the entire southern work force. "Each of us knows ten illiterate people full of good sense and ten university professors [who are] perfect idiots outside their classrooms," Salvemini argued, in opposing the existing law. He was confident that the southern workers, given the vote, would quickly educate themselves to the realities of local politics. They would use political power as all people do, to address their own interests.[18]

Universal suffrage clearly threatened the status quo, including the leadership of the PSI. Salvemini and a number of southern socialists began to call for the PSI to expand the party aggressively into the South as a mechanism to liberate poor southerners from the oppression of the landlord system.[19] In these exchanges with Turati, Salvemini was the first to propose a bold political solidarity between northern industrial and southern agricultural workers. He saw a political potential in the southern peasants that Turati and the PSI leadership did not. In September 1908, Salvemini travelled to Florence to address the Tenth PSI Congress. In an impassioned plea on behalf of disenfranchised southerners, he told the delegates: "Give us the one proof of useful solidarity you can give us, the only one . . . worthy of free men. Help us to be free, to win . . . *universal suffrage*; and the rest we will figure out for ourselves."[20]

The leadership ignored his appeal. The proposal created a dilemma for the Socialist Party because its leaders, northerners like Turati, believed that universal suffrage would weaken them in the Mezzogiorno. Turati had written of the "two Italies," one northern, in the process of industrialization and modernization, the other southern, a "feudal, medieval" society of "barbaric putrefaction." To introduce the universal vote in the South, Turati insisted, would risk manipulation of the peasants by Catholic candidates and landlords who would simply use the newly acquired power against the socialists. More important, to Turati, the Socialist Party could not succeed in the South until the region industrialized.[21] To Salvemini, Turati's assumptions were arrogant and riddled with stereotypes.

Salvemini and other southern socialist writers argued that the franchise was the one instrument by which poor southerners could assert their own political power.[22] Salvemini, for whom political parties were always merely a means by which to achieve change, would have liked to use the PSI as a mechanism to liberate the South, particularly to win the votes to achieve land reform. In this sense it can be said that Salvemini was first a southern radical, second a democratic socialist, and a PSI partisan only when useful. His inability to convince the PSI leadership to accept universal suffrage would drive him further away from the party.

Also central to Salvemini's reform program was his call for sweeping economic changes. Salvemini's economic views reflected the empirical positivism of his university years, now evolved into a moderate, pragmatic socialism. Moving away from Marxism, he struggled through a temporary loss of confidence. When he recovered, what emerged was a more mature and original set of ideas.[23]

Never a theoretical socialist, Salvemini rejected most of the tenets of turn-of-the-century liberal capitalism as well. He argued that the fallacy of liberal capitalist theory was that its celebrated freedom failed to reach all of society. The proletariat (a term he readily applied to the southern *braccianti*), lacking property, could not share in society's freedom to pursue economic gain.

It was Salvemini's distrust of theory that also led him to caution socialists against economic panacea. The utopian socialists had failed, he warned Turati, because they had withdrawn from society in order to pursue social perfection. Economic reforms must be realistic. In Salvemini's articles and letters, one finds the specific components of economic reform designed to replace liberal capitalism with a system of collective ownership of property and the means of production.[24] His lack of interest in developing his ideas in more systematic fashion was simply a part of his concrete approach to public issues.

Among the most radical of his economic proposals was his call to redistribute land and income in favor of poor southern farmers. He advocated selective expropriation of the *latifondi*, and restoration to the original smallholders of lands confiscated because of unpaid taxes. He favored a system of producer cooperatives if adequately capitalized. However, he opposed collectivization of the farms, warning Turati of the enormous problems that would be caused by abandoning private land ownership altogether. Here his predilection for small proprietorship, learned as a youth in Apulia, is obvious. On this issue, as on others, his reform proposals stopped well short of state socialism, whose centralized power, he believed, would surely not serve the South well.[25]

By 1902, Salvemini's political ideas had evolved as well. No longer did he entertain the idea of an Italian revolution, as he had in the crisis of 1898. His analyses of the French Revolution and Mazzini had taught him that a "great national revolution" must be built upon "the force of thought, upon a vast moral renewal" and a firm economic base.[26] He was convinced that no such conditions existed in Italy, and thus he moved to a position of political reform more closely aligned in concept with Turati and the *Critica* faction who saw the revolution as a long-term acquisition of political power by the working class. However, he continued to criticize the PSI's approach.

His politics, like his economics, were part principle and part revolt against abstraction and theory, especially his frustrations with the vague verbiage of the PSI program: "All this mystification can happen only because they do not discuss a concrete program." Progress was being blocked by specific laws, he argued, and could be overcome only by specific laws.[27] In early 1903, Salvemini admonished Turati in *Critica* to abandon democratic rhetoric in favor of specific proposals designed to achieve democratic results. Together, his social and economic proposals can be called Salveminian *concretismo*, or concrete reform.[28]

One month before, Salvemini had spelled out his demands to the party in "A Program for the Socialists of the South," directed primarily to Turati. He called for the abolition of the hated *dazio* (tax) on grain and other obsolete taxes; reform of agricultural credit and of the tax structure, including a 50 percent reduction and a moratorium on property taxes for small landholders; limitation of the excessive power of the prefects; and, finally, universal suffrage, at least in local and provincial elections.[29]

It has been argued that his distaste for theory, and particularly economic theory, limited his intellectual and political impact. His opposition to liberal capitalism was impassioned, but in its place he offered only individual reforms. Some contemporaries dismissed Salvemini as a man whose ideas were too narrowly regional to have significance outside the South. He disagreed. Although his program was regional in emphasis, he was convinced that the future of Italy rested on its ability to address these issues and thereby to reconcile the profound historical discrepancies between the regions. He did not want to be known simply as an apologist for the South. He warned that the government's continued discrimination against the South would lead to the formation of an ugly antinorthern movement with frightening reactionary potential. At the same time, he argued that the democratic parties of the North could be convinced that improving conditions in the South would contribute to the development of the national economy. The destructive system of *trasformismo* rested on the restricted franchise. Until the government established universal suffrage, it could never hope to correct such abusive policies as the *dazio* on grain and the high protective tariff and could not, therefore, begin to evolve toward a modern state.[30]

Salvemini's influence on Italian political thought derives substantially from the originality of his concrete agenda. The direct and unequivocal approach of his numerous turn-of-the-century polemics—as well as the freshness of his ideas—established him as a strong voice for change and thus as a rival to Marxists, revisionist socialists, and liberals alike. His polemical exchanges with spokesmen for these groups made him the subject of criticism from the Right as well as the Left.

Salvemini's *concretismo* argued for a socialism that was Italian, pragmatic, rational, decentralized and democratic, designed to tip the balance of economic and political power in the direction of southern workers and away from northern industrialists, labor leaders, and politicians. Although he advocated a socialist economy that would redistribute property among the general population, he nevertheless showed little interest in developing a comprehensive plan to reach that ultimate goal.[31]

Although Salvemini did not develop his program from ideological premises, it does represent a more synthesized proposal than has generally been acknowledged. In fact, Salvemini's was the most systematic of all the southern reform proposals of the day. He hounded Turati not only for using empty rhetoric but also for advocating a piecemeal approach to Italian politics that lacked conceptual and methodological foundations. This same reprimand, ironically, would be leveled at him by his own critics. In fact, in their positivism and rejection of ideology, Salvemini and Turati used very similar political attacks.[32]

Salvemini expressed his views with great regularity at the rate of about one published article each month and several politically substantive letters each week. With the exception of several personal crises, he maintained this staggering pace through most of his adult life. For a man struggling to establish himself in his profession, this productivity constitutes a remarkable achievement.

In fact, this profusion of political ideas seems to have exacted consequences in the form of physical and psychological stress.[33] He often expressed these strains as the results of familial pressures, all of which he internalized. He was "nervous about being alone" and then sick from moving. He was frequently frustrated, sometimes by his younger brothers, whom he supported. One married "without a cent to live on"; the other "wasted" two years at a university. When Salvemini was well, it seemed that his wife or his children were sick.[34]

At times, his frustration was the consequence of career failures and self-doubts, the cumulative result of a decade of fruitless job searches, first for a university position, then for a transfer to a better institution. After four years at Messina, Salvemini was once again sensing futility in his career. He found the university community small, limited in scholarly resources, provincial in attitude, and insulated from "intellectual contact." He complained that his students were lethargic. He tired of grading exams and especially of student papers that demonstrated the depth of "imbecility and human ignorance."

At the same time, he experienced bouts of neurosis and depression and described his "dark side" as caused by a type of "neurasthenia" that he could sense as it approached. The realization that poverty forced him to take a job reading exams for fifteen lire a day put him in "a great, heavy melancholy." In 1902, as he struggled with his changing political ideas, he experienced a "period of distressing aridity" that included an entire month in which he "did not have a single good moment." Tearing up page after page of his drafts made him feel "inert and useless." It was a "psychological desert" that lasted ten months.[35] Frustrated at his failure to advance in his profession, Salvemini contemplated abandoning his studies. Carlo Placci, attempting to bring him to his senses, called such an idea "silly and senseless" and urged his friend to slow down. "To this point, your career has been exceptionally accelerated and happy." Such words were little reassurance to a man who felt ignored by his professional community and impeded by an academic bureaucracy he could not penetrate.[36]

Salvemini's frustration influenced his politics as well. He attacked contemporary issues with a passion easily rising to a pitch of righteous indignation. This man who prided himself in reasoned analysis was also a man of strong emotions who readily personalized political campaigns. This advocate of empirical methodology was also prone to moral rigidity. He grew comfortable in the role of political outsider.

Salvemini's opposition to political parties not only evoked contempt but often led him to bitter condemnation of his adversaries. The popular parties were "a great hodgepodge of cretins" and the *estrema sinistra* were "imbeciles" with "intellectual and moral deficiencies." Of all the parties, the PSI was "the least stupid, but always stupid enough not to be good at anything." In general, the moderates were "much more stupid than the democrats."[37] At times, in letters to friends, frustration with socialist party leaders led to pouting, as was the case when he threatened on several occasions to abandon the PSI in favor of anarchism or republicanism. His bitterness and the harshness of his political judgments sometimes alienated friends. He understood the price he paid for the rigor of his criticism, but he prided himself in the "hard courage" to criticize the PSI "on the basis of facts." Sometimes his friends cautioned him to cool his rhetoric and control his impatience. "It appears to me," wrote Francesco Papafava, "that you exaggerate a little your hatred [of political factions]."[38]

Although Salvemini and Turati could maintain their equilibrium and their mutual self-respect in the face of Salvemini's persistent condemnation of Turati's tactics and policies, others found his friendship too difficult. In the fall of 1901, his long and close association with Archangelo Ghisleri ran aground on differences of politics and political integrity. Defending his criticisms of Ghisleri for changing his political positions and associating with some "egregious men" in the PRI, Salvemini explained philosophically: "True courage does not prove itself by assailing adversaries, but by criticizing friends." Ghisleri responded defensively, and after years of intensive correspondence, the two never wrote again.[39]

Ultimately, Salvemini's growing contempt for political parties heightened his alienation from mainstream politics. Once he became interested in a federalist movement, he expressed pride that his success occurred outside the major parties. "We are all an intellectual proletariat," he wrote to Placci. It was a classic statement of the European intelligentsia that often defined itself as a class separated from society in self-conscious isolation.[40]

One of Salvemini's responses to the intensity of these rhetorical political battles and the stress of family and career was to retreat even further philosophically. His alienation gave him a more objective outlook that signaled a healthy personal maturation. "Politics are without doubt a great humorous comedy," he mused in 1904—this from a man not given to satire. Placci had noticed the change: "You are slowly becoming a political agnostic." Salvemini was quite aware of the transformation in his basic political approach. "I am becoming more contemplative," he observed in June 1908. "Perhaps some external incident will redirect my practical tendencies, remove me from my uninterested study, and make me a political man."[41]

The painful maturing of Salvemini's political views at Messina was accompanied by changes in his perspective as a professional historian. Absent in his historical publications of this period was the fiery Marxist analysis of everything from medieval Florence to nineteenth-century Molfetta. In its place developed a broader interest that began to incorporate a more positivist, "scientific" perspective. If the influences of Marxism were clear, so was his effort to move beyond its limitations. While attempting to establish himself in his profession and qualify for a promotion and a better job, he explored new topics for research. He had essentially left behind in Florence his study of medieval history and now focused almost exclusively on the modern era.

On the afternoon of November 19, 1901, Salvemini stood before an audience of students, faculty, and secondary school teachers to deliver his first university lecture, an introduction to his course in modern history. The lecture, "History Considered as Science," raised a number of issues about the philosophy and methods of history, incorporating some of the most recent literature from the new field of social sciences. He organized his presentation around the rhetorical question: Is history art or science? The issue created a flurry of interest on campus.[42]

He took direct issue with a thesis of the idealist philosopher Benedetto Croce, who, in his view, made a false distinction between art and science by arguing that artists limit themselves to the particular, whereas scientists generalize. The real contrast, Salvemini insisted, was that the scope of scientific research is confined to reality, whereas the scope of art, as Tolstoy wrote, is to "provoke the senses" by using both reality and fantasy. Salvemini's disagreement with Crocean idealism would broaden and deepen as time passed.

Departing from the literary and artistic tradition, Salvemini championed history as science. Like natural scientists, historians must study the particular in order to generalize. A historian cannot generalize about the conditions of the working class, he noted, without studying the individual worker.

Salvemini's lecture made a strong case for the new social history, the "true history," deviating markedly from the political and biographical studies that had dominated the field in the nineteenth century. He questioned whether any man could be "representative" or "symbolic" of an age, as in "The Age of Dante"; "scientific historiography," he argued, must be "collective" and "social." The historian could be an artist, and his books could make people laugh and cry, but his investigation must be scientific and social.[43]

This lecture was remarkable in several respects. It demonstrated a maturing of his historical views at the same time he was rethinking politics. Placci praised his friend's change in approach from a "solely materialistic" to a "more eclectic" interpretation.[44] "History Considered as Science" was also one of the few occasions on which Salvemini articulated a philosophy and methodology of history. It was certainly a more systematic treatise than he had ever produced, and he would continue to expand and rethink it throughout his career.[45]

At the same time, he drafted two historical manuscripts in the hope that publication would boost his career. In December 1904, Salvemini officially opened the academic year with the first of a series of lectures entitled "The Thought and Action of Giuseppe Mazzini." Mazzini was one of the historical figures whom Salvemini most admired. The Risorgimento hero had become the subject of controversy particularly between Marxists, who considered him a bourgeois intellectual, and republicans, for whom he represented the great "lost cause" of Italian history. For many Italians he remained a bold, romantic hero whose mystical image and grandiose style had made him a cult figure.[46]

Salvemini found another, more complex person behind the Mazzini myth and developed one of the first scholarly analyses of his subject. His interpretation stressed the contrast between Mazzini's politics and his theology. What alarmed Salvemini about this "Man of Action" was the irrational quality of much of his thought. Salvemini noted that Mazzini searched for truth among "the secrets of an intuition that defies analysis . . . in the most secret aspirations of the soul." Salvemini, product of a rational education, found this religious mysticism repugnant.[47]

From this mysticism, Mazzini had developed his political ideal of a unified, theocratic republic. He based this unity of religion and state on the assumption that the popular will represented the true interpretation of divine revelation. The centralization of power, a direct contradiction to Cattaneo's federalism, alarmed Salvemini as much as its religious base. Italian liberals could accept Mazzinianism only if they chose to ignore his most basic precept.

Though rejecting this commitment to centralized theocracy, Salvemini was profoundly influenced by Mazzini's life. Mazzini's "heroic vision" and his suffering had inspired generations of Italians, and his "single-minded obstinacy" had made an indispensable contribution to Italian unification. This was for Salvemini the Mazzini paradox: one could be a Mazzinian while ignoring many Mazzinian ideas. Croce disagreed. Later, he would contradict Salvemini's self-description as a "Mazzinian socialist," noting that Salvemini's was a "Mazzinianism without Mazzini and socialism without Marx."[48]

Meanwhile, three job openings appeared at Italian universities, making publication and promotion all the more imperative. In July, after being nominated for promotion, Salvemini received a disturbing letter from his former mentor at the University of Florence. Professor Villari wrote that he planned to retire but that his position had been filled by Carlo Cipolla, a veteran of twenty-three years at the University of Turin. "Naturally," wrote Villari, the faculty had discussed Salvemini, "our old and talented disciple who had brought honor to the university." However, they had considered his too-recent nomination to full professor status, his political activity, and his lack of serious publication in his field enough to disqualify him.[49]

Salvemini was crushed. He believed that Cipolla was the wrong man for the job because, in spite of his well-earned reputation, he lacked analytical methodology. What seemed unfair, he claimed, was that "the professors at the university . . . excluded me not because my academic value was inadequate . . . but because they were afraid that politics would distract me from my teaching duties."[50]

Shortly after this rejection, Salvemini learned of positions at the Universities of Milan and Turin, where, in contrast to Florence, there would be a formal process of competitive application. He hoped that the publication of his second book of the year would force the Ministry of Public Instruction to take his candidacy seriously. Unfortunately, *The French Revolution* received some bad reviews and therefore raised questions about his competency as a scholar.

The book, much bulkier than his *Mazzini*, was a synthesis of several interpretations that treated the French Revolution as a series of political and economic changes. It conformed to his empirical, positivist method, rejecting the abstract notion of a revolution: "We can say the Revolution did away with feudal dues, so long as we remember that . . . it was the peasants who refused to pay them, the Constituent Assembly that failed to enforce them, the Legislative Assembly that formally abolished almost all of them."[51]

He knew that the book was not highly original, but he believed that his approach had not before been "applied systematically" to the entire Revolution. When several critics labeled it "secondhand," he was furious. In a letter to Villari, who had praised the book, Salvemini berated the "little people with little minds who in our universities pass themselves off as historians. . . . This is not a book for erudite idiots; it is a book for the intelligent public."[52] This attitude, partly defensive, was also indicative of a profound distaste for intellectual pretense and a philosophical commitment to write simply and directly for a mass audience.

Just before Christmas 1905, Salvemini got the news: he was eliminated from the competition for both appointments at the Universities of Milan and Turin. He felt like a "victim of bullying." To exclude him from the two positions, he protested, the Ministry had ranked him third. "If there had been three, they would have ranked me fourth." In retrospect, he recalled with irony that he should have written two versions of *The French Revolution*, "one for the socialists and one for the competition."[53]

After the anger had subsided, Salvemini began to experience, once again, profound personal self-doubts. As much as he had blamed the Ministry for his rejection, he also began to believe that he was failing to meet his own expectations as a historian. Placci reassured him that the jobs would come to him in time, that he believed Salvemini would become a great historian, but the kind words provided little reassurance. Salvemini responded with uncharacteristic self-importance: "The academic rabble confines me to Messina and deprives me of all significant means of research, [thus] denying me success—given that I have the stuff—as a great historian."[54] More and more, he felt stranded in Messina indefinitely. As much as he wanted to leave, he did not wish to compete again for a job because he would have to campaign. "I am not cut out for this kind of exercise," he complained. "I have competed for jobs ten times in ten years. I have the right to be tired."[55]

He was told that his pursuit of a new professorship had suffered in part because of his activities as organizer of the teachers' union. Five years earlier, he had joined the venerable Giuseppe Kirner, "the lovable father of all [Italian] teachers" of his day, in organizing the National Federation of Middle School Teachers. The Federation provided Salvemini the opportunity to test some of his most important ideas in a political framework that offered less resistance than Parliament and the political parties.[56]

Since Salvemini was the driving force behind the teachers' federation, he could hope to control its direction. It conformed to Salvemini's model of decentralized, anti-authoritarian structure, giving him the opportunity to strike a blow at the centralized bureaucracy of the Ministry of Public Instruction in Rome. As a union, it allowed him to demonstrate to the PSI that elements of the population they had neglected—in this case, part of the exploited and underpaid lower middle class—could be organized into an effective political force. As a voice for educational reform, the Federation could reshape the Church-dominated, elitist school system to serve the greater interests of society. At best, it would be grassroots, secular democratic socialism at work.

Salvemini addressed the Federation's first congress in Florence. Rising to his feet, with the zeal and militancy of youth, he exhorted the nation's schoolteachers to plunge into active political life:

We will mingle in the life of our time, not afraid of losing our political virginity; we will flirt with all the political parties in order to dominate them without binding ourselves to any; we will fight anyone who opposes the rights of the schools. To be afraid of politics is to isolate ourselves from the world, to split ourselves from the currents of modern life.[57]

Salvemini was an unlikely candidate to lead a drive for educational reform because he had very little interest in educational philosophy or pedagogy and little patience for the educational bureaucracy. However, he believed that education played an absolutely crucial role in society. In a book destined to become a classic in the annals of Italian education, he wrote, "Every scholastic question is, in the final analysis, a social and political question. . . . All teaching . . . must always come around to a social purpose."[58]

To make the school system an instrument for social reform, he called for teachers to abandon the "the fetishism of scattered facts," the tradition of ency-clopedic accumulation of information. What Italian education needed was to teach students to observe, analyze, reflect, and assimilate. It should be "antidogmatic" and should teach a sense of "proportion" and "perspective" and a tolerance for contrasting ideas. Then, and only then, would the system en-courage the development of a true culture. The social function of education, he argued, was to prepare the citizenry to make intelligent political choices. This was a view that reflected both classical and modern values, a Socratic axiom long forgotten, a modern democratic conviction not yet accepted.[59]

By 1905, Salvemini's protestations on behalf of reform had won the attention of the educational establishment. The Minister of Education, Leonardo Bianchi, appointed him to the three-man Commission for the Reform of the Middle Schools. The appointment took him to Rome, Florence, and Milan, requiring a leave of absence from the University of Messina for most of the 1905–1906 aca-demic year. In January 1906, he left the Commission for a temporary return to Messina upon the birth of his fourth child, Ughetto. All the while, he managed to participate actively in the PSI and the teachers' federation.[60]

In Naples in September 1907, standing before the organization he had cre-ated six years earlier, Salvemini told his audience that all educational questions begin with the fundamental issue of "general culture." He explained: "[Educa-tional] culture . . . consists of . . . the need for logical and clear ideas; of the en-thusiasm for personal and critical initiative; of the strength and courage of thought."[61] To achieve these cultural goals, Italy would have to move away from the confessional schools toward secular, lay education. Secular schools could best instill in students the antidogmatic, critical spirit.

The noted philosopher Giovanni Gentile, who had his own following at the convention, openly challenged Salvemini on this issue. Gentile argued that the secular schools should adopt a philosophy and should teach religious values. Salvemini retorted that the schools should teach religion in the same critical spirit as politics and should eliminate altogether the dogma of the catechism. Salvemini, bristling at what he saw as Gentile's tendencies toward orthodoxy and indoctrination, argued that the teachers of the Federation would find unity in the freedom of their critical perspective: "For me, academic freedom is the means, and the end, and everything."[62]

Then, with rising emphasis, Salvemini attacked the Italian tradition of the remote, learned professor. The ideal lay teacher, he declared, "would carry to the school such a spark of fire that it would illuminate and consume humanity; . . .

would abandon the noble toga of the professor to wear the humble shirt of the teacher."[63]

Salvemini committed great energy to practicing these lofty values. His students at Messina were only the first among many who would applaud his enthusiasm for teaching. He spent long hours writing his first lectures, while teaching five days each week in three of the university's colleges. His view of secular education as a process for teaching independent, critical thinking was an idea he lived by; he could not have known then that it would eventually cost him his career.[64]

When the teachers' convention adjourned, he returned to Messina, where he would remain for the next two years. In spite of his dissatisfaction with Italian politics and his frustration at being trapped at the University of Messina, Salvemini did find a certain personal happiness during his years in Sicily. He had become almost comfortable in his role as a critic of Italian public life without losing his passion for participation. He had finally been awarded his promotion and the accompanying stipend; and in October 1907, Maria presented him with their fifth child, Elena. Even material privation could not deaden the richness of family. In the fall of 1908, he proclaimed, "In my family life I am so happy that I am frightened."[65] To this day, the letter invokes an eerie sense of foreboding.

Three nights after Christmas 1908, Salvemini walked along the Viale della Libertà, across from the long seaside park, where on warmer nights local residents strolled to feel the breeze blowing in off the Straits of Messina. In the vast harbor, ships swayed at anchor. He walked briskly, anxious to retire after an especially long day. Arriving at a large, rectangular edifice at the Piazza Cairoli, he wearily climbed the five flights of stairs to the top floor where his sister, wife, and five children lay sleeping.

Just before dawn, awakened by the cries of his daughter Elena, Salvemini lifted her from her crib and gently transported the infant to his wife's breast. As he did, they were both startled by a prolonged and terrifying rumble, accompanied by a torrential rain. Dogs howled in anguish, gas street lamps flared and died, and electric bells chimed a surrealistic chorus, a certain indication that the night silence would be shattered again. Instantaneously, he felt a reeling sensation in his stomach and heard sinister sounds in the street. He leaped to his feet, bolted in his nightshirt to the nearest window, and flung open the shutters into total darkness. Everywhere beams moaned and squeaked; walls, cornices, and chimneys shivered and fell; tile roofs slammed to the ground. Sensing a wall collapsing behind him, he lunged instinctively for the window. At that moment, the whole house crashed down, the crumbling wall carrying him along as he clung desperately to the window frame.[66]

The successive shocks of earthquake and tidal wave that battered Salvemini's house buried his entire family in the rubble. Emergency workers, including British, Russian, and American sailors, knew that Messina had suffered unthinkable devastation, along with much of Sicily and Calabria. The first newspapers to report the tragedy estimated that 90 percent of the city had been demolished. Later estimates placed the death toll at 60,000.[67]

Il Corriere della Sera, the largest Italian daily, reported in bold print in its January 2 edition, "THE DEATH OF PROF. SALVEMINI." The story that followed, based on a report from a colleague at the university, included an obituary of the "beloved" professor.[68]

Seven hundred miles to the north of Messina, in the small Italian Riviera town of Oneglia, a twenty-five-year-old teacher and socialist editor read, among the details of a newspaper account, "The family of Professor Gaetano Salvemini was completely destroyed." Moved by the tragic loss of such a well-known intellectual and fellow partisan, he sent a telegram expressing his grief: "In Gaetano Salvemini passes one of the greatest men of Italian socialism. Benito Mussolini."[69]

NOTES

1. GS, "La questione meridionale e il federalismo,"*Opere* IV (2), 157–158.

2. GS, "La questione meridionale e il federalismo," *Opere* IV (2), 157–158.

3. GS to Carlo Placci, December 12, 1901, *Opere* IX (1), 196; Denis Mack Smith, *A History of Sicily* (New York, 1968), 495, *passim*; Michela D'Angelo, "Salvemini a Messina" in GC, *Sal*, 278–279.

4.ET, *Sal*, 27; AGh to GS, October 7, 1901, *Opere* IX (1), 196; D'Angelo, "Salvemini," 292– 294.

5. DeG, *IL*, 8–9.

6. DeG, *IL*, 9; JM, *EMP*, 13–20; DiS, *DIS*, 11–38.

7. GS, "Contributo alla riforma del programma minimo: I–II," *Opere* IV (2), 52–59; DiS, *DIS*, 1– 10, 31–32, 39–66; MLS, *Sal*, 61–68; DeC, *Sal*, 117–119.

8. JM, *EMP*, 7, *passim*; DeG, *IL*, 5–14, *passim*; DiS *DIS*, *passim*.

9. On the issue of PSI organization, see JM, *EMP*, 41–53.

10. JM, *EMP*, 13–14; DiS, *DIS*, 104–105, 141–142.

11. GS, "I partiti politici milanesi nel secolo XIX," *Opere* II (2), 29–123; "L'*Opera Omnia* di Cattaneo e la ristampa dei documenti inediti," *Opere* VIII, 223–224; Luigi Lotti, "Nella linea del pensiero democratico," *La Voce Repubblicana*, December 20–21, 1967.

12. GS, "La questione meridionale, I," *Opere* IV (2), 71–74.

13. GS, preface to *SSQM*, xvi; to AGh, April 29, 1899, *Opere* IX (1), 91; Giuseppe Giarizzo, "Gaetano Salvemini: La Politica," in GC, *Sal*, 14.

14. GS, "La questione meridionale e il federalismo"; to AGh, January 16, 1900, *Opere* IX (1), 127.

15. GS, "La questione meridionale e il federalismo," 106; "Il federalismo di Cattaneo in uno scritto di Salvemini," *La Voce Repubblicana*, December 20–21, 1967.

16. GS to Francesco Papafava, March 11, 1900, *Opere* IX (1), 147–148; to AGh, March 25, May, and July 13, 1900, *Opere* IX (1), 151, 154, and 157.

17. GS, "Un programma per i socialisti del Sud," *SSQM*, 138–140; "Per il suffragio universale," *SSQM*, 370–372; "Il suffragio universale e le riforme," *SSQM*, 229–337; DeC, *Sal*, 136–145; MLS, *Sal*, 68–73.

18. GS, "La questione meridionale e il federalismo," 90–92.

19. GS, "Nord e Sud nel partito socialista italiano," *Opere* IV (2), 239–248.

20. GS, "Suffragio universale, questione meridionale e riformismo," *Opere* IV (2), 331–352 (emphasis added).

21. FT, "Tattica elettorate," quoted in LB, *Sal*, 72–79; GA, *SSI*, 132; DiS, *DIS*, 112–119.

22. Ettore Cicotti, "Mezzogiorno e Settentrione d'Italia," *Rivista popolare di Politica Lettere e Scienze Sociali*, August 15 and 30, September 15, 1898.

23. GS to Placci, October 6, 1902, *Opere* IX (1), 221–224; Angelo Ventura, "Gaetano Salvemini e il partito socialista" in GC, *Sal*, 49–51.

24. GS to Papafava, September 20, 1899, *Opere* IX (1), 105–106.

25. GS to AGh, January 30, 1900, in *Opere* IX (1), 137.

26. GS, *La Rivoluzione francese (1788–1792)* (Milan, 1905) quoted in Giarizzo, "Salvemini," 6–7.

27. GS to Papafava, January 29, 1900, *Opere* IX (1), 132.

28. GS, "Sempre polemiche meridionali! II" *SSQM*, 175–182; to Papafava, January 29, 1900, 132; to AGh, January 30, 1900, 136–138, *Opere*, IX (1); DiS, *DIS*, 114.

29. GS, "Un programma per i socialisti del Sud," *Opere* IV (2), 235–239; "Sempre polemiche meridionali: I," *Opere* IV (2), 270–278; *Programma amministrativo dei partiti popolari di Molfetta* (Molfetta, 1902), WL.

30. GS, "La questione meridionale e il federalismo," 72 ff. For an evaluation of Salvemini's proposals, see LB, *Sal*, 71 ff; DeC, *Sal*, 19–40, 83–104, 208–223; MLS, *Sal*, 59–89.

31. GS, "Sempre polemiche meridionale! II," 278–283; "Un programma per i socialisti del sud," *Opere* IV (2), 239; "Nord e Sud nel Partito socialista italiano," and "Riforme sociali e riforme politiche," *Opere* IV (2), 239–248 and 299–313.

32. GS, "Contributo alla riforma del programma minimo: I–II," *Opere* IV (2), 52–59.

33. GS to AGh, October 4, [1899] and July [13], 1900, 110–111 and 156; to Papafava, July 23, 1900, 159; to Placci, October 6, 1902, 221–222, *Opere* IX (1).

34. GS to AGh, May, July (13) and August 1900, 153, 156, and 164; to Papafava, July 23, 1900, 159; to Placci, June 5, 1899 and April 10, 1902, 92 and 213, *Opere* IX (1).

35. GS to AGh, August 6, 1900, 163; to Placci, October 6 and 7, 1902, 221–222, *Opere* IX (1).

36. Placci to GS, January 20, 1906 (especially n. 1), 334–335; GS to Placci, January 21, 1906 and June 24, 1908, 336 and 387, *Opere* IX (1); ET, *Sal*, 59.

37. GS to AGh, August 13, 1900, 164; to Papafava, December 21, 1900, *Carteggi*, 171–172; to Giuseppe Kirner, January 7, 1904, 295; to Placci, April 19, 1903, 266, *Opere* IX (1).

38. Papafava to GS, July 28 and December 23, 1900, *Opere* IX (1), 161 and 174.

39. GS to AGh, October 9, 1901, 186–190; AGh to GS, October 13, 1901, 190–193; FT to GS, September 1, 1907, 363, *Opere* IX (1).

40. GS to AGh, July [13], 1900, 156–157; to Placci, April 19, 1903, 267, *Opere* IX (1).

41. GS to Placci, January 31, 1904, 295; Placci to GS, [April 1], 1904, 305, *Opere* IX (1).

42. D'Angelo, "Salvemini a Messina," 281; GS to Placci, December 12, 1901, *Opere* IX (1), 197.

43. GS, "La storia considerata come scienza," *Opere* VIII, 107–135. It would be revised in various forms, including a series of 1938 lectures at the University of Chicago, published as *Historian and Scientist* (Cambridge, 1939), translated as *Storia e Scienza* (Florence, 1948).

44. Placci to GS, August 22, 1902, *Opere* IX (1), 219.

45. GS, "La storia considerata come scienza."

46. D'Angelo, "Salvemini a Messina," 285–286.

47. GS, *Mazzini* (New York, 1962), 17. The 1905 version was published as *Mazzini* (Messina, 1905); Giarizzo, "Salvemini," 18–27; AGG, *Salvemini e Mazzini* (Messina, 1981), *passim*; and *Archivio Trimestrale* (July–December 1982), *passim*.

48. GS, *Mazzini*, 100–103,130–131, 158; Croce, "Il partito come giudizio e come pregiudizio" in BF, *L'U*, 30.

49. GS to AGh, Dec. 13, 1899, 116, n. 3; PV to GS, July 14, 1905, 321, *Opere* IX (1).

50. GS to PV, July 18, 1905, *Opere* IX (1), 322–326.

51. GS, *French Revolution*, 11–12; see Antonio Marando, "I filosofi dei lumi a la 'Grande Rivoluzione,'" *La Voce Repubblicana*, December 20–21, 1967; Leo Valiani, *L'Historiographe de L'Italie Contemporaine*, French translation by Maurice Chevallier (Geneva, 1968); ES, "Lo Storico" in ES, *ACGS*, 3–37.

52. GS to Placci, August 21, 1903, 281; to PV, November 30, 1905, 328–329; PV to GS, November 27, 1905, 328, *Opere* IX (1).

53. Papafava to GS, December 18, 1905 (especially n. 1), 330; GS to Papafava, December 26, 1905, 331, *Opere* IX (1).

54. GS to Placci, January 21, 1906, *Opere* IX (1), 336–337.

55. GS to Placci, January 21, 1906, 337; to PV, July 27, 1906, 342, *Opere* IX (1).

56. See Lamberto Borghi's Preface, *Opere* V, ix-xxx; Borghi, "Educazione e Scuola in Gaetano Salvemini" in ES, *ACGS*, 197–239; Giovanni Maria Bertin, "L'idea di cultura educativa negli *Scritti sulla scuola* di Salvemini e la sua attualità" in ES, *ACGS*, 241–270.

57. L. Ambrosoli, *La Federazione Nazionale Insegnanti Scuola Media dalle origini al 1925* (Florence, 1967), 66, quoted in Bertin, "L'idea di cultura educativa," 251–252.

58. GS and Alfredo Galletti, *La riforma della scuola media* (Palermo, 1908), in *Opere* V, 567.

59. GS and Galletti, *La riforma della scuola media*, 293–304.

60. GS to Placci, January 21 and September 1, 1906, 336, 344; to PV, July 27, 1906, 342, *Opere* IX (1).

61. GS, "Che cosa è la coltura?," *La Cultura Contemporanea* (Rome), March 1–16, 1910, 89, Pusey.

62. GS, "Che cosa è la laicità," *Opere* V, 881–896.

63. GS, *Cultura e laicità* (Catania, 1914), 64, cited in Borghi, "Educazione e Scuola in Gaetano Salvemini," 207 ff. See also Bertin, "L'idea di cultura educativa," 242.

64. D'Angelo, "Salvemini a Messina," 282 ff.

65. Lidia Minervini, "Amico e Maestro." Salvemini's children were Filipetto, Corrado, Leonida, Ugo, and Elena.

66. Jay Henry Mowbray, *Italy's Great Horror* (n.p., 1909), 34–35.

67. Minervini, "Amico e Maestro"; HC interview, August 13, 1991, Leeds, Massachusetts; HC to Killinger, September 24, 1991; Mowbray, *Italy's Great Horror*, *passim*.

68. "La morte del prof. Salvemini," *CdS*, January 2, 1909. See also in the same edition, Giuseppe Ricchieri, "Notizia biografica su Salvemini creduto perito durante il terremoto."

69. Minervini, "Amico e Maestro." See also Salvemini's own description in D'Angelo, "Salvemini a Messina," 300 n.; MLS, *Sal*, 22; Iris Origo, *A Need to Testify*, 144–145.

Chapter 3

The Making of a Reformer

On New Year's Day 1909, *Critica Sociale* featured a compelling tribute from its editor, Filippo Turati: "He lived and lives—yes, *lives* . . . the strong, combative and generous soul of Gaetano Salvemini; the best educated, the best equipped of the Italian socialists."[1]

The eulogies had proven premature. Three days later, *Il Corriere della Sera* reported from Catania, "Salvemini lives." This time it was correct.[2]

Salvemini miraculously survived the collapse of his house. In desperation, he had clutched the window, which remained attached to the architrave, and thereby to the structure of the exterior wall. The wall had slowed his descent and protected his head, depositing him on a mound of rubble and sparing his life. Stunned but not seriously injured, desperate for a sign of life, Salvemini feverishly combed the debris, his brother-in-law at his side. The two found only death. Eventually, rescuers uncovered the bodies of four of his children, but those of his wife, his sister Cammilla, and his son Ugo were never found.

Salvemini and the few survivors from his extended family sought temporary shelter in a cottage on the Via Dogali along the Piazza Cairoli, an area partially spared. A shell of the five-story residence, devoid of the top two floors of its facade, provided a pitiful reminder of the catastrophe. The family recovered only the scantiest personal possessions: a sock, several mangled books, a few of the children's school papers, a primer, and a child's dress.

Surviving neighbors and crews from ships docked in the port provided some clothing and food. At the dinner table of the cottage, Salvemini sat, fork in hand, immobile, a fixed stare revealing the shock of his devastating loss.

"Gaetano, have you eaten?" someone asked.

He remained motionless and silent. No one who consoled him saw the familiar, broad smile. Some said it would never again appear so readily.[3]

It is impossible to overstate the destruction of the earthquake that brought the ancient city to its knees. The University of Messina closed, depriving Salvemini of his job at the same time that he lost his family and his possessions. He left Sicily immediately for Florence, always his second home. There he stayed with friends and resumed part-time lecturing at the university. The intellectual activity scarcely helped.

He was particularly haunted by the failure to find the body of Ugo, the toddler he affectionately called "Ughetto," whose third birthday neared. Two weeks after the earthquake, Salvemini wrote Giovanni Gentile that he would return to Messina as soon as he could acquire permission to search for Ugo. If he did not find the child alive, he wrote, "Just to find the body would put my soul at peace."[4]

In March, visiting friends in Milan, he heard a story of a young orphan in a Palermo hospital who answered to the name Ugo. Startled, he immediately dispatched a telegram to Gentile: "CONFIRM CHILDREN'S HOSPITAL IF UGO BENSAI IS TRULY BENSAI OR IF HE BEARS OTHER SURNAME." The reply, confirming the child's name as Ugo Bensai, broke Salvemini's heart.[5]

Friends worried about psychological damage. Croce feared for his sanity.[6] In April, Salvemini expressed the pathos of his profound loss:

If I had ever been able to imagine a horrible calamity striking me, I would never have thought of this one. If only one of those children . . . remained for me, at least Filipetto!

I go forward, I work. . . . I go on living. . . . I am a poor wretch, without a roof and without a hearth, who has seen destroyed in two minutes the happiness of eleven years.

I have on my table a few letters from my poor wife, my sister and the children. . . . And after reading a few, I must stop, because a great, desperate crying attack overcomes me and I want to die.[7]

On several occasions, he accepted invitations to stay with friends in France, but he remained distraught, near madness and suicide. In May, he wrote to Placci from Grenoble:

In this tranquil, methodical, homely life that takes me back to happy days and gives me nearly the illusion of having a family, my health improves. . . . But during the intervals, the past seizes me. I see it before me in living fragments that give me an atrocious illusion of reality! I dream of it. It seems at times that . . . this is leading me toward insanity. These moments pass; . . . But they hurt me very much.[8]

The disaster changed him, and in a sense he never fully overcame the staggering memory. Writing in a diary days after Christmas 1922, Salvemini remembered:

Now fourteen years have passed, to the day, on which I saw my previous life destroyed in a single moment. And I have not succeeded yet in thinking of that tragedy without feeling unable to control the bewilderment of my soul. The memory of that which I lost . . . is still intolerable. And yet more frightening was the year that followed my misfortune. How I did not lose my sanity, I do not know. . . . It is impossible for me to think of it. My sanity is linked to my successful effort not to remember, not to think.[9]

For years, Salvemini advertised in Russian newspapers for Ughetto in the vain hope that the Russian crew had rescued the child from Messina. Many years after the disaster, while staying with friends in both Italy and the United States, he was heard crying in his sleep: "Maria! Maria! Maria!"[10]

Some people who knew of his emotional fragility, like Benedetto Croce, expected Salvemini to crack. In the immediate aftermath, expressing his suffering acted as a temporary balm. He even published a brief description in *Avanti!* just days after the earthquake. For months he was trapped in utter despair. For a year he failed to shake the abiding melancholy, and he shrank from ever again speaking of the tragedy. Emotionally scarred, he no longer readily addressed his own fears and anxieties. Enzo Tagliacozzo, an intimate for many years, wrote that "a veil of sadness and pessimism covered his life." Yet somehow Salvemini resumed teaching and rediscovered his zeal for politics. In the process, he found a measure of personal happiness.[11]

His productivity as a writer did not noticeably suffer. Before the disaster, he had already begun to publish at the rate of two articles per month, and he maintained that steady pace through 1909. By 1911, he had doubled that rate and by 1912 he was publishing more than three articles per week. The next year, before war distracted the European population, he produced more than 220 articles, a rate he would never surpass. When he wrote to his friend Ernesta Bittanti that he was "occupied from morning to night with all my various work," she knew him well enough to understand that he was not exaggerating.[12] He returned to active politics as well, committing enormous energy to winning for all Italians the right to vote—hardly the campaign of a cynic. His work may have been his salvation.

As his attacks on the political establishment intensified, some sensed a prevailing negativism induced by the tragedy. Anna Kuliscioff, who responded with sensitivity and intelligence to many broadsides Salvemini fired at the Socialist Party leadership, warned him in early 1910, "Be careful, Salvemini, that you do not abandon yourself to skepticism."[13] However, there is no evidence of a clear psychological break. He had chosen the pseudonym "The Pessimist" by age twenty-six, in the winter of 1899. His criticism of the status quo, often perceived as negative, was the product of his usual self-conscious perspective as outsider. Well before his personal tragedy, many Italian politicians had become quite familiar with the sting of Salvemini's rhetorical vehemence.

Several friends saw a more reluctant smile and a dimming of his eyes, but others, even years later, recall his roaring laugh and zest for life. Franco Venturi, historian and fellow exile, remembered "this lust for life, this explosion of vitality, of protest, of revolt" that continued to accompany his friend's "violent and rebellious" temperament. Notably little had changed. Within months of the earthquake, Salvemini resumed his political activities with a vengeance, and the next decade would bring a depth and variety of new experiences he could never have anticipated.[14]

The years after 1908 were among the most politically tumultuous of Salvemini's life. Just months after his great loss, some friends, perhaps sensing in him a need for activity, encouraged a run for office in the approaching general election. He knew that candidacy was premature, but his friends had scarcely missed the mark. Declining the offer, he proposed instead to monitor the election in his home region of Apulia in the town of Gioia del Colle, infamous for electoral violence and fraud. It was a fateful decision.

Salvemini understood the local politics of Apulia, and he chose Gioia del Colle because it exemplified Giovanni Giolitti's version of *trasformismo*. Giolitti, the astute Piedmontese politician, was serving his third of five terms as prime minister. In national politics since 1882, he had recovered from the bank scandal that had destroyed his first government by building a power base as Giuseppe Zanardelli's Minister of Interior. Giolitti used patronage to mobilize the prefects in a clientele system that provided the parliamentary votes for his program of economic development and moderate reform throughout the period 1903–1914. So dominant was he that this decade is called the "Giolittian Era." It was his moderate reforms, designed in part to co-opt the Left—and especially his corrupt methods—that invoked Salvemini's opposition. By dramatically confirming his views of Giolitti, this local election pushed Salvemini in a political direction he would maintain for most of his life and made Giolitti Salvemini's singular *bête noire*.[15]

On the evening of March 6, 1909, Salvemini and two respected journalists, Ugo Ojetti and Luigi Lucatelli, arrived at the small town in the Trulli district, about forty miles inland from Bari. They had discussed the local political machine, controlled by a former merchant named Vito De Bellis, a typical sergeant in Giolitti's political army. Salvemini believed that it was Giolitti's ability to control hundreds of such southern towns by political influence and electoral fraud that enabled him to victimize and exploit poor southerners to the advantage of both their landlords and the northern businessmen and politicians—including PSI deputies—who were their allies in Giolitti's parliamentary organization. In a sense, then, this otherwise obscure political event became for Salvemini one of greatest significance.[16]

As the three men stepped off the train at the Gioia del Colle station, all speculation ended. A crowd of club-wielding men waited in silence on the platform. As they stood, face-to-face, with De Bellis's thugs, they understood the reality of small-town politics. The *mazzieri* (club wielders) escorted the aliens to their hotel, where a number of them stood vigil. Complaints to the local police went unanswered. Instead, responding to a knock at their door, Salvemini found a man who identified himself as a plainclothes police agent. Purporting to speak on behalf of his captain, an infamous political operative named Ettore Prina, the agent advised them to leave town on the next train because he feared a massacre. They refused, demanding that they be guaranteed police protection. A little later, Salvemini ventured out the front door, only to be confronted by the threatening crowd. Before he could react, he was whisked to safety by a deputy and another plainclothes officer.[17]

Salvemini and the two journalists remained in Gioia del Colle for the duration of the campaign, and their observations and interviews confirmed all that they had suspected about provincial political corruption. Groups of *mazzieri* created an atmosphere of intimidation calculated to deliver victory. They warned the wives of the anti–De Bellis party that their husbands took great risks if they voted, and they patrolled the streets on election day to emphasize the point. They painted threatening graffiti on the headquarters of the local League of Peasants, and the implied violence silenced most opposition. Salvemini interviewed as many people as he could, but he could find few willing to criticize the De Bellis organization.[18]

The notes he made from the campaign became the raw material for one of Salvemini's best-known works. A year later, *La Voce* of Florence published *Il Ministro della mala vita* ("The Ministry of the Underworld"), the collection of essays by which Salvemini established himself as Giolitti's nemesis. In it he described the abuses he saw on election day in Gioia del Colle:

The soldiers and the *carabinieri* occupied all the streets leading to the voting places, leaving free only one entrance at each place. The voters, who had to pass all of them to reach the entrance, were drafted by the partisans of the government's candidate. . . . The delegates let their friends pass or stopped their enemies. The ones who protested or insisted on getting through were beaten by the *mazzieri* or were arrested for resisting an officer of the law and were forced outside until . . . the polls were officially closed.[19]

The tainted victory of Vito De Bellis and the Giolittian slate of candidates in Gioia del Colle provided Salvemini, by firsthand observation, solid proof of what he had believed about Giolitti's tactics. The tentacles of Giolitti's political organization did, in fact, manage to strangle the political freedoms of southern villagers. With such a small electorate, political hacks like De Bellis, with the support of the local prefects of the Interior Ministry and the local police, could easily "fix" any elections they could not otherwise win by the use of political influence. What was needed, Salvemini was convinced, was nothing less than a radical change in the election laws. Only universal suffrage would create a large enough mass base of voters to overturn Giolitti's machine. He emerged from the 1909 election more firmly committed than ever to expanding the vote.

Salvemini's persistent advocacy of universal suffrage reveals much about the man. In a sense, this campaign and his continuing efforts to oppose the Giolitti organization are the defining events of Salvemini's maturing political life. In fighting these prewar battles, Salvemini developed his own political identity to the point that he became an icon of idealism and moralism, a personified rejection of the political process. At the 1908 PSI convention in Florence, he had told the delegates:

When we ask for something we always take care to say that we shall be satisfied with a half, a quarter, or an eighth of it.... Thus, in practice, we do not make a compromise, but the compromise of a compromise of the compromise.[20]

Compromise, inherent in the political process, was incompatible with the idealism of this rigid moralist. With greater visibility in the prewar era, Salvemini became, as one friend called him, "The anti-Machiavelli of contemporary society."[21] In a sense his unmitigated condemnation of Giolittian tactics tended to create a simplistic dualism of politics and ethics, cynicism and idealism, good and evil. Neither Giolitti nor Salvemini understood that the political battles they fought, for all their imperfections, were to be the last exercises in Italian democracy for more than two decades. Their failure to build a stronger commitment to democratic institutions was fatal.

Giolitti employed his political acumen to build a working consensus of liberals and moderate socialists by sponsoring gradual reforms and tolerating a degree of public opposition. For all his ability to command political power, however, Giolitti lost ground in the general parliamentary elections of 1909, especially to the left-wing parties. As a result, after a futile attempt to strengthen his hand, he ended his "long ministry" in inimitable style by asking King Vittorio Emanuele III to replace him before he lost a vote of confidence. Sidney Sonnino succeeded Giolitti, forming his second cabinet, this time exclusively right of center. These events caused a great stirring of anticipation within the PSI as the leadership welcomed the opportunity to gain at the expense of a government less likely to undercut their support.[22]

The fall of Giolitti's "long ministry" elevated Salvemini's campaign for universal suffrage to the informal agenda of the PSI and gave him his best chance to win the party's endorsement. Turati resisted, arguing that extending the franchise to illiterates would deliver the South to the Catholics.[23] Salvemini countered Turati's opposition with a vigorous propaganda initiative in *Avanti!* and other national organs, including Turati's own *Critica Sociale*.[24]

Salvemini also continued to address numerous audiences on the topic. In Rome, he spoke to the Chamber of Labor and several other groups in February. At a theater in Bari, he pled with local socialists to break Giolitti's control of the South by expanding the vote. "We will not pass our lives in vain," he exhorted the crowd, "if we contribute . . . to this work of justice and morality." His master plan called for a "half year of agitation" followed by "a great demonstration in Rome in May 1911 and obstructionism in the Chamber."[25]

Despite his political agitation, in early 1910, after a year of lecturing in Florence, the Ministry of Education reassigned Salvemini to the nearby University of Pisa. His socialist militancy almost cost him the appointment. Finally, over the objections of a divided Faculty Council dominated by older conservatives, the Minister intervened personally to order the appointment. A number of students, more sympathetic with Salvemini's politics, had learned of the dispute and were excited by the news.

On an afternoon in February, his first class met. Not aware that students had campaigned on his behalf, he crossed campus from the library to the lecture hall with distinctive short, quick steps and entered the classroom. The twenty or more students greeted him with enthusiastic applause. He thanked them. Their warm display gave him comfort, he told them. However, sensing the political implications, he decided that he must warn them that inside the classroom he was only a professor of history. All political activity must remain outside.[26]

In spite of this precarious debut, the College of Letters promoted Salvemini to professor of history in less than one year. One of his students remembered his distinctive teaching style: less pretentious than most, his lectures were simple and clear, emphasizing scientific rigor and "concreteness" while challenging all abstractions and projecting values of human freedom and dignity. He respected his students, involved them directly in presentations and discussions, "became a friend, a thoughtful counselor," and inspired them to lives of thought and action. He welcomed students to his house daily, and consequently it became a hub of intellectual activity for young scholars. It was in Pisa and in nearby Florence, where he would return in a few years, that he began to build a following of history students and political activists that would become known informally as the "Salvemini school" of scholars.[27]

In April, shortly after he moved to Pisa, a coalition of democratic parties invited Salvemini to run for Parliament in Albano, an electoral district southeast of Rome known for its political corruption and violence. His recently published *Ministro della mala vita* had given him new exposure as a champion of election reform, and the leaders of the Radical, Republican, and Socialist Parties hoped to make a symbolic statement. It was a formula for disaster.[28]

As events would soon reveal, Salvemini should have followed his initial instincts. He declined the offer on principle, only to relent when reassured by local leaders that they wanted to conduct a reform campaign on a high moral plain. It was, he said, an invitation he "did not have the right to refuse." As soon as he committed, the local coalition fell apart, but he refused a PRI request to drop out and began to campaign feverishly in the twenty-one towns that stretched from the Apennine Mountains to the Tyrrhenian Sea. Each day he delivered four or five speeches, focusing on tariff reform, literacy, and, of course, universal suffrage. On April 13, *Avanti!* reported one of his speeches:

I do not promise personal favors because I will not give them. I do not have money. I do not have any inheritance other than my ideas. If I commit improprieties I will immediately remove myself from the ballot. . . . Likewise, . . . I will expose [my adversaries] at the first sign of treachery on their part.[29]

His moralistic appeal found an audience. Mussolini reported that the Socialists of Forlì invited Salvemini to speak to them on universal suffrage in April 1910. Nonetheless, the campaign never managed to overcome its initial difficulties. Charges triggered countercharges; irregularities appeared from the start. Eventually he heard that local Republicans were plotting to "stuff the ballot box" to assure his victory, then replace him with a Republican after having the results overturned. His protests led to further controversy until, two days before the election, after a sleepless night, Salvemini withdrew from the race.[30]

Salvemini's rhetoric and behavior in the Albano campaign illustrate a quixotic approach to politics that suggests that remaining on the sidelines would have been a wiser choice. At best, he generated further publicity for election reform; at worst, he brought ridicule upon himself and thereby to his cause. He admitted, shortly thereafter, that he had made mistakes. He realized that he should have avoided a campaign in an unfamiliar district, but, having entered, he should have remained in the race and resolved the improprieties after the votes had been counted. Perhaps they were only the mistakes of a political novice, but observers had to ask whether Salvemini possessed the psychological durability to withstand the rigors of political campaigning. When he returned to the University of Pisa, his students, ignoring his earlier warning to abstain from politics in the classroom, once again rose to their feet in applause, indicating their support for his campaign. The academy provided a refuge from the ordeal of Giolittian politics.[31]

Salvemini's unsuccessful campaign of 1910 reaffirmed his distrust for political parties and did little to mend his deteriorating relationship with the PSI. As its leaders were still discussing the debacle at Albano, Salvemini sharpened the tone of his criticism of the PSI parliamentary delegation. In March, economist and former Treasury Minister Luigi Luzzatti replaced Sonnino as prime minister and began to propose reform measures, including election reforms and an expanded franchise. In April, over the opposition of Kuliscioff and Turati, the PSI parliamentary group agreed by a narrow vote to support Luzzatti's program, a tactic known as "ministerialism." Salvemini was furious, believing that the Socialists were continuing to sell their ideals for political gain and, in the process, undercutting universal suffrage with meaningless, piecemeal reforms.[32]

Acerbic exchanges with socialists heightened Salvemini's anticipation of the Tenth PSI Congress, scheduled for Milan in October 1910. It was to be a turning point in his political career, and a great deal of attention, then and later, was focused on his actions and his attitude. One person who supported Salvemini's condemnation of patronage in the socialist cooperatives was revolutionary socialist Costantino Lazzari, who, along with Mussolini, challenged the revisionist leadership of Turati's forces.[33]

As an independent socialist, Salvemini was courted by other factions as well. Reformist Fausto Pagliari warned Salvemini of a "lynching" campaign and, in a flurry of enthusiasm, promised support, urging him to attend the Congress: "You have a sturdy back, a strong head, and a heroic pen; do not let them reduce [you] to silence."[34] By the time he received Pagliari's vote of confidence, Salvemini was in Milan meeting with Kuliscioff and others to map strategy in support of universal suffrage.

Salvemini placed himself on the left of the socialist spectrum. The right, he told a friend, would be led by Leonida Bissolati and Ivanoe Bonomi; the center right, by Turati. "We are the left," he continued; and the extreme left, the "verbose and apocalyptic" revolutionaries, would be led by Lazzari—not even Salvemini anticipated the emergence of the young extremist socialist from the Romagna, Benito Mussolini, who stood with Lazzari on the extreme left. Mussolini's first party convention would be Salvemini's last.[35]

Salvemini anticipated the Congress with high expectations.[36] Kuliscioff pled his case before Turati, providing Salvemini with an opportunity to convince the party to endorse a national campaign of agitation for universal suffrage. By late summer, however, his expectations had begun to diminish, and by fall Kuliscioff was dampening his hopes, warning of an impending power play by the revolutionaries that might indirectly be abetted by Salvemini's initiative. She wrote in September, "I do not believe that the center left that you represent . . . can dominate in northern Italy. Your contingent must be recruited in southern Italy under the banner of universal suffrage."[37] As the Congress neared, he wanted to abandon politics in favor of research: "I have lost all faith in the men who today dominate the party. . . . I go to Milan without enthusiasm and without hope. I feel absolutely alone."[38]

On October 21, 1910, the PSI Congress opened at the Casa del Popolo in Milan. In spite of doubt and frustration, Salvemini approached the meeting with characteristic vigor and with the unrealistic assumption that the moral rectitude and social justice of his cause could carry the convention. It was the classic Salveminian posture, and in a sense the unfolding of events provided no surprise. Turati, undoubtedly with the encouragement of Kuliscioff, gave Salvemini the forum he wanted by naming him keynote speaker. It was his long-anticipated opportunity to convert the PSI to a vehicle of democratic reform.[39]

The huge crowd of more than 20,000 delegates spilled into the hallways and anterooms, still negotiating political tactics on the second day of meetings. In the main hall the thirty-seven-year-old professor rose to deliver the speech of his life. Those who recognized only the name Salvemini from the periodical press must have noticed the unique, if rather undistinguished, appearance: a prominent, prematurely balding forehead; a dark beard that brought the roundness of his head to an angular finish and accentuated his teeth. It was a Socratic head on a peasant's frame.

As the delegates listened, the words in a sense confirmed the contradictions of the visual impression. They heard the simple, direct style that he always claimed, with some pride, to have developed in conversations with the peasants and fishermen of Molfetta. As he built his case, however, the uncompromising logic and precision of his attack displayed the analytical wit of a superior mind. Even those who had debated him, like Turati and Bissolati, had difficulty in distinguishing style from substance or delineating emotion from intellect.[40]

The PSI, he told them, had in the past made important gains by recruiting northern workers, but the party's leaders were drifting toward a conservative position destined to relegate it to failure. From the rostrum, he directed his comments to the party leader:

Turati, notwithstanding the fact that he suspects that I am slightly mad, does not deny that on some points I am correct: in denouncing the danger of localism, of corporativism of the leadership groups. He says, "That is the way things are." If we must accept things as they are, why do we hold a Congress?

It was his choice to move the party out of this complacent posture. "That," he emphasized, "is why I can be quiet no longer: I protest your indifference."[41]

Then he moved through a sharp analysis of the party that brought a stir of uneasiness to the crowd. The PSI was now dominated by a privileged elite from the Genoa-Milan-Ravenna triangle that delivered government benefits to their constituents while ignoring the masses of laborers in the rest of the country. It was a ringing call for the party to find its moral compass and to rediscover its obligation to provide justice for the entire Italian working class, peasant as well as industrial, southern as well as northern.

The only solution radical enough to redirect the party, and thus to save the party from obscurity, he warned his audience, was to extend the vote to all women as well as men. Knowing that various moderate reform options had been floated by the government, Salvemini drove his point to an emotional climax that rejected all compromise. "Pure and simple universal suffrage" must be achieved only as the product of proletarian demand, not as a tainted gift from Giolitti, "the minister of the underworld." If Giolitti offered to expand the vote, Salvemini roared, "I would reject universal suffrage because, if granted on such a condition and by such a man, universal suffrage would come into the world dishonored." Shouts of favor came from the left-wing faction amid a din of comments and heckling.[42]

By agreeing to allow this militant voice to open the convention, Turati also assured that its impact would be deadened by many successive speeches and endless political maneuvering. Turati's objective was to hold the majority of the delegates together in a broadly based coalition committed not to specific proposals or to reorganization but to party unity.[43]

As speakers droned on for two days, only one voice focused the crowd's attention as Salvemini had. Leonida Bissolati, a party founder, contributor to *Critica Sociale*, and now editor of *Avanti!*, stepped to the front to harangue an appreciative crowd. Like Salvemini, Bissolati emphasized the failures of the party, but the main thrust of his speech served as a direct rebuttal to his former friend, whom he accused of Jesuit-like legalism. Universal suffrage, Bissolati told the crowd, was not the solution; in fact, it would probably be counterproductive. What the party needed was greater latitude for its legislators, including the authority to support the government.[44]

Salvemini was angry and hurt, particularly because of the personal nature of Bissolati's criticism. For months he had seen his friendship with Bissolati unravel, unable or unwilling to stop the deterioration. Bissolati had been leading the right-wing socialists toward ministerialism and had thrown his support behind the PSI legislators, whom Salvemini blamed for most of the party's problems. Their disagreement had become more personal and now was public.

When the great hall was finally still, the delegates cast ballots on three conflicting proposals. Salvemini categorized his motion, presented by his friend and political ally G. E. Modigliani, as "democratic socialism" or "dissident reformism": it called for an end to election corruption and violence and for universal suffrage supported by a comprehensive campaign of agitation. Lazzari proposed an uncompromising, "revolutionary" alternative, emphasizing organization and propaganda among the proletariat and rejecting ministerialism. Turati moved to adopt a moderate, "reformist" compromise that endorsed universal suffrage and tolerated ministerialism but did not endorse the existing government, thus appealing to all socialist elements to form a harmonious, comprehensive party. When the ballots were counted, the Salvemini-Modigliani motion won more than 4,500 votes; the revolutionary motion, almost 6,000; both were swamped by the response to Turati's initiative, which won more than 13,000 votes. Thus Turati had managed to keep control of the Congress in the hands of the reformist leadership.[45]

As a token of reconciliation to Salvemini and his supporters, Turati introduced a motion to adopt "cornerstones for future action," the first of which was a commitment to universal suffrage. Salvemini was not pleased. This "ascetic of politics" deplored such gestures and harbored little patience for the promises and concessions that are the currency of politicians. The ultimate outcome had been a resounding public rejection of his stubborn idealism, destroying any remaining faith in the PSI leadership and deepening his cynical view of parties.

Salvemini took the defeat personally. When he walked out of the Casa del Popolo in Milan on October 25, 1910, he would never again participate in the activities of a political party. Above all else, his contribution to organized socialism had been to make the case for the masses of poor southerners, whose needs the party leadership had ignored. It had been to Salvemini, as one historian saw it, an updated version of the medieval class struggle, and the people had lost.[46]

Reflecting on the whole affair a few days later, he complained bitterly to Giustino Fortunato: "Politics, my dear friend, disgusts me." He felt great tension between his political ideals and his personal well-being. Exhausted, he felt like "throwing everything [political] to the wind and returning to my studies. And then," he concluded, "I must hear near me the voices of the few people whom I love, who must correct me when I have erred and tell me that I must continue."[47]

Although he had made the emotional break with the PSI after the convention, the reality surfaced only gradually. Once apparent, it erupted in controversy. In January 1911, when Turati endorsed the Luzzatti government's proposal for limited election reform, Salvemini denounced the party position in both *Critica* and *Avanti!*, arguing that, by maintaining literacy requirements, the compromise would not significantly broaden the franchise in the south. Rebuking the PSI parliamentary group, he called for a general strike and a campaign of obstruction in support of universal suffrage.[48]

When Giolitti formed his fourth government to replace Luzzatti in March, he approached the reformist socialists for support, offering Turati and Bissolati portfolios in the cabinet. The offer was rejected. Nevertheless, the mere fact that Turati had appeared to consider the offer provoked Salvemini's wrath and widened his breach with the PSI.[49] By the end of the summer, he delivered an obituary on the party to its leader, advising Turati to abandon ministerialism and cooperatives in favor of "concrete questions." He was now convinced that it was necessary to create a new vehicle outside the old parties. "What? I do not know," he continued. "If I knew now, the new party would already exist. But it is necessary to search, and in searching, we will find it."[50]

In appealing to the Left, Giolitti announced support for a suffrage law that would increase the eligible voters from three million to eight million. This proposal might have pleased Salvemini had it not come from his nemesis, but he could not trust Giolitti, and such a partial proposal threatened to defuse his campaign. As a result, he maintained the position he had held for years: simple universal suffrage for both sexes. Giolitti's "gift" was "lunch at 8:00 P.M." Nonetheless, Giolitti had won a psychological edge that made Salvemini's objections seem legalistic and self-serving.[51]

Another casualty of Salvemini's celebrated departure from the Socialist Party was his friendship with Bissolati. Oddino Morgari, a trusted friend and PSI deputy, had warned Salvemini nine months before the convention that Bissolati would not help in the universal suffrage campaign and was a "socialist in name only."[52] In July, Salvemini referred to Bissolati with saddened resignation:

In this whole campaign, this hurts me most: that the friendship between Bissolati and me is finished; because Bissolati, notwithstanding the mistaken impression he has of me because of the ignoble style of [my] polemicizing, I respect. And when a friendship of this type is broken, it is as if a part of us dies. But what to do? Life is full of sadness of this sort.[53]

The incident is another example of Salvemini's sacrifice of friendship for political principle. The personal and the political were, for Salvemini, inexorably entwined. He understood this, consciously relinquishing one for the other, resigned to his fate. Each time, he believed that he was upholding principle while others around him more readily abandoned theirs for political gain. He valued, above all else—and he despaired to find, and he tried to be—an "honest man." Repeatedly he found himself disappointed and politically isolated.

This was not completely rational behavior. It is difficult to accept his view that he made conscious choices in each case, as with Bissolati, or that he always occupied the high moral ground; or that he alone was consistent. In this instance Bissolati shares blame for publicly labeling Salvemini's insistence on universal suffrage as "Jesuitism." However, it is just as likely that Salvemini lost friends not because he stood on principle but for appearing self-righteous and intolerant. He did find that the intemperate tone of his political rhetoric hurt his friends as well as his enemies. Many, though not all, could have accepted the rigidity of his political values had he been more tolerant.

If he could not completely control this tendency, he did indeed recognize it, as was the case when he referred to his "ignoble style of polemicizing" with Bissolati. He knew that he suffered for this reason, and he was not indifferent, for he truly valued friendship. To his credit, he eventually mended his personal relationship with Bissolati.[54]

It was not to the press or to political groups that Salvemini looked for approval of his ideas, but to friends, his "second conscience."[55] "If I did not feel loved and approved by a group of personal friends of diverse parties," he wrote, "I would feel alone. . . . Fortunately that is not the case."[56]

Among those he counted as friends were his disciples. Salvemini was a man who attracted intense devotion. "We are the warriors," Lombardo Radice had told him before the convention. "You must be the general."[57] Two months later, Pagliari proclaimed, "You are a visionary and a heretic. . . . You are Don Quixote."[58] That he lived his values explains that devotion, but in defending those same values he would not, or could not, modify the tone of his rhetoric. His tendency to engage in intemperate personal attacks against political opponents would periodically continue to disrupt his personal relations. Toward those who disappointed him, he was seldom forgiving. Much later, in the twilight of his life, he wrote to an old friend, "You cannot know how old and tired I feel. Above all it has been the defection of men . . . that has disheartened me."[59] It is not surprising that one who held others to the same rigid standards to which he held himself would, in the end, be disappointed.

In a bizarre turn of events, within months after the convention, Salvemini was offered the editorship of *Avanti!*, the PSI paper. The party's revolutionary faction, led by Lazzari, forced out Bissolati as editor and offered the job to Salvemini, whose independent, militant voice and prestige promised to counterbalance Turati's moderation. This presented Salvemini with the opportunity to assume a significant role in Italian political journalism; the nationwide circulation of *Avanti!* made it a major vehicle for shaping opinion. However, Salvemini declined the offer, telling Lazzari, in language undoubtedly designed to signal his opposition to the revolutionary wing of the party, that he was "not only a reformist, but a reformist of the right" and thereby in conflict with Lazzari's revolutionary wing. It may also have confused Lazzari to think of Salvemini in such terms.[60]

One cannot help but pause to reflect on this curious exchange. His refusal was part of his withdrawal from the PSI and his general retreat from organized politics. More comfortable on the sidelines, he would consider assuming a position of political responsibility only on exceptional occasions. What if Salvemini had accepted? Editorship of the PSI newspaper would have offered him ample opportunity to publicize his ideas, such as universal suffrage. Certainly his refusal is not surprising. A man who would not accept universal suffrage from Giolitti would, on the same principle, not accept the editorship of *Avanti!* from a revolutionary socialist. When he refused, the party turned to Claudio Treves. Within two years, when the revolutionaries took control of the party, Benito Mussolini took the position and used it as a platform from which to rise from obscurity.[61]

One impact of Salvemini's rebuff at the Congress was to reaffirm his identity as a southerner. He could easily attribute his political failure to a northern elitist campaign, and resuming the advocacy of the southern cause would provide a means by which to recuperate. It was further evidence of the resiliency that carried him through many of life's travails. Some northern socialists reaffirmed their support by soliciting his candidacy. His answer was decisive: "I do not intend to accept candidacy outside southern Italy. . . . I do not wish to 'expatriate' myself; I intend to remain linked to my country. . . . When the peasants are voters, then I will be a deputy."[62]

The emergence of pressing foreign policy issues led Salvemini into further confrontation with the PSI that finally forced him out. One troubling international issue was irredentism. A few irredentists had periodically created furor, demanding war with Austria, opposing Italy's partnership in the Triple Alliance with Germany and Austria, and aligning themselves at times with the growing nationalist movement. A few Italian socialists supported irredentism, including his former classmate at the University of Florence, Cesare Battisti, and, more recently and to a lesser degree, Leonida Bissolati.

Since 1899, in a departure from his youthful support for Mazzini and Imbriani, Salvemini had generally rejected irredentism as "madness" that meant war with Austria.[63] It was primarily his interest in domestic reform that convinced Salvemini that any such foreign adventurism was "craziness" that would drain the budget and at the same time strengthen the hand of the military and the House of Savoy—as had historically happened—and thus undercut democratic reforms. In January 1900, he had published the first of a series of articles criticizing irredentists for their reactionary politics and calling for the democratic parties to renounce irredentism. As other expansionist causes surfaced, Salvemini became increasingly disappointed in the inability of the Socialist Party to remain focused on the reform of the political and economic system.[64]

The Libyan War provided the particular forum for Salvemini's final rift with the PSI, whose reformist leadership was now badly split between supporters and opponents of Giolitti's policy.[65] Salvemini, along with the rest of the Left, was caught short by rapidly moving events. As Giolitti pushed a larger military budget, popular enthusiasm built in response to growing nationalist propaganda. Throughout August and September 1911, Salvemini warned that North Africa would fail to be the "promised land" its sponsors were seeking. Such arguments could not, however, offset the mounting hysteria fueled by the nationalists in *Il Regno*, *L'Idea Nazionale*, and the Italian Nationalist Association.[66]

In October 1911, Italian forces bombarded and occupied Tripoli as the Giolitti government moved on the Turkish Empire to protect Italy's North African aspirations against the prospect of French colonial expansion. Salvemini was particularly exasperated by the "silence and indifference" of the PSI, which spoke out, he noted, only after Giolitti declared war. Finding his warnings about Libya ignored, he recalled, "All my work fell into a black hole. At that point, I did not wish to have anything further to do with the Socialist Party."[67]

Salvemini's disappointment at his inability to influence the party is understandable but unrealistic. At the very time he was penning his opposition to the impending conflict, Turati was trying to persuade reformist leaders to oppose Giolitti's military policy.[68] Salvemini's steady criticism undermined Turati and contributed to the ultimate rise of the revolutionary socialists. By the time the socialists opposed the war with a half-hearted strike, the fighting had started.[69]

His disagreement with the PSI on the Libyan conflict—like his differences with them over universal suffrage—illustrate that Salvemini was essentially a man of ideas and not of politics. Once again, his actions clarify his basic apolitical character. After he publicly left the party, how could he hope to influence its decisions? This was Salvemini the idealist, believing that his ideas should prevail because of their fundamental rectitude and justice. This was Salvemini the intellectual, whose influence would be limited to his ability to convince others, through the written and spoken word, of the merit of those same ideas. To expect such an apolitical approach to succeed was illusory. His words could stimulate thought and excite emotions; his courage and strength could inspire; but they were not likely to produce ready results in the political arena. A man of more stoic temperament might have accepted those limitations.

He recalled later that among his reasons for leaving the party was Turati's "bad faith." To stay would have meant leading a movement against Turati that would inevitably turn personal. "Remembering our past friendship," he reflected, "I preferred to leave him in charge and let him chart his own destruction."[70]

Salvemini's departure did not signal his failure to take control of the party, as one critic has written. Political leadership was not his calling. His failure was his inability, on the strength of his ideas, to redefine socialism and reshape the party. He did not challenge Turati for power; in fact, he never really intended to do so, but he fought him at every juncture over universal suffrage, the role of the southern peasantry in the party, and other issues. As much as he would have liked to prevail, maintaining his integrity was more important. Viewing the political process as inherently hypocritical, he simply refused to play the requisite political games because they too often required compromising ideas and principles in order to succeed. In October 1911, he wrote to Giuseppe Prezzolini, "From the Socialist Party I am now irrevocably divided."[71] Much later, pondering this watershed decision, he recalled with some pleasure, "I abandoned the Socialist Party . . . but I did not abandon the 'proletariat'—that is to say, the southern peasants."[72]

An even more fundamental issue is Salvemini's tendency to remain, throughout his life, a critic of the given political establishment, a heretic against all orthodoxy. In this case, as a critic of the PSI leadership, he was a minority within a minority. Was this a matter of choice or of psychological necessity? His advocacy of unpopular positions cast him inevitably in such a minority. His criticism of Cavour, Crispi, Giolitti, and then Mussolini was a response a continuous stream of antidemocratic governments in Italy. He also had a need to be an outsider, and this need preceded particular political circumstances. On the occasion of Salvemini's departure from the PSI, Morgari addressed this tendency, very directly, as only a friend could do:

Your head is cracked. It makes you hypercritical, suspicious, pessimistic, difficult to please, intractable, perpetually quarreling with half the world. Your destiny is to remain isolated. But, in the final analysis, you are so noble and sincere that I will continue to be your admirer and your friend.[73]

Salvemini's polemic against the Libyan War in 1911 and 1912 invoked the wrath of the Italian nationalist movement. The nationalists celebrated the annexation of Libya in November 1911 and the occupation of Rhodes and the other Dodecanese Islands in May 1912. The signing of the Treaty of Lausanne in October 1912 ended the war, solidifying Italian claims to Tripoli in return for evacuation of the islands.

Meanwhile, the clouds of a more threatening war gathered over Europe. As European powers scrambled to solidify alliances, update war plans, and stockpile weapons, nationalist political groups gained influence in many capitals. Italian nationalists, living in the shadow of the humiliating defeat in Ethiopia in 1896, were no exception. Writers such as Enrico Corradini and Gabriele D'Annunzio led a chorus of strident chauvinism.[74] As they campaigned, Salvemini hounded them with steady opposition to two nationalist tenets: imperialism in North Africa and participation in the Triple Alliance.[75]

The Libyan War also led Salvemini to break his ties with *La Voce*, the influential Florentine journal to which he had contributed regularly since returning to Tuscany after the earthquake. Although he had been a collaborator in the publication, he had never enjoyed a comfortable relationship with *Voce*'s other leading figures: Giovanni Amendola, Giovanni Papini, and its editor, Giuseppe Prezzolini. Salvemini had begun writing for *La Voce* after distancing himself from Turati's *Critica Sociale*, and for almost two years he found it a convenient forum for his views on Italian public life.

The difficulties that emerged were both philosophical and political. At one level, Salvemini objected to *Voce*'s literary and cultural emphases, its use of aesthetic analysis, and its somewhat mystical tone. He preferred to use the journal to address more pressing issues of political reform in a more direct, realistic manner. This ever precarious relationship worsened with the advent of conflict in North Africa.[76]

The fact that Salvemini wrote regularly about the Libyan conflict in *Voce*'s pages only exacerbated matters. Amendola, Prezzolini, and especially Papini were all nationalists, and all felt uncomfortable in implicitly supporting Salvemini's antiwar crusade. "On Tripoli, enough now," Prezzolini wrote to him in September 1911. The next month he wrote, "As for politics, we are saying: be quiet for now. The belief that with a few articles in *Voce*, at 3,500 copies each, [we can] destroy a movement created by three million copies of the major journals is ridiculous." Salvemini, to whom such an argument was irrelevant, never submitted another article to *Voce*.[77]

The next day, he declared, "My decision to break with *Voce* is now definite. The substance of these last four issues reveals among the others of *Voce* a state of mind that is absolutely not mine." The break reflected a fundamental and irreconcilable disagreement in editorial policy and an unwillingness on Salvemini's part to subject himself to the limitations under which Prezzolini had placed him. Prezzolini's ultimatum was tantamount to dismissal.[78]

More important, Salvemini's break with Prezzolini represented a profound disagreement between intellectuals, a very different matter than his dispute with politicians such as Turati and Treves. As an intellectual, Salvemini could view the latter group with disdain for their tendency toward Machiavellian manipulation. However, his differences with Prezzolini were not the product of contrasting perspectives. Both were intellectuals, evenly matched, whose stock and trade was ideas and values. In this case the disagreement was a more fundamental one that revolved around the nature of Italian culture itself. In his final departure from *Voce*, Salvemini explained the following to Prezzolini:

[Your friends at *Voce*] find that it is not "culture" to occupy themselves with Tripoli, and it *is* culture to occupy themselves with Picasso. For me, true culture today consists of speaking of Tripoli. All the rest today is not culture, it is literature.[79]

This elementary disagreement clearly was sharpened by personal discord, so often the case with Salvemini. Instead of sulking or engaging in counterproductive recrimination against Prezzolini, however, Salvemini immediately began exploring the possibility of founding a new publication.

Failing to convince the Laterza publishing house to back his effort, Salvemini found success at the villa of his friend, Senator Fortunato. Fortunato agreed to invest in the endeavor along with Croce and the editor and radical deputy Antonio De Viti De Marco. All were prominent southerners. By the end of the month, Salvemini had begun to solicit articles and had named the new journal *L'Unità*, dedicated to those who had fought for the "true unification of the country."[80]

Two months later, in December 1911, the premier issue of *L'Unità* appeared. Salvemini would serve as its editor, administrator, and intellectual force throughout its nine years of publication. If the PSI, *Critica*, and *La Voce* all had recoiled from his hard-hitting, "concrete" approach to politics, *L'Unità* would provide him the ideal platform.[81]

Salvemini intended to create a journal that would focus the most intelligent minds of Italian democracy on issues of fundamental Italian political culture. "*L'Unità*," he wrote, "must be a school and a guide for the discontented and for the reformers of all the democratic groups." Readers and contributors alike recognized his unmistakable hand and the journal's singularity of tone—direct, unadorned, and devoid of philosophical abstraction or rhetorical flourish. Much later, Salvemini explained, "In reading his manuscripts, I assumed the point of view of a worker, even an unlettered peasant, convinced that if we were to be true democrats and not priests of arcane rituals, they had the right to understand."[82] It was a standard of political communication that Salvemini would apply for the rest of his life.[83]

In spite of a circulation that never exceeded 1,200 and deficits that stretched Salvemini's meager resources, *L'Unità* endured. The journal persisted in sounding the familiar themes of Salveminian "concrete" radicalism: universal suffrage; reform of elections, the educational system, and the tax structure, including the protectionist tariff; secularization of the state; and opposition to the Libyan War. The writers frequently emphasized the impact of all of these issues on the South. The coherent message that *L'Unità* sounded from the start was a reaffirmation of democratic ideals against the counterweight of Giolitti's politics.

The changing international climate soon brought a new emphasis to *L'Unità*: the liabilities of Italian partnership with Germany and Austria in the Triple Alliance and, in general, the dangers of nationalism. Warning that German militarism threatened the future of Italian democracy just as it threatened democracy throughout Europe, Salvemini called for a fundamental reorientation of Italian diplomacy. He hoped that through *L'Unità* he could provide a unified vision to Italy's fragmented and provincial political culture, in a sense completing the drive for democratic unification that had been lost in 1870. In the process, he aspired to forge a new national leadership group, perhaps even a new party. *L'Unità* enjoyed some success in focusing the views, at least, of a small group of young Italian political activists for whom the paper became a source of inspiration and Salvemini a kind of role model. In retrospect, the *L'Unità* group nurtured an exceptionally fertile environment for the development of political thought.[84]

In a sense, the new journal was the logical conclusion of the growing nonconformity of Salvemini's prewar politics. It is perhaps typical of the intellectual to work best alone. In his own publication, Salvemini could express his unique views without the frustration of disapproval by others. *L'Unità* offered Salvemini the ideal situation: he benefited from the intellectual stimulation of collaboration without the indignity of being told by an editor to "tone down" his approach or to avoid certain issues. The publication provided him with his best opportunity, in his role as political educator, to make an unfettered contribution to Italian public life.[85]

While editing *L'Unità* and lecturing at the University of Pisa, Salvemini once again entered the political arena when Giolitti dissolved Parliament in September 1913. Perhaps it would have been more prudent to resist the invitations of friends to enter the race. However, in declining a similar offer just two years earlier, he had sworn that he would become a candidate "when the peasants could vote," and Giolitti's expansion of suffrage had forced his hand. The general election of 1913 would test Giolitti's ability to maintain his organization in the face of an electorate swelled by the 1912 law that added all veterans and all males over thirty; conversely, it would finally prove whether expanded suffrage would provide the democratic corrective that Salvemini had advocated for so long.

He accepted this invitation to candidacy from a group of peasants and fishermen in the district around Molfetta. Much later, he recalled the decision with some nostalgia:

One evening, at the country home of my best friend, we were talking in a small group, under the stars, with the sweet freshness that follows a summer day. A farmer [in the group] said to me: "You have never deceived us." Those words, pronounced in the darkness, were engraved in my soul and have never disappeared.[86]

Salvemini recognized among the Molfettese a sense of resignation and powerlessness, reflective of southern attitudes forged by centuries of poverty and oppression. It was the regional psychological impediment that his political reforms ultimately would have to overcome, but he simply could not accept the status quo. Thus he ventured again into the troubled waters of the electoral politics of the liberal state.

Determined to avoid the mistakes of his disastrous 1910 episode in Albano, Salvemini was buoyed by the much greater familiarity with his native region. The peasants of Bitonto and Terlizzi, two towns in the Molfetta district, formed a "Salvemini Movement," and he responded with a campaign designed to appeal to the southern peasantry, challenging them to take a leadership role among the Italian working class and to use their votes to reduce the heavy burden of protectionism and to wipe out illiteracy. It was a vote of confidence in their ability to overcome the psychology of apathy his friends felt.

Nevertheless, the inevitable perils of violence and corruption soon dragged his campaign off the lofty peak of idealistic reform. He, above all others, must have expected this. In fact, his anticipation of problems led him to invite several friends to join him in Molfetta to scrutinize the campaign and document irregularities. One of them, Ugo Ojetti, had been with Salvemini to observe the 1909 election in Gioia del Colle, but nothing had prepared these veteran observers for the 1913 campaign.[87]

Salvemini won the endorsement of the anti-Giolittian *Il Corriere della Sera,* for which Ojetti wrote, and of many women who, although they could not vote for him, saw his candidacy as a promise that they would win that right. In his early enthusiasm, Salvemini underestimated the support the Giolitti government would give his opponent, a Republican lawyer named Pietro Pansini who was the incumbent in the district. However, expecting trouble from pro-Pansini "thugs," Salvemini urged his supporters to avoid violence at any cost.[88]

Soon he began to understand even better the methods by which Giolitti's machine maintained its support in the South. One of the favored subterfuges was for Giolitti's Interior Ministry to employ its prefects, who commanded local police and had power to remove local elected officials from office. He heard from friends that the Interior Minister had run a systematic disinformation campaign against him through the Prefect of Bari; and that he had transferred police commissioners to the towns of Bisceglie and Molfetta and mobilized the commissioner of Terlizzi for the express purpose of stopping him. Others told him that priests had opposed him even in the confessional booth, accusing him of supporting divorce laws and wishing to destroy religion.[89] Years later Salvemini recalled the experience:

... The police, in league with the government supporters, enrolled the scum of the constituencies and the underworld of the neighboring districts. In the last weeks before the polls, opponents were threatened, bludgeoned, besieged in their homes. Their leaders were barred from addressing meetings, or even thrown into prison.... Voters suspected of upholding the opposition were refused polling cards. Those favoring governmental candidates were given not only their own polling cards, but also those of opponents, emigrants, deceased voters, and were allowed to vote three, five, ten, twenty times.[90]

In September, his friend Fortunato, an experienced hand at southern campaigns, wrote to reassure him:

The last issue of *Puglia del Popolo* had your magnificent leading article, inspired by a vivid accent of desperation: "Is it not possible to have a decent, honest, human election campaign down here?" I wanted to telegraph you: "No, it is not possible!"[91]

As the election approached, violence intensified throughout the South. On October 6, after addressing a large crowd of sailors in Molfetta, Salvemini supporters met a counterdemonstration by Pansini partisans who waited by the local socialist headquarters. A brawl ensued and shots were fired, leading to great confusion. Local authorities interceded, restored order, and made some arrests.[92]

Just weeks before the election, when Salvemini arrived to campaign in Terlizzi, he found that the police commissioner had banned speeches by opposition candidates. To challenge the decision, he returned quietly in the late afternoon of October 13 with a group of anti-Giolitti candidates in an automobile.

Pansini's supporters were waiting. In a stroke of fortune, a bus arrived in the town square ahead of them, and the government's thugs, mistaking the passengers for Salvemini's supporters, fired pistols in the air, creating great confusion.

Into the midst of the chaos arrived the opposition candidates, and one of the government's rogues, recognizing Salvemini's distinctive appearance, moved purposefully toward him. At close range, he leveled his revolver and squeezed the trigger. He then turned and fled into the customs office, waving his arms excitedly and shouting, "I shot Salvemini!"

The more sober customs agent grabbed the weapon and examined it. He saw that, in the excitement of the moment, the would-be assassin had failed to notice that the gun misfired. Salvemini, shaken but sound, left Terlizzi and declined to return in the final weeks of the campaign. So corrupt was the system that the police department falsified the report of the incident, gave perjured testimony, and eventually charged Salvemini and his supporters with instigating the scenario by firing weapons.[93]

Election day, October 26, 1913, proved uncannily reminiscent of previous southern elections in the Giolittian era. In a newspaper article, Ojetti called it a "Sunday of passion." Progovernment thugs roamed the streets, clubs in hand, and clustered threateningly around the polling places with apparent license from local police. Their presence took its toll on the turnout, which ran slightly more than 60 percent, a low figure even though many were first-time voters. In spite of numerous irregularities, all of which seemed to favor the government's candidate, Salvemini came within 102 votes of victory in his hometown, out of more than 5,000 votes cast. He lost the race, however, managing to win only about 41 percent of the votes in the province. In all, he emerged as an even more bitter opponent of Giolitti, whose "ministry of the underworld" had taught him that his political influence would be limited to words.[94]

The night after the election, about 100 peasants and sailors who had been ruled ineligible to vote took their electoral certificates to Salvemini's house. There they noticed Pansini's men, the same ones who had denounced Salvemini during the campaign. The Pansini partisans, previously accused of similar force, unleashed a barrage of stones and gunshots on the house, dispersing Salvemini's supporters. The *carabinieri* broke up the mob, but there were no arrests.[95]

Although he had expected problems, Salvemini found the campaign irregularities to exceed his worst fears. Immediately after the election, his supporters began checking details in anticipation of launching an official inquiry. The same week, he wrote from Molfetta, still burning with disgust from the misadventure: "How wonderful to be back in this place where there is such a scarcity of men of integrity and character!"[96]

He filed a protest with the elections commission detailing all the irregularities, but to no avail. Reflecting on the political depravity of the Giolittian system, he complained, "War is war. But it is a true disgrace that a European country must stoop to this level."[97] Months later, when the final investigation confirmed the results, he vented his utter frustration: "I am disgusted with everything and everybody. I do not believe there is any justice. Above all there is swelling in me a hatred for northern Italy."[98]

On November 1 in Molfetta, Salvemini's supporters staged a rally on behalf of their vanquished native son. Thousands filled the streets, marching in defiance of local authorities. Police were alarmed to witness a crowd that stretched as far as they could see, Salvemini carried above the fray, shaking a defiant fist in the air. When a Bari photographer displayed an enlarged photo of the demonstration, local police forced him to remove it in the name of public security. That same day, in *La Ragione*, a local newspaper, editor Giacinto Panunzio published a tribute that reflected the agitation of Salvemini's supporters: "Gaetano Salvemini is a secular saint who martyred himself on behalf of an entire people who beckoned his rebellious spirit against the violence and fraud of the self-righteous republic."[99]

In Milan, Benito Mussolini, the thirty-year-old revolutionary socialist who for a year had edited *Avanti!*, reported that local socialists were threatening a general strike to denounce election violence.[100] Meanwhile, in Rome, it was said that when Prime Minister Giolitti heard the news of Salvemini's defeat in this highly publicized race, he rubbed his hands together and exclaimed, "Here's to fraud!"[101]

NOTES

1. "Lutto di patria, lutto di famiglia, forse!," *CS*, January 1, 1909.

2. "I professori scampati a Messina," *CdS*, January 4, 1899.

3. Lidia Minervini, "Amico e Maestro"; MLS, *Sal*, 22; HC interview; HC to CK, September 24, 1991.

4. GS to Giovanni Gentile, January 15, 1909, *Opere* IX (1), 396.

5. Telegram, GS to Gentile, March 24, 1909, *Opere* IX (1), 399, n. 1; to GLR and Gentile, April 1, 1909, *Opere* IX (1), 226.

6. Benedetto Croce to Karl Vossler, January 5, 1909, *Carteggio Croce-Vossler, 1899–1949* (Bari, 1951), 114.

7. GS to Gentile, April 1, 1909, *Opere* IX (1), 399.

8. GS to Carlo Placci, May 27, 1909, *Opere* IX (1), 403; to Placci, July 21, 1909, *Opere* IX (1), 405; ET, "Nota biografica," 225.

9. GS, "Memorie e Soliloqui (18 novembre–24 settembre 1923)," *Opere* VI (2), 61.

10. MC interview; HC interview; HC to CK, September 24, 1991. Iris Origo, *A Need to Testify*, 146.

11. GS in *Avanti!*, January 8, 1909 quoted in Michela D'Angelo, "Salvemini a Messina," 300 n.; ET, *Sal*, 78–79; DeC, *Sal*, 150.

12. GS to Ernesta Bittanti, January 1, 1910, *Opere* IX (1), 419.

13. AK to GS, January 28, 1910, *Opere* IX (1), 427.

14. Franco Venturi, "Salvemini storico," *Il Ponte*, December 1957, 1794–1795.

15. AWS, *IGE, passim*; GS, *Il Ministro della mala vita* (Rome, 1919), *Opere* IV (1), 73–141.

16. LB, *Sal*, 85 ff.

17. GS, "Parlamento, governo ed elezioni meridionali nell'Italia giolittiana," *Opere* IV (1), 53– 212; ET, *Salvemini*, 117 ff.

18. GS, "L'opera nel Mezzogiorno," *Opere* IV (1), 73–107; ET, *Sal*, 121, n. 1.

19. GS, "L'elezione di Gioia del Colle," *Opere* IV (1), 73–107; ET, *Sal*, 118 n. 2; Denis Mack Smith, *Italy* (Ann Arbor, 1969), 284.

20. AWS, *IGE*, 69; *Suffragio Universale, Questione Meridionale e Riformismo* (Milan, 1909), WL.

21. Ettore Rota, "Una pagina," 323.

22. AWS, *IGE*, 23–33, 38–41, 58–61.

23. DiS, *DIS*, 113–118; LB, *Sal*, 78 ff.

24. GS, "La legge Daneo-Credaro per la scuola popolare," *SSQM*, 441–452; to Oddino Morgari, January 2, 1910, *Opere* IX (1), 419 and September 2, 1913, *Cart 1912*, 375–376n.

25. GS, *Pel Suffragio Universale* (Bari, 1909), 35, WL; to GF, February 14 and 15, 1910, *Opere* IX (1), 430, 431; to Morgari, March 6, 1910, *Opere* IX (1), 432.

26. Augusto Torre, "Alcuni miei ricordi su Salvemini," *Rassegna Storica Toscana* IV (April–June 1958), 205–206.

27. Lamberto Naldini, "Salvemini Maestro a Pisa," *Belfagor* XII (1957), 697–700; Torre, "Alcuni miei ricordi," 205–206; ER, "Il nonconformista," *Il Mondo* (Rome) September 17, 1957.

28. GS to Morgari, March 30, 1910, *Opere* IX (1), 436.

29. GS, "Le memorie di un candidato," *Opere* IV (1), 163–212; ET, *Sal*, 123.

30. BM, "Note Forlivesi," *OO* III, 215; GS, "Memorie di un candidato," 194–195; MLS, *Sal*, 23.

31. Torre, "Alcuni miei ricordi," 206; GS, "Memorie di un candidato," 205–212; to Giustino Fortunato, April 30, 1910, 437–438; to GLR, May 20, 1910, *Opere* IX (1), 441; ET, *Sal*, 125; DeC *Sal*, 164 ff.

32. GS, "Nord e Sud nella riforma elettorale Luzzatti," I–III, *Opere* IV (1), 459–469; "In tema di riforma elettorale," I-VI, *CS*, January 16, February 1 and 16, 1911; "La nuova crisi del partito socialista mentre si prepara il Congresso di Milano," *Opere* IV (2), 354–358. JM, *EMP*, 116; GA, *SSI*, 133–144; DiS, *DIS*, 114–119; DeC, *Sal*, 169.

33. Costantino Lazzari to Salvemini, June 24 and 29, 1910, *Opere* IX (1), 450 and 451–452; GA, *SSI*, 138–148; DiS, *DIS*, 112–119.

34. Fausto Pagliari to GS, July 2, 1910, *Opere* IX (1), 452–453.

35. GS to GLR, July 7, 1910, *Opere* IX (1), 457; LB, *Sal*, 127; BM, "Dopo il Congresso di Milano," *OO* III, 254.

36. GS, "La nuova crisi del partito socialista," 358; to GLR, July 7, 1910, *Opere* IX (1), 458; DeC, *Sal*, 175.

37. AK to GS, September 16, 1910, *Opere* IX (1), 466.

38. GS to Rodolfo Savelli, September 28, 1910, *Opere* IX (1), 466–467; DeC, *Sal*, 175.

39. JM, *EMP*, 127–131; DiS, *DIS*, 118–119.

40. EG, "Gaetano Salvemini nella società del tempo suo" in ES, *Sal*, 153.

41. *Resoconto stenografico dell'XI Congresso Nazionale del Partito Socialista Italiano* (Rome, 1911), 59–70; *Suffragio universale* (Rome, 1910), WL; LB, *Sal*, 113 ff; AWS, *IGE*, 56; JM, *EMP*, 242; DiS, *DIS*, 118–119.

42. *Resoconto dell'XI Congresso* (PSI), 59–70; AWS, *IGE*, 56 and JM, *EMP*, 242.

43. JM, *EMP*, 128–132.

44. *Resoconto dell'XI Congresso* (PSI), 174–189; GA, *SSI*, 133 ff.; AWS, *IGE*, 56 ff.; JM, *EMP*, 126–132, 229; DeG, *IL*, 22–24; DiS, *DIS*, 118–119.

45. GA, *SSI*, 143–146; JM, *EMP*, 126–131; LB, *Sal*, 126–127; DiS, *DIS*, 118–119.

46. AWS, *IGE*, 55–58; GA, *SSI*, 133.

47. GS to Fortunato, October 29, 1910, *Opere* XI (1), 469.

48. GS and FT, "*Che fare*," *Opere* IV (1), 215–226; GS, "Nord e Sud nella riforma elettorale Luzzatti," I–III, *Opere* IV (2), 459–469; "In tema di riforma elettorale," I–VI, *CS*, January 16, February 1 and 16, 1911.

49. GA, *SSI*, 146 ff.

50. GS to FT, August 6, 1911, *Opere* IX (1), 495–497; AWS, *IGE*, 58–59.

51. GS, *SSQM* xxii; Mack Smith, *Italy*, 255; DeC, *Sal*, 177 178; DiS, *DIS*, 116–121.

52. Morgari to GS, January 3, 1910, *Opere* XI (1), 423; LB, *Sal*, 75 ff.

53. GS to GLR, July 7, 1910, *Opere* XI (1), 458.

54. GS to Fortunato, October 29, 1910, *Opere* XI (1), 469–470; to Placci, August 12, 1910, *Opere* XI (1), 464.

55. GS to GLR, May 20, 1910, *Opere* XI (1), 441.

56. GS to Fortunato, April 30, 1910, *Opere* XI (1), 438.

57. GLR to GS, June 11, 1910, *Opere* XI (1), 445.

58. Pagliari to GS, July 2, 1910, *Opere* XI (1), 452–453.

59. GS to ER, December 4, 1944, translated by PC in GS, *IFAUS*, vii.

60. GS, "Riepilogo," *Opere* IV (2), 679–680; *Cart 1912*, 271n.; DeF, *il riv*, 133–134; GA, *SSI*, 164; LB, *Sal*, 79, ff.

61. GA, *SSI*, 136–137; DeG, *IL*, 24ff.; JM, *EMP*, 95; Gherardo Bozzetti, *Mussolini direttore del'Avanti!* (Milan, 1979), 155; DeF, *il riv*, 133–176.

62. GS to Alessandro Schiavi, March 16, 1911, *Opere* XI (1), 479.

63. GS to AGh, April 29, 1899, December 29, 1899, and January 30, 1900, *Opere* IX (1), 89–90, 123, 136.

64. GS, "L'irredentismo," "A proposito di 'irredentismo' "; *Opere* III (1), 3–16. Even then, however, aligning himself with Bissolati, Salvemini had endorsed a limited form of Mazzinian irredentism of the Risorgimento era, as long at it confined itself to the protection of Italian language groups outside the country; Torre, Preface to *Opere* III (1).

65. RC, *Leonida Bissolati* (Milan, 1958) 172 ff.

66. *Storia dell'Avanti!, 1896–1926*, GA, ed. (Milan, 1956), 93; DeF, *il riv*, 104; ADG, *The Italian Nationalist Association and the Rise of Fascism* (Lincoln, 1978);

Franco Gaeta, *Il nazionalismo italiano* (Naples, 1965); Ronald Cunsolo, *Italian Nationalism from Its Origins to World War II* (Malabar, FL, 1990).

67. GS, "Tripoli e i socialisti"; "Socialismo e tripolismo," *L'U, Opere* IV (2), 498–509; to Morgari, September 13, 1913, *Cart 1912*, 392; BF, *L'U*, 14–15.

68. JM, *EMP*, 145.

69. BF, *L'U*, 14–15; MLS, *Sal*, 79–81.

70. GS to Morgari, September 13, 1913 in *Cart 1912*, 392.

71. GS to GP, October 6, 1911, *Opere* IX (1), 523.

72. GS, Preface to *SSQM*, xxvi. DeC, *Sal*, 191–192.

73. Morgari to GS, September 19, 1913, GS, *Cart 1912*, 397.

74. Alcio Riosa, *Il Partito Socialista*, 152 ff.; JM, *EMP*, 141–146; DiS, *DIS*, 125–146; GA, *SSI*, 134; Torre, preface to *Opere* III (1); AWS, *IGE*, 99–103.

75. See, for example, Salvemini's articles in *L'U* in 1911 and 1912.

76. See Salvemini's correspondence with Giuseppe Prezzolini and Giovanni Amendola in *Opere* IX (1). See also BF, *L'U*, 12ff.; ET, "Nota biografica," 229ff; MLS, *Sal*, 24; DeC, *Sal*, 154ff.

77. GP to GS, September 26 and October 20, 1911 in *Opere* IX (1), 504, 539; ET, *Sal*, 138; Michele Pellicani, "Gaetano Salvemini," 790–793.

78. GS to GF, October 21, 1911, in *Opere* IX (1), 541; DeC, *Sal*. 193 ff.

79. GS to GP, September 28, 1911, *Opere* XI (1), 506–507.

80. GS to GF, October 21 and 29, 1911 *Opere* XI (1), 542, 543; ET, *Sal*, 138; BF, *L'U*, 15.

81. BF, *L'U*; Cesare Vasoli, "*L'Unità* di Salvemini," *Il Ponte* XIV (1958), 1382–1406; Paolo Spriano's review of Beniamino Finocchiaro's book, *Rinascità*, SV (1958), 539–541; Gennaro Sasso, "*L'Unità* di Gaetano Salvemini," *Nord e Sud*, March 1959; Rosario Villari, "Il meridionalista" in ES, *Sal*, 128 ff.; DeC, *Sal*, 197ff.; GF, *L'U*, March 9, 1912 in ET, *Sal*, 138 n.

82. BF, *L'U*, 16–18n.

83. GS to Guglielmo Zagari, September 3, 1913, *Cart 1912*, 380.

84. BF, *L'U*, *passim*; EG, "Salvemini," in ES, *Sal*, 192–210; *La cultura italiana del '900 attraverso le reviste* (Turin, 1962), *passim*.

85. ET, *Sal*, 231.

86. GS, Preface to *SSQM*, xxviii. Translation by Daniela Giufridda.

87. BF, *L'U*, 19.

88. GS, "L'elezione di Molfetta," quoted in ET, *Sal*, 127.

89. GS, "Gli incidenti di Molfetta" in BF, *L'U*, 280–282; Introductory Essay, AWS, *IGE*, xiv-xix; ET, *Sal*, 127–136.

90. GS, Introductory Essay to AWS, *IGE*, xix.

91. Fortunato to GS, September 17, 1913, *Cart 1912*, 395.

92. "Incidenti elettorali: Tumulti, ferimenti ed arresti nei vari collegi di Puglia," *CdS*, October 7, 1913; "Un telegramma del prof. Salvemini," *CdS*, October 9, 1913.

93. The assailant was identified by witnesses as Raffaele di Michele De Leo. Corte di Appello di Trani, Sezione d'Accusa (1915), "A Difesa del Prof. Gaetano Salvemini contro Francesco Vicario, Carlo Fumarola ed altri," WL. (The document contains a note in Salvemini's handwriting: "Written by G. Salvemini except the first two pages); "La elezione politica di Molfetta alla camera dei deputati: Relazione della

minoranza della Giunta delle elezioni," (Molfetta, 1915), personal archive of Carmine Spadavecchia, Molfetta; GS, "Intorno alle elezioni giolittiane. Un poliziotto assassino," *Opere* IV (1), 346–351. See also "Episodi di violenza e tumulti durante la propaganda elettorale," October 14, 1913; "La lotta elettorale nelle Puglie e in Calabria," October 17, 1913; "Effervescenza in provincia di Bari," October 20, 1913; "Stranezze elettoriali nelle Puglie," October 22, 1913; "Un ferimento a Molfetta," October 25, 1913. "Il memoriale dei riformisti sulle sopraffazioni elettorali nel Mezzogiorno," October 6, 1913, all in *CdS*; ET, *Sal*, 127 ff.

94. *Il Corriere della Sera* reported the following on October 27, 1913: registered: 18,236; voted 8,695; Pansini (Rep) 5,067; Salvemini (Soc Ind) 3,599. See also GS, "Frammenti di vita italiana: Gli amici dell'on Giolitti, *L'Unità*," in BF, *L'U*, 284–289; "Elettori e deputati," *Opere* IV (1), 333–341; "Intorno alle elezioni giolittiane. Un poliziotto assassino"; "San Michele Arcangelo candidate," *Opere* VIII, 430–432; GS, *La elezione di Molfetta. I documenti pansiniani* (Florence, 1914), WL, 14ff.; *La elezione di Molfetta del 1913: memoria per la Giunta delle elezioni* (Florence, 1914), WL, 9ff.; *La elezione di Bitonto; memoria per la Giunta delle elezioni* (Florence, 1914), WL; "Come procedette la lotta elettorale: Episodi di violenze e di brogli in parecchie località" and "Nuovi risultati delle elezioni politiche di ieri," *CdS*, October 27, 1913. See also ET, *Sal*, 133; DeF, *il riv*, 175 ff.; UO, *Ricordi di una domenica di passione*; RC, ed., *Gaetano Salvemini e Molfetta: un rapporto civile, politico, morale* (Bari, n.d.); "La elezione politica di Molfetta alla camera dei deputati."

95. "Violenze, prepotenze e intimidazione: Rivoltellate e sassate a Molfetta," *CdS*, October 28, 1913.

96. GS to Morgari, September 2, 1913, *Cart 1912*, 375; see also "Nella Puglia Rossa," BM, *OO* IV, I, 218–221.

97. GS to Gino Luzzatto, August 31, 1913, *Cart 1912*, 375.

98. GS to Z-B, July 13, 1914, *Cart 1914*, 7; GS, *Cart 1914*, 135 n. 1.

99. Giancinto Panunzio editorial, *La Ragione*, November 1, 1913 in *Gaetano Salvemini e Molfetta: un rapporto civile, politico, morale*, RC, ed. (Molfetta, 1988), BCM.

100. UGM to GS, September 6, 1913, *Cart 1912*, 387.

101. ET, *Sal*, 134.

Chapter 4

In the Trenches of the Great War

> For two hours the Italian artillerymen and the Austrians have been ex-
> changing grenades that are passing over our heads. We are separated from
> the Austrians, in certain places, by ten meters of space. So far the Austrian
> grenades have missed. There is an obligatory passageway that we call the
> pass of death; anyone who has to go through there runs for it, and all the
> others watch to see if he makes it. This morning . . . I went through there
> calmly, as if I were the king of the universe. War is a game of chance in
> which we are continually picking numbers.
>
> Gaetano Salvemini, 1915[1]

Nine months after the stinging defeat in the 1913 parliamentary election, the
voters of Molfetta and Bitonto, without incident, decisively elected Salvemini
provincial councilman. Although the council hardly provided him a forum
equivalent to the Chamber of Deputies, he continued to air his views in the
pages of *L'Unità*. The national election just a memory, more profound problems now beckoned, both at home and abroad.[2]

In the spring and summer of 1914, new signs of peril appeared. In June, a
wave of riots swept Italy. "Red Week" began with antidraft demonstrations led
by socialist Piero Nenni and anarchist Errico Malatesta in Ancona, where police response provoked the insurgents to call a general strike and seize control
of the city. Rebels built barricades in Rome and flew a red flag at the city hall in
Bologna. Around the country, rioters looted shops and destroyed railroad
tracks and telegraph lines. In some places, seizing control of local governments, they abolished taxes and lowered prices by decree. Elsewhere, insurrec-
tionists assaulted churches and villas and, in Ravenna, even overwhelmed an

army general. Eventually the government restored order by a show of massive armed power.

Red Week shook the settlement by which Giolitti had presumed to disarm such left-wing violence through his electoral machine and his reforms. The trauma deepened divisions within the political system, as in the aftermath both Right and Left heaped blame on Giolitti. In *Avanti!*, while Mussolini brazenly took credit for Red Week, Salvemini voiced his disapproval of what he called a counterproductive series of incidents of "vandalism *without purpose*."[3]

The antidraft, antimonarchy, antinationalist tone of Red Week spawned counterdemonstrations from the Right. Vigilantes assisted police in Bologna, and although candidates of the Left benefitted most, nationalists and Catholics also won several local elections. Reflecting a polarization that fused partisan politics with foreign policy, Red Week presaged the divisive debate over Italy's position in the approaching conflict as the international crisis burst upon Italy. While European powers scrambled to strengthen alliances, Salvemini thrust *L'Unità* into the midst of the accelerating controversy.[4]

Since 1900, when he had called for a national debate on foreign policy, Salvemini had opposed Italy's participation in the Triple Alliance (known as the "Triplice"). He had argued that the aggressive German challenge to the British made a future war likely and friendship with both impossible; that a German victory would strengthen militarism, monarchism, and reactionary movements throughout the continent and give the Hohenzollerns a presence in the Adriatic and an alliance with the Vatican. Thus, Italian withdrawal from the Alliance was "an absolute and urgent necessity." As Italian diplomats negotiated with both Germany and France in the next decade, and as Anglo-German hostilities deepened, Salvemini called for cooperation with the democracies, Britain and France. This opposition to Germanic autocracy and militarism provided the foundation of Salvemini's democratic interventionism.[5]

Salvemini's campaign against the Triple Alliance placed him on a collision course with socialists, nationalists, and pacifists. Responding to nationalists, Salvemini argued the strategic benefits of a policy of support for the Entente that would free France to move regiments to its German border and require Austria to dispatch troops to the Russian front, thus strengthening the Entente powers and serving Italy's long-range interests.[6] He chided pacifists for being sentimental in their advocacy of "peace at any price" and simplistic in their indifference to the outcome of war.[7]

Amid the debate on the Triple Alliance, Salvemini sided with the irredentists on two specific points. The Trentino, the area around the city of Trent between Lake Garda and Bolzano, was culturally and economically Italian, but it remained part of the Austrian Empire. His standards of national self-determination led him to advocate the acquisition of the Trentino, including as small a

German-speaking population as possible. He considered strategic necessity, noting that the language line approximately separating the Trentino from the Alto Adige ran along a chain of mountains that afforded Italy a sound defense.[8]

Salvemini also agreed with the irredentists on the city of Trieste, based on its overwhelming Italian majority. In the process, he spelled out his basic criteria for resolving border disputes: Ethnic-linguistic lines should be given highest priority, but defensible borders should not be neglected.[9] This careful geographical scrutiny would later place Salvemini in line with Woodrow Wilson's approach to international politics and in direct opposition to the nationalists' call for territory on the Dalmatian coast.

Because Salvemini had come to accept ultimate Italian control of Trentino and Trieste, it has been argued that he "converted" to the irredentist movement. In fact, the logic of his basic position had not changed since 1900, when he embraced the "democratic irredentism" of Bissolati. This position was instead a manifestation of the limited irredentism of the Risorgimento and the national self-determination of Mazzini. His willingness to advocate this position more forcefully by 1909 reflects the influence of Battisti, his own advocacy of an anti-Austrian policy, and his assumption that war would generate territorial changes. However, it would be a mistake to believe that Salvemini had become an irredentist. He was distrustful of the movement's leadership and of their zeal for expansion that took them well beyond Mazzini; nor did he approve of their ideology, especially after they began to accept the broader nationalist program. Growing Hapsburg-Hohenzollern aggression relieved any concern that his finite irredentist program would provoke a war that was, for more profound reasons, becoming ever more likely.[10]

By the time Salvemini had founded *L'Unità* at the end of 1911, he had begun to present a coherent foreign policy that would reorient Italy toward the Entente. In this way, he hoped to check Austrian expansion in the Balkans through Slavic independence and to deprive the Hapsburgs of the ethnic Italian regions of Trentino and Trieste. At the same time, friendship with Britain would stabilize Italy's Mediterranean interests and solidify its support for the democratic powers. A policy of liberty at home and national self-determination abroad would strengthen democracy while checking Prussian militarism and imperialism.[11]

Readers of *L'Unità* in 1912 and 1913 noticed a new emphasis on the spreading European peril: Franco-German hostility; the strengthening of the Anglo-French Entente; Austrian discord with Russia over the Balkans; and the resulting division of Europe into hostile camps. The mounting antagonism between Triplice and Entente propelled the continent toward disaster, and Italians to the moment of truth.[12] Salvemini advised against the 1912 renewal of the Triplice that would, he predicted, make war more likely and eventually reduce Italy to "*a vassal of Germany and Austria.*"[13] On December 5, 1912, despite growing differences with Austria over the Balkans, the Marquis di San Giuliano, Giolitti's foreign minister, renewed the treaty. Simultaneously, General Alberto Pollio, Italian chief of staff, coordinated Italian contingency plans with his Germanic counterparts.[14]

When the Balkan Wars broke out in 1912, tempting both Austria and Russia to intervene, Giolitti and San Giuliano distanced Italy from the Hapsburgs and began quietly to explore rapprochement with Britain and France. In October 1913, Serbia yielded to an Austrian ultimatum and withdrew from Albania. As Austrian aggression threatened to alienate Italy further, ethnic tensions between Italians and Slavs in Trieste fueled chauvinist emotions.

In November, after the general election in which Salvemini had lost in Molfetta, Giolitti assembled another government. The Gentiloni Pact, the agreement between Giolitti and the Catholic leader Count Vincenzo Gentiloni, made the prime minister dependent on Catholic support. This new alliance between clericals and liberals, Salvemini wrote later, was an attempt to short-circuit the new suffrage law.[15] Temporarily, the pact produced for Giolitti another working majority. In *L'Unità*, Salvemini lectured the new Chamber on "The Specter of War," warning of economic nationalism and the burgeoning arms race.[16]

In March 1914, when Kaiser Wilhelm II met with King Vittorio Emanuele in the splendor of Venice, it was perhaps Italy's last indulgence in the old-world fantasy that the alliance system guaranteed security. In toasting military cooperation, the king assured the kaiser that Italy's diplomatic relationship with Austria was sound.[17] In reality, neither the heads of state, their heads of government, nor their military commanders were fully confident in the Triple Alliance.

That same month, Giolitti's coalition fell apart and Antonio Salandra accepted the king's offer to form a new government. The Italian navy continued its frenzied program to build four super dreadnoughts to match Austria, while San Giuliano and his diplomatic corps counted the many issues on which Italy's interests clashed with those of Austria.[18]

Whereas Italian newspapers variously defined Italy's interests, *L'Unità* expressed the Salveminian view, advocating national independence for the Balkan subject peoples, opposing expansion by either Austria or Italy, and supporting the democratic powers of the Entente. As for Albania, Salvemini wrote in the summer of 1914, both Italy and Austria "must keep their hands to themselves; . . . no division into spheres of influence."[19]

It was, in fact, the very issue of nationalism among the Hapsburg subject peoples in the Balkans that began the war Salvemini had anticipated. On July 28, a month after a young Bosnian nationalist assassinated the Austrian Archduke at Sarajevo, Austria declared war on Serbia. Italy's exact obligation under the Triple Alliance was not clear. Salvemini was particularly alarmed that the Austrians and Germans would drag Italy into conflict, in violation of both Italy's interests and its treaty obligations. Meanwhile, the Salandra government, preoccupied with domestic problems, was caught unprepared for the spreading crisis. Salandra and San Giuliano preferred to avoid discord with Austria while hoping to win certain territorial concessions in return for honoring the alliance—as was Italy's right under Article 7. The Austrians stubbornly refused to promise territory and concealed their intent to vanquish the Serbs.

Within days of the Austrian declaration, the war spread. On August 1, the French and German governments ordered full mobilization and Germany declared war on Russia. The next evening, Germany delivered an ultimatum to Belgium and on August 3 declared war on France. That night, the German First and Second Armies crossed the Belgian border. When the Germans refused a British ultimatum to respect Belgian neutrality, Britain declared war on Germany. Within weeks, the German forces moved relentlessly toward Paris. Failing to close the Channel ports, they enabled the British expeditionary force to land and support its beleaguered ally. At *L'Unità*, Salvemini proclaimed, "As anti-imperialists and democrats, we wish with all ... our soul that this crisis will end with the defeat of the Austro-German bloc." He ended the article with a solemn decree that, in the event the Italian government abandoned neutrality, he would "suspend publication of the journal and wait in disciplined silence for the end of the crisis," a pledge that friends discouraged and some readers must have doubted.[20]

Privately, Salvemini responded with exalted enthusiasm that he was "very optimistic": The world will not be preyed upon by Teutonic militarism. 1814 signaled the end of the medieval world. 1914 will signal the dawn of the new world of national and social justice. ... Let us work together for the destruction of imperialism and the triumph of international democracy.[21]

A month later he proclaimed to his old friend Ernesta Bittanti Battisti: "War is today the only way to make peace and to curtail military spending in the aftermath."[22] In thus advocating the defeat of the Triple Alliance, Salvemini anticipated the central diplomatic choice now confronting the Italian people in what would be known as the neutrality debate. It would be Italy's first nationwide campaign of mass propaganda.

Not only was Salvemini among the first to advocate Italian military support for the Entente, but within a week of Austria's declaration of war on Serbia, he began to express a personal commitment: "If war comes with Austria, I will go."[23] It was a pledge that he repeated to a number of friends.[24]

In the midst of a series of German victories in the last week of August, Salvemini staked out his basic position on the Great War. The article he entitled "The War for Peace" was a ringing endorsement of the Allied cause. To end war and prevent the menace of Austro-German imperialism, Allied victory was essential. Italians must make certain, however, that the war did not end without

liberating the Italian ethnic regions of Austria and without clarifying Italy's relations with the Slavic regions of the Adriatic.[25] In thus championing the circumscribed goals of Mazzinian irredentism, he hoped to steal the territorial
issue from Sonnino and the nationalists, who, he believed, ignored these re-
straints in pursuit of a dangerous illusion:

We are not, and will not be . . . that "great power" that the nationalists are deliriously pursuing. We should want to be certainly at least the first of the small powers, renouncing
the dangerous position of being the last of the great powers.

Did such modest war aims deprive Italy of a role in the war? In relative
terms, Italy could contribute to the Allied military effort:

Our maritime intervention can add useful power to the naval superiority of England and
aid in the destruction of German naval power. The intervention of our ground forces, coordinated with those of the Balkans states, can deliver the decisive blow against Austrian military power.[26]

This was the foundation of "democratic interventionism" that would expose
Salvemini to the wrath of both imperialists and socialist internationalists.[27]

World War I forced Italians to make an agonizing decision. The struggle over
intervention traumatized the country for nearly ten months, leaving Italy the
most badly divided of the European states. Most Italians applauded neutrality,
including Giolittians, socialists, union and Catholic political leaders, and many
democrats. In opposition, some nationalists, militarists, and conservatives, expecting a German victory, demanded that Italy honor its commitment to the Triple Alliance. On the Left, dissident factions pressed Italian leaders to commit to
the Entente. As the war continued, divisions deepened, further fragmenting socialists, Catholics, liberals, nationalists, and other groups. The press aired the
debate daily, while behind the scenes powerful industrialists pressed for intervention. In the piazzas, D'Annunzio, Mussolini, and other interventionists incited crowds to direct action against the government. Italy was in crisis.

When the French stopped the German offensive at the Marne, one factor was
the transfer of French troops from the Italian border and from North Africa, fa-
cilitated, as Salvemini had predicted, by Italy's refusal to support Austria. The
stalemate at the Marne enabled the Italian government to worry less that a rapidly victorious Austro-German power would punish Italy for quitting the Triple
Alliance. More important, Salandra and San Giuliano anticipated a longer and
less decisive war in which Italian participation might influence the outcome.
Thus, within weeks of the Battle of the Marne, the Foreign Minister quietly approached the British and the French to negotiate terms of Italian intervention.
The public debate now shifted to focus on the question Salvemini had ad-

dressed six weeks earlier: Neutrality or armed intervention in support of the Entente?[28]

Salvemini's most influential role in the politics of Giolittian Italy was his advocacy of Italian intervention in World War I. Second only to Bissolati, Salvemini provided intellectual direction to the democratic forces who called for Italy to join the war in support of democratic principles. In fighting for democracy abroad, Italy would rediscover its own democratic roots.[29] He wrote later that the campaign for democratic intervention revived the Mazzinian tradition "from the grave where it had rested for fifty years."[30]

As the neutrality dispute sharpened, Salvemini electrified his followers by announcing the suspension of *L'Unità*. He was weary of "recycling the same ideas," he told his friends.[31] In a candid article entitled "We Have Nothing More to Say," the editor explained his decision: "To write of anything other than war would be ridiculous . . . Today events speak so clearly that our comments would be superfluous. . . . When the tempest is finished, . . . then we will again take up the work and rally our old friends."[32]

Ignoring the pleas of friends and associates, Salvemini stopped publication with the September 4 issue. This decision reflected the exhaustion of a man driven to influence Italian policy, overworked by writing most of the text of the weekly journal and worrying about its financial problems, and well aware of his limitations.[33] He now wrote only an occasional commentary and gave infrequent speeches, a pace greatly reduced from the average of four articles he had been writing in each weekly issue of *L'Unità*.[34] "My brain is tired from three years of excessive work," he complained, "and in these conditions I have become incapable of producing ideas." Had he continued to write, he reflected, he would have been reduced to "calling the nationalists scoundrels and the socialists imbeciles. Would it be worth it?"[35] However, within six weeks he began to reconsider reopening the journal.[36]

In November Salvemini delivered a lecture in Milan entitled "The Origins of the War." Rising before the imposing crowd at the People's University in the Beccaria School's large lecture hall, he explained the European alliance system, originated by Otto von Bismarck in an attempt to secure Germany in the aftermath of the Franco-Prussian War. Subsequently, the young Kaiser Wilhelm II had launched both an aggressive colonial expansion and a menacing naval program that alarmed the British. Consequently, the British cleared the air with France and agreed to the Entente Cordiale of 1906. Simultaneously, they accelerated their own naval buildup and recalled their fleets from distant waters. Meanwhile, Germans, Austrians, and Italians renewed the Triple Alliance. "From 1908 until this day," he thundered, "the Austro-German alliance functioned . . . as a revolutionary machine of militaristic threat and of international change." It was the same German people who now "thrust themselves beyond their borders with all the fury of the ancient barbarian migrations . . . crying their *Deutschland, Deutschland über alles.*"[37]

The lecture in Milan marked a broadening of Salvemini's campaign for intervention and attracted a notable new ally to the cause. The speech alone proved less significant than its coverage in the first issue of *Il Popolo d'Italia*, the new daily newspaper founded by the revolutionary socialist Benito Mussolini. Salvemini had known of Mussolini since the 1910 PSI Congress in Milan, where the twenty-seven year-old had debuted in national party politics with a furious speech just when Salvemini, ten years older, had exited.

Later in Florence, Prezzolini had introduced the two after Mussolini had returned from the Austrian-controlled Trentino region where he had worked in labor and nationalist agitation with Battisti. Salvemini's first impression had been favorable, and he had then observed Mussolini's rapid ascent—from participant in the revolutionary socialists' takeover of the PSI at the Reggio Emilia Congress in July 1912, to a position in the party directorate, and, by November of that year, to editor of *Avanti!*.[38] For several years, though wary of Mussolini's brand of revolutionary socialism, Salvemini and his cohorts welcomed him as a new socialist voice who promised to provide the party a needed focus. His polemics gave him political notoriety and provoked continuing discussion among the collaborators at *L'Unità*.

In February 1914, Salvemini and his friend Fernande Luchaire attended a lecture on "The Historical Worth of Socialism." When Mussolini spoke to 3,000 Florentines, Salvemini and Fernande responded enthusiastically.[39] Several months later, Salvemini wrote an optimistic article entitled "Socialist Rebirth," in which he declared that Mussolini was the man to articulate "the need for a sincerely revolutionary movement in our country."[40] This article, published on May Day, the socialist holiday, signaled Salvemini's closest approach to revolutionary socialism since 1898.

For a time, Mussolini and Salvemini cooperated on trade policy.[41] Mussolini had followed Salvemini's political commentary and selectively championed Salveminian positions without becoming a disciple. Salvemini's split with reformist socialism, his support for universal suffrage, and his opposition to Freemasonry particularly influenced Mussolini, who published several of his articles. Mussolini was especially interested in his ability to tap the latent revolutionary potential of the Mezzogiorno, the magnitude of which Salvemini had called to his attention. Evaluating Red Week of June 1914, Salvemini referred to Mussolini as a "serious" revolutionary.[42] The relationship between these bitterest of future enemies was, in its early stages, one of mutual regard.[43]

In February 1913, and again a year later, Mussolini supported Salvemini as a socialist candidate for the Chamber of Deputies from the fourth district of Turin. In the first instance, he wrote the following:

Yesterday evening the secretary of the socialist section of Torino spoke to me about . . . your candidacy. . . . I immediately declared my enthusiasm for these reasons: 1) Giolitti detests you . . . ; 2) Because your great cultural, political and moral qualities in the Chamber would be good; 3) (The most important) Torino—*the most civilized city in Italy*—would provide magnificent proof of civil and political solidarity to your poor and genuine plebes of Puglia.[44]

When Salvemini had, in fact, run for the Chamber from Molfetta, Mussolini had pledged active support, including a general strike.[45] Meanwhile, Mussolini campaigned for the Chamber from Forlí. Both lost.[46]

The second of these invitations proved more controversial, particularly in retrospect. In early 1914, when a vacancy appeared in Turin's fourth district seat, a group of young left-wing Turinese socialists invited Salvemini to offer his candidacy. It was an effort to demonstrate socialist solidarity with southern peasants and to retaliate against Giolitti for "stealing" the 1913 election from Salvemini in Bitonto and Molfetta. Acknowledging Salvemini's estrangement from the PSI, the young socialists assured him that, once in the Chamber, he could represent the peasants of Apulia and avoid the PSI parliamentary group.[47] Although moved, Salvemini declined. He did not want the people of Molfetta to think that he was abandoning them in favor of new political ties in the North. Furthermore, he was no longer a member of the PSI, and would not reenter the party to run for office. To do so would be improper and immoral.[48]

That Salvemini refused the offer is no surprise. The controversy arose only in the ideologically polarized 1950s, when a posthumous publication of Italian communist patriarch Antonio Gramsci alleged that in declining the offer, Salvemini had proposed the candidacy of Mussolini.[49] Salvemini indirectly refuted Gramsci. Although most historians accept the Gramsci rendition, the incident remains ambiguous.[50]

Of greater importance is the influence that Salvemini exerted on Gramsci, Palmiro Togliatti, Tasca and other young left-wing socialists of Turin, the future founders of Italian communism. The power of Salvemini's personality and intellect and the boldness of his political positions had created a strong following within the ranks of Turin's Socialist Youth Federation. Gramsci and Tasca had contributed to *L'Unità,* and they regularly followed its editor's writings. The Turinese socialist press frequently quoted and reprinted its articles.[51]

Some within this group were, at least for a time, convinced by Salvemini's example that it was possible to pursue democratic socialism without being co-opted by the leadership of the bourgeois parliamentary system. Some were attracted to the analytical precision of his methodology of *concretismo,* although Gramsci and other more "idealistic" socialists dissented. Some saw Salvemini as a sympathetic victim of Giolitti's electoral machine; others identified both Salvemini and Mussolini as zealous socialists and role models in their independent rejection of the party leadership. Of greatest significance was the plan to recruit Salvemini as a means to bring southern peasants into the party. This idea, apparently originating with Gramsci and considered also by Mussolini, addressed one of the core issues of twentieth-century revolutionary socialism, the role of the peasant class in revolution.[52]

The invitation to candidacy, as all parties acknowledged, was a sincere gesture designed to illustrate the common ground occupied by northern and southern proletarians, a point that Salvemini had been emphasizing for years. In response to the gesture, Salvemini traveled to Turin to campaign for the PSI candidate. Gramsci believed that the cooperation between Salvemini and northern socialists was an important step in the development of the party.[53]

By 1914, despite some degree of mutual interest and respect, Mussolini and Salvemini, two bold critics of the liberal state, disagreed markedly on many issues and would never become friends.[54] Most notably, they differed on the approaching war in Europe. Mussolini was a well-known advocate of neutrality, the official position taken by most of Europe's socialist parties; Salvemini was a leading voice for democratic interventionism.

Since 1912, when the revolutionary wing had won control of the PSI and had named him editor of *Avanti!*, Mussolini had led a campaign to drive the reformist socialists from the party. A major part of his program was rigid neutrality in Europe. However, a growing fear that the party might isolate itself in a futile neutralist campaign led Mussolini to reconsider the intervention issue in the fall of 1914. On October 18, in a now famous article, he announced a fundamental shift "From Absolute to Active Neutrality."

Salvemini responded to the article enthusiastically. "Dear Mussolini," he scratched on a postcard the evening the fateful article appeared:

While on the train, I read your magnificent article on *non*-absolute neutrality, and I feel the need to send my congratulations. Once again your sound and strong instincts have led you in the right direction. It is no small act of courage to violate the letter, in order to salvage the spirit, of internationalism in this country.[55]

By publishing the text of the postcard, *Avanti!* established Salvemini's support and consequently generated mixed responses from several of his associates.[56] Two days after Mussolini rejected the party's neutrality doctrine, PSI directors, in a tumultuous meeting, forced Mussolini to resign as editor of *Avanti!*.[57] Within days, Mussolini wrote a letter published in *Il Corriere della Sera*, entitled "New Facts," in which he justified his shift on the basis of changed conditions.[58] Mussolini's rejection of the socialist dogma of "absolute neutrality" pleased the interventionists among Salvemini's friends and sparked continuing exchanges on the war.[59]

In the first issue of Mussolini's new publication, *Il Popolo d'Italia*, he published the text of another postcard from Salvemini congratulating him for making the transition to interventionism and for having "broken the Marxist paralysis." Mussolini wrote that he was encouraged by the approval of such a "maestro" as Salvemini.[60] Within ten days, the PSI had expelled Mussolini.[61] Soon he received a dramatic telegram from Giuseppe Prezzolini, Lombardo Radice, and other former Salvemini associates at *La Voce*: "The Socialist Party expels you. Italy welcomes you." The separate endorsements from Prezzolini and Salvemini accompanied numerous statements of support from the revolutionary Left, including those of Tasca and Gramsci.[62]

When the first issue of *Il Popolo d'Italia* appeared on November 15, 1914, two slogans crossed the masthead: "Whoever has iron has bread" (Louis Blanchi); and "Revolution is an idea that has found bayonets" (Napoleon).[63] The Prefect of Milan, reporting on the political scope of the new paper, described an "eclectic collaboration" that included Salvemini, who functioned at first as a kind of informal member of its editorial board.[64] In the first six months, Mussolini's paper won a large following and played a significant role in the interventionist campaign.[65]

With the first issue of Mussolini's paper came charges in *Avanti!*, now substantiated, that *Il Popolo d'Italia* was subsidized by the French in an effort to encourage Italian intervention in the war.[66] Mussolini denied the charges as the German press quickly amplified them. Salvemini, in Milan at the time, sought out Mussolini at his house and advised him to exonerate himself from the charges. Mussolini assured him that the issue would soon be resolved.[67]

On top of the French subsidies to Mussolini's press, there is no doubt that French intellectual and cultural influences helped to fuel the Italian interventionist campaign, and that Salvemini was one of their chief targets.[68] One influence that fortified Salvemini's pro-French sympathies was his friendship with the family of a French literature professor, Julien Luchaire, director of the French Institute in Florence, and his wife, Fernande. Salvemini lectured on intervention in several Italian cities in conjunction with Julien Luchaire and the Belgian socialist and patriot Jules Destrée.[69] However, it is even clearer that Salvemini's commitment to the ideals of Western democracy—in contrast to Mussolini and Gramsci—and his opposition to Austro-German authoritarianism were deeply rooted. At best, any immediate prewar influence from French sources only reaffirmed Salvemini's commitment to protecting Anglo-French democratic political culture. In contrast, the change that brought Mussolini into the camp of interventionism has been described as a "conversion" determined not by French funds but by Mussolini's "political crisis." Salvemini believed that the change was sincere.[70]

When Mussolini left the Socialist Party and founded *Il Popolo d'Italia* in November 1914, he also began to organize revolutionary socialists and syndicalists in northern and central Italy into "*fasci* for revolutionary action." At the same time, he joined the growing interventionist movement that attracted a wide range of groups. While *Il Popolo d'Italia* took a radical position of intervention for the sake of revolution, others supported the cause for different reasons, including the conservative *Il Corriere della Sera* and the Turin socialist weekly *Il Grido del Popolo*. After September, when the German forces bogged down at the Marne, Italian nationalists, maintaining their enthusiasm for belligerency and territorial acquisition, simply changed sides, many following D'Annunzio's siren song. In contrast, reformist socialists, led by Bissolati, hoped to strengthen democratic forces in England and France as well as in Italy and anticipated the need to participate in the postwar settlement to ensure that the world would change its ways. Like Salvemini, all supported intervention. In early 1915, *Il Popolo d'Italia* observed that the interventionists all had "boarded the same train by accident and were bound for different destinations."[71]

The Salandra government and its liberal supporters held to their position of official neutrality throughout the fall of 1914. Salandra announced that Italy would be guided in negotiations by her *sacro egoismo* (sacred self-interest). All the while Italy quietly mobilized and built stockpiles in the event that war came. In November, Salandra named Sonnino foreign minister, and the two resumed secret negotiations with Austria-Hungary in which they spelled out their terms for maintaining neutrality. When the Austrians refused to offer enough territory, Sonnino instructed his ambassador in London to pursue negotiations with the Entente powers.[72]

Meanwhile, three weeks before Christmas, 1914, encouraged by readers and friends, Salvemini resumed the publication of *L'Unità* and thus rejoined the movement for intervention on the side of the Entente powers.[73] The second *L'Unità* would be shored up with new funds and moved from Florence to Rome where Antonio De Viti De Marco would share editorial responsibility.[74] Disturbed by the socialists' "absolute neutrality" and the nationalists' flawed interventionism, Salvemini proclaimed: "We have no right to be silent." The time had now arrived to resume the important work of educating the young generation:[75]

If this war ends with the prostration of the Triple Entente and with the victory of the Austro-German bloc, the neutral states, not less than the losers, will become subjugated to the winners. . . . [In contrast], victory of the Triple Entente will not diminish the national independence of Italy or any other European state.[76]

Salvemini's legacy to the campaign was twofold. The revived *L'Unità* made a Salveminian case of concrete issues within an idealistic framework: In return for their great sacrifice, Italians could expect specific benefits, while at the same time serving the greater interests of democracy. Thus, though small in circulation, *L'Unità* complemented the pro-intervention campaign mounted by *Il Corriere della Sera* and such influential papers as *Il Secolo*.

Second, Salvemini joined Bissolati in offering democratic interventionism with circumscribed territorial goals. Thus, Italians could support intervention without having to accept the imperialistic agenda of the nationalist movement; they could complete the Risorgimento without acquiring alien nationalities and territory the army could not defend. A persistent anti-imperialist, Salvemini limited himself to a confined irredentist agenda consistent with Mazzini and Battisti, favoring an expanded Slavic state rather than a trans-Adriatic Italy.

The best-known and most controversial example of Slavic independence he offered was his support for Dalmatia. He applied to the Adriatic coast the same Mazzinian nationalities argument, based on ethnography and justice, that he had applied to the Brenner Pass and the Tyrolian Alps. Luigi Federzoni struck back. An old antagonist from the Libyan War and one of Italy's leading nationalists, Federzoni spoke in Florence on "The National Idea."[77] Federzoni's impassioned rejoinder foreshadowed the abuse that the Dalmatian issue would bring Salvemini.

The year 1915 began with little movement on the western front. Reading the news one evening in mid-January, Salvemini learned of new attempts by the major powers to break the stalemate. The Austrians changed foreign ministers while the Russians sought British naval support on the Turkish front. On the same page a report of a disaster revived shocking images. An earthquake in the Abruzzi had killed 30,000 and destroyed hundreds of villages.[78]

Within hours Salvemini headed a volunteer team that boarded a train for Rome, carrying medical supplies, blankets, bread, and milk. When the party reached Rome, Senator Leopoldo Franchetti provided his automobile and they proceeded to the remote village of Balsorano, where they found a desperate situation. The town was partly destroyed and totally without official assistance. Amid torrential rains, the volunteers implemented their plan, plagued by problems from the first day.[79]

Excavation was already in progress. Salvemini wrote to Ojetti what must have been an agonizing reminder of his own Messina tragedy: "Yesterday [in a nearby town] they dug from the ruins *living* children. For another fifteen days there is hope." Soon others joined the effort, including Aldo Rosselli, a young man from Pisa whose brothers were destined to play a major role in Salvemini's life.[80]

Salvemini's stay in Balsorano reaffirmed some of his most basic values. The simple folk of this isolated village were the southerners for whose interests he had been fighting throughout his adult life. Many assumed that the earthquake was the apocalypse, that the entire earth had suffered a similar shock. "The Madonna wishes to reward us in Paradise, Mister Florentine," explained a woman in accepting her ration of bread. After two weeks, Salvemini left the Abruzzi for Florence, where he continued to solicit supplies. The rescue attempt, for all its pain, served as partial redemption for the failure of his Messina rescue.[81]

Returning to Florence at the end of January, Salvemini evaluated Italy's diplomatic status. In the midst of secret diplomacy and divisive debate, he continued to present the case for the Entente powers. In January he published *War or
Neutrality*, a long pamphlet that presented a pragmatic case for intervention.[82]
Later that same month, he laid blame for the growing neutrality crisis at the feet
of "The 'Boss' of Italy," his old nemesis, Giovanni Giolitti.[83] In late February, in
the face of advanced protests against his appearance, he accepted an invitation
from former student Pietro Silva, professor at the Naval Academy at Livorno, to
address the local People's University on the causes of war.[84]

All through the winter and spring, Sonnino secretly negotiated with both
sides. Making little headway with the Austrians, he speeded up negotiations
with the Entente, demanding territorial concessions from both.[85] When the
Austrians made an unsatisfactory counteroffer, Sonnino signed the secret Pact
of London on April 26, 1915, whereby the British met virtually all his demands
in return for Italy's promise to enter the war within one month. Although
Salvemini did not know then, he would discover that the treaty promised to
transfer to Italy the Trentino, Tyrol to the Brenner frontier, Trieste, Gorizia,
most of Istria, northern Dalmatia, and the nucleus of Albania.[86] The territory included nearly one-quarter million German-speaking Austrians and almost
three-quarter million Slavs. Thus the Pact's terms of both northern and eastern
border settlements violated Salvemini's Mazzinian sense of international justice. For Sonnino, the realistic prospect of increasing Italian security by controlling the Adriatic warranted entering the war; for Salvemini, such motivation
demeaned the very ideals for which he endorsed intervention. Count Carlo
Sforza, experienced career diplomat and future foreign minister, told Sonnino
that he agreed with Salvemini and Bissolati on democratic intervention.
Sonnino responded, "They are mad, they are idealists."[87]

Terms of the Pact of London remained carefully guarded, and as Salandra
juggled his political options in a deeply divided government, Salvemini continued to promote democratic intervention. Salandra had one month from the
signing of the Pact of London to convince the Parliament and the public to support the Entente. Neutralist opinion dominated the Chamber of Deputies, and
not once did Salandra present the Pact or lead a debate. Outside, interventionists were more aggressive. The open confrontation among neutralists and interventionists built to violence in the piazzas of major cities. On the fourth day of
the month, Italy renounced the Triple Alliance.[88]

Nationalists, democratic interventionists, and socialist internationalists
clashed in the escalating strife known as "Radiant May." Salandra's time ran
short. In Milan, Mussolini called for a popular uprising: "War or revolution!" In
Rome on May 12, nearly 100,000 swarmed the train station to greet
D'Annunzio. From his hotel balcony, he harangued, "It is no longer time for
speeches, but for action! . . . If it is a crime to incite people to violence, I boast of

now committing that crime." The next day, Salandra held a portentous meeting with the parliamentary party leaders to test support for his policy. When only Bissolati voted for war, and only sixty votes could be counted, Salandra handed his resignation to the king.[89]

Salvemini observed the crisis with a sense of disbelief and dread. "The resignation of the prime minister is our liquidation," he wrote the same day. "Now there is only one thing to do: intensify the anti-Giolittian demonstrations to the brink of revolt, and threaten the king."[90] He saw that interventionism had the upper hand, not as the result of a national consensus on policy, but because of a breakdown in the political system and because of the manifestation of superior power to which he had contributed. Then the irony came full circle. Because Salandra could not govern, the king turned for political salvation, as Salvemini feared, to Giolitti, Italy's power broker for a generation and now the leading neutralist. Salvemini's campaign had unwittingly helped to tip the scales in favor of his *bête noire*.[91]

By offering little explanation or alternative plan to the press or the public, Salandra abandoned center stage to the king and to extraparliamentary forces. As interventionist demonstrations against Giolitti turned violent in many major cities, Mussolini warned the king that to ignore the people's will would cost him the throne. Demonstrators invaded the Chamber of Deputies.

In this revolutionary atmosphere, things moved quickly. Giolitti declined the king's request to form a government, as did other potential prime ministers. The king, believing the monarchy to be in jeopardy, spoke of abdicating unless Parliament supported war. On May 16, the king refused Salandra's resignation and recalled him to his post. Four days later Salandra asked the Parliament to approve war. In an astounding about-face, he won overwhelming endorsement and on May 22 ordered mobilization of Italian forces. Two days later, Italy went to war with Austria-Hungary, and an Austrian destroyer bombarded Barletta near Salvemini's boyhood home.[92]

True to his word, Salvemini suspended publication of *L'Unità* on May 28, proclaiming in the final issue that to continue criticizing policy would interfere with Italy's focus on military victory. However, once "a systematic work of concrete discussion" appeared useful, he would resume publication.[93] He had also promised a number of people that he would enlist. He would volunteer for the infantry, preferably with a unit from Apulia, if the need existed.[94]

As Italian soldiers left for the front and he searched for a way to contribute to the war effort, Salvemini entered another period of personal crisis. This time, Fernande Luchaire was at his side to give him caring support and love. Salvemini counted Fernande and her husband, Julien, as among his oldest and dearest friends. When he had returned to Florence in 1908, distraught over the loss of his family, they had consoled him. While recuperating from the trauma, he had rested in Grenoble, where the Luchaire family vacationed. Fernande had been especially comforting. Later, he had joined the family at the Tuscan hill town of Abetone.[95]

The Luchaires, who now lived near Salvemini on the Via San Gallo, moved in Florentine literary and political circles that included Prezzolini, Amendola, Papini, Placci, the well-known art historian and critic Bernard Berenson and his wife, Mary, and the eminent jurist Piero Calamandrei. Although Salvemini was never entirely comfortable in the salon culture, often a victim of his well-known impatience and his distaste for pretense, the others in the Florentine group respected him for his forthrightness and his searing intelligence, enjoyed his humor, and frequently invited him.[96]

Salvemini found himself drawn to the Luchaire children, Jean (whom he lovingly called "Giovannino") and Corinne, who helped to fill the void left by the Messina tragedy and gradually became a kind of surrogate family. By the summer of 1910, having spent many hours in the company of the family, he began to express a romantic interest in Fernande.[97]

Fernande Luchaire was a woman of culture. Her French university education had prepared her to participate actively in the political life of prewar Florence where she had won respect for her intellect. Nicky Mariano, Berenson's librarian and lifelong companion, remembered Fernande as a serious conversationalist but less charming than Salvemini and "very pedantic." Fernande had once returned to Berenson a borrowed Proust volume in which she had extensively corrected the author's style and syntax. What to the friend seemed overly meticulous and pretentious, Salvemini found appealing. Apparently, like Salvemini, she was not fully at ease among the free spirits of the Bloomsbury group who frequented "I Tatti," Berenson's villa outside Florence. Mariano remembered the embarrassment Fernande experienced on the occasion of a later visit of Vanessa Bell, John Maynard Keynes, and Duncan Grant. As Grant painted by one of the ponds, the poet Robert Trevelyan emerged from the water and proceeded to dry himself by walking around naked. Just then, Fernande walked through the garden gate toward the lemon house. She was dismayed, she told Mariano, "to have found a completely nude savage who walked around . . . as if it were the most natural thing in the world."[98]

Perhaps because neither was drawn to salon society and both were more serious than playful, Fernande and Gaetano grew closer. In her cerebral energy and political vigor, she was becoming the intimate intellectual companion and soulmate that Ernesta Bittanti had been in his university days, when the two had regularly discussed Marxist ideology and Italian politics late into the night. The contrast to his beloved Maria, the traditional southern wife and mother, could not have been greater.

Fernande, in turn, was drawn to Salvemini's engaging wit and warmth, something other women understood. Nicky Mariano recalled Salvemini's vigor, impetuosity, and passion: "Gaetano's laughter was irresistible and his whole personality life-enhancing."[99] Hélène Cantarella, who met him later, re-called:

Salvemini was (in his leonine way) an eminently attractive man. He had a great capacity for friendship, . . . [was] monumentally kind. . . . He had also one of the most endearing smiles in the world; and his laugh was irresistible. . . . Add to this a dazzling mind, an incisive wit, encyclopedic knowledge, yet an unusual candor. . . . The result was absolutely beguiling.[100]

By 1914 Fernande had become his confidante and adviser. Toward the end of that year, she and Julien legally separated and began divorce proceedings in France. By November 1915, the divorce was final.[101]

In the summer of 1915, as Salvemini considered volunteering for the infantry, Fernande urged him to schedule a physical examination with a private physician. Although he was forty-one, his powerful body compacted on a short frame, a paunch, spectacles, and premature balding gave the appearance that he was fiftyish and in poor condition. Nonetheless, he felt strong, and in spite of a past history of recurring episodes of depression, he was anxious to serve. When in July a doctor rejected him for military service, Salvemini was beside himself with rage: "The son of a bitch found a scar on the apex of my right lung . . . with a hiss in an important vein near the scar. Therefore it would be better if I stayed at home hiding behind Mama's skirt."[102] Unwilling to accept this fate, Salvemini went to the Hospital of Santa Maria Nuova to consult a group of doctors he knew. Examining new x-rays, they confirmed the initial diagnosis: "sclerosis of the upper lobe of the right lung that had changed the size of the large venous vessels." The examining physician advised Salvemini against enlisting as a volunteer. Confidentially, the doctor informed the professor that if he marched off to war, a few weeks in the heat and humidity would land him in the hospital.[103]

As Salvemini waited, still hoping to be accepted into the army, 400,000 Italian troops attacked stalwart Austrian defenses over mountainous terrain in the face of superior firepower. The failure of the Russian-Serbian offensive indicated trouble, because the Austrians were able to concentrate forces on Italy's borders at the Trentino and the Isonzo River. On both fronts, Italian troops advanced slightly during the summer months and paid dearly for every mile gained.

In July, Salvemini passed a physical examination given by a professor at the University of Bologna Medical School. "My *disability* was a false alarm by an overly conscientious doctor," he explained.[104] He bided his time working in a press office, assigned the gruesome task of dispatching notices of soldiers' deaths, "an exercise very unsuited to prepare the spirit for killing." The experience forced him to contemplate the implications of his interventionist campaign:

There are moments when I feel overcome by doubt, faced with such human sorrow, [wondering] if . . . German tyranny would not be preferable to . . . such carnage. And if there were not in me something that rebels invincibly against servitude and places justice and liberty above life, I confess to you that I would repent for having wanted war.[105]

On July 31, he was appointed to cadet officer school and now awaited orders to report.[106]

By the middle of July, the second of eleven successive battles had begun for control of the Isonzo River along a sixty-mile front. Casualties mounted, Italian munitions ran short, and the weather worsened. The commander, General Luigi Cadorna, like his French and English counterparts, now had to face the reality of a war of attrition. The war that the generals and politicians had expected to end by Christmas 1914 threatened to stretch out indefinitely. Strategic victory would be elusive; instead of lightning movements, foot soldiers would slug it out in the trenches in a tactical struggle over a few miles of blood-soaked turf. Salvemini had shared in the "short-war illusion," originally predicting an October conclusion.

His expectations for training also proved unrealistic. He hoped to train in Florence where he would have access to his books; instead he was assigned as a second lieutenant in the 70th Infantry Regiment at Arezzo. By the first week in August, he had begun training at the Tiber River town of Sansepolcro in Tuscany. In two months of training, Salvemini adjusted with surprising ease: "I have accepted the rule of questioning nothing and obeying everyone," he explained in October. "Thus I am perfectly happy and I am placing my trust in destiny." Such adaptation, combined with a severe shortage of officers, earned him a rapid promotion to cadet commander of a company.[107]

The military training experience proved to reenforce his sense of self-identity. An intellectual never completely at ease among intellectuals, Salvemini rediscovered his peasant roots. He truly enjoyed comradeship with the soldiers. "I am," he wrote a friend, "profoundly '*popolo*' [of the people]. To be with the *povera gente* [ordinary folk] puts me at ease. They make you laugh, sing, tell jokes. Basically, I think they like me and instinctively respect me."[108]

The good will and humor of these young recruits eased the transition of their middle-age professor-lieutenant. "Since I do not know how to give orders," he observed, "I can make a serious mess of a march through the city." To compensate for this shortcoming, Salvemini worked out an arrangement at the suggestion of one of his men. The soldier would whisper the proper order, then Salvemini would bark it out with a thunderous command, pleased that he was creating a fine martial image. Occasionally, this system failed. One day while marching his troops through Florence, he rested them at the Piazza del Duomo. Then came a command to move them to the nearby Borgo San Lorenzo. "To San Lorenzo, march!" he shouted, only later laughing at the abortive order. Several days thereafter, his troops in formation, instead of saying "Right face," he shouted with authority, "Face the street!" The soldiers broke up in laughter, he along with them. Recalling such incidents, he mused to a friend with character-istic democratic stoicism, "Ah, these are good people, docile, intelligent, affec-tionate. When will we find a leadership class worthy of such heroism?"[109]

While training, he managed to publish nearly an article each week, two of them in Mussolini's *Il Popolo d'Italia*, continuing to concentrate on foreign policy issues. It was not easy. "The life of a 'warrior' does not leave sufficient time for intellectual occupation," he complained. He did manage a few days' leave, which he spent with Fernande and friends.[110] Just before he finished training, the Luchaires' divorce nearing conclusion, he told a few good friends of his intention to marry Fernande. He explained to Umberto Zanotti-Bianco, perhaps somewhat disingenuously, that he did not cause the divorce:

The divorce was given at the Signora's [official] request, but because of her husband, who wished to resolve a sad situation, one that goes back to a distant time before I knew the Signora. She freed herself from that relationship . . . and since then she and I are free to organize a new way of life for ourselves. [She and her husband] maintain cordial per-sonal relations, in spite of the divorce, in the interest of the children, who will continue to remain with her and who will make up my new family.[111]

For the moment, the realities of wartime training prevailed over personal considerations. One month past his forty-second birthday, overweight, psycho-logically vulnerable, and with no previous firearms experience, Salvemini des-perately needed training. What he encountered was extensive lecturing, military instructors methodically diagraming on blackboards the banal tactics of trench warfare. He could not help but think of the enemy machine-gun fire that would render absurd the instructor's neat, rectilinear sketches. Not once in nearly three months at Sansepolcro did Salvemini hold a weapon in his hand.[112]

On November 4, 1915, the call finally came: he would command a platoon of the 121st Infantry, First Company, Macerata Brigade, a unit of Venetians and Florentines. Disappointed that he was separated from the Apulians, he boarded a train of reinforcements that crossed the River Piave, passing the busy city of Udine to the ancient town of Cividale, a few miles from the front. Then he heard the guns.[113]

Italian armies had now launched offensive after offensive, raiding Austrian positions at the cost of more than 100,000 casualties. Salvemini did not know that the third battle for the Isonzo River had ended the day before, as indeci-sively as the rest. Nor did he know that he was headed into the teeth of the most intense military action of the entire conflict.[114]

Historians would later write of this campaign that Italian foot soldiers were victims of disastrous planning and command decisions: undertrained and underequipped, they were ordered to assault barbed wire-protected trenches in the face of heavy artillery and automatic weapons fire. Cadorna and his staff had learned little from the carnage of the campaigns fought the year before on the western front. For Salvemini, the failures of command materialized before his eyes.[115]

He found the 121st Infantry in the Carso, mired in mud amid fierce fighting, trying to breach Austrian lines and take the bridgeheads of Gorizia and Tolmino. The Italians were penned on a barren hillside between Mount San Michele and Mount Sei Busi. He joined them, thirty yards from the Austrian positions, armed only with a baton.[116]

Within days, the Italian command ordered the fourth Isonzo offensive. The trench became his hellish new home, his office, and his sanctuary. The Austrian grenades never let up, exploding all around. The first day, as he crossed the route known as the "passage of death," he felt a certain calm, a momentary invincibility, a sense of floating above the fray. That night, he handed out cartridges in preparation for the impending assault. The activity drew Austrian fire. "Down, flat!" he ordered his troops. Then he tapped them, one by one, in the darkness with the butt of his newly acquired rifle, and they crawled to the relative safety of the trenches. The fire did not let up until daybreak. No longer did he entertain notions of invincibility.

Soon fatigue set in. He managed two hours' rest the next day, recovering from the night's rigors, to sleep only two hours the following night. "The trench is nothing but a cauldron of mud, and we wallow in it up to our helmets," he recorded. "We sleep in beds formed by sacks of earth, naturally damp." During the day, he worked under constant fire, sensing the rounds passing just above his head.

He found this "strange adventure" so interesting, and the relentless pounding so exhausting, that he had to force himself to focus, lest a lapse in concentration cost him his life. In a moment of contemplation, he observed a surreal quality: "What is indeed amusing is the insane cheerfulness of people who live in these conditions." Being shot at, he recorded in his diary, reminded him of the Molfetta election.[117]

Day after day the artillery rounds and the grenades exploded all around and the machine-gun fire formed an invisible, deadly ceiling. Steady rain aggravated the misery in the trenches, thunder and lightning replicated the artillery, and when the rain stopped, mist further impaired visibility. Across the entire front, cholera spread.

On November 11, the 121st Infantry supported the renewed offensive. Fighting erupted in a fury of artillery and rifle fire and a bayonet charge. It was a "diabolical night." In front of him charged reinforcements, sidestepping the returning wounded. The water in the trench reached his knees. Finally the rising sun brought a lull in the action. A calm settled over him, and for a moment he sensed the fighting was finished forever.

That night was his initiation. No longer did his letters to Fernande reflect the same naive fascination or the false sense of security. He felt at the same time an awareness of reality and a new stoicism. He entered the following in his diary:

Whoever proclaims the beauty . . . of war I wish were [here] on the mountain we are occupying, in our trenches! But they have chosen to stay home. As for me, right in the midst of real war, not [the war] of the *literati*, I am happy that I came. If I had not come, I would suffer remorse and humiliation about it for the rest of my life. I could die on the front myself.[118]

The throb of artillery and the report of rifle fire became so commonplace that Salvemini found himself adjusting to the trenches and engaging in some semblance of normal conversation with men of differing political views. One morning a major in his battalion, a zealous irredentist, ordered an attack, saber drawn, shouting as if to strike fear into the Austrians: "Savoy!" It was the old monarchist battle cry. Somewhere in the trenches was D'Annunzio, and just to Salvemini's left flank, in the 120th Infantry, the young syndicalist Filippo Corridoni lost his life.

On the night of November 13, Salvemini headed directly into frontline action as his unit carried munitions to the advanced troops. In the dark, soldiers told of miraculously surviving Austrian carpet fire. As he stepped over the dead, still where they had fallen, he sensed an imminent counterattack. Everyone around him prepared. He removed his rifle from his shoulder, unsheathed and fixed his bayonet for hand-to-hand combat, and waited in the darkness for the charge. It did not come. Six days later, the Austrians launched their counteroffensive under a furious artillery assault and overran the positions of the 121st Infantry. The last letter Fernande received from the front was dated the thirteenth.[119]

When Salvemini's next letters arrived, they came from the Third Army Field Hospital at Perteole. He was not wounded, he explained, but ill. With badly swollen feet and severe intestinal problems, he had been hospitalized the day before the Austrians overwhelmed the 121st Infantry. What he did not tell friends was that his condition was so severe that the hospital's director, who knew him, had failed to recognize him. Furthermore, although he joked that he hoped to be well in a few days, doctors told him that he was suffering from serious heart, liver, and circulation problems. The demands of war in the trenches had overwhelmed his body, just as his physician had predicted. He was then moved by train from the field hospital across the border to the Red Cross Hospital in Padua and was soon granted a medical discharge.[120]

While recuperating, Salvemini experienced guilt, "humiliated" at having left the front after twelve days mired in the mud. "In all of this, there is nothing either of greatness or heroism," he wrote. He could not shake the self-doubt.[121] Rereading *War and Peace* helped to restore his perspective. Tolstoy's condemnation of war, through the eyes of simple peasants, reinforced the tragedy and futility Salvemini had so recently experienced, and he understood the profound malaise that would soon settle among this generation of European youth who had borne the weight of war.[122]

Released from the hospital just in time for Christmas 1915, Salvemini returned to the Florence home of the Marchesa "Donna Titina" Benzoni, daughter of Ferdinando Martini, Minister of Colonies. Salvemini took advantage of this new opportunity, a kind of intimacy with power to which he was unaccustomed, by urging the Minister to pursue two causes: military reform and an investigation of Italy's obligations under the Triple Alliance. In addition, he asked the Minister to intercede on behalf of his old friend Ernesta, who was struggling to feed her three children while her husband, Cesare Battisti, was fighting in the Trentino.[123]

Salvemini's transition to civilian life stretched through the spring of 1916. A low-grade fever lingered, and his body recovered slowly from the stresses of war.[124] Jokingly, but with some frustration at the pace of his recovery, he wrote in February, "I have pains in my head, pains in my feet, pains in my kidneys, pains in my heart, pains in my wallet: all the pains in the universe."[125]

He did resume his job, but even the short commute from Florence to the University of Pisa to lecture consumed most of his energy. He resisted requests to resurrect *L'Unità*, feeling the need to accomplish some "original, scientific work" before returning to journalism. This was but one expression of the continuing dilemma of the scholar-political activist that would produce tension throughout his life. In this instance, he was consciously balancing the roles. He clearly understood the need to regenerate his career as historian, and yet the issues of Italy's role in war and peace demanded his attention as never before.[126]

NOTES

1. GS to Fernande Dauriac, after November 13, 1915, entry dated November 9, *Cart 1914*, 214–215.

2. GS to ED, October 22, 1914, *Cart 1914*, 57.

3. S-W, *ILF*, 394; GS, "Una rivoluzione senza programma," *Opere* IV (1), 382–384.

4. GS, "Per la nuova Albania," June 19 and July 3, 1914; "Sciopero generale e guerra," July 24, 1914; "La neutralità 'assoluta,'" August 7, 1914; "I patti della Triplice Alleanza e la questione balcanica," August 21, 1914, all in *L'U*.

5. GS, "La Triplice Alleanza e gl'interessi politici dell'Italia"; "La conferenza d'Algesiras"; "La politica estera dell'Italia"; "Il gioco della Germania," *Opere* III (1), 25–95.

6. GS, "La politica estera dell'Italia," *Opere* III (1), 33–36.

7. GS, "La politica estera dell'Italia e il pacifismo," *Opere* III (1), 49–50.

8. GS, "Il problema dell'Alto Adige," *Opere* III (1), 444. See also the attached "Lettera di Salvemini a Cesare Battisti."

9. GS, "Irredentismo, questione balcanica e internazionalismo," *Opere* III (1), 63.

10. GS, *La politica estera dell'Italia dal 1871 al 1915* (Florence, 1944) in *Opere* III (4), 509–514.

11. GS, "La nuova Triplice," *Opere* III (1), 213.

12. GS, "Il problema delle alleanze," *Opere* III (1), 230–231.

13. GS, "La Nuova Triplice," *Opere* III (1), 208; "Alleanza tedesca e alleanza inglese," *Opere* III (1),157–166; "La Turchia e la Triplice," *Opere* III (1), 173; "Il problema della alleanze," *Opere* III (1), 228–236; "Postilla a 'L'imperialismo della paura,'" *Opere* III (1), 278.

14. S-W, *ILF*, 396–409; JB, *LMV*, 6–17; L&M, *IFP*, 130–132.

15. GS, "Proporzionale e suffragio universale," *Opere* VIII, 663.

16. GS, "Lo spettro della guerra," *Opere* III (1), 308–312.

17. From LA, *Venti Anni di vita politica*, quoted in S-W, *ILF*, 408.

18. S-W, *Italy*, 408–409; JB, *LMV*, 17–19; L&M, *IFP*, 133–136.

19. GS, "La nuova Albania," *Opere* III (1), 340; "Per la nuova Albania," *Opere* III (1), 336–338.

20. GS, "Fra la grande Serbia ed una piú grande Austria," *Opere* III (1), 348–350.

21. GS to PS, August 9, 1914, *Cart 1914*, 17.

22. GS to EBB, September 7, 1914, *Cart 1914*, 35.

23. GS to Z-B, August 5, 1914, *Cart 1914*, 15.

24. GS to GP, August 5, 1914, 16; to PS, August 9, 1914, 17; to UO, August 11 and 14, 1914, *Cart 1914*, 18 and 21.

25. GS, "La guerra per la pace," *Opere* III (1), 359–361.

26. GS, "La guerra per la pace," 360–361.

27. GS, "Non abbiamo niente da dire," "Offerte insidiose," *Opere* III (1), 362–368.

28. GA, *SSI*, 198; JB, *LMV*, 25–31; S-W, *ILF*, 413–430; L&M, *IFP*, 133–159.

29. See, for example, GS, "La neutralità 'assoluta'," "Fra la grande Serbia e un più grande Austria," and "Il problema delle alleanze," August 7, 1914 and subsequent articles in *L'U*; "La Dalmazia," November 9, 1914, *Il Secolo*.

30. GS, *Dal Patto di Londra alla Pace Di Roma* (Turin, 1925), *Opere* III (2), 732; S-W, *ILF*, 421.

31. GS to PS, August 28, 1914, *Cart 1914*, 30.

32. GS, "Non abbiamo niente da dire," 366.

33. GS to PS, August 28, 1914, *Cart 1914*, 30.

34. UGM to GS, October 19, 1914, *Cart 1914*, 56.

35. GS to PS, October 14, 1914, *Cart 1914*, 52.

36. GS to ED, October 22, 1914, *Cart 1914*, 57.

37. GS, "Le origini della guerra," 374–394.

38. ET, *Sal*, 163.

39. Carlo Placci to GS, July 3, 1914, *AGS*; GS to Guglielmo Zagari, December 16, 1913, *Cart 1912*; DeF, *il riv*, 129, 161, 185.

40. GS, "Rinascita socialista," *Opere* IV (2), 551–553.

41. GS to Zagari, December 16, 1913, *Cart 1912*, 456–457; GS, "La lotta antiprotezionista e il partito socialista" (interview), *Opere* IV (2), 553–556.

42. GS, "Una rivoluzione senza programma."

43. DeF, *il riv*, 86ff. and chapters four and seven; "Mussolini e *La Voce*," *Il Borghese*, June 11, 1964.

44. BM to GS, February 18, 1913, *AGS*, "Mussolini."

45. UGM to GS, September 6, 1913, *Cart 1912*, 386–387; G. M. Serrati to GS, March 10, 1913, 314; Arturo Vella to GS, July 19, 1913, 347; UGM to GS, July 21, 1913, 352; Agostino Lanzillo to GS, September 20, 1913, 400; UGM to GS, November 4 and 20, 1913 and March 14, 1914, *Cart 1912*, 432, 440–441 and 477–478.

46. DeF, *il riv*, 175.

47. No primary sources from 1914 can be found to document this incident fully. See Ubaldo Formentini to GS, February 2, 1914, *Cart 1912*, 463–464; Antonio Gramsci, *La questione meridionale*, 15; Paolo Spriano, *Torino operaia e socialista*, 270–273; Ottavio Pastore to editor, "Salvemini candidato," *Il Contemporaneo* (Bari), 1955, n. 41, BCM; Angelo Tasca, "La storia e la preistoria," *Il Mondo* (Rome), August 18, 1953; DeF, *il riv*, 198–200; UGM to GS, February 20, 1914, *Cart 1912*, 471; DeG, *Angelo Tasca* (Milan, 1985), 30–31.

48. GS to Formentini, February 4, 1914, cited in DeF, *il riv*, 199; Pastore to Spriano, June 16, 1958, cited in Spriano, *Storia di Torino operaia e socialista*, 271; GS, preface to *SSQM*, xxiii; AWS, *IGE*, 24.

49. Gramsci, *La questione meridionale*, 15–16; Spriano, *Storia di Torino*, 270–273.

50. GS, *SSQM*, xxiv-xxv. On Gramsci, see his *Scritti giovanili* (Turin, 1958); John M. Cammett, *Antonio Gramsci and the Origins of Italian Communism* (Stanford, 1967); GA, *SSI*, 240 ff.; Alastair Davidson, *Antonio Gramsci* (London, 1977); Aldo Romano, "Antonio Gramsci tra la guerra e la rivoluzione," *Rivista storica del socialismo*, I, n. 1 (1958), 405–410; Domenico Zugàro, "Antonio Gramsci all'Università di Torino, 1911–1915," *Società* (Milan) VIII (December 1957), 1091–1111.

51. For an evaluation of Salvemini's following among the young socialists of Turin, see Cammett, *Gramsci*, 31–34. See also Spriano, *Storia di Torino operaia e socialista*, 262–264; DeG, *Tasca*, 30–31; Aldo Agosti, *Palmiro Togliatti* (Turin, 1996), 9–20; GA, *SSI*, 243 ff.

52. Spriano, *Storia di Torino*, 262–264. See also Cammett, *Gramsci*, 34 and 116 n.; BM, "Concretiamo il partito!," *OO*, V, 98–102.

53. Cammett, *Gramsci*, 34; DeF, *il riv*, 199–200; Gramsci, *La questione meridionale*, 15; MLS, *Sal*, 25; GA, *SSI*, 200; GS, *SSQM*, xxiv.

54. ET, *Sal*, 164: "A true friendship never developed between Salvemini and Mussolini."

55. GS to BM, October 18, 1914, *Cart 1914*, 55. This note was published in *Avanti!* October 21, 1914, and appears in BM, *OO* VI, 416.

56. Giovanni Malvezzi to GS, October 23, 1914, *Cart 1914*, 57–59; GF to GS, October 22 and 25, 1914 in *Cart 1914*, 57, 59. See also DeF, *il riv*, 265n.

57. DeF, "Benito Mussolini," in PC, ed., *Historical Dictionary of Fascist Italy* (Westport, Connecticut, 1982), 359; BM, "Dalla neutralità assoluta alla neutralità attiva ed operante," *Avanti!*, October 18, 1914; DeF, *il riv*, 221–287; GA, *SSI*, 165 ff.

58. GS, *Cart 1914*, 59n.

59. GP to GS, November 4 and December 8, 1914, *Cart 1914*, 71, 93; GS to GP, December 7, 1914, *Cart 1914*, 91; GP entries of November 8, December 3 and 6, 1914 *Diario, 1900–1941* (Milan, 1978), 140–141; DeF, *il riv*, 265–267; DeC, *Sal*, 248–249; MLS, *Sal*, 94; ET, *Sal*, 162–164.

60. GS to BM, October 16, 1914 cited in GS, *Cart 1912*, xxxv.

61. DeF, *il riv*, 269–287.

62. DeF, *il riv*, 266–267; Cammett, *Gramsci*, 37–38.

63. GA, *SSI*, 185.

64. Michele Vaina to GS, November 11 and 23, 1914; Enzo Maria Gray to GS, November 16, 1914, *AGS*; DeF, *il riv*, 289–290.

65. DeF, *il riv*, 277–290; DeF, *il riv*, 288; S-W, *ILF*, 423.

66. The article, raising the question of subsidies, appeared in the November 19 issue of *Avanti!*. For a discussion of the issue of French contributions, see DeF, *il riv*, 276–278.

67. ET, *Sal*, 163.

68. Jean Richard Bloch to GS, August 8, 1914, *Cart 1914*, 17; Paul Sabatier to GS, December 15, 1914, *Cart 1914*, 97; GS to ED, March 26, 1915, *Cart 1914*, 143; Luigi Vojnovich to GS, May 18, 1915, *Cart 1914*, 151–152.

69. Bloch to GS, August 8 and October 27, 1914, 16–17 and 61–66; Sabatier to GS, December 15, 1914, *Cart 1914*, 97–98; GS to Ferdinando Martini, August 6, 1915, *Cart 1914*, 175; GS to ED, February 16, 1915, *Cart 1914*, 128.

70. DeF, *il riv*, 287; GS, *The Origins of Fascism in Italy*, tr. RV (New York, 1973), 101. This book was first published as *"'Lezioni di Harvard': L'Italia dal 1919 al 1929" in Opere* VI (1), 299–655. See also ET, *Sal*, 164n.

71. *Pd'I*, April 19, 1915; S-W, *ILF*, 424; Cammett, *Gramsci*, 37.

72. JB, *LMV*, 25–31; S-W, *ILF*, 413–430; L&M, *IFP*, 133–159.

73. UGM to GS, September 8, 1914, 35; PS to GS, September 9, 36–37 and October 13, 1914, 48–51; GF to GS, September 9, 1914, 37; Zagari to GS, October 5, 45–46 and October 27, 1914, *Cart 1914*, 67–68.

74. BF, *L'U*, 15–16. See also Zagari to GS, *Cart 1914*, 45–46.

75. GS, "Ripresa," *L'U*, December 4, 1914 in *Opere* III (1), 397.

76. GS, "Per l'indipendènza d'Italia," *Opere* III (1), 399–402. Emphasis in original.

77. GD to GS, November 13, 1914, *AGS*.

78. "Il ministro degli esteri austro-ungarico Berchtold sostituito da Burian"; "La guerra della Turchi"; "Il violento terremoto id ieri nel lazio, negli Abruzzi e in Campania," *CdS*, January 14, 1915.

79. GS to UO, after January 14, 1915 in *Cart 1914*, 112–113; ET, *Sal*, 167–168.

80. GS to UO, January 18, 1915, *Cart 1914*, 114–116; ET, *Sal*, 167–168.

81. GS to ED, March 10, 1915, *Cart 1914*, 138; ET, *Sal*, 167–168; GS, "Dopo il terremoto," February 26 and March 19, 1915; "Il Comitato della Leonardo da Vinci a Balsorano," May 28, 1915, *L'U*; GS to UO after January 14 and January 18, 1915; to ED, February 16, 1915; to Vito De Bellis, February 5, 1915; GF to GS, February 1 (2 letters) and February 4, 1915.

82. GS, *Guerra o neutralità?* in *Opere* III (1), 455–474. See also DeF, *il riv*, 294.

83. GS, "Il 'boss' d'Italia," *Opere* IV (1), 390–392.

84. PS to GS, February 20, 1915, *Cart 1914*, 131–132.

85. JB, *LMV*, 21–22.

86. Rene Albrecht-Carrié, *Italy at the Paris Peace Conference* (New York, 1938), 334–339; S-W, *ILF*, 430–436; JB, *LMV*, 22–25; L&M, *IFP*, 151–159.

87. Carlo Sforza, *Contemporary Italy* (New York, 1944), 208.

88. S-W, *ILF*, 431–436; JB, *LMV*, 28–30; L&M, *IFP*, 155–159.

89. S-W, *ILF*, 444–445.

90. GS to UO, May 13, 1915, *Cart 1914*, 152.

91. GS, "Il tranello," *L'U*, May 14, 1915, *Opere* III (1), 511–513.

92. S-W *ILF*, 446–449; JB, *LMV*, 28–29.

93. GS, "Oportet studuisse," *Opere* VIII, 468.

94. GS to Gina Dallolio, June 5, 1915, 161; GS to UO, August 14, 1914, *Cart 1914*, 21.

95. GP to GS, February 3, 1909, 396; Carlo Placci to GS, June 23, 1909, 404; GLR to GS, October 2 and November 20, 1909, 406 and 412, *Opere* IX.

96. Julien Luchaire, *Confession d'un Francais Moyen*, I (1876–1914) (Florence, 1965), vii.

97. GS to GLR, July 7, 1910, 455; to Placci, July 14, 1910, and October 8, 1911, 460 and 524; GP to GS, October 20, 1911, 539, 540, *Opere* IX.

98. Nicky Mariano, *Forty Years With Berenson* (New York, 1966), 30.

99. Mariano, *Forty Years*, 30.

100. HC to CK, March 4, 1992.

101. ET, *Sal*, 180; GS to Zanotti-Bianco, October 6, 1915, *Cart 1914*, 207–208.

102. GS to Z-B, July 11, 1915, *Cart 1914*, 165.

103. Medical report, Prof. Giuliano Daddi, July 17, 1915, Appendix I, 553; GS to Z-B, July 11, 1915, *Cart 1914*, 165.

104. GS to ED, July 27, 1915, *Cart 1914*, 168.

105. GS to PS, July 30, 1915, *Cart 1914*, 171.

106. Edoardo Giretti to GS, August 2, 1915, 172; Ester De Viti De Marco to GS, August 3, 1915, *Cart 1914*, 173.

107. GS to ED, August 4, 1915, 174; PS to GS, August 8, 1915, 179; GS to Z-B, August 31, 1915, 186–187; to PS, September 3, 1915, 190; GF to GS, September 16, 1915, 195; GS to GP, October 1, 1915, 201; to ED, October 1, 1915, *Cart 1914*, 202.

108. GS to ED, October 1, 1915, *Cart 1914*, 201–204; DeC, *Sal*, 258–259.

109. GS to ED, October 1, 1915, *Cart 1914*, 202.

110. GS to ED, October 1, 1915, 201; to GLR, October 3, 1915, *Cart 1914*, 204.

111. GS to Z-B, October 6, 1915, *Cart 1914*, 207–208.

112. ET, *Sal*, 175.

113. GS to UO, November 4, 1915, *Cart 1914*, 213–214; to PS, September 3, 1915, 190; to ED, October 8, 1915, *Cart 1914*, 209–210.

114. Luigi Cadorna, *La guerra alla front italiana* (Milan, 1924), I, 156.

115. S-W, *ILF*, 451–452.

116. ET, *Sal*, 175–176.

117. GS to Dauriac, after November 13, 1915 [entries of November 9 and 10], *Cart 1914*, 214–215; Fernande Luchaire to ED, November 18, 1918 (sic) in Iris Origo, *A Need to Testify*, 148. Emphasis in source.

118. GS to Dauriac, after November 13, 1915, entries of November 12 and 13, 216; Dauriac to Z-B, November 16, 1915, 217, *Cart 1914*.

119. GS to Dauriac, after November 13, 1915, entries of November 11 and 13, *Cart 1914*, 215–217; ET, *Sal*, 176.

120. GS to ED, November 20 and 24, 1915, *Cart 1914*, 218, 219; ET, *Sal*, 176.

121. GS to PS, December 8, 1915, *Cart 1914*, 224.

122. Leo Tolstoy, *War and Peace* (Garden City, N.Y., 1949). See ET, *Sal*, 177.

123. GS to Martini, December 1, 1915, *Cart 1914*, 220.

124. GS to ED, December 16 and 26, 1915, *Cart 1914*, 229–232; to Z-B, February 8, 1916, *Cart 1914*, 237.

125. GS to Z-B, February 8, 1916, *Cart 1914*, 237.

126. GG to GS, December 3, 1915, *Cart 1914*, 221; GS to Z-B, February 8 and 16, 1916, *Cart 1914*, 237–238.

Chapter 5

The Strains of War and Peace

> The experience of life has made me pessimistic and suspicious. And it has
> convinced me of the necessity of clear positions.
>
> Gaetano Salvemini, 1917[1]

While riding a tram through the streets of Florence in 1919, Ernesto Rossi recognized a fellow passenger as a well-known history professor from the university. Rossi, a young law student, noticed the black cape, long out of style, that enveloped Salvemini's stubby torso, and the black sugarloaf hat that betrayed southern peasant origins.

Just then, a startling shout interrupted Rossi's observation: "*Rinunciatario* [traitor]!" Rossi recognized the invective that zealous nationalists reserved for their most hated opponents. Someone had leaned out from the platform of a passing tram to hurl the insult more fiercely in the face of the professor.[2] Nationalists had invented the epithet precisely for Salvemini and those who dared to propose limits on Italy's postwar expansion. The caustic tone typified the new nationalism and heralded the arrival of a broader movement grounded in similar passions. The day approached when intimidation would turn to outright violence and Salvemini's position would become increasingly dangerous.

The spring and summer of 1916, the half-year after Salvemini's release from the Red Cross Hospital, proved to be seasons of fitful recuperation. Fernande Luchaire wrote the following to Elsa Dallolio in April:

[Gaetano] needs rest, but he won't accept it . . . and when he sees me looking sad, he says "I don't feel well"—sometimes it is the only phrase he utters for hours at a time. . . . Perhaps when we are married and I can have him close to me, I shall be able to look after him better.

Eventually he returned to the political wars, battles for which he was better pre-pared than those on the Isonzo front. As he regained his energy and began to stalk his familiar opponents—Sonnino, Giolitti, and the nationalists—he rel-ished the caring support and companionship of Fernande.

Fernande noted that, although many people disapproved of her pending mar-riage, she would defer to him: "Salvemini loves me and I love him, so it's up to him to decide, both the date and the marriage itself, which he does so obsti-nately want. For him, the sooner the better."³ On June 22, the two married. After eight years of loneliness, he was again surrounded by wife and children. A number of friends would later note the intensity of his love for his new children, "a pretty little girl" and a "highly intelligent schoolboy of 14." His second fam-ily contributed to his recovery.⁴

Three weeks later, Salvemini heard shocking news about Cesare Battisti, husband of Ernesta Bittanti. Two decades before, Battisti had been a member of the close-knit student group in Florence. In the intervening years, he had edited a socialist newspaper in the Trentino, which, in spite of an Italian popu-lation exceeding 95 percent, remained a part of the polyglot Hapsburg Empire. He represented the Trentino at the Austrian parliament in Vienna, and there, as elsewhere, used every opportunity to advocate Italian acquisi-tion of his native region. By the time the war began, Battisti was the best-known *irredentista* in the Trentino, audaciously calling for the destruc-tion of the empire. In 1914, his political activism had forced him to flee to It-aly with his family. Salvemini, too poor to satisfy Ernesta's pleas for money, had attempted to publish Battisti's irredentist writings and to find a job for Ernesta.

In May 1915, Salvemini heard that Battisti had volunteered for the Italian army and was fighting the Austrians on the Alpine front, an especially risky venture for an Austrian citizen. Salvemini worried, consoled Ernesta, but heard little news until July 1916. Then, to his horror, he learned the worst. On July 10, the Austrians had captured Battisti and had transported him to Trent, where the next day an Austrian military tribunal had convicted him of treason and con-demned him to death. Two days later, Cesare Battisti was hanged.⁵

For Salvemini, Battisti's execution was a severe blow, yet another episode in what would be a life filled with tragedy. "My dear Ernesta," he wrote,

This tormented and desperate anguish which has overtaken me I have experienced a few times in my life, only on the occasions of great sadness and of great misfortune. . . . I wish that I could be with you in these days, to make you feel how my heart has kept for you intact and fresh and pure all the fraternal affection of twenty-five years.⁶

He penned an impassioned tribute, only the first of many such eulogies delivered by a man who would outlive many of his friends and students.[7]

Battisti's influence was significant, primarily in convincing Salvemini of the justice of the Italian claim to the Trentino, now an integral part of his position on national boundaries. Nonetheless, because of his general campaign against the nationalists and his outspoken aversion to Italian expansion in the Adriatic Sea and the Balkan Peninsula, opponents labeled him "anti-Italian."[8]

Just the week before Battisti's execution, Salvemini broke his self-imposed wartime silence with a series of articles on the Triple Alliance. Inspiration for the new work came before he left Florence for military training. The previous year, Placci had taken him to the home of Count Edmondo di Robilant, son of General Carlo di Robilant, the former Minister of Foreign Affairs who had negotiated the secret 1887 revisions of the Triple Alliance in favor of Italy. The elder Robilant had given the original documents in a sealed envelope to his son with the stipulation that they were to be opened only if Italy terminated the treaty. Within days of Italy's renunciation of the Triple Alliance, and after a moratorium of twenty-eight years, Robilant opened the documents in Salvemini's presence. In a rare moment of exhilaration in his career as a historian, he was amazed by what he saw.

Poring over the documents with great excitement, Salvemini discovered that in 1912 the Giolitti government had fundamentally altered Italy's foreign policy by renewing the Triple Alliance without simultaneously renewing the Mediterranean agreements with England that had protected Italy's freedom of action. Salvemini believed that Giolitti's failure to renew the Anglo-Italian agreements made Italy virtually servile to Germany, costing Italy leverage and making war more likely.

Most alarming was the revelation that Italy's neutrality had been legally justified under the terms of the Triple Alliance. In Article 7, Salvemini discovered language requiring Austria to give prior notice before modifying the status quo in the Balkans or the Adriatic. If contemplating an accrual of territory by conquest, the Hapsburgs were likewise obliged to offer Italy compensation. In sending their ultimatum to Serbia, tantamount to a declaration of war, the Hapsburgs had done neither. On the strength of this revelation, Salvemini now believed that Austria, not Italy, was guilty of breaking the Triplice. This discovery lent historical evidence to his anti-German, anti-Austrian position, refuted German and Austrian claims of Italian treachery, and confirmed his own interventionist campaign. Presented to the public in convincing fashion, the documents could lend needed support to the government's decision to intervene on behalf of the Entente powers. He copied them feverishly. He then requested from Sonnino, through Ferdinando Martini, permission to publish the text of the Triple Alliance along with the Anglo-Italian agreement, allowing for certain omissions in the interest of national security. Sonnino refused.[9]

Salvemini bristled under this constraint, knowing that he possessed information that the Italian people had a right to know and that strengthened his own case. "Here it is the historian who speaks," he wrote to Martini, explaining that he had rights as a writer that had to be reconciled with his duties as a citizen.[10] He told Luigi Albertini, publisher of *Corriere della Sera*, that Sonnino's ruling seemed completely unjustified, and he hoped that Albertini would publish the material. Albertini replied that Prime Minister Salandra would not grant permission without consent from Foreign Minister Sonnino.[11]

As a result of the official barriers to publication of the documents, Salvemini composed a general history of the Triple Alliance in four parts, the "original, scientific work" that he wanted to accomplish before resuming publication of *L'Unità*. By the end of March, although convinced that the censors would cut it, he had completed the first installment. Salandra's fall gave him little hope of approval, because the vacancy was filled by the seventy-eight-year-old caretaker, Paolo Boselli, who retained Sonnino as foreign minister.[12]

Increasingly frustrated by what he believed to be the censor's bias, Salvemini amplified the problem of the historian as political activist: "I ask myself if it would not be better simply to write the history of other people's mistakes than to exhaust myself uselessly in trying to prevent them."[13] Thus the old tension between history and politics resurfaced even as he delayed the reopening of his journal in a conscious attempt to devote himself to writing "scientific" history. The results of this effort were, at this point in his life, predictable. The first part of his meticulously researched work on the Triple Alliance appeared in July.[14] Once the censors allowed it to be published in full, it would provide an original contribution to the diplomatic history of that era.[15]

Salvemini's passion to reveal the truth again elevated a work of history to the plane of high intrigue. In this attempt to refute "official history," he was now writing contemporary history, a field destined to take on greater importance in the mid-twentieth century. As would be the case for the remainder of his long career, in writing history he would provoke controversy, not only within governmental circles but also from organized political groups. The anti-Salvemini campaign initiated by the nationalists now became personal and threatening.

The issue that focused Salvemini's opposition to the nationalists was the postwar status of the people of the Hapsburg empire, especially the Slav populations of the Dalmatian coast and the islands in the Adriatic Sea. Dalmatia was part of the volatile Balkans, including Serbia, Croatia, Montenegro, Herzegovina, and Bosnia, where an assassination had started the war. Dalmatia had long been an objective of Italian expansionists, and in 1915 part of it had been promised to Italy in the Pact of London. A key point of contention was the future status of the port of Fiume.

Few issues better illustrated the interrelationship of war, diplomacy, and public opinion than Dalmatia. In 1915 and 1916, with a stalemate on the west-

ern front, the Allies pursued diplomatic initiatives that turned military attention
from France to the periphery. Cooperation of Serbia and Italy against Austria
would have advanced the Allied cause, but it was inhibited by mutual suspicion
based in part on a common desire for Dalmatia. Dalmatian ports would open the
Adriatic either to Serbs or Italians. Further complicating strategic cooperation
was the position of Foreign Minister Sonnino, who preferred a weak Hapsburg
Empire to a strong Russian-backed Serbia. From Sonnino's perspective, Italian
domination of the Adriatic, including Dalmatia, was the only legitimate basis
for Italian belligerency.[16]

As early as the spring of 1915, Salvemini had begun to address the Dalmatian issue.[17] Of all his work since Italy's entry into the war, this topic most directly challenged Italian diplomacy and attracted the attention of the censors.
Throughout the spring and summer of 1916, he assembled chapters of an anthology, circulating proofs among friends. The censors intervened.[18]

While Salvemini battled the censors over foreign policy, the Italian Third
Army renewed its Isonzo offensive. In early August 1916, Italian forces captured Austrian forts near the front where Salvemini had served, crossing the
Isonzo River and occupying Gorizia. Italian morale soared at the news of an impressive success. Bissolati described it in his diary as "the first, great, *authentic*
Italian victory."[19] Although Salvemini's private response may have been
equally celebratory, he published an article two weeks later in which he called
for the Italian administration to protect the rights of Slav minorities living in the
newly conquered territory around Gorizia.[20] Bissolati wrote, expressing his
agreement on the matter.[21]

As Italian troops kept up the Isonzo offensive and Sonnino pushed the Allies
to honor the London Pact's provisions, Salvemini renewed his own campaign
while Bissolati reaffirmed the goals of democratic interventionism.[22] Encouraged by the naming of his colleague Bissolati to the new cabinet, Salvemini resolved to go to Rome in an attempt to influence foreign policy.[23] More
realistically, he redoubled his efforts to revive *L'Unità*. In soliciting support, he
laid out his case: "The review must ... excite discussions of problems that today
are either not discussed or are discussed [only] in glib phrases and journalistic
nonsense."[24]

The new *L'Unità*, he argued, was necessary to support the cause of democracy in Italy and in Europe. It would support reform and would contribute to the
victory of the Allied powers, and in the process it would oppose the ambitions
of Italian nationalists, standing solidly for the principle of national self-determination. With this program, Salvemini attracted a new group of collaborators,
including such luminaries as Leopoldo Franchetti, Archangelo Ghisleri,
Gaetano Mosca, and Piero Gobetti. On December 8, 1916, Salvemini and Antonio De Viti De Marco opened publication of the new *L'Unità*. Within two
months it had aquired more than 800 subscribers.[25]

In soliciting support for the revival of *L'Unità*, Salvemini visited Benedetto Croce, accompanied by Giustino Fortunato, who had withdrawn his subsidy during the intervention campaign.[26] The two arrived at Croce's house to find him disheartened by the war. Because the Allies had no philosophy, Croce argued, they could not defeat the Germans. Salvemini, ever the pragmatist, expressed his disdain for such reasoning.

"Listen, Don Benedetto, wars are won by he who has more soldiers, cannon, and major economic resources, not by he who has a better philosophy."

Croce remained unconvinced.[27]

Primarily in the pages of the second *L'Unità*, Salvemini began to delineate his wartime political views with a vigorous defense of Dalmatia and an independent Yugoslavia. Soon, nationalist adversaries labeled him "*Slav*emini" in a personalized war of words that established an ominous tone of rhetorical violence.[28]

Nationalist and socialist criticism aside, however, in this instance reputation approached reality. Through Bissolati, Salvemini's democratic interventionism reached the highest levels of national politics. In a war in which every military campaign carried territorial implications, Salvemini's commitment to an independent Yugoslavia assumed growing international importance. Much later in life, he would remember the campaign with some pride, telling his wife that the inscription on his tomb should be "He fought the annexation of Dalmatia."[29]

The last months of 1916 offered the hope of Allied military advance. The British and French launched a major offensive on the Somme River, Romania joined the Alliance, and, two years after Italy had declared war only against Austria-Hungary, the Boselli government ended the ambiguity by declaring war on Germany. However, the new Allied optimism quickly faded as the Somme offensive mired in mud and death. By mid-November, the Allies had pushed ahead about seven miles at the cost of almost 600,000 casualties. The Romanian offensive backfired, and the Russians were too fatigued to assist.

As the stalemate dragged on, Salvemini attracted greater scrutiny from government censors. They suppressed *L'Unità*'s rendition of his five-city lecture tour advocating the dismantling of the Hapsburg Empire and a long letter about Dalmatia written to the Roman journal *Azione Socialista*. By 1917, when he had learned the rules of the censor's game, he sent the *L'Unità* article to Edoardo Giretti, who retitled, signed, and published it in a Milanese paper. The next month, Salvemini published the article, under the new title and author, as a reprint in *L'Unità*.[30]

The failures of the Allied initiatives in the fall of 1916 gave the Central Powers an apparent edge, partly offset by the death of the old Austrian emperor, Francis Joseph. When his grandnephew Charles, successor to the Hapsburg throne, announced a desire to end the war, the German chancellor offered to negotiate. One week later, President Woodrow Wilson asked the belligerents to state their terms for peace. The British, French, and Italians met in Rome in January 1917, refused the Austro-German offer to negotiate, then planned their 1917 offensive and responded to Wilson with their own set of war aims.

This diplomatic maneuvering focused world hopes on terms of postwar settlement, as the belligerents were generally ambitious for territorial gain around the globe. The Allies' demands, to which Sonnino had given his approval, included "the liberation of the Italians, as also of the Slavs, Roumanes and Czecho-Slovaks from foreign domination."[31] The ambiguous statement, given primarily as a public response to Wilson's request, ignored the territorial aspirations of the belligerents, and particularly those promised to the Italians in the secret Pact of London.

The emergence of Wilson gave Salvemini hope for a just peace. Wilson's "self-determination of nations" principle, his espousal of "peace without victory" and his vision of a League of Nations were in direct contrast to the imperialism of Italian, Slav, British, and French nationalists. Salvemini had admired Wilson since his election as president. In 1913, he had reviewed Wilson's first inaugural address, comparing it favorably to Garibaldi's exhortation to his volunteers. He had described Wilson as "a man of faith," a man of "poetry and reality, thought and action, idealism and concretism."[32] In the intervening years, Salvemini had espoused principles similar to those of Wilsonian diplomacy, and by 1917 he had become one of Wilson's strongest European supporters.[33]

Shortly before the beginning of 1917, fate allowed Salvemini to fulfill a primary aspiration of his professional life. Historian Carlo Cipolla fell ill, creating a temporary vacancy at the University of Florence, which Salvemini filled in mid-November. Cipolla's subsequent death led the university to appoint Salvemini Professor of Medieval and Modern History. At age forty-four, he had returned to his intellectual home. It is one of the ironies of his life that a major university in a centralized system of higher education would extend him an offer at a time when his articles were being censored and his journal had been earmarked for its criticism of the foreign minister. Apparently his reputation for controversy and political candor was less a liability during the war than it had been earlier in his career during peacetime. Undoubtedly Boselli felt less need than Giolitti to exploit the patronage system. Moreover, the presence in the cabinet of several Salvemini partisans—Bissolati, Ivanoe Bonomi, and Senator Francesco Ruffini—may well have worked in his favor.[34]

The new faculty appointment did not deter Salvemini's activities on behalf of a Yugoslav Dalmatia. As war weariness spread throughout Italy and the military command launched yet another Isonzo offensive, *L'Unità* pressed its assault on Italian nationalists. Whereas the Italian Socialist Party maintained its innocuous position of "neither support nor sabotage"of the war, more extreme Italian socialists aligned with Lenin's revolutionary ideology.

Meanwhile, major events promised to break the strategic deadlock on the battlefields of Europe. On February 1, Germany unleashed its submarines in the war zone against neutral ships and belligerents alike. Wilson severed diplomatic relations two days later, and the sinking of American ships in February and March alerted the world to impending American belligerency. In March, the Russian Revolution emboldened Italian militants, and in the streets of northern Italian cities, protests against economic conditions mingled with antiwar rallies. Revolutionary syndicalists and socialists hoped to emulate Russian socialists in converting war to revolution. Events on the domestic front now upstaged those on the Austrian front. Throughout the spring and summer, public pressure mounted against the Boselli government to take Italy out of the war, and it appeared that, once again, as in 1914, policy might be made in the piazzas.

In the midst of escalating internal discord, Salvemini noticed a widening rift among the interventionists of the Left. He had found it particularly difficult to cooperate with those he despised, especially some nationalists, while opposing men such as Turati, whom he respected. Among those with whom Salvemini had coalesced on war issues was Benito Mussolini, who in general shared the common ground of leftist interventionism. However, in the spring of 1917, a shift in the editorial position of Mussolini's newspaper announced a separation from Salvemini and others of the democratic Left.[35]

Since its founding, Mussolini's *Il Popolo d'Italia* had been a voice for left-wing and democratic interventionism. When Mussolini began to endorse a movement of Italian dissident socialists to counter the impact of the PSI, *Il Popolo d'Italia* drew the wrath of other leftist journals.[36] In early March, Salvemini backed the paper's efforts to unify support for the war, but he made a strong appeal to correct its logic. The real differences among interventionists were those separating democrats from nationalists.

If the interventionists . . . have had a common program of war, they have also had opposing programs for peace. . . . And [waiting] at the end of the war, there is between the nationalists and the democrats an abyss. . . . This necessity to differentiate between nationalist and democratic interventionists becomes ever more urgent and more visible as we approach the final crisis.[37]

Thus, in spite of Salvemini's conciliatory appeal to *Il Popolo d'Italia*, he had laid down a clear challenge. When in 1917 Mussolini began to move toward accommodation of the nationalists, he knew he would risk losing the support of Salvemini and other democrats.

The issue that opened the breach, as might be expected, was Dalmatia. In late 1916 and the first months of 1917, Mussolini moderated his stance on the Adriatic question, moving away from the Salvemini-Bissolati position of

Wilsonian "self-determination" toward the nationalist position.[38] In April, Salvemini was convinced that on the Adriatic question, *Il Popolo d'Italia* was on the nationalists' side.[39] By summer, Salvemini had written off Mussolini. He wrote candidly to Prezzolini: "You are right that *Il Popolo d'Italia* is infected with imperialism."[40]

As Salvemini's polemic with Mussolini sharpened, the United States entered the war against Germany. Meanwhile, as the German submarine campaign took a heavy toll on British shipping, the Royal Navy countered with new tactics, including the convoy system. On the Austrian front, Italian General Luigi Cadorna launched the tenth battle of the Isonzo. Shortages in artillery and ammunition had limited the Italian advance to about ten miles after two years of fierce fighting.

In August, Salvemini returned to Molfetta to attend a provincial meeting in Bari, where he had been elected councilor. He found the council meeting a sobering reintroduction to the realities of local politics. Nonetheless, finding the group focused on diplomacy, he participated enthusiastically. When a colleague introduced a motion to endorse Italy's right to annex Dalmatia, Salvemini objected, explaining that the Slavs, who would soon form an independent state directly across the Adriatic, would make ideal trading partners. He urged direct Italian negotiations with the Slavs to encourage cooperation against Teutonic aggression.[41] By reframing the issue, Salvemini established the connection between international and provincial politics, fusing wartime diplomacy with the postwar economic interests of Bari. Robbed of a national parliamentary forum, he made the provincial council chambers his occasional political stage. Salvemini's motion to cooperate with the Slavs won majority support.[42]

On the "internal front," in the third week of August, insurrection raged in Turin. Revolutionary socialists rallied to cries of "Lenin!," workers erected barricades in their neighborhoods, looters broke into shops, and insurgents attacked churches and police stations. On August 23 the army employed tanks and machine guns to restore order. Economic desperation in Turin and elsewhere increased the pressure on the government to produce results and compounded the impression that public support for the war effort was dissipating further. PSI leaders now raised the pitch of their cry for peace. In mid-August, after almost two years of public silence, former Prime Minister Giolitti joined the chorus.

Military victory would have boosted sagging morale and served to undercut the socialist peace initiative. Cadorna had assembled fifty-one divisions, almost a three-to-one advantage over the Austrian armies, in his attempt to deliver a knockout blow. Inexplicably ignoring a British offer of artillery support, Sonnino and Cadorna were doomed to face the Hapsburgs alone. Thus, on August 18, when Cadorna gave the order for the eleventh battle of the Isonzo, he did so with less firepower than he needed. The offensive went well, but the lack of Allied artillery prevented Italian forces from exploiting the initial gains.[43]

As the Austrian armies clung desperately to their positions, the German command reinforced their war-weary ally in order to keep the Hapsburgs in the war. The collapse of the Russian army allowed German General Erich Ludendorff to contribute six German divisions for an Austrian offensive. The Italian Isonzo offensive failed, even at the expense of 200,000 casualties. Consequently, spirits sagged; desertions, surrenders, and mutinies spread in the Italian ranks; and the number of courts-martial rose dramatically.

All the while, Salvemini kept up support for the war in *L'Unità*, reminding readers of the necessity of defeating Germany and Austria, and countering neutralists, clerics, and the mounting clamor of Giolittians in Parliament and in the press. Salvemini, Bissolati, and a relatively few democratic interventionists sustained the drive for Allied victory in the face of mounting odds. Following a conflicting vision of postwar settlement, Mussolini pursued his campaign, but Salvemini knew that, as a small weekly, *L'Unità* had a limited impact. He thus conducted his own private effort to win the support of Albertini in *Il Corriere della Sera*. Albertini supported the government on the war but had not taken an editorial stance in favor of a Wilsonian postwar settlement. Salvemini sent Albertini the proofs of his censored anthology, *La questione dell'Adriatico*, in an effort to explain the case for a South Slav state and to discourage any support for the nationalist campaign to extend Italian territory across the Adriatic: "We have conscientiously studied the theme from all its sides. And if policy is to be made on the basis of *reality* and not mystification, we feel that we have created a useful work."[44] Later in 1917, *Il Corriere della Sera* accepted Salvemini's position on Dalmatia, giving him great satisfaction.[45]

As summer turned to fall, the prospect of Italian victory collapsed at Caporetto. On October 24, the Germans fired their artillery and launched a concentrated infantry charge designed to break through Italian defenses, divide their armies, cut supply lines, and force a retreat. Poor Italian morale, panic, confusion, and command indecision contributed to an even greater rout than Germany had anticipated. Italian forces retreated first to the Tagliamento River, then to the Piave.

At the lowest point of the Caporetto retreat, Italian soldiers discarded their weapons and deserted. Nearly half a million refugees from occupied Italian territory joined the troops in chaotic flight, and the command lost contact with its remaining forces. Cadorna issued a press release, picked up by international press services, that blamed the defeat on cowardice in the ranks of his own Second Army. Austro-German forces pushed the front to within fifteen miles of Venice, retaking all the territory lost to the Italians in more than two years of fighting. Once the Italian command had recovered, it counted enormous losses:

40,000 casualties, 300,000 prisoners, an additional 350,000 soldiers unaccounted for, and innumerable weapons lost.[46]

For Salvemini and the democratic interventionists, Caporetto meant political disaster as well. Defeatism spread, finger-pointing accompanied partisan infighting, and various factions debated the question of Cadorno's removal. Would Italy be knocked out of the war? The entire Italian war effort was in peril. On October 25, the Boselli government resigned, replaced the next week by former Interior Minister V. E. Orlando, who appointed a new commander, General Armando Diaz.

In the wake of the retreat, Salvemini reaffirmed the necessity of fighting Germany in an article entitled "Looking at Reality." In a guardedly optimistic assessment of Italy's position, he reminded his readers that this conflict was destined to alter the map of Europe. Caporetto had clarified the situation: "Anyone still obstinate enough to consider the Italian war as simply a duel with Austria, . . . and to consider the monstrous possibility of an Italian-German reconciliation, must by now . . . have opened his eyes." In this sense, the attack by German forces at Caporetto had strengthened the argument of the democratic interventionists to fight a coordinated war with the Allies against Germany as well as Austria. In an appeal to rally support to the Allied cause, Salvemini asked Italians to persevere so that "everything can be saved."[47]

Salvemini now redoubled his efforts to support the embattled Italian forces. He defended the reputation of Italian soldiers, placing blame at higher levels, launching a series of Sunday lectures to soldiers, which he followed by visiting a refugee shelter. He intervened on behalf of a wounded eighteen year-old Molfettese infantryman, attempting to move this "baby" to a hospital nearer home. He asked the contributors to *L'Unità* for articles supporting the war and called for a renewed Italian unity. Privately he later wrote: "Almost all our generals are deficient and cowardly, in contrast to our soldiers."[48] This view, expressed repeatedly, was in part a defense of the foot soldier against General Cadorna's allegations of cowardice. It was also a manifestation of democratic faith, of the Salveminian worldview of the moral superiority of simple folk.

In the immediate aftermath of the military retreat, the interventionists themselves retreated. The defeat extracted a heavy personal toll on Salvemini's friends. Bissolati was depressed. On November 4, Leopoldo Franchetti took his own life. Salvemini published a brief tribute to the prominent Tuscan and *L'Unità* collaborator, extracted from a speech in which he credited Franchetti with a significant contribution to his country.[49]

By late 1917, the Italian defeat at Caporetto had driven Salvemini into profound despair. The only remedy to the great sadness was "solitude, silence, contemplation," he wrote. "We are all leaves tossed about by the wind."[50] To Bernard Berenson he described three dreadful weeks that he would remember as "the saddest of my life after those—greater than all human strength—of Messina."[51]

Caporetto converted many Italians to nationalism. In Salvemini's case, he found a new focus in addressing his country's problems. He spoke less now of protecting Allied democracy against Germanic tyranny and more of Italy's borders. He more clearly defined the geographic differences between the Adriatic policies of the Slav leadership and his own, complaining that Slav nationalists were misrepresenting history.[52] He became more openly pro-Italian in tone, continuing to address Italian troops and designing a propaganda campaign for Italians in the trenches.

In March, he went to Rome to lecture on the topic "Mazzini Now." He justified a Mazzinian approach to foreign policy, not on the basis of idealism but of enlightened self-interest. However, the invocation of a national hero did not entirely satisfy nationalists in the crowd. As he turned to the question of Dalmatia, hecklers interrupted, reflecting the growing volatility of the issue of postwar boundaries. Reading news reports, Salvemini concluded that the nationalist press exaggerated the disturbance. "We need to discredit these lies," he wrote, because the nationalists were trying to demonstrate that "the lunatics are the majority and we, the minority."[53]

In the midst of crisis, Italian forces rallied. In early November, and again in early December, Austro-German forces, with vast superiority of troops and firepower, opened their final offensive on the Piave. The reinvigorated Italian army wavered but did not yield. On Christmas 1917, the enemy offensive ended.

As the troops held, a surge of patriotism swept the home front. In Parliament and the press, critics of the war made gestures of support to the government and urged the citizenry to follow their lead. In *L'Unità*, Salvemini published soldiers' letters asking their families and friends to resist the enemy.[54] The patriotic rally of November and December stiffened the resolve of those determined to fight on, especially the democratic interventionists who believed, like Salvemini, that they desperately needed to hold on until the postwar settlement. Ironically, it was the rabid nationalists, Salvemini's most vocal opponents, who eventually turned adversity to political advantage by seizing the banner of national defense.[55]

In February 1918, after months of obstruction by the censors, Salvemini managed to publish his long pamphlet on Dalmatia, *La questione dell'Adriatico*, minus one chapter and featuring a number of blank pages. A collaboration with the geographer Carlo Maranelli and other experts, the work made a reasoned case on behalf of South Slavs in an attempt to undercut the campaign of the Italian nationalists that had spilled even into the mainstream press. Through detailed evidence, they countered claims by Sonnino and others that the cities of Dalmatia were "purely Italian."[56] They argued that Dalmatia would be difficult to defend from the east and was therefore a military liability, an argument largely supported by the army's general staff. Instead of annexing Dalmatia and making the Adriatic an "Italian lake," as the nationalists and the admirals urged, Italy would be better served by maintaining free trade there and protecting the rights of Italians in Dalmatia by making Fiume and Zara "free cities."[57]

In a futile attempt to change the government's views, Salvemini sent page proofs to Salandra, expressing the hope that the former prime minister would forward them to Sonnino: "I am afraid sometimes," Salvemini wrote, "that the Honorable Sonnino is badly informed on the real elements of the Adriatic problem." He clearly was exercising great restraint and entertained little hope that the foreign minister would read the book.[58]

The book and its authors met immediate and vicious assault in the nationalist press. In April 1918, the nationalist deputy Giovanni di Cesarò questioned his patriotism by lodging a formal inquiry into the "danger" of Salvemini's association with the English Institute of Florence.[59] Throughout the spring, nationalists labeled Salvemini a *rinunciatario* for "renouncing" Italy's rightful claim to any spoils victory might bring. The outlines of the myth of "mutilated victory" were already discernible.[60]

A few months after Caporetto, the initial surge of patriotism waned and political divisions resurfaced. V. E. Orlando, the new prime minister at the head of a national cabinet, maintained the commitment to resist the enemy and stand fast behind the Allies. However, in Parliament, the nationalists were growing in strength, Giolitti was emerging from the shadows, and socialists, energized by the Bolshevik Revolution, lionized Lenin from the floor.

As economic conditions worsened, rumors spread of a separate peace with Austria. In fact, British, French, and American diplomats had contacted the Austrians, as had Orlando.[61] *L'Unità* steadfastly opposed any hint of a separate peace. Coincidentally, so did Sonnino. Although censors omitted passages, they left untouched Salvemini's exhortation to his countrymen to persevere in the struggle against Germany and Austria.[62] He also distanced himself further from Mussolini, who now was engaging him in open polemic over Dalmatia and calling Wilson a "dictator."[63] At the same time, Salvemini sharpened his criticism of Giolittians and nationalists in a campaign that he himself described as "relentless."[64] By avoiding moral platitudes and addressing Italy's interests in classic Salveminian style, he made a direct and well-documented case.

In early 1918, the Salvemini-Bissolati position was given a boost by President Wilson's Fourteen Points address that affirmed the arguments of the Italian democratic interventionists. They especially embraced Point Nine, in which the president declared his intention to readjust Italy's frontiers "along clearly recognizable lines of nationality." Although gratified by this apparent commitment to the dismantling of the empire, Salvemini was profoundly disappointed at the failure of the United States to declare war against the Hapsburgs until October 1918.[65] The great danger was the possibility that the Allies would pursue a separate peace with the Hapsburgs, blocking Italy's acquisition of Italian ethnic areas from Austria. However, in spite of reservations on the Austrian issue, Salvemini generally resumed his support of Wilson after the Fourteen Points speech.[66]

At about the same time, the new Bolshevik government deepened Italian political divisions by publishing the text of the Pact of London. In February, an Italian nationalist deputy read it aloud from the floor of the Chamber. Nationalists demanded that the Allies reward Italy in accordance with the document's terms; socialists condemned it. Salvemini remained uncharacteristically quiet on the Pact of London in these critical months, preoccupied with editing *L'Unità* and focused on themes that would only indirectly undercut the treaty.[67] Privately, he found numerous defects in the treaty and, more important, believed that Italian occupation of the Balkans would be a blunder.[68]

More and more, Salvemini directed criticism at the foreign minister. Baron Sidney Sonnino, committed nationalist and advocate of the conventional diplomacy of power politics, had negotiated the Pact of London with the Allies in 1915 as the premise for Italian belligerency. As foreign minister for three successive governments, he dominated foreign policy and remained committed to the full implementation of the London Pact. Salvemini grew increasingly uncomfortable sharing support for the war with Sonnino, convinced that, as a sympathizer with Germany and Austria, Sonnino too readily directed the conflict against the Slavs.[69]

Salvemini found the difficulty of cooperating with a supporter of the Triple Alliance compounded by Sonnino's persistent censoring of *L'Unità*'s articles, particularly on the Adriatic. With a degree of paranoia induced by months of official scrutiny, Salvemini believed that Sonnino had given the censor specific orders to monitor *L'Unità* and his work in particular.[70] This political disdain was sharpened by growing personal animosity. "That man," he wrote Zanotti-Bianco in January 1918, "I hate him . . . as the most incurable, idiotic usurer that history has ever seen." With a stroke of ironic hyperbole, he noted that Sonnino's "idiocy" was converting him to a Giolittian.[71]

In his criticism, Salvemini impeached Sonnino's character, an uncommon criticism, because even Sonnino's adversaries conceded his integrity. However, what sounded like a moral gauge was to Salvemini a measure of *intellectual* integrity. He could give no higher compliment than to refer to someone as an "honest man." The Salveminian measure of character was the degree to which a person lived his ideals. Few politicians met this lofty standard—out of necessity to compromise—and thus Salvemini's tolerance for politics remained low. This was his anti-Machiavellian soul.

When Salvemini discovered that the foreign minister, in his newspaper, *Giornale d'Italia*, had altered a quotation from Mazzini to justify Italy's acquisition of Dalmatia, he was outraged.[72] Steadily he attributed more of his own "internal rage" and "agony" to Sonnino.[73] This penchant for intermingling personality and politics would prove a perennial liability in Salvemini's efforts to influence political decisions.

Salvemini's chronic psychological struggle sharpened under pressure from the nationalists and the self-imposed stresses of his dual career in academics and journalism. He was convinced that the days he spent in the trenches had destroyed his health.[74] He was also becoming so preoccupied with the journal that teaching had become burdensome. The consolation was that teaching paid his salary and thus enabled him to go to Rome to "save Italy."[75] The life of the scholar–political activist taxed his spirit.

L'Unità's awkward logistics became increasingly difficult to manage, and he remained disappointed at the journal's inability to influence Italian opinion. It earned prestige by being regularly quoted by other journals, but its readership lagged.[76] He always functioned as an activist editor, and, consequently, preparing *L'Unità* weekly had become torturous.[77] In the summer of 1917, he explained his perseverance in stoic terms: "We are doing our duty. If nothing else, we have saved the peace of our conscience."[78]

Compounding Salvemini's difficulties was the added frustration caused by his Slav associates. Leaders of the pan-Slav independence movement, as well as pan-Serbs such as Serb Prime Minister Nikola Pǎsić, tended to be as aggressively expansionist in their pursuit of territory as were the Italian nationalists. Salvemini compared Pǎsić to Sonnino.[79] In fact, when addressing the issues of the future of the Balkans, Salvemini was evenhanded and reasonable. He argued that excessive Slav nationalism did not excuse Sonnino's imperialism. In fact, Salvemini supported negotiation of Italo-Yugoslav differences and thus took a much more centrist, flexible, pro-Italian position than the tone of his attack on Italian nationalists would suggest, and more than they would acknowledge.[80]

Contemplating the prospects of peace, Salvemini began to anticipate the nationalist propaganda that later labeled Italy's peace terms the "mutilated victory." He explained to Berenson the resentment Italians would feel if deprived of all territorial gains in the face of major concessions to their allies, the British and French. He also believed that the Bolsheviks' publication of the secret treaties may have helped Italy's cause by showing Wilson and the world that the British and French governments were as imperialistic as the Italian government. To invoke general Mazzinian principles to solve the Adriatic problem was not enough, he wrote. He hoped for a few courageous souls to speak out for "concrete" positions. This tough, pro-Italian stance neither separated him from Wilson nor convinced the nationalists that he was anything but "*Slav*emini."[81]

In April 1918, Salvemini met Italian and Yugoslav nationalists face-to-face at the Congress of Oppressed Nationalities in Rome. Orlando agreed to the meeting as a vehicle for open support of Yugoslav independence. If successful, the meeting would bolster Slav opposition to the Hapsburg armies, contributing to the dismantling of their empire, and rewarding Italy in the postwar settlement with its *terre irredente* at their expense. At the same time, Orlando was quietly supporting the agenda of the Italian nationalists.[82]

Salvemini plunged into the proceedings, hoping that the conference would indeed turn into an official diplomatic parley and that, if his "concrete" nationality positions prevailed, Allied governments would accept the recommendations. The Rome conference thus seemed to offer a rare opportunity for him to participate in quasi-official diplomacy. [83]

Although he understood the opposition of the Italian nationalists, he did not fully realize the duplicity of Orlando's game, nor did he know the degree to which the agendas of the other participating groups were firmly at odds with his. The prevailing concern for Allied unity required that the Allies avoid antagonizing any of the nationality groups, something that "concrete" Salveminian commitments were likely to do. In turn, those groups—Serbs, Yugoslavs, Czechs, Poles, and Romanians—demanded their right to independence in a postwar world. If pushed to "concrete" commitments, their demands would clash, not only among themselves but also with the Treaty of London and with the more modest Salvemini-Bissolati irredentist demands. Thus the logic of the occasion drove most of the participants toward ambiguous general solutions that would protect their future prospects. Salvemini would be forced to temper his optimism as soon as he understood these dynamics.[84]

The Italian democratic socialist and liberal group, generally supportive of Slav independence and opposed to Sonnino, included Bissolati, Salvemini, Albertini, Ojetti, Silva, Ruffini, and Amendola. They were, however, divided on specifics.[85] The unofficial British delegation, headed by R. W. Seton-Watson and Henry Wickham Steed, though sympathetic with the views of the Italian Left, had to avoid being drawn into a Mazzinian-Wilsonian position that would threaten British imperial interests.[86]

The South Slavs, assured by Sonnino that the meeting was merely a political expedient, followed Sonnino's advice to keep their options open until the end of the war, when they figured to fare better. Accordingly they maintained their distance from Salvemini, who suspected that they themselves harbored imperialist ambitions.[87] Seton-Watson observed that Salvemini's group risked isolation.[88]

From the start, Salvemini played an active role at the Rome conference. With the exception of the Bari council, it was the first time he had shown an interest in direct political participation since his ill-fated general election candidacy of 1913. He was frustrated by the delegates' lack of specificity on territorial issues, and his impatience with ambiguities revealed a predictable deficiency in diplomatic temperament. Only his group, he wrote Fernande, was prepared to make "a *concrete* accord" with the Slavs. He soon would discover that not even the Slavs were willing to reciprocate.[89]

On April 6 Salvemini spoke at length with British delegates Seton-Watson, publisher of *The New Europe*, and Steed, foreign editor of *The London Times*, both of whom had acted as liaisons between Italians and Slavs in London. He tried to forge a working alliance with them in order to achieve a breakthrough in negotiations. The next day, the Slav delegation joined them, led by Ante Trumbić, leading spokesman for the Yugoslav London committee. Salvemini took the offensive, demanding substantive progress. "Steed was embarrassed," he boasted to Fernande. "He wished to avoid this sharpness of positions. I was relentless."[90]

For Salvemini, this play within a play was his bid to upstage Sonnino, who clung doggedly to the existing Pact of London and refused any diplomatic exchange until the end of the war. On behalf of the democratic Left, Salvemini attempted to wrest control of this question from Orlando's cabinet. If he succeeded, he would isolate Sonnino. Suspecting such a motive and convinced of the futility of Italian-Yugoslav cooperation, Sonnino refused to attend the meeting.

Salvemini proposed a quid pro quo, whereby the Italian delegation would renounce Italian claims to Dalmatia in return for Yugoslav concessions on Italian ethnic areas of Istria, a promising initiative. Albert Thomas, former French Minister of Munitions, endorsed the Salvemini approach, whereas Steed seemed to waver. His hands tied by his own government, Steed, like others, avoided specific territorial commitments and thus frustrated Salvemini by his apparent equivocation.[91] To Salvemini's dismay, Steed supported Trumbić: "Italy can be sure that at the moment of the peace treaty, the Allies will resolve the Italian-Yugoslav territorial questions on the basis of justice and equity."[92] What Salvemini did not know was that Steed had cleared his statement with Sonnino.[93] As Salvemini began to discern the subtleties of the diplomatic game, he repeatedly reproached both Italian and Slav chauvinists.[94]

It was largely the work of Salvemini, Bissolati, and the democratic Left that, by applying enough pressure, produced the Pact of Rome of April 10, 1918. In the document, the nationalities of the Hapsburg Empire agreed to continue a "joint struggle against the common oppressors." The Italian delegation committed to the "unity and independence of the Yugoslav nation" and the amicable and just settlement of ethnic problems on the basis of self-determination. For the moment at least, the democratic Left had sent a clear message to a recalcitrant government for a peaceful resolution of the Dalmatian problem along Wilsonian lines. The gauntlet had been thrown down to Sonnino and the nationalists.[95]

In his plunge into quasi-diplomacy, Salvemini failed to win the specific commitments he believed essential, in particular, Italian ethnic areas of the Istrian peninsula. The Pact's provisions were sufficiently vague so as to imply mutual territorial concessions without actually making them; thus they served the propaganda interests of the Allies without foreclosing the territorial aspirations of the various nationalist groups. Sonnino—even in his absence—may have been the real winner among the Italians in the negotiations, because the Pact of London remained intact. Ironically, in settling for broad statements of principle, Salvemini was forced to accept the position of his nationalist opponents on both sides of the Adriatic because, in their ambition, they all wanted to keep their options open.[96]

Given the duplicitous behavior of Trumbić, Steed, and Orlando, it is remarkable that Salvemini reacted with such restraint in the aftermath of the Congress. He spent little time expressing his regrets over the outcome, convinced that global forces, especially the collapse of the Russian military, had made his task impossible. Instead, he used *L'Unità* to insist that Sonnino not be allowed to "sabotage" the principles of the Pact of Rome—which, according to Steed's memoirs, is exactly what Sonnino proceeded to do.[97]

Meanwhile, Salvemini continued his efforts to boost the morale of Italian troops. He spoke at a munitions plant, lectured soldiers at training sites, and addressed officers on the subject "Why Can Germany Not Win?" Taking a typically direct approach, he invoked statistics to show the industrial-military superiority of the Allies, especially after the American entrance into the conflict. He suggested to the officers that they use similar directness when addressing their troops. From his days in the trenches, he recalled that his comrades did not respond at all to the propaganda of the glory of the war. Instead, they fought to spare their families from Germanic aggression, to avoid suffering the fate of the Belgians and the Serbs.[98]

In mid-June, as Salvemini sought to bolster the spirits of Italian officers, the Austrian armies assaulted reinforced Italian positions on the River Piave in a desperate, final offensive. The Austrians crossed the river on a fifteen-mile front and reached the final line of Italian defenses, but Italian forces held, counterattacked, and drove the Austrian troops into full retreat. The battle cost Austria 100,000 casualties and immeasurable morale, as a sense of defeatism spread in the ranks and among the dispirited civilian population.

"The battle of Piave," Salvemini said, "was magnificent from the point of view of the conduct of Italian soldiers, but was a monument to stupidity from the point of view of the General Staff." Allowing the retreating Austrians to rebuild bridges on the Piave and to escape, he calculated, cost about 100,000 potential prisoners, men who could fight another day.[99]

As he used *L'Unità* to press the government, the censor's scissors trimmed his work.[100] In July he again encountered authorities, who denied him a passport to travel to Paris for a meeting with a European anti-Austrian group.[101] Meanwhile, he searched for an avenue to publish the secret diplomatic documents from the Triple Alliance. In September, De Viti De Marco presented the case to Sonnino, justified in terms of strengthening Italy's position under international law. Sonnino once again withheld permission, citing the danger of enemy propaganda.[102]

The day before refusing Salvemini's request, Sonnino suffered a rare setback in the cabinet. Under Bissolati's influence, the government voted to endorse Yugoslav independence, thus confirming the achievement of Salvemini and the democratic Left at the Congress. This vote was to prove the high watermark of official Italian endorsement of Wilsonian policy and thereby of Salvemini's work.[103]

That same week, their government in disarray, the Austrians joined the Germans in asking Wilson for an armistice based on his Fourteen Points. The Italian cabinet, sensing the impending end of the conflict, debated an offensive designed to drive the Austrian armies out of Italian territory. Reluctantly, General Diaz ordered the attack.

On October 24, 1918, the anniversary of Caporetto, Diaz launched the offensive. For five days, Italian forces hammered Austrian defenses. Riddled by mutiny and desertion, and assaulted by the renewed Italian charge, the Austrian armies collapsed. Italians took Vittorio Veneto on October 30, then pursued the fleeing Austrians, taking Udine, Trento, Trieste, and Fiume in the chase. On November 3, the two sides signed the armistice at Villa Giusti.

The celebrated triumph at Vittorio Veneto transformed the political climate. Victory brought a resurgence of nationalist pride and, at the same time, a breakdown of the patriotic unity to which Italians had rallied after the humiliation of Caporetto. In this politically charged setting, the revolutionary socialists still hoped the war would bring upheaval, and the nationalists clamored for even more territory than Sonnino. Salvemini sounded the cry from the near Left, maintaining rhetorical pressure on Sonnino, the nationalists, and the government.

The disagreement among Italian political factions focused on the issue of postwar boundaries. On this, Italy's most critical interest at the approaching Paris Peace Conference, the Orlando cabinet maintained contradictory positions based on Sonnino's Pact of London, Wilson's Fourteen Points, and the Pact of Rome, advocated in the cabinet by Bissolati. Orlando, with no apparent commitment to any of these diplomatic positions, searching at best for a politically favorable solution, appeared to take a neutral position between Sonnino and Bissolati.

With the Italian government divided, Wilson entered the fray. He opposed the Pact of London as the archetypal secret alliance, and his closest adviser considered Sonnino "a reactionary." He thus reached for support to the democratic Left, the one Italian political faction closest to his ideological positions and his hope for building a popular base. Bissolati, now vice-premier in the Orlando government, was Wilson's most prominent Italian advocate.[104]

By 1918, Bissolati was aligned with Salvemini on territorial points, arguing that Italy should renounce the Pact of London, and with it the Dalmatian coast (except the predominantly Italian city of Zara), the Brenner frontier, and the Dodecanese islands. In fact, although it was not generally noticed, Salvemini argued not to "abandon" the treaty but to "substitute" an agreement of superior quality.[105] As American diplomats and Wilson aides opened channels of communication with the Italian democratic Left, Bissolati succeeded in countering Sonnino while reinforcing Wilson's belief that the Dalmatian coast was unnecessary for the postwar defense of Italy. Salvemini had consistently taken this position.[106]

When Wilson arrived in Paris, he read diplomatic reports of his popularity in Italy and of maneuvering within the cabinet.[107] While the American ambassador in Rome pled for a Wilson visit, the president heard that four of Orlando's left-of-center cabinet members had resigned in protest, hoping to force Orlando to send Bissolati to Paris to counterbalance Sonnino.[108] Encouraged by the reports, Wilson decided to take his case to the Italian people in a bold new initiative.[109] A week before Wilson departed, Bissolati made his own dramatic exit from government.[110]

On January 3, 1919, Wilson arrived in Italy to launch his campaign before the Italian public. They responded with wild enthusiasm. In Milan, reformist socialist mayor Emilio Caldara endorsed Wilson's diplomacy while cheers of "Viva Wilson!" rang through the piazzas. However, the socialists divided on the question of endorsement, and the trip produced its share of frustration as Orlando and Sonnino sabotaged Wilson's public appearances to prevent his undercutting their political support.[111]

In addition to addressing mass audiences, the president was most interested in forging an informal political partnership with elements of the democratic Left, including some reformist socialists, labor leaders, and newspaper editors. His advisers suggested that he consult Bissolati, Albertini, Turati, Treves, and Salvemini, among others. The president succeeded in meeting with Albertini and Bissolati, the latter perhaps overstating the popularity of Wilson and his peace plan.[112] The president then returned to Paris, moved by his popular support. Two weeks later the Peace Conference opened.

Sensing the crucial timing of international negotiations, Salvemini refused to ease the pressure. He criticized Sonnino and the nationalists for their blustering and called for the Italian government to pursue American cooperation and to denounce any intention to control the Adriatic.[113] In Parliament, Turati and Treves generally advocated the Wilsonian positions of Salvemini and Bissolati over those of Sonnino. Orlando rode out the storm by remaining noncommittal.

Troubles within *L'Unità* hindered Salvemini's campaign. He complained that the journal was destroying him week by week. "Perhaps Italy is not capable of understanding my work," he wrote in frustration. "But I cannot be silent; I am what I am." Searching for solutions, he sought to relocate the publication, offered joint editorship to Prezzolini, and considered converting it to a newspaper. In the spring of 1919, he moved *L'Unità* to Florence.[114]

Victimized by his inability to refrain from denigrating those who disagreed with him, Salvemini undermined his own effectiveness. Albertini made the point by declining to sponsor an additional printing of Salvemini's book on the Adriatic. Not only did the noted journalist disagree with Salvemini on Fiume, but he thought the polemical tone of the book was unfair to those who had supported his moderate position at the Rome Congress. "They would rightly resent my cooperation," he explained to Salvemini, "in the distribution of pages in which they are vividly attacked." This was the voice of the successful man of public affairs lecturing the anti-Machiavellian intellectual.[115]

Disagreements with political allies were tame by comparison to Salvemini's heated engagements with his adversaries. The nationalists persevered in the polemical barrage they had initiated in 1916 when Francesco Coppola, a founder of the Nationalist Association, had first attacked Salvemini in response to an article on Dalmatia. By 1918 the war of words had escalated to a bitter and personal anti-Salvemini campaign. Energized by military success, they labeled Salvemini unpatriotic.[116]

Within days of the victory at Vittorio Veneto, he had attracted their attention by launching a new series of articles called "New Duties," warning that "victory must not cause us to forget all kinds of responsibility." He cautioned the readers of *L'Unità* that the war would have occurred in vain "if the terrible experience . . . did not teach us all the deficiencies of our culture and of our national character."[117] Nationalists regarded such introspective analysis as untimely and disloyal. In that same issue, advocating a "just peace" that guarded against destruction of Germany, Salvemini urged all Italian democrats to join forces politically against Italian Germanophiles (a thinly veiled reference to Sonnino) with the same vigor they had marshaled in the military effort.[118]

As Salvemini won further notoriety as an advocate of negotiation with the Slavs, the nationalists stepped up the vehemence of the attacks. When members of Parliament arrived on December 10, a number of them found copies of an anonymous, typewritten pamphlet containing scurrilous charges: "Finding himself in the lines at the beginning of the war and reaching the moment of danger, the volunteer Gaetano Salvemini abandoned his post, turned his back and dared to run." For confirmation, the pamphlet urged readers to consult several nationalists, including Corradini.[119] In *L'Idea Nazionale*, the nationalists amplified the accusations of desertion.[120]

A month later, Ernesto Rossi observed the incident on the tram in which an enraged nationalist shouted *"Rinunciatario!"* in Salvemini's face. The shouting incident was a manifestation of the growing threat by nationalist zealots against Salvemini and his cohorts of the democratic Left, those most closely associated with Wilsonian internationalism. The incident also signaled that the nationalist impulse had spread from intellectuals like Federzoni, Corradini, and Coppola to the general public, and that the nationalist press had succeeded in broadening the base of the movement. The increasingly personal quality of their campaign hinted strongly at the violent attacks that would soon begin.

Salvemini was not impervious to nationalist assault. In accentuating his differences with Slav nationalists and protecting Italy's rights in the Italian-inhabited areas of the Istrian peninsula, he also amplified his own form of Italian nationalism. He pointed out the hypocrisy of the British and French who blocked Italian expansion while indulging in their own, complaining that they expected Italy to be "the only immaculate lamb in the world."[121] He thus defended himself against charges of being anti-Italian, which would follow him much of his life.

In January 1919, Salvemini resigned as a contributor to R. W. Seton-Watson's journal *The New Europe*. Part of the protest by Italian correspondents against what they perceived to be an anti-Italian bias in the journal, Salvemini's exodus was directed against Trumbić as well.[122] Salvemini still resented the scheming of Slav imperialists, who, with the tacit assistance of Seton-Watson and Steed, had disrupted his plan to solidify postwar territorial commitments at the Rome conference. Salvemini's withdrawal from *The New Europe* marked the end of the semiofficial diplomatic cooperation between English and Italian democrats that had peaked nine months before.[123] Mussolini seized the opportunity to cite his letter of resignation as evidence of Slav imperialism.[124]

Nationalist protest now surged to a new plateau of violence directed at the Italian supporters of Wilson. First, the nationalist press assailed Bissolati for criticizing Sonnino in an interview in a British paper. Then *Il Popolo d'Italia* attacked Bissolati as a *rinunciatario*.[125] That night, anti-Bissolati posters appeared on the walls in Milan, where he was scheduled to speak at a Wilsonian rally.

The next day, January 11, 1919, Bissolati addressed a capacity audience at La Scala in Milan. It was to be the grand public defense of his resignation, and in a larger sense a kind of justification of his political life. A slender man of sixty-two, surrounded on the stage by supporters, Bissolati showed the strain of war wounds and political conflict. He began his endorsement of the League of Nations and a Wilsonian peace, calling for restraint and the support of international freedom and justice: "Italy," he declared, "would be among European nations the vanguard of the Wilsonian movement."[126]

Gradually noise from a box to Bissolati's right became a distraction. It was now apparent that opponents, including Futurists, nationalists, irredentists, and black shirted Arditi shock troops had broken security and found seats.[127] Each time Bissolati made a point, the Futurist Filippo Marinetti shouted a sarcastic "Amen!" Then, as Bissolati began to address the issue of Italian borders, the noise swelled. Initiated by a signal from Marinetti, his followers began a shrill chorus of howling and whistling. Streamers and thousands of pamphlets sailed down from the balconies. Cries of "Croats no!" and "vile *rinunciatario!*" punctuated the din, giving it anti-Yugoslav, anti-Wilson political focus. When Bissolati supporters, including wounded veterans, attempted to restore order, nationalist and Futurist zealots roughed them up.[128]

Then Bissolati recognized among the shouting mob the distinctive visage and baritone voice of Benito Mussolini, a political associate of Marinetti and his Futurist Party. Bissolati turned to friends on the stage and said, with a sense of resignation and quiet dignity, "That man, no! I will not fight with that man!" He folded his papers and left.[129]

In the aftermath of his failed attempt to deliver his "spiritual and political testament," Bissolati and the democratic interventionists endured further abuse. Fanatics, spilling out of La Scala after disrupting the Wilsonian rally, shattered windows at the offices of *Il Corriere della Sera* and *Il Secolo*. Meanwhile, Bissolati took the failure with great distress, saying, "I have closed my life with this act of duty and faith."[130]

Salvemini found himself both disgusted and saddened by the events at La Scala. Hearing that the incident had devastated Bissolati, he took Zanotti-Bianco to visit their compatriot at his small tenement, now guarded by *carabinieri* because of threats against his life. They found him in bed, prostrate, disheartened, and bitter, particularly because his former ally Ivanoe Bonomi, who replaced him in the cabinet, no longer supported his positions. Bissolati died sixteen months later.[131]

Of greatest significance to Salvemini and to all Italians was Mussolini's participation in the agitation at La Scala. His public confrontation of Bissolati, combined with his editorial condemnation of the previous day, marked Mussolini's final break with the democratic interventionism that Salvemini had so fiercely advocated. As Mussolini denounced *rinunciatari*, he propounded the thesis of "the mutilated victory," in which he argued that Italy was being unjustly deprived of its rightful reward of territorial gain. For almost a year, he had been referring to *rinunciatari* of the "Salvemini type."[132]

Salvemini had endured a continuing barrage of criticism similar to that which virtually destroyed Bissolati. However, in 1919, a number of writers rallied around Salvemini and his work, and the praise bolstered his sagging spirits. Within a few months appeared laudatory biographical sketches by Prezzolini, Silva, Jules Destrée, and Ettore Rota, and a historiographical sketch by Croce.

"I am not indifferent to the affection and esteem of men like you," he wrote to Prezzolini, "just as I am not indifferent to the insults of so many others."[133]

The day after Bissolati's fateful speech, Salvemini addressed a League of Nations rally in Pisa. The next week he defended Bissolati in *L'Unità*. During the war, Sonnino and the Italian government had hidden behind the "mask of democracy," he wrote, but Bissolati "ripped off the veils." For this reason, Bissolati's opponents had castigated him. "Our duty, friends of *L'Unità*, is clear: to continue to rip off the veils." He warned his readers of ominous dangers if Italian foreign policy should be influenced by those who shouted down Bissolati: "The war for peace will be succeeded by the peace for war, because a peace like this cannot be anything but preparation for new war."[134] However, in this all-important battle for public opinion, Bissolati, Salvemini, and the Italian Wilsonians were quickly losing ground to a more potent and aggressive coalition. Within a week, irredentists and nationalists held pro-Fiume, pro-Dalmatia rallies, attended by blackshirted Arditi, and Mussolini stepped up his furious attack against "Yugoslav imperialism" and *rinunciatari*.[135]

NOTES

1. GS to GP, December 24, 1917, *Cart 1914*, 348.

2. ER, "Il nonconformista." The invective "Rinunciatario!" translates literally as "renouncer." In the portwar context the connotation is "turncoat" or "traitor."

3. Fernande Luchaire to ED, April 12, 1916, quoted in Iris Origo, *A Need to Testify*, 150.

4. FS to Romain Rolland, August 3, 1916, *AGS*; Iris Origo, *A Need to Testify*, 150.

5. EBB to GS, September 4, 1914 and May 9, 1915, 32–33 and 151–152; GS to EBB, September 7, October 15 and 16, 1914 and July 13, 1916, 35, 54–55, and 266–267; to Cesare Battisti, December 7, 1914 and October 25, 1915, 93 and 212; to Ferdinando Martini, December 1, 1915, *Cart 1914*, 220.

6. GS to EBB, July 13, 1916, *Cart 1914*, 266–267.

7. GS, "Cesare Battisti," *Opere* VIII, 82–85.

8. GS, "Lettera di Salvemini a Cesare Battisti," *Opere* III (1), 447; "Brennero o Salorno? Lettere inedite di Salvemini ai Battisti," ET, ed., *Il Mondo*, June 13, 1961; "Il problema dell'Alto Adige," *Opere* III (1), 441–446.

9. Martini, *Diario, 1914–1918*, Gabriele De Rosa, ed. (Milan, 1966), 492; Delio Cantimori, *Conversando di storia* (Bari, 1967), 186; ET, *Sal*, 178; GS to Martini, August 6 and 14, 1915, *Cart 1914*, 175–178, 182–185; to Donna Titina Benzoni, July 30, 1915, 170; Martini to GS, August 9, 1915, 181, *Cart 1914*; GS, series on the history of the Triple Alliance in *Opere* III (4), 3–103; Martini, *Diario*, 492; Augusto Torre, preface to GS, *Opere* III (4), x ff.

10. GS to Martini, August 14, 1915, *Cart 1914*, 185.

11. GS to LA, September 2 and 14, 1915; LA to GS, September 15 and 26, 1915, 189, 192–194, 200; Edmondo di Robilant to GS, September 26, 1915, *Cart 1914*, 200.

12. GS to Z-B, February 8 and 13 and March 28, 1916, 237, 238, 244–245; Robilant to GS, February 23, 1916, *Cart 1914*, 238–239.

13. GS to ED, October 19, 1916, *Cart 1914*, 284; to Benedetto Croce, December 15, 1914, *Cart 1914*, 95.

14. GS, "La Triplice Alleanza: I. Le origine," *Rivista delle Nazioni Latine*, July 1, 1916, WL.

15. The remaining installments of the seven part series are found in *Opere* III (4), 3–103; see also *La politica estera dell'Italia dal 1871 al 1915* (Florence, 1950), *Opere* III (4), 291–451.

16. S-W, *ILF*, 432; JB, *LMV*, 40–67.

17. GS, notes on Francesco Evoli's article "Problema adriatico e problema mediterraneo," *Opere* III (1), 476–483; introduction to Carlo Maranelli's "Il problema dell'Adriatico," *L'U*, March 12, 1915; "La campagna per la Dalmazia," *L'U*, May 14, 1915; "Per l'amicizia italo-jugoslava," *L'U*, May 21, 1915.

18. GS to Z-B, March 28, April 7, 16 and 27, June 18, 1916, *Cart 1914*, 244, 250–251, 252–253, 255–256, 262.

19. LBi, *Diario di guerra* (Turin, 1935), 69. Translation from S-W, *ILF*, 459.

20. GS, "Gorizia e l'Italia," *Opere* III (2), 12–15.

21. LBi to GS, August 25, 1916, *Cart 1914*, 268; RC, *Bissolati*, 233; Ugoberto Alfassio Grimaldi and Gherardo Bozzetti, *Bissolati* (Milan, 1983), 191–192.

22. LBi, "Commemorazione di Cesare Battisti," *La politica estera dell'Italia dal 1897 al 1920* (Milan, 1923), 358–372; DeF, *il riv*, 332–333.

23. GS to Z-B, September 24, 1916, *Cart 1914*, 274.

24. GS to UO, April 6, 1916, *Cart 1914*, 248.

25. GS to Z-B, March 12, April 13 and September 24 , 1916, 241, 251–252, 275; to PS, March 12 and October 4, 1916, 241–242, 277; to UO, March 12 and April 6, 1916, 242, 248; to GP, April 6 and September 26, 1916, 249, 275–276; to ED, October 19, 1916, 283; to AGh, October 25, 1916, *Cart 1914*, 285–286; to R. W. Seton-Watson, February 10, 1917, *Cart 1914*, 296; DeV, "Perchè rinasce *L'Unità*" and "Circolare agli amici dell'*Unità*," "*L'Unità,*" "*La Voce Politica,*" 479–481; DeF, *il riv*, 335–336.

26. GS to ER, October 7, 1922 in "Carteggio Salvemini-Rossi, 1921–1925," Umberto Morra, ed., *Il Mondo*, January 26, 1960.

27. ET, *Sal*, 186 n. 1.

28. See, for example, "Salvemini, jugoslavo di razza!," *L'Impero* (Rome), n.d. 1925 in SPD, CR, "Salvemini."

29. ET, "Nota biografica," 258.

30. GS, "Il congresso di Parigi e i socialisti interventisti," *Pd'I*, August 31, 1916 and "Non complichiamo le cose!," *Pd'I*, September 15, 1916; "L'Italie et la Serbie," *Opere* III (2), 15–17.

31. H. W. V. Temperly, *History of the Peace Conference of Paris*, quoted in S-W, *ILF*, 460.

32. GS, "Il discorso di Wilson," *Opere* VIII, 407–409.

33. GS to UO, April 6, 1916, *Cart 1914*, 247–248; "Wilson e gli imperi centrali," *L'U*, December 29, 1916.

34. GS to UO, November 7, 1916, *Cart 1914*, 286; ET, *Sal*, 180.

35. Alceo Riosa, "L'interventismo democratico e la questione adriatica tra l'armistizio e la marcia su Fiume," *Storia e politica*, October-December 1965, 517.

36. DeF, *il riv*, 340–345.

37. GS, "Interventismo nazionalista e interventismo democratico," *Opere* III (2), 51–54.

38. DeF, *il riv*, 344–345.

39. GS to AGh, April 18, 1917, *Cart 1914*, 302.

40. GS to GP, July 8, 1917, *Cart 1914*, 314.

41. GS to Z-B, August 10, 1917, *Cart 1914*, 320.

42. "Gaetano Salvemini: Consigliere provinciale," 8–9; RC, "Gaetano Salvemini e Molfetta" (Catalogue, Mostra documentaria, Commune di Molfetta, October 1988, Bari, n.d.), 16; GS, "Italia e Francia," "Italia e Inghilterra," "Il pericolo tedesco," "Per discutere utilmente," *Opere* III (2), 94–126; "La politica estera dell'on. Giolitti," *Opere* III (2), 133–137; "I trattati segreti," *Opere* VIII, 483–484; "Una macchina per volare," August 23, 1917, *Opere* IV (1), 418–419.

43. S-W, *ILF*, 460–461.

44. GS to LA, August 6, 1917, 317–319; LA to GS, August 8, 1917, 319; *Cart 1914*, 326–327.

45. GS to PS, August 27, 1917, *Cart 1914*, 327.

46. S-W, *ILF*, 477–479; DeF, *il riv*, 365–366, 392; V. E. Orlando, *Memorie*, Rodolfo Mosca, ed. (Milan, 1960), 230–232.

47. GS, "Guardando la realtà," and "Particolarismo," *Opere* VIII, 297–298 and 301–302.

48. GS to GP, October 26, 1918, 429; to UO, October 26 and November 13, 1917, 334, 337; to PS, November 7, 1917, 335; to BB, November 25, 1917, 339, *Cart 1914*.

49. GS, *L'U*, November 15, 1917.

50. GS to Sofia Cammarota Adorno, November 20, 1917, *Cart 1914*, 338–339.

51. GS to BB, November 25, 1917, *Cart 1914*, 339.

52. GS to GP, March 20, 1918, *Cart 1914*, 364–365.

53. GS to Z-B, March 17, 1918, 362–363; to UO, March 23, 1918, 367, *Cart 1914*; JB, *LMV*, 147–163.

54. ET, *Sal*, 190.

55. DeF, *il riv*, 362–382.

56. Quoted in Antonio Salandra, *L'intervento 1915* (Milan, 1930), 168. See also RV, *Il dopoguerra in Italia e l'avvento del fascismo (1918–1922)* (Naples, 1967), 175–177.

57. Carlo Maranelli and GS, *La questione dell'Adriatico* (Florence, 1918).

58. GS to Salandra, April 18, 1918, *Cart 1914*, 383–384.

59. GS to PS, April 18, 1918, *Cart 1914*, 382–383; "Il duca di Cesarò," *L'U* April 20, 1918.

60. RV, *Il dopoguerra*, 176–178.

61. Charles Seymour, ed., *The Intimate Papers of Colonel House* (Boston, 1928) III, 277; JB, *LMV*, 138–163.

62. GS, "Austria e Dalmazia," *L'U*, January 17, 1918 (censored); "Il problema dell'Adriatico," *L'U*, January 24, 1918.

63. "Discussioni," BM, *OO*, X, 261–163; GS, "I nazionalisti e la Dalmazia," *L'U*, January 17, 1918; "Il fronte unico morale," *Opere* III (2), 161–165.

64. GS to GP, February 1918, *Cart 1914*, 358; to Seton-Watson, February 10, 1917, *Cart 1914*, 295; "Lucro emergente, danno cessante," *L'U*, February 16, 1918; BM, "Wilson, dittatore," *OO*, XI, 88–90.

65. Henry Wickham Steed, *Through Thirty Years, 1892–1922* (New York, 1924), 179–183; JB, *LMV*, 97–120, 127–142; S-W, *ILF*, 463–464; Albrecht-Carrié, *Italy*, 36–39.

66. GS, "Particolarismo," *L'U*, November 22, 1917; "Austria e Dalmazia," *Opere* III (2), 147–150; to BB, November 27, 1917, 341; to Z-B, January 10 and 12, 1918, *Cart 1914*, 350–352.

67. GS, "Le condizioni della pace in Germania," February 16, 1918; "Un nuovo verbo," February 23, 1918; "Facile contentatura," March 2, 1918, *L'U*; to Z-B, January 10, 1918, *Cart 1914*, 350–351.

68. GS to PS, August 21, 1915, *Cart 1914*, 324; Maranelli and GS, *La questione dell'Adriatico* (Florence, 1916).

69. GS to UO, January 26, 1917, *Cart 1914*, 293; to PS, August 21, 1917, *Cart 1914*, 325.

70. GS to UO, April 24, 1917, *Cart, 1914*, 303.

71. GS to Z-B, January 10 and 12, 1918, *Cart 1914*, 350, 351.

72. GS, "L'abitudine delle bugie," *Opere* III (2), 178–179.

73. GS to UO, January 26, 1917, *Cart 1914*, 294.

74. GS to AGh, May 24, 1917, *Cart 1914*, 310.

75. GS to ED, November 27, 1917, *Cart 1914*, 345.

76. GS to Z-B, July 1, 1917, *Cart 1914*, 313.

77. GS to Adorno, November 20, 1917, 338; to ED, November 27, 1917, *Cart 1914*, 345.

78. GS to PS, August 16, 1917, *Cart 1914*, 321.

79. GS to Seton-Watson, February 10, 1917, 296; to PS, August 21, 1917, *Cart 1914*, 322.

80. GS to PS, August 16, 1917, *Cart 1914*, 322; JB, *LMV*, 150–154.

81. GS to BB, November 27, 1917, 341–344; to AGh, December 13, 1917, *Cart 1914*, 347–348; "Salviamo l'Istria," *Opere* III (2), 85–91; "Sul problema militare della Dalmazia," "L'Italia e la Società delle Nazioni," *Opere* III (2), 188–191.

82. JB, *LMV*, 147–154; S-W, *ILF*, 494–497; Steed, *Through Thirty Years*, 208–216.

83. JB, *LMV*, 148–150; RV, *Il dopoguerra*, 169 ff.; GS to UO, July 13, 1918, *Cart 1914*, 402–403; to FS, April 6, 8, 9, 1918, *Cart 1914*, 372–381; "Il congresso di Roma," *Opere* III (2), 179–182.

84. Steed, *Through Thirty Years*, 179–183; JB, *LMV*, 147–154; S-W, *Italy*, 494–497.

85. Translation of Confidential Statement Obtained from Bissolati, December 30, 1918, *WWP*, LC, Series 5B, Reel 387. See also DeF, *il riv*, 380–384; Giuseppe Borgese, *Goliath* (New York, 1938), 128–129; RC, *Bissolati*, 252–253; JB, *LMV*,

147–154; S-W, *ILF*, 494–497; Grimaldi and Bozzetti, *Bissolati*, 234–238; Riosa, "L'interventismo," 515–517.

86. Steed, *Through Thirty Years*, 173–216; Seton-Watson, *R. W. Seton-Watson and the Yugoslavs: Correspondence, 1906–1941* (London, 1976) I, 30–31; JB, *LMV*, 147–154.

87. GS to Seton-Watson, February 10, 1917, 296; to PS, August 21, 1917, *Cart 1914*, 322; to UO, March 23 and 27, 1918, 367–372; to FS, April 6, 8, 9, 1918, *Cart 1914*, 372–381; PS, Appendice II, April 6–11, 1918, *Cart 1914*, 563–570; S-W, *ILF*, 494–495.

88. Quoted in Hugh and Christopher Seton-Watson, *The Making of a New Europe* (Seattle, 1981), 262.

89. GS to FS, April 8, 1918, *Cart 1914*, 374.

90. S-W, *ILF*, 494; JB, *LMV*, 148–149; GS to FS, April 9, 1918, *Cart 1914*, 377.

91. Steed, *Through Thirty Years*, 185–196; JB, *LMV*, 147–148.

92. PS, April 10, 1918, Appendice II, GS, *Cart 1914*, 566.

93. Steed, *Through Thirty Years*, 210.

94. DDI, 5, IX, 42, Sidney Sonnino to Carlotti, September 12, 1917. See also JB, *LMV*, 129–131; GS to R. W. Seton-Watson, November 10, 1917, *R. W. Seton-Watson and the Yugoslavs*, I, 289–290.

95. Rene Albrecht-Carrié, *Italy*, 347–348. See also Steed, *Through Thirty Years*, 184–185; JB, *LMV*, 151–154.

96. JB, *LMV*, 153–154.

97. GS, "Il Congresso di Roma"; "Le cose a posto," *Opere* III (2), 226–232; Steed, *Through Thirty Years*, 213–215.

98. GS to Z-B, September 22, 1917, 329; to ED, November 27, 1917, 345; to UO, March 27 and June 24, 1918, 370–371 and 396; to GP, May 10, 1918, 359; L-R to GS, February 20, 1918, 358–360; Peyrelli to GS, June 25, 1918, *Cart 1914*, 396–397; ET, *Sal*, 201.

99. ET, *Sal*, 203.

100. GS, "La propaganda in America," June 1, 1918; "I nervi a posto," June 29, 1918, *L'U*.

101. GS to PS, July 13, 1918, 402; to UO, July 22, 1918, 408 and July 26, 410; to AGh, August 10, 1918, 417, *Cart 1914*.

102. Torre, preface to *Opere* III (4), x-xii.

103. Albrecht-Carrié, *Italy*, 46; Arno Mayer, *Wilson vs. Lenin: Political Origins of the New Diplomacy* (Cleveland, 1964), 198; Alfassio Grimaldi and Bozzetti, *Bissolati*, 243–245; Translation of Confidential Statement Obtained from Bissolati, Reel 387, 2.

104. Seymour, *Intimate Papers* III, 283; Albrecht-Carrié, *Italy*, 55, 90 ff.

105. GS, "Le cose a posto," *Opere* III (2), 226–232; "'Austria delenda' o 'Austria servanda,'" *Opere* III (2), 224; RV, *Il dopoguerra*, 181.

106. Telegram, Ambassador to Italy (T. N. Page) to Secretary of State (Lansing), January 21, 1918, *FRUS, 1918, the World War*, supplement 1, I (Washington, D. C., 1933), 35; Confidential Digest of the President's Conference with On. Bissolati, Page to Wilson, January 7, 1919, *WWP*, Series 5B, Reel 388, LC. See also RC, *Bissolati*,

235–239; GS, "Sul problema militare della Dalmazia," *L'U*, February 23, 1918, 37–38.

107. Steed, *Through Thirty Years*, 216; GS to UO, July 26, 1918, *Cart 1914*, 410–413; JB, *LMV*, 159–163.

108. RV, *Il dopoguerra*, 211 ff; RC, *Bissolati*, 265–271.

109. Ray S. Baker to E. M. House, November 1, 1918, *BP*; Baker to House, November 22, 1918, 856.00/213, RG 59, NA; Baker to House, December 6, 1918, 856.00/214, RG 59, NA.

110. Page to Amission, Paris, December 30, 1918, Series 5B, Reel 387, *WWP*, LC.; Alfassio Grimaldi and Bozzetti, *Bissolati*, 249–252; Oldino Malagodi, *Conversazioni della guerra, 1914–1919*, Brunello Vigezzi, ed. (Milan, 1960), I, 450–466.

111. Bruno Tobia, "Il partito socialista italiano e la politica di W. Wilson (1916–1919)," *Storia contemporanea* V (1974), 295; Arno Mayer, *Politics and Diplomacy of Peacemaking* (New York, 1967), 214; F. Colgate Speranza, *The Diary of Gino Speranza, Italy 1915–1919* (New York, 1941) II, 238–239.

112. Page to Wilson with Enclosure, January 7, 1919, *WWP*, LC, Vol. 53, 639–644; Translation of Confidential Statement Obtained from Bissolati. See also Mayer, *Politics and Diplomacy*, 212–215; Tobia, "Il partito socialista," 295.

113. GS, "Sui margini della vittoria," *Opere*, VI (1), 222–223; "Il nuovi doveri," *Opere*, VI (1), 232; "La flotta ex-austriaca," *Opere*, VI (1), 228. See also, Mayer, *Politics and Diplomacy*, 203.

114. GS to Z-B, October 20, 1918, 425; to UO, October 25, 1918, 426; to Z-B, November 6, 1918, 433; to GP, November 6 and December 10, 1918, 433 and 438; to Z-B, December 11, 1918, 441; to GLR, March 13, 1919, *Cart 1914*, 453. See also Fabio Grassi, "Salvemini e l'ultima *Unità*" in Gaetano Cingari, ed., *Gaetano Salvemini* (Rome, 1986), 329–363.

115. LA to GS, October 25, 1918, *Cart 1914*, 427; JB, *LMV*, 150–157.

116. GS to Z-B, September 24, 1916, *Cart 1914*, 275; to AGh, May 11 and July 16, 1918, *Cart 1914*, 387, 403.

117. GS, "Nuovi doveri," *Opere* III (2), 265.

118. GS, "La guerra e la pace," *L'U*, November 9, 1918.

119. GS, "Un anonima sconcezza," BF, *L'U*, 726.

120. MC, *Bibliografia*, 143; BM, "Il margine alla polemica," *OO* XI, 314.

121. GS to BB, October 26, 1918, *Cart 1914*, 428.

122. Giuseppe Bruccoleri to R. W. Seton-Watson, December 11, 1918; DeV to R. W. Seton-Watson, December 12, 1918, R. W. Seton-Watson, *Correspondence* II, 10–11; LA, "Troppo Zelo," *CdS*, December 6, 1918; LA to Emanuel, November 14 and December 4, 1918, *Epistolario 1911–1926*, Ottavio Barrié, ed. (Milan, 1968) III, 921 and 929; GS, "Al sig. R. W. Seton-Watson," *L'U*, January 18, 1919; to the Publisher of *New Europe*, January 7, 1919, *Cart 1914*, 443.

123. JB, *LMV*, 147–166; RV, *Il dopoguerra*, 180–181.

124. BM, "Confessioni tardive," *OO* XII, 164–166; BM, "Liquidazione," "Pro Fiume e Dalmazia," "Equivoco o malafede," "L'aperatura," "La parola di Poincare," *OO* XII, 134–158.

125. BM, "Il Nuovo 'Parecchio' di Bissolati," *OO*, XII, 125–130.

126. Ivanoe Bonomi, *Leonida Bissolati e il movimento socialista in Italia* (Rome, 1945), 220.

127. DeF, *il riv*, 487.

128. LBi, *La politica estera dell'Italia*, 394–414.

129. Borgese, *Goliath*, 140–143; Mayer, *Politics and Diplomacy*, 218–221; RC, *Bissolati*, 272–279; Grimaldi and Bozzetti, *Bissolati*, 256–257.

130. Bonomi, *Bissolati*, 221.

131. RC, *Bissolati*, 273; GiS, *Diary* II, 246–250; "Brennero o Salorno? Lettere inedite di Salvemini ai Battisti," ET, ed., *Il Mondo*, June 13, 1961; Riosa, "L'interventismo," 522–534; Grimaldi and Bozzetti, *Bissolati*, 261; GS, "Il problema di Fiume," *L'U*, November 23, 1918; "La difesa degli italiani di Dalmazia," *L'U*, January 25, 1919.

132. BM, "In margine alla polemica," *OO*, XI, 314.

133. GS to GP, December 10, 1918, *Cart 1914*, 438. See PS, "Gaetano Salvemini," *L'Italia che scrive* (Rome), June 1918, 1–2; Rota, *Una pagina di storia contemporanea: Gaetano Salvemini* (Milan, 1919); Jules Destrée, *Gaetano Salvemini* (Altamura, 1919); PS, *Chi è Gaetano Salvemini* (Florence, 1919); Benedetto Croce, *Storia della storiografia italiana nel secolo XIX*, (Bari, 1921).

134. GS, "Il discorso di Milano," *Opere* III (2), 485–487.

135. BM, "Liquidazione," "Viltà e menzogna," "Il delitto," "Equivoco o malafede," "L'apertura," "La parola di Poincarè," "Confessioni tardive," *OO* XII, 134–136, 137–140, 141–143, 153–155, 156–158, 161–163, 164–166. See also DeF, *il riv*, 489–491.

Chapter 6

One Man Alone

The revolution of October 1922 was now the fact that belied the political forecasts of Salvemini. And he, then, assigned to the distant future the task of destroying it.

Benito Mussolini, n.d.[1]

As the extremists shouted down Leonida Bissolati at La Scala, the victorious Allies opened the peace conference in Paris that would determine the shape of the postwar world. In the first week of February 1919, after an extended struggle to acquire a passport, Salvemini arrived in the French capital, eager to influence the Allied diplomats and to challenge the Sonnino position.

In Paris, he encouraged members of the American delegation to accept a Wilsonian settlement that awarded Italy Fiume but not Dalmatia. He had now abandoned his earlier support for Fiume as an "open city" for a more pragmatic position of acquiring central Fiume in exchange for Dalmatia, applying Wilsonian criteria to each. The American diplomats, dissatisfied with the official position of the Italian delegation and aware of its internal divisions, listened to Salvemini's views, knowing all the while that he represented only a dissident faction. He returned to Florence without knowing that the threats aimed at Bissolati would soon shroud Tuscany in a web of violence and force him to forestall a similar return voyage from Paris three years later.[2]

Exhausted from his trip, Salvemini nonetheless delivered to the readers of *L'Unità* a comprehensive account of the League of Nations charter, giving a cautious endorsement, supporting both German disarmament and German membership in the League.[3] Meanwhile, he organized in Florence the first meeting of the "Friends of *L'Unità*." These "Unitari" had been meeting in various cities during the war, and some hoped to convert the group to a political party. In April, they met for three days in Florence and formed the Democratic League for National Renewal, expressing reservations to the Paris treaty and committing themselves to democratic reforms. In spite of the specifics, their manifesto was as much a general condemnation of the political status quo as a formula for action. Salvemini hoped that he could recruit young people: "They have faith in us . . . ," he wrote. "We have with us the better part of the youth."[4] However, he never contemplated launching a mass movement. "We must focus on *facts*, on *action*," he wrote Prezzolini. "It is better to be a few, compact and with clear ideas, than many with contradictory ideas."[5] The League thus lacked a demographic base, with the result that its influence, like that of its journal, was confined to the realm of intellect.[6]

By voicing "repugnance toward the old parties," Salvemini committed the Democratic League to the same critique of the politics of the liberal state he had expressed in *L'Unità*. If, however, the democratic interventionists could recruit the "better part of the youth" to a mass political movement, and perhaps cooperate with democratic socialists like Turati and Treves, they could renew Italy's political institutions. Like the democratic socialists, Salvemini and his group were explicit in their condemnation of left- and right-wing alternatives they saw as antidemocratic. Yet the bitter legacy from the intervention crisis made cooperation between Salvemini and Turati unlikely. In the face of mounting violence, Salvemini issued a call for calm.[7]

Several weeks before the Unitari met in Florence, Benito Mussolini launched the Fascist movement in Milan. On the morning of March 23, 1919, in a small conference hall at the Piazza San Sepolcro, Mussolini announced to a meeting of his supporters the founding of the Fasci Italiani di Combattimento. On hand for the subsequent rally were Filippo Marinetti, Roberto Farinacci, Michele Bianchi, and a heterogeneous crowd of more than 100 Arditi, other veterans, former socialists, syndicalists, revolutionary interventionists, and Futurist intellectuals who would collectively be called "Fascists of the First Hour."

The disruption of Bissolati at La Scala, led by Marinetti and Mussolini, proved to be the first postwar political violence and the beginning of the end of politics as usual in Italy. In the spring of 1919, Fascists began to confront socialists in the streets, and in April, in one of their first "punitive expeditions," blackshirted Arditi ransacked and burned the offices of *Avanti!*. Some of the business elite of Milan, fearing an Italian Bolshevist revolution, applauded the attacks and began to accept the myth that only the Fascists could prevent revolution from the Left. The government took no action. Mussolini's open gestures to workers and his claims to leadership of a revolutionary movement, perhaps even as an Italian Lenin, indicated that he rejected the counterrevolutionary role. The disparate Fascist movement grew, especially among young men in the cities, held together by the audacity of violent action and by a common disillusionment with the boredom of bourgeois society and a rejection of the institutions of the liberal state.

Salvemini responded to the destruction of the *Avanti!* offices not by sounding an alarm of impending danger from Fascist squads but by noting the weakness of revolutionary socialism. "A revolutionary movement, of a more or less Bolshevist type, cannot succeed in Italy," he wrote. "*Avanti!* has been brutally burned down without any . . . revolutionary outbreak."[8] Salvemini's initial public response to Fascism, therefore, was to replay an old theme—the weakness of the extreme Left—without warning of this new peril. In this, he was not alone, for there was a general failure to recognize the danger lurking in early Blackshirt violence. Yet privately he revealed a grave concern, predicting violent political reaction would spread throughout Italy within a year.[9]

Three months later, food riots in Forlí led to a general strike throughout the Romagna and the Marches. Within days plundering spread through the country. Among the cities hit hardest was Florence, where looting persisted for several days. *La Difesa*, the local socialist newspaper, hailing the "dictatorship of the proletariat," urged its readers: "Forward! Toward Communism." In the midst of chaos, Salvemini walked the streets, looking for signs of the revolution. What he saw confirmed his view that revolution was unlikely. He noted little evidence of Bolshevik organization, but he saw "good-natured, jolly people" who went home carrying several flasks of wine, shoes, and other stolen merchandise. "There was no heroic and revolutionary exaltation in anyone," he wrote in *L'Unità*. "There was no will to set up a new social organization. . . . Everywhere there are crowds ready to revolt. There does not exist anywhere a class equal to a revolution."

Nevertheless, Salvemini worried. The middle and upper classes—angry, damaged, and threatened—might strike back at the workers. Once the city wearied of the food riots, he wrote, "the police will no longer be indulgent. . . . Then machine guns will blaze in the streets." He sensed growing danger as the socialists, incapable of delivering revolution, persisted in the use of revolutionary rhetoric. He foresaw a terrible reaction from the military.[10]

As strife spread throughout the spring and summer, the economy worsened in response to the cessation of Allied credits and controls. The lira fell, food and fuel shortages spread, the cost of living climbed, industrial production faltered, and strikes multiplied. In the countryside, peasants seized uncultivated land from estates and rallied to socialist and Catholic insurgency.[11]

While diplomats reported the surge of political violence and the growing threat of revolution in Italy, the Big Four hammered out the terms of the Versailles Treaty. Wilson refused to award Italy land at the expense of Slavs and insisted that Fiume was essential to the economic viability of Yugoslavia, an apparent contradiction of his own principle of nationality. A divided Italian delegation made its official demands on the same day that Wilson recognized the state of Yugoslavia. Many Italians regarded Wilson as pro-Slav and anti-Italian and vented their wrath on Salvemini and Wilson's other Italian supporters. In Paris, the Italian delegation grew more frustrated at Wilson's rigidity on the issues of Fiume and Dalmatia.

In December Orlando added Fiume to Italy's demands. Unlike most of the other Italian territorial claims, the city had not been promised to Italy in the Pact of London and therefore had no place on Sonnino's agenda. Orlando, feeling his support weaken in his own cabinet and threatened by Bissolati's Wilsonian program, finally decided to come down firmly on the side of Sonnino against the democratic program. To strengthen his own political base, especially among the nationalists, Orlando embraced Fiume. Inadvertently, he gained allies in Salvemini and Bissolati, who were likewise urging "Fiume *italianissima*." Sonnino was appalled by the addition of Fiume. Unable to resolve the issue between Sonnino and Orlando, the Italian delegation simply asked for "The Pact of London plus Fiume."

From opposite political poles, both nationalists and democrats now demanded Fiume. Whereas Orlando's motive was to make political capital, Salvemini and Bissolati lodged the claim on the basis of ethnicity. Inadvertently, this coincidental agreement identified Salvemini with the nationalists. This unintended link between Salvemini and Orlando's nationalist following would be only one of many ironic twists in the life of a man accused of being anti-Italian.[12]

On April 23, Wilson published an appeal to the Italian people to reject the expansionist position of their government and join him in creating a "new order" based on peace and justice for all. Orlando, regarding Wilson's appeal as an invasion of domestic politics and a threat to his political support, walked out of the peace conference. Six days later Orlando and Sonnino entered Parliament to shouts of "*Viva* Italian Fiume! *Viva* Italian Dalmatia! Annexation! Annexation!" Only the socialist deputies withheld their applause.[13] Nationalists and irredentists countered Wilson's plea by trumpeting their campaign against a "mutilated victory" in which Italy had been deprived of the rightful spoils of territorial expansion promised in the Pact of London.

The Italian Wilsonians faced a paradox. They found themselves trapped by Wilson, who now opposed them on Fiume when he rejected most Italian territorial claims. This placed Salvemini in an untenable position: attacked by the Right as a *rinunciatario* and undercut by Wilson on the Fiume case. In April, Mussolini attributed Wilson's message to the "vulgar campaign of the *rinunciatari*." As the political offensive against Wilson's Italian supporters spread, Salvemini became frustrated and outraged.[14] In May, he lashed out at Wilson in *L'Unità*:

From the ground of right, [Wilson] shifted to that of opportunity. But in this field the wolves and the foxes of the old European diplomacy were stronger than he. . . . Why does he want to impose what he considers *absolute justice* on the Italian people alone? Why does he not first issue a message to the English people to deny [them] the German colonies and ask that they be all entrusted to the League? Why does he not send a message to the French people . . . to the Yugoslav people . . . to the American people?[15]

It has been argued that Wilson's failure to support his Italian followers was a "personal tragedy" for Salvemini, whose commitment to Wilsonian solutions had culminated in great disappointment.[16] His characterization as "opportunistic" of a president generally considered overly rigid in his idealism reveals the lofty standards by which Salvemini gauged his contemporaries. Once Salvemini swung against Wilson on Fiume, his opposition underscored the utter feebleness of the American president's remaining support in Italy. As in the intervention campaign, Salvemini found himself in the uncomfortable position of occupying common ground with his major adversaries, the nationalists. The man who had been called a "Mazzinian without Mazzini" was now a Wilsonian without Wilson.

On May 7, the Italian delegation returned to the Paris Peace Conference. Within a month negotiations between the Italians and the Allies were deadlocked on the Adriatic question. In a heavily censored article entitled "The Protests," Salvemini increased the pressure: "We intend to protest not only against French and English diplomats, but above all against our own."[17] As disillusionment spread over Italy's faltering status at the peace negotiations, democratic criticism focused on the prime minister. He had failed to build popular support for the moderate Salvemini-Bissolati position and had cast his lot with Sonnino and the nationalists. The liberal state strained under mounting pressure from Bolsheviks, Catholics, and aggressive nationalists. On June 19, Orlando lost a confidence vote in the Chamber of Deputies and promptly resigned.[18]

F. S. Nitti, the new prime minister, named a centrist cabinet, including a number of Giolitti's supporters. Those choices confirmed Salvemini's skepticism that Nitti would either break the Giolittian client system or achieve any success in addressing Italy's pressing needs.[19] Nitti immediately faced demonstrations, a general strike, and an abortive coup.

By late summer, while Nitti focused on domestic economic problems, his Foreign Minister Tommaso Tittoni managed to win support among the British and French for Italian control of Fiume. In early September, however, Wilson denied Nitti's appeal and signed the Treaty of St. Germain, confirming the breakup of the Hapsburg Empire and leaving Fiume outside Italian territory. Dissatisfied with the status of Fiume, Salvemini was nonetheless pleased that Italy had emerged from the war in a relatively strong position. During this period of strident bombast, his was a voice of moderation and reason. In contrast came shrill demands from the Right. Notwithstanding that the dismantling of the Hapsburg Empire had greatly enhanced Italy's security, Italian nationalists intensified their "mutilated victory" propaganda by demanding Dalmatia and imperialist domain in Asia Minor and Africa. Fiume became their cause célèbre.

On September 12 an expedition of 1,000 Italian volunteers, commanded by the nationalist poet and decorated aviator Gabriele D'Annunzio, seized Fiume without opposition from the Allied Occupation forces. A local Italian council ratified the coup by voting to give the flamboyant writer unlimited powers; defying Italian and international authority, D'Annunzio pledged to remain until Italy annexed Fiume. This poet-campaigner introduced the blackshirted uniforms, salutes, bonfires, night rallies, and other public symbols that the world would soon recognize. Another 7,000 nationalist volunteers streamed to the port city. Mussolini, both impressed and resentful, became D'Annunzio's primary advocate in Italy.[20]

Nitti opposed annexation in the face of growing nationalist hysteria. Salvemini found himself in a continuing dilemma over Fiume. In a September 18 article entitled "The Fiume Incident," he expressed dismay at the prime minister's lack of sympathy for D'Annunzio's followers. At the same time, he shared Nitti's apprehension of the serious threat represented by this episode of militarism that enjoyed the support of military authorities. He believed that the incident confirmed the prediction of his book on the Adriatic: unless the city of Fiume were annexed to Italy, it would be a source of continuing conflict. The blame, Salvemini wrote, should rest not primarily with D'Annunzio but with the military command. He hoped the poet could be convinced to return to civilian life. The great respect owed D'Annunzio for his wartime heroism, he wrote, did not give him the right to drag millions of Italians into a new war. He sensed an element of real danger in D'Annunzio's audacious adventure.[21]

The week after Salvemini's article appeared, the Italian government reacted to the Fiume incident with mixed signals. A Crown Council backed Nitti's opposition to annexation; three days later the Chamber of Deputies passed a resolution endorsing the *italianità* of Fiume. That same week, after winning a vote of confidence against the supporters of D'Annunzio on the Fiume issue, Nitti dissolved Parliament and called for general elections. He warned Allied diplomats of spreading danger and offered a compromise that appealed to David Lloyd George and Clemenceau. Wilson, however, remained adamantly opposed to conceding Fiume.[22]

Salvemini maintained a position of some subtlety in the face of an issue he recognized to be complex. Faulting Nitti and others for oversimplifying the events at Fiume as an empty scheme, he nonetheless detected selfish adventurism among soldiers who exploited the incident to prolong the material benefits of active duty after the armistice. All the while, he deplored the irresponsibility of government officials for allowing the military to make policy. He saved his most vehement reproach of Nitti for the prime minister's tolerance of Admiral Enrico Millo, military governor of Dalmatia, who had publicly recognized D'Annunzio and had vowed never to remove his forces.[23]

In Salvemini's most original analysis of the incident, he praised the motives of those, especially young officers, who went to Fiume with selfless enthusiasm. In doing so, he identified in the fall of 1919 an authentic popular impulse to pursue a cause and to fight for Italy's honor. If the seizure of Fiume was to prove a "dress rehearsal for Fascism," as some have argued, then Salvemini's perception of genuine commitment to Fiume indicated a sensitivity to the human forces—the peculiar Italian admixture of frustrated nationalism and idealistic sacrifice—that inspired young men to heroic deeds. At the same time, although he repeatedly condemned the seizure of Fiume, his critics would later twist his admiration for the enthusiasm of the young participants and his advocacy of an Italian Fiume as early sympathy for proto-Fascism.[24]

By the time Nitti dissolved Parliament, Salvemini had once again become interested in entering active politics. For more than a year he had advocated proportional representation in order to break down the old Giolittian system of manipulation and replace it with a truly democratic alternative.[25] Parliament passed the law in August, with broad support that included the new Catholic Popolari (PPI), reformist socialists, and nationalists as well as the Salvemini-Bissolati group. Passage of the law promised fairer elections, particularly in the South, where Salvemini now could run a campaign free from interference by the Giolittian machine and its local operatives, Vito and Angelo De Bellis.

At the same time, Salvemini had been forging a reform movement that could serve as a vehicle to influence the long-anticipated general elections. By July, he had proposed a merger of the Democratic League with the veterans' association known as the Combattenti as a means of enlarging the League's base and submitting to the voters a list of candidates without actually forming a political party. It was clear by the summer that Salvemini's name would appear on the list that would include reform candidates outside the ranks of the existing parties.

Salvemini's attempt to lead a political movement of veterans challenged the status quo. He sensed among the returning soldiers the kind of energy that he had admired in the more altruistic followers of D'Annunzio. Recalling the "spirit of the trenches," he believed that he shared with the young veterans a visceral revulsion for the old parties. Within their ranks he recognized the potential for leadership in the new generation, believing that "the corporals, sergeants and lieutenants of the war would be the corporals, sergeants, and lieutenants of peace."[26] He recalled from the front a "feeling of solidarity combined with the will to a new kind of political action that, freed from the entanglement of the old political parties, could prove truly useful to the country." In avoiding the old parties, he hoped to entice the Combattenti from the abstractions of tired rhetoric to his own issue-oriented *concretismo* and to field a list that balanced more experienced League members and young political novices.[27]

In the young veterans' energy and will to action, however, Salvemini also sensed a darker side. He was particularly alarmed by the publications of the

Florentine Combattenti. "It is Mussolinism and nothing else," he wrote to Ojetti, "nationalism that regards itself as revolutionism, or better put, a nationalistic state of mind in foreign politics, and a revolutionary state of mind in domestic politics."[28]

Oddly, for a man who became a staunch republican, Salvemini did not support the replacement of the monarchy with a republican constitution. As discussion of the institutional question penetrated the campaign, he opposed the calling of a constituent assembly to revisit the issue, making the conventional case for the usefulness of the monarchy as moderator among the parties. His response to an interviewer was quite pragmatic and couched in the careful phrasing of the candidate. The key issue, he answered, was fundamental reform: of peasant landholding, bureaucracy, and education. Reform had to be achieved "with the monarchy if possible, with a republic if necessary."[29]

This first postwar campaign took place in a swirl of uncertainty. In October, with D'Annunzio entrenched in Fiume, the first Fascist Congress met in Florence. In this setting of economic crisis, inflation and unemployment mounted, strikes and labor violence spread. In a message infused with nationalist overtones, the Fascists sounded a revolutionary socialist call to seize property, including factories and farmland. In spite of the list of Fascist candidates, Mussolini insisted that they were not a party but a "movement," an "antiparty," an "organization not for propaganda but for battle."[30]

It was this hypernationalism of the early Fascist movement that first caught Salvemini's attention and drove him into opposition. He was not among those who gave credence to the radicalism of early Fascism; instead, he identified the movement as anti-Bolshevist and imperialist, for no true movement of the Left would earn the implicit sympathy of state authority and bourgeois conservatism.[31]

As the Fascists met in Florence, the PSI gathered in Bologna. The revolutionaries, aroused by the Russian Bolshevik success, won control of the party under the leadership of G. M. Serrati. Their platform advocated violence, but their full slate of candidates for Parliament indicated the strength of their revisionist tradition and their reluctance to be orthodox Marxist revolutionaries.

A major competitor at the polls for the first time was the PPI, the first mass-based Italian Catholic party, launched by Sicilian priest Don Luigi Sturzo with the approval of the Vatican. In an attempt to counter the PSI, the PPI ran a campaign of reform that supported the rights of workers and small landholders and, like Salvemini, supported women's suffrage, proportional representation, and the League of Nations. When Pope Benedict XV lifted the *non expedit*, the forty-four-year-old prohibition on voting, he vastly improved the chances of the PPI to compete in November.[32]

The emergence of mass parties in the campaign suggested a genuine political upheaval. Salvemini's small Democratic League-Combattenti movement not only repudiated the traditional parties but also rejected the PPI and the PSI by name. In turn, nationalist candidates attacked the PPI, the PSI and *rinunciatari*, including Salvemini, as "anti-Italian."

By the second week of August, Fernande had gone to Paris for vacation while her husband solicited money for his campaign. Meanwhile, he escaped the oppression of the Florence summer for the town of Cavalese, nestled in the Dolomite mountains between Trento and Bolzano, where he delivered a series of ten lectures on the Risorgimento to the teachers of Trentino. Before returning to Florence, he stopped to see his old friend Ernesta Battisti, and, finding that she was struggling to publish her deceased husband's works, vowed to assist her. The escape to the Alto Adige provided him a final respite before what he knew would be a grueling campaign in Bari province.[33]

To prepare his campaign for Parliament, Salvemini targeted a number of people around Bari for a *gratis* mailing of *L'Unità*, to be followed closely by a speaking tour of the province. Salvemini arrived in Bari in the first week of September with a comprehensive and hard-hitting message, only to be confronted with the inevitable campaign intrigues. Rumors of desertion in the face of enemy fire followed him, as did the nationalist epithet *rinunciatario*. In Giolitti's *La Stampa*, irredentists of the Trento and Trieste Society labeled him the "saboteur of our victory." He also quickly found himself physically taxed by the rigors of campaigning. "The problem is," he wrote Ghisleri, "that I am no longer young. The forty-six years are beginning to weigh me down. I can no longer make more than three meetings a day!"[34]

In the political arena, he utilized historical arguments, once again walking the line between history and political activism. For Salvemini, however, this had never presented a dilemma. He readily employed historical studies in the pursuit of a cause with a clear conscience, never worrying that he could be accused of distorting the past for political gain. Thus he debated the battle of Caporetto, including a private exchange with former prime minister Salandra that he ended with Salveminian flair. After expressing his enduring gratitude for Salandra's accomplishments, he noted that the Prime Minister had also made the "great error" of signing the Pact of London.[35] Similarly, while the nationalists used the "legend" of former Prime Minister Francesco Crispi as a tool of nationalist propaganda, he published a small book called *The Foreign Policy of Francesco Crispi* that he hoped would dismantle the nationalist arguments piece by piece.[36]

Salvemini officially launched his campaign in his hometown of Molfetta on October 5, 1919, with a major address on "Combattenti and Proletariat" delivered to a large and enthusiastic crowd. The next week he received a formal endorsement from the Workers Society of Molfetta, a coalition of unions including stonecutters and ceramic workers. Their statement of support included a rebuttal of the charges that Salvemini had been a "shirker" in the Great War.

For two weeks the campaign intensified but remained peaceful. Then, in the third week of October, violence erupted, a haunting reminder of his narrow escape from assassination during his campaign of 1913. Salvemini's supporters found themselves intimidated, provoked into bloody confrontations, and arrested, all with the apparent complicity of the prefect and local police. Finally, they struck back. The target of their retaliation was the infamous "boss" of the Giolittian machine, "King" Nicola Ungaro, who once again was attempting to undermine Salvemini's campaign. At Bitonto, on October 18, some Salvemini campaigners killed "King Nicola."[37]

A war of words followed, Giolitti's *La Stampa* attributing a premeditated conspiracy to Salvemini's supporters, Salvemini denying everything in great detail in *Il Corriere della Sera*. Salvemini immediately took the offensive, firing off a telegram to the prime minister. He blamed the prefect for allowing the intimidation of Salvemini's supporters that had provoked the bloody incident, and he implored Nitti to restore order. In the exchange, Salvemini reminded Nitti that Giolitti's *mazzieri* (thugs) had cost him the election in 1913. The prime minister replied by assuring Salvemini that he was immediately dispatching an inspector general to Bitonto. The local press and the Bari nationalists and Combattenti joined the fray by exchanging countercharges.[38]

Salvemini was frustrated and angry. All he had asked for was an election free from corruption and violence, and once again the De Bellis brothers had victimized him. With the election less than one month away, the prospect was disturbing: more intimidation, arrests, and beatings of his supporters; a criminal investigation headed by a Giolittian judge and the bad publicity it might generate; and, ultimately, the potential destruction of enough voting certificates to deprive him of an election he expected to win. Even with Giolitti in temporary retirement, his shadowy regime had struck. Still, in the face of this tribulation, Salvemini kept up his spirits. In a letter thanking Luigi Albertini for his editorial support, Salvemini predicted: "the killer of King Nicola will be acquitted by the jury."[39]

By the first week in November, his campaign regained its momentum as he addressed a large Sunday morning rally at the piazza in front of the Bari train station. He made a tour around the electoral district, traveling by automobile from one poor Apulian village to another: to Casamassima, Cellamare, Montrone, Triggiano, Carbonara. At every stop, the Florentine intellectual reminded crowds of peasants and fishermen in very direct language that he was one of them, both by birth and in spirit, and that in Rome he would never violate their trust. It was for Salvemini a kind of immersion in a life he had left behind; it was a way to act out his political ideals, to abandon the office of *L'Unità* for the crucible of political warfare. He was, in a sense, back in the trenches.

He ended his campaign on November 15, election eve. Two days later, when the vote count was completed, Salvemini had won the election to the Chamber of Deputies on the crest of a resounding 28,000 votes cast for the Combattenti list while personally winning 16,000 preferential votes, making him the second-highest vote-getter in Bari province. He outpolled the top Socialist Party candidate by a wide margin, and the Combattenti won an absolute majority in many towns. However, this provincial success enjoyed by the Combattenti was overwhelmed by national results that made this one of the most significant elections in Italian history.

The old Liberal Party, the oligarchy that had controlled national politics since the Risorgimento, suffered a shocking defeat. The greatly expanded electorate, using the proportional system for the first time, handed victory to the mass parties, Socialists, and the PPI, who together won a slim majority of the 508 seats in the Chamber of Deputies. The Fascists made a great deal of noise in the campaign, but they failed to win a single seat in Parliament. The Combattenti won more votes in Bari than the Fascists won in Milan, where Mussolini lost his race. In little more than a month the number of *fasci* (local chapters) had dwindled to thirty-one, with a combined membership of fewer than 1,000.[40]

Exhausted from the campaign, Salvemini read his congratulatory telegrams and prepared to depart for the capital where he had called a meeting of the Combattenti deputies. Within days he was swamped with invitations from towns around the province, all stressing the urgency of his visit. "What do they want me to do," he wrote Tomasso Fiore, "work the miracle of St. Antonio?" A request to meet with the deputy from Altamura, Pasquale Caso, for whom he held little respect, led him to contemplate his new career:

I cannot kill Giolittismo by myself. I am one man alone. . . . I cannot work miracles. I did not promise them. I promised to work *in Rome* to defend the interests and the rights of Apulian workers; I promised to answer to them for my work.[41]

Among the more repugnant prospects of the new career was the thought that he would be expected to work with the likes of Caso to form some sort of "solid front" for the region, the very kind of political activity that had led him to label Giolitti the "Minister of the Underworld."

In fact, Salvemini went to Rome with expectations that were, at least in part, unrealistic. Although he knew that he could not destroy the Giolittian machine, he was determined to defy the unwritten rules by which it had manipulated the liberal state. He was particularly intent on defying the tradition of deputies procuring favors for their constituents. He had told campaign crowds an anecdote about voters expecting their deputies to run errands for them, one man asking a deputy to carry a pair of shoes to his wife, another asking that the deputy sell his wine for him: "If you elect me deputy, . . . do not occupy me with either shoes or . . . wine. If you want not a deputy but an errand boy, vote for someone else." He expected a political career focused on making policy, and he tried to avoid the role of agent for his constituents. "I have always blamed deputies who occupy their time asking favors," he wrote. "And now I do not wish to descend to the level of Caso [in order] to fight Caso: no, no, no."[42]

That expectation was doubly improbable because Salvemini occupied a position in a small, isolated parliamentary faction. The mass parties, the PSI and the PPI, held center stage, but their ideological incompatibility assured that Giolitti would regain the reins of policy. Some of the minor parties and factions would find a role to play with the PPI in Nitti's coalition government. However, the Combattenti were themselves divided between nationalists and Salvemini's *rinunciatari* and would thus be relegated to deeper obscurity. Unwilling to cooperate with either the PSI or the PPI, and unyielding in his opposition to Giolitti, Salvemini was destined to a political career as outsider.[43]

Shortly after his arrival in Rome, Salvemini won a minor victory. The Combattenti national committee had hoped to unify its factions behind a call for the annexation of Dalmatia. Challenging the group's right-wing faction, Salvemini won a vote in committee against annexation. This minor intramural struggle was not what he had envisioned in Parliament, but it proved revealing. He had told the voters of Bari to send him to Rome to make policy; he would spend much of his time on less noble endeavors.

Influencing policy would be particularly difficult in light of the growing crisis that rendered Parliament incapable of governing. The PSI, the largest single party, was now dominated by its revolutionary wing, which was committed to subverting bourgeois institutions; the extreme right-wing delegates abetted that antiParliamentary effort for their own reasons, blocking action and disrupting debate. Salvemini warned that Parliament might soon be caught in a torrent of nationalist and revolutionary socialist activity.[44] In response to the growing stalemate, Nitti governed by decree. This presented Salvemini with the frustrating task of reading and reacting to lengthy proclamations drafted by the bureaucracy, instead of writing laws to reform the system. It was his misfortune to join Parliament at a time when it was rapidly failing to function.

On December 21, 1919, Salvemini stepped to the podium to deliver his first parliamentary speech. With high expectations that he could bring his influence to bear, he urged the government to play a productive role in a restless postwar world. The delegates to the Paris Peace Conference, he told the deputies, were producing a "disgusting spectacle of bad faith and bad will" that troubled and disilllusioned the Italian people. The Allies and the Italian government were both being unreasonable. As he spoke, he could hear comments from various areas of the Chamber. From the extreme Left, the ranks of the revolutionary socialists, came spirited interruptions that quickly deteriorated into a shouting match with those on the extreme Right.

When he endorsed the League of Nations, he committed himself once again to an essentially Wilsonian agenda. The verbal barrage resumed. He called for the admission of Germany, international limitations on arms, termination of private arms manufacture, and protection of national minorities.

From the extreme Left came the cry, "As long as there is capitalism, there will be war!" Speaking over the interruptions, he called for Italy to take "the Mazzinian initiative of true peace." Amid the shouting, Salvemini interjected the issue of Fiume, which he addressed as a simple breakdown of military discipline. He especially blamed Nitti for failing to discharge Admiral Millo. This failure reinforced the growing public perception that order was breaking down, that anyone, by implication, could defy the government with impunity: "Popular disturbances [and] unrest in the military . . . are largely the result of the general belief that in our country no one has the duty to obey, because no one has the moral right to command."[45]

Two months into the session, Salvemini forced his first confrontation with Giolitti, who had resurfaced with his widely publicized Dronero speech of October 1919. It was a face-to-face manifestation of the campaign Salvemini had conducted in one of his best-known books, *Il Ministro della mala vita*, already in its second edition.[46] On the floor of the Chamber, the professor-turned-legislator combined precision with a sense of moral outrage. He confronted Giolitti by accusing his former foreign minister of a sinister prewar deal: "May 8, 1913, as we read in the document published by the Bolsheviks, . . . San Giuliano and the Austrian government agreed to divide Albania . . . with the right of military occupation."

As comments spread around the Chamber, Giolitti replied: "There had to be complete independence from Austria and there was an agreement with Austria on the same point."

"There is a document published by the Bolsheviks, and its authenticity has not been denied," Salvemini retorted.

"That is absolutely false," answered the former prime minister to enthusiastic applause.[47] However, the mere opportunity to lodge a public challenge gratified Salvemini and, in a sense, substituted for policy making. Benito Mussolini would later render his own evaluation: "Salvemini saw Parliament as a university faculty."[48]

Quickly such difficulties in the Chamber were overwhelmed by economic troubles and growing strife in Italy's streets and factories. As industry reconverted to peacetime production, serious shortages reappeared in coal and foodstuffs, and inflation mounted. The Nitti government revived rationing, tried to save the lira, and sponsored social reform legislation in an attempt to win support of the moderate working class.

Economic problems exacerbated political discord, and Italy began to experience its worst industrial violence since the turn of the century. Anarcho-syndicalists led railroad and postal strikes. Sit-down strikes froze production in many factories, and a general strike followed in Turin. Agricultural strikes and peasant land seizures spread from Lombardy to Sicily, while anarchists disrupted northern cities.

Throughout the spring, Nitti made gestures to labor and to socialists as the PPI threatened his coalition. The PSI showed no more interest in supporting the prime minister than did the nationalists, and on May 11, the PSI and the PPI brought down his government. Nitti reshuffled his cabinet, but his popularity waned in the face of rising bread prices and socialist demonstrations against arrests of nationalist protesters. On June 9, Nitti resigned to cheers from both Left and Right.

In July, King Vittorio Emanuele brought back Giolitti and the liberals to govern. This return to power of Salvemini's nemesis marked the supreme irony of his brief parliamentary career. He had criticized Nitti but gotten Giolitti in return. In advocating reform of the system, he was now destined to confront the man he considered most responsible for corrupting it. While others looked to the venerable five-time prime minister to save Italy from the brink of anarchy and economic collapse, Salvemini could foresee only more Giolittian manipulation.

In August 1920, Salvemini delivered an impassioned address on behalf of Bari province, documenting at length the suffering of his constituents in the face of growing food shortages, bureaucratic ineptitude, and political manipulation. "The martyrs are our women," he pled, "who keep bread out of their own mouth to give it to the man who works and the baby who must grow."[49]

By the time Giolitti assembled his final government, Salvemini had isolated himself almost entirely within the Chamber. Ideological differences had driven him further from the Combattenti. He had warned them against the anti-Bolshevist trap, against competing with the nationalists to lead the conservative charge against the proletariat.[50] In February, he resigned from the group, citing their support for the Pact of London and the prevalence of "Fascist types" in its leadership.[51]

Bissolati's untimely death had created a real void, leaving only De Viti De Marco as a trusted ally in the Chamber, and a few, including Turati, whom he respected.[52] His opponents relentlessly assailed him from the floor and in their press, the nationalists using the "anti-Italian" label and suggesting that he should serve instead in the Yugoslav parliament. Anonymous pamphlets now circulated, accusing him of "desertion" from the front. He discovered that Sonnino's *Giornale d'Italia* so badly distorted his speeches that he was forced to reprint them in *L'Unità* for accuracy.[53]

In general, Salvemini found far too many absentee legislators, friend or foe, who merely returned to Rome in response to telegrams from their parties calling them to vote, and far too few intelligent, informed public servants. The elections of 1919 had brought many newcomers into government service and a great deal of raucous behavior to the Chamber, but little evidence of wisdom.

He experienced legislative obstruction and bureaucratic tyranny that could be resolved only by fundamental reforms. As he grew more discouraged, he looked forward to resuming his life as professor-journalist.[54]

While dining at a Roman *trattoria*, Salvemini encountered Turati and his longtime collaborator and lover, Anna Kuliscioff, whom Salvemini "adored." Past political differences set aside, they talked. Kuliscioff expressed her gratitude for Salvemini's work in *L'Unità*, a gesture he would not forget. Turati understood all too well Salvemini's frustrations in the Chamber, having told Kuliscioff that the new socialist deputies knew only how to "hurl insults and make uproar."[55]

In July, Salvemini delivered a hard-hitting speech in which he extended a contentious "greeting" to the returning prime minister. The occasion was the presentation of Giolitti's cabinet and legislative program, which had led a number of orators to lionize the historical import of the event. Salvemini countered with an ironic analogy, quoting Cosimo de' Medici. Asked when he would return to Florence from exile, Cosimo had responded, "When the errors of the opposition party have made them forget my own errors."

Although his historical wit provoked little response, he scored a direct hit with his criticism of Giolitti's past practices. He raised the issue of universal suffrage, which he had supported for a decade before Giolitti had sponsored a restricted version in 1911 that had benefitted the South very little: "Honorable Giolitti, when you produced universal suffrage, perhaps you did not calculate..."

"I did it deliberately!" interrupted the prime minister.

"Then why did you interfere with the vote in 1913?" Salvemini retorted. To confront his nemesis on that campaign, in which Giolitti's thugs had tried to murder him, provided a needed catharsis.

As he launched a frontal assault on Giolittian policy and politics, the presiding officer repeatedly demanded order to quell the tumult. Summarizing Italy's serious crises, Salvemini offered a vote of confidence, not in the new government but in the Italian people:

Today there is a general prostration, and all the prostrate spirits draw close to you, Honorable Giolitti, hoping that you will save them. I am not prostrate. I have no faith in you. I am certain that Italy will save itself and will not need saviors. Therefore, I will vote against you.

Clamorous demonstrations of support roared from the left of the Chamber. Salvemini had delivered a severe reprimand to the "Minister of the Underworld," much to the delight of Giolitti's opponents.[56]

Pleased with the speech and its response, Salvemini nonetheless sensed the futility of public life. "This life is too tiring and painful for me," he wrote to Tomasso Fiore. "And I feel old. I cannot remount an election campaign. Last November's left me sick for six months. My heart, since the arthritis of the

Carso, is no longer young." As his term approached its final months, he reaf-firmed the decision. "It is evident," he concluded, "that I am a fish out of wa-ter!"[57]

Within the same week when Salvemini confronted Giolitti, he challenged Luigi Federzoni, the Chamber's leading nationalist voice who would soon emerge as a supporter of Mussolini's Fascism. Federzoni was speaking from the floor in support of the Pact of London, arguing that Italy needed the Dalma-tian coast for security reasons. As proof, he offered Austria's use of Dalmatia as a staging area for bombardment of the Italian coastline.

Salvemini interrupted, "When did they bombard it?"

"At Ancona, May 24," Federzoni responded.

Salvemini countered that the bombardment of May 24 had been attributable to the negligence of the Adriatic commander, Count Thaon di Revel: "Once we prepared, they never challenged us again."[58]

Salvemini's stormiest parliamentary confrontation came not with antago-nists of past and present, Giolitti and Federzoni, but with his future archenemy, Benito Mussolini. In the debates over the Treaty of St. Germain with Austria, Salvemini delivered an address summoning the foreign policy of Mazzini and Bissolati in a call to revise the Italian position. Deputies became raucous as he criticized first Sonnino and then D'Annunzio, the latter for his disgraceful mis-government of Fiume. As evidence, he offered incidents of corruption and theft by the poet's associates.

"From the contributions for Fiume," he alleged, "Mussolini subtracted 480,000 lire for campaign expenses." Lively comments in the Chamber hinted at the impending controversy that would accompany the publication of Salvemini's speech. D'Annunzio, said to be indignant, called Mussolini a "thief."[59]

Mussolini's response was more bellicose. Accusing Salvemini of injuring his honor, he issued an ultimatum, nominated two seconds, and challenged him to a duel. Salvemini responded by naming his own seconds, who, meeting with Mussolini's proxies, took the position that their man had documentary evi-dence and that the alleged indignity would be proven in the court of public opin-ion. Mussolini's seconds rejected the plan, and he now turned *Il Popolo d'Italia* against Salvemini in a more personal attack, renewing the nationalists' charges of cowardice in the trenches.

The incident would be easily relegated to the realm of trivia if not for the growing significance of violence and intimidation. Shortly after the Mussolini feud, D'Annunzio sent two agents to confront Salvemini. They failed to find him. But in an Italy where threats of physical attack now had to be taken seri-ously and nationalism was becoming more aggressive, Salvemini would not likely escape unscathed if he persisted in his aggressive rhetoric against the na-tionalists.[60]

That polemic heightened in November 1920, when the nationalists began to campaign against the Treaty of Rapallo, negotiated with Yugoslavia by Giolitti's foreign minister, Count Carlo Sforza. The treaty resolved the major Yugoslav-Italian border issues, vindicating Salvemini's positions on Adriatic diplomacy and thus rewarding a decade of writing and campaigning. He wired congratulations to Sforza, pledged his support in Parliament, and opened an offensive in *L'Unità*.[61]

On November 24, Salvemini opened parliamentary debate on the treaty with a motion of endorsement. As he systematically defended its terms, a shout from the poet and Calabrian deputy Luigi Siciliani interrupted: "Go tell this to the parliament in Belgrade!"

"If it were necessary to go to Belgrade to tell the truth," Salvemini fired back, "it would be a bad sign for the Italian parliament and for Italy." Recovering quickly, he spelled out his position, rebutting hecklers while invoking Cattaneo, Mazzini, and even Abraham Lincoln on behalf of the justice of the treaty. He would remember his support of the Treaty of Rapallo as the one bright spot in his legislative career.[62]

In the fall of 1920, the more immediate threat of violence and disorder appeared to come not from D'Annunzio's disciples, the nationalists, or the Fascist squads, but from the Left. Strikes had persisted throughout the spring and summer, and in September workers had seized factories in northern cities, and their councils continued production while red flags flew over the plants. Soon the "occupation of the factories" spread to include 500,000 workers throughout Italy. Gramsci interpreted the event as the workers' seizure of the means of production, the most revolutionary act in Italian history. In rural areas, armed peasants seized land with the support of the socialist farmworkers' organizations. Resentment built among property owners in the face of what many saw as a Bolshevik threat.[63]

Giolitti's reliance upon his proven practice of strategic inaction produced mixed results. His pressure on industrialists led to increases in wages and improvements in working conditions that, in turn, undermined the "occupation." The deterioration of the insurgency revealed the weakness of the Left, which, having identified itself with the uprising, now had to take blame for its failure. November's local elections confirmed Giolitti's strategy. Socialist candidates, using the slogan "war against the state," lost ground to nationalists.

Salvemini reacted skeptically. He saw little hope that labor organizations could succeed in mobilizing the resources to conduct business. Seven years later, in reaffirming that point, he would see the "occupation" also as a bungled opportunity for revolution. "The bankers, big industrialists, and big landlords," he wrote, "waited for the social revolution as sheep wait to be led to the slaughter." However, the perceived Bolshevist danger was not real. Instead of seizing the factories, the labor and socialist leaders should have occupied government

offices, postal and telegraph offices, and railroads. Failure led to disillusionment, hurling the workers and socialists into bitter recrimination. In Giolitti's
response, although the prime minister tried to appear "more socialist than the
socialists," his game was always fundamentally conservative, designed to keep
power in the hands of the same groups who controlled it throughout his career.
To the extent that the failure of the occupation had split the socialists, Giolitti
enjoyed a temporary triumph.[64]

Offsetting the failure of the Left was the general perception of Giolitti as ir-
resolute. The government's refusal to respond decisively in the face of illegal
violence and property seizure gave the impression of its own weakness, and
class resentment heightened. In December 1920, defending his vote to con-
demn Giolitti for antiworker policies, Salvemini strengthened his denunciation
of both Fascism and official complicity in Blackshirt violence. Successive governments had tolerated the violence of the squads because it had served the governments' purpose of intimidating socialists. Most importantly, industrialists
and rural landowners feared left-wing violence and began to consider financial
support for anti-Bolshevik groups. As Fascists exploited these anxieties,
Salvemini confirmed his belief in the reactionary nature of Fascist politics.[65]

In fact, the major recipient of the political contributions of the industrialists
was Benito Mussolini. Many of the socialist, syndicalist, and Futurist radicals
had left the movement after the Fascist failure in the 1919 election, and the
growing middle-class membership both challenged Mussolini's control of the
movement and forced him to accommodate its right-wing sources of strength.
By 1921, Mussolini began to redirect the movement toward goals committed to
the protection of private property and capitalism. At the same time, he began to
convert Fascism to a party structure. In March 1921, he defined its objective.
The historic purpose of Fascism, he wrote, was "to govern the nation."[66]

Giolitti, convinced that the political process was correcting itself, relied
upon his prewar clientele system. Economic threats, in the form of mounting
inflation and worries of impending depression, convinced him to retain his
1919 Dronero program of expropriation of war profits, heavy taxation of the
rich, and cuts in the military budget. By 1921 the harvest returned to normal, the
lira strengthened, and the deficit narrowed. By most measures, Italy appeared
to be recovering from the worst of its postwar travail.

Confident that the voters would applaud the recovery, Giolitti dissolved the
Chamber and called for a general election. He assembled a National Bloc, appealing to a wide range of parties, including the Fascists. Mussolini agreed and,
amid violence and intimidation, the campaign developed an antisocialist tone.

Giolitti's decision plunged Salvemini into the midst of personal crisis:
Would he pursue politics or return to academia? With little warning, he was
forced to consider his own campaign for re-election. He had lost his organized
base when he resigned from the Combattenti movement and he regretted not

having established his own newspaper in Bari province. Now he suffered the consequences of limited exposure—most of it negative—in his home region. At the same time, he was drawn back to private life. A recent recess had allowed him to resume academic work and had reaffirmed his tentative decision to return to the university. Still, he tested the waters. He agonized, projecting a best case in which he could win 9,200 votes out of the 10,000 he thought would be necessary. The prospect of candidacy in the proportional system without benefit of party affiliation was so bleak that he even let it be known that he would accept a place on the list of the Bari PSI. They stalled before answering him, not surprising in light of his unrelenting criticism of the party; and when the party finally agreed to readmit him, he rebuffed them. He could not contain his disappointment that no supporters had stepped forward to organize a public campaign to draft him.[67]

In fact, even as he discussed his prospects, he had decided against running. He was recoiling from the past two years in government at the same time he was searching for organized support and calculating the chances of winning without it. "No one feels the need to thank me for what I have done in the Chamber," he wrote Giacinto Panunzio. "Why ruin my health? Why subject myself to all this disgusting defamation and all this violence at the hands of the dregs of the country?" Giolittians would expose Salvemini and his supporters to arrests, beatings, and worse. If he could find a mass following, he would commit the "last shreds of health and dignity. But where are these masses?" he reflected.[68]

As he experienced this visceral reaction to the politics of 1921, Salvemini developed a deeper self-awareness. In saying that he would fight Giolittians and Fascists, given popular support, he also faced reality, knowing that he was no longer young enough to be quixotic. He felt that his morose outlook might not be permanent, but a consequence of having been mired too long in militant politics. At the same time, he expressed a more generalized cynicism.[69]

It is significant that at the most critical period in modern Italian history, Salvemini had acquired a loathing for politics and had begun to experience one of his chronic bouts with emotional distress. Emotional problems now accompanied physical illness, as had often been the case. He was exhausted from the rigor of his routine: commuting 175 miles between legislative sessions in Rome and lectures in Florence, trying to sleep on the train; traveling regularly 280 miles to Bari province to address his constituents' needs; and all the while publishing a weekly journal. By the time he recovered from an acute liver attack, he had become "morally tired." He wrote to Giuseppe Donati that he had "lost faith in many things":

I do not feel in myself the communicative force of Mazzini; and I do not have Marcus Aurelius's capacity to insulate himself from his ego. Mazzini detested humanity, but he had the heroism to remain among them and to work with them *for* humanity; Marcus Aurelius concentrated within himself as in a cool and immobile cloud where human stupidity did not disturb him. I do not know how to be either one or the other. It appears to me that I have lost the best thirty years of my life. And now that I want to return to academics, the spring of my intellectual energy is weakened.[70]

On May 15, on ballots without Salvemini's name, voters returned a new Chamber that deviated only marginally from the old: the PSI and Giolitti's coalition lost votes, the PPI gained, and the Fascists won their first thirty-five seats. Giolitti's gamble had failed. Mussolini now took his seat and began to conduct himself more as a conventional member of Parliament than as an insurrectionist.[71]

In spite of Giolitti's disappointment, as he reorganized his government he had reason to believe that he could preside over Italy's continuing progress. The one anomaly that disrupted the trend toward recovery was the surge of right-wing violence. Incidents of Fascist *squadrismo* spread from Venezia Giulia and Emilia to Venezia, Lombardy, Tuscany, and Umbria, as young Blackshirts assaulted socialists and destroyed party and labor union offices in the name of patriotism and order. In March, three truckloads of Fascists attacked the Chamber of Workers in Siena, supported by a police armored car, and burned down the office. In Scandicci, after authorities used artillery fire to put down an insurrection by villagers, a Blackshirt punitive expedition arrived from nearby Florence to wreck the workers' headquarters. That night, Florentines cheered the return of the triumphant procession of soldiers and Fascists. In April, truckloads of Fascists overwhelmed a small town near Arezzo, looting the offices of the mayor and of the unions of both peasants and workers and burning their furniture in a bonfire in the piazza. By election day, the death toll had surpassed 100, and much of northern Italy faced civil war.[72]

Official response was ineffective. Local prefects, police, and military commanders tolerated Blackshirt violence and in some instances supported it.[73] At the national level, while ordering the Ministries of Interior and War to punish illegal violence, Giolitti planned to co-opt the Fascists just as he had co-opted the socialists. Traditional politicians of the liberal state still opposed one another, failing to recognize the need to join forces. In discussions with other political leaders and with the king, Giolitti intimated that Mussolini could be brought into the cabinet and controlled when necessary. In response, Mussolini promised to rein in Fascist violence. Not once did Giolitti call out troops. Instead, as was his custom, his working majority now thin, he beat a strategic retreat, taking refuge in resignation, assuming he would return. It had worked before. Minister of War Ivanoe Bonomi replaced Giolitti, lost support, then encountered a damaging banking crisis. Amid the ministerial crisis, the old Giolittian Luigi Facta agreed to form a government, expecting to step aside at the proper time to facilitate his mentor's return.[74]

Just as Giolitti and his supporters underestimated Fascism, so too did Salvemini initially make a similar misjudgment. In August 1920, responding to spreading Fascist violence in northern Italy, he told Parliament that he had seen it all before. The assaults, he observed, were "identical to the painful history of southern Italy. The formula is always the same. One party assails the other with arms, and the security forces let them go."[75] Ojetti, familiar with Salvemini's prediction of the spread of political violence, observed that he tended to judge the entire peninsula on the basis of Apulia.[76]

Reacting in September to Blackshirt violence in Venezia Giulia, Salvemini blamed a passive middle class, a weak press, and the lingering Austrian political legacy for the lack of opposition. Again, he saw in this region the Giolitti government's collusion with Fascist violence as a factor.[77]

Salvemini employed a similar analysis when Fascist violence reached Florence in early 1921. In February, after a *carabiniere* shot a railway worker, Fascist assaults on unions increased as a gesture in support of "law and order." The same day, a Fascist squad broke into the offices of the Communist Union of Disabled Soldiers and murdered Spartico Lavagnini, a communist railway worker, secretary of the Union, and city councilman. Strikes spread through the city, accompanied by industrial warfare in which both police and Fascists attacked workers. On March 1, a sixteen-year-old named Giovanni Berta, wearing a Fascist badge, wove his bicycle through a crowd of workers gathered on a bridge over the Arno. The agitated crowd, believing the boy to be a Fascist messenger, surrounded him, stabbed him, and threw him into the river. Violent exchanges between Fascists and unions intensified.[78] Two days after the murder of Berta, Salvemini described the violence in Florence. He did not know which side was more brutal. The communists were stupid; the Fascists were treacherous and had *carte blanche* from the government: "This is the way Giolitti prepares *his* elections," he explained. "At one time the phenomenon of the *mazzieri* was localized in the Mezzogiorno. Today the *mazzieri*, calling themselves Fascists, are spread all over Italy and are more malicious."[79]

It is ironic that Salvemini understood Fascist violence in the context of Giolitti's normal electoral practices, while Giolitti assumed, perhaps because the methods did seem familiar, that he could control the movement when necessary. Salvemini also tended to regard the Fascists within a traditional context because of the movement's nationalist ties. He viewed official indifference to Blackshirt violence as the government's implicit support for the nationalist agenda. It is worth noting that nationalists and industrialists made a similar judgment.

Given the general lack of alarm at early Fascist violence, Salvemini's restrained reaction is unusual only in the light of his later anti-Fascist vehemence. As late as 1921, Fascism was too small and weak to be a political force.[80] Salvemini correctly estimated its lack of impact and perceived the Fascists as a threat only to the extent that conservative forces supported them and the authorities let them act with impunity. The fact that the movement was growing escaped the notice of most observers. At the November 1921 Fascist Congress, Mussolini converted the decentralized movement into the more highly structured Fascist National Party (PNF) and adopted a more explicitly conservative program. Thus, in a sense, Mussolini fulfilled Salvemini's political expectations by moving Fascism further from its radical roots.

By the time Fascism had assumed threatening proportions, Salvemini had already begun his temporary exit from active politics. After nine years of tedious editing, while authoring an average of three articles every week, he terminated *L'Unità* at the end of December 1920, consoling himself with the realization that he had made a singular contribution to Italian political journalism. "Ten years of ideas put in circulation among the youth," he wrote Rossi, "I believe should be useful indeed. Within ten years it should prepare a couple of thousand men, between twenty-five and thirty-five years, who could form the leadership class in all the parties." Knowing that his greatest success came not as a politician but as an educator, he concluded that political education was the only work worth doing. He also began to sense that the sun might set on Italian democracy before this new leadership class could save it; in fact, his hope of building a new group of leaders went largely unfulfilled.[81]

In retrospect, *L'Unità* had subjected virtually every major public issue—and most public figures—to lively, independent, intelligent scrutiny and had thus expanded the limits of political education. It provided intellectual direction and an alternative to the politics of the liberal state. In that sense, the journal prepared the Italian democratic Left to brace itself for the arrival of Fascist oppression. However, the contribution of *L'Unità*, whatever its merit, was inadequate to prevent the eventual demise of the leadership of the democratic Left, which collapsed along with the liberal state. Three decades later, reinterpreting his impact on Italian politics and reassessing his criticism of Giolitti, Salvemini would regret having contributed to the weakening of emerging democratic institutions.[82] Whether they thereby eased the rise of Fascism, the *L'Unità* collaborators would play an important part in the opposition after the March on Rome, and in turn many would be targeted by the Fascists and victimized by assault, imprisonment, and exile.[83]

Having ended his brief parliamentary career and rid himself of the oppressive obligation of publishing, Salvemini left Florence to join Fernande in Paris, where she had gone to stay with her son Giovannino, his wife, and their infant daughter. He stopped first for two weeks at Chianciano, a Tuscan town known for its thermal spas whose sulphur and calcium springs were recommended for treatment of liver disorders. The vacation provided a needed respite.

As Salvemini rested in the Tuscan hills, removed from the crucible of politics, all around him Fascism grew in new and threatening directions. By the end of 1921, membership swelled to nearly one quarter million, many newly recruited from the ranks of the lower middle class. The movement diversified geographically as well. Originally an urban phenomenon, Fascism now spread rapidly through the countryside in opposition to rural socialist organizations. Fascist squads ransacked hundreds of offices of labor groups, cooperatives, and peasant leagues. Violence spread even as Prime Minister Luigi Facta called for order. Throughout the spring and summer of 1922, Fascist squads—now numbering 140,000—blanketed north and central Italy with a systematic campaign of terror. Under the command of authoritarian Fascist *ras* (local chiefs) such as Roberto Farinacci, Italo Balbo, Leandro Arpinati, and Dino Grandi, Blackshirts swept from town to town, seizing town halls, banks, railroad stations, union headquarters, post offices, and major roads, then releasing control and moving on. In August, Fascists expanded their campaign to new major urban centers, stunning the authorities in Livorno, Genoa, and Milan. When 60,000 Blackshirts forced the removal of the Prefect of Bologna, Balbo called the event "a dress rehearsal for revolution." Farinacci explained that the revolution demonstrated the inability of the state to exercise its authority.[84]

It was just at this precise point, as Fascism grew in political magnitude in 1921, that Salvemini failed to appreciate its importance as an independent force. He criticized the government and the political leadership class for tolerating Fascists as well as the nationalists and industrialists for supporting them. He understood Fascism as a reactionary movement, dependent on traditional sources of support, unlikely to last. He could not then explain—or perhaps even understand—the broader implications of the growth and diversification of the movement, and he underestimated its revolutionary quality. It was Italy's tragedy that Salvemini was not alone in his failure to recognize the extraordinary nature of Fascism.[85]

Salvemini returned from France in October 1921 in time for classes at the University of Florence. He already was working on four books, all of which would be in print by the end of the next year. Yet he returned to academia against a menacing background of political violence. "Italy gives me a feeling of nausea that I have never before experienced in my life," he wrote to a friend.[86]

At the same time, he found new interests that rejuvenated him. He found Giovannino's daughter a delightful paradigm of beauty and health. He felt at the same time melancholic and joyous as he admired his young stepson tenderly playing with his child. Salvemini even loved the marionettes, the dolls, and the handcrafted baby carriage, all the trappings of infancy he so vividly remembered from happier days in Messina. Describing his beloved Giovannino, he burst with paternal pride: "He also involves himself in politics, naturally of the Left, and even gives lectures!!!" In this surrogate son, Salvemini found a great source of love and optimism.[87]

It was also in the fall of 1921, as Blackshirt violence spread, that Salvemini developed one of his most enduring and closest friendships. Ernesto Rossi, a twenty-three-year-old wounded veteran, law graduate, and economist, had introduced himself and was quickly accepted. Within a few months, Salvemini had begun to take Rossi under his wing, advising him particularly on the study of the South. He cautioned Rossi to employ concrete analysis and to avoid haste: "Look, examine, criticize."[88] The relationship with Rossi was warm and candid from the start, providing Salvemini with a sounding board that he intuitively trusted. "As for the contrast that you observe between my sentimental actions and my analytical mind," he wrote, "what can I say? I have noticed this myself."[89]

In March 1922, Anna Kuliscioff had lunch with Salvemini in Rome. Reporting her observations to Turati, she noted that he looked at least ten years older than he was, but that his retirement from Parliament had begun to regenerate his energy and return him to the Salvemini of old. She reminded Turati of Salvemini's intelligence and originality and said that she had invited him to return to *Critica Sociale* as a collaborator.[90]

Salvemini once again fled the Florence summer, seeking therapy at a thermal spa near Pisa before joining Fernande in Paris. By this time, the extended periods of separation had begun to produce stress as he attempted to overcome his wife's jealousy. Their 1922 correspondence contains an undercurrent of her suspicion, which he playfully dismissed as unfounded. Responding to one of her inquiries, he explained that the woman in question was a black-eyed twenty-seven-year-old. He wrote Fernande that in order for her suspicions to be justified—whether they were is unclear—he would have to be herculean. Still, while he employed humor in his letters, he also tired of her insecurity.[91]

En route to Paris, he stopped at Lake Como—an "earthly paradise"—to take notes on documents from Luigi Corti, former Minister of Foreign Affairs, then laid plans for a trip to England that would enable him to learn the language while making various political and academic contacts. Arriving in England in late August, he was captivated. He stopped in Hyde Park, listening for hours to speeches, pleased that he understood the language. Finding that many Londoners spoke Italian to him, he returned to Hyde Park to listen and practice his English. Seeing a group singing hymns, he joined them, reading the words from the hymnal. On his final evening in London, he revisited Hyde Park and was fascinated to hear an African preaching on the immaculate conception, while nearby a group of rowdy Sinn Feiners sang Irish nationalist songs. He found himself observing the city with the wide-eyed interest of a child: "London appears to me to compare to Florence today in the same way that thirty years ago Florence compared to Molfetta." With the exception of the food and the tea, he liked his "new world" more every day, particularly in contrast to Italy, where he felt he had been suffocating.[92]

In September he rented a beachfront room in Brighton, airy and light, where the landlady gave him dictation and lectures after lunch each day. Brighton presented the ideal opportunity to learn the language, because there "not even a dog knows a word of Italian or French." For a man who described his own religious views in skeptical terms, Salvemini found surprising inspiration in Brighton's parish churches—albeit a kind of linguistic, rather than spiritual, salvation. He found that he could follow the liturgy while pronouncing the words. In his first English language letter, he wrote to Bernard Berenson that he would leave the town renowned as "Saint Gaetano of Brighton":

I leave a church and I enter another. I seize all at once upon a prayers [*sic*] book; and sing and pray with all my breath, . . . often out of tune. . . . I should have many others thing to tell you about my English life and experiences, and the orrible cookering [*sic*] and the lovely country, and the various faces of his [*sic*] wonderful people. But to write this letter I have been . . . fighting with a whole library of dictionaries and grammars. And I am tired like the Creator of nature after six days of his work. And I also rest like him. Blessed be his name. Amen![93]

Language difficulties aside, his contacts with Berenson and English intellectuals now began to pay rewards as he was asked to lecture in Cambridge, Leeds, and London. Within three weeks he had accepted an offer to pay all his expenses in return for delivering a series of eight English-language lectures on Italian foreign policy at Cambridge University in the fall of 1923. Meanwhile, he published an article on the Vatican in London's *Contemporary Review* and began revising some articles to submit to *The Manchester Guardian*.[94]

As the Fascist threat mounted in the fall of 1922, Salvemini was forced to glean information from friends' correspondence. He knew that the socialists remained in disarray, weakened by the founding of the Italian Communist Party the previous year. In parliament, neither maximalist socialists nor communists would participate in an attempt to block the Fascists. In September, writing to Rossi, Salvemini amplified his blame of the entrenched interests that made up the PSI. His prediction of a further split materialized when, at the party's Rome Congress, the PSI expelled the reformists who, in turn, founded the Partito Socialista Unitario (PSU).[95]

While the Left debated, Mussolini cleverly used his position in Parliament to divide the opposition. He exacerbated tensions among Catholics by attacking in turn the Vatican, then PPI leader Don Luigi Sturzo, whom he labeled as "antipope," then the PPI itself, which he called "socialist." From the right, Salandra assembled a conservative effort to bring the Fascists into the government, an idea supported by Albertini and many others of the ruling class. The Duke of Aosta, military commander and first cousin to the king, openly supported Fascism. As Blackshirt violence raged, Mussolini waited and implicitly threatened Parliament, saying that although he preferred a peaceful solution, he could not guarantee peace if his demands went unfulfilled. His first demand was for elections so that Fascists would gain the representation they deserved.[96]

In September D'Annunzio reappeared, with a reputation and political connections that challenged Mussolini. After having been evicted from Fiume, the poet had faded from public attention. Now he was talking about leading his troops in a march on Rome, and he was negotiating with both union leaders and his friend Luigi Facta to reenter public life. The prime minister persuaded D'Annunzio to appear in Rome at a rally of veterans planned for November. Mussolini, threatened by the poet's great popularity, began to plan his own march. On a September speaking tour of northern towns, Mussolini reaffirmed his objective: "We intend to govern Italy." Meanwhile, he reassured Giolitti that he did not intend to seize power illegally.[97]

Giolitti could have returned to power. Most parties would not have blocked the move, for which Facta was simply waiting. Giolitti stalled and negotiated behind the scenes, as was his habit. He was willing to bring the Fascists into the government, but Mussolini was growing impatient. By October, Mussolini was talking openly of Fascist insurrection. At the same time, he reiterated his assurances that a Fascist government would avoid radical economic changes.

In London, as Salvemini prepared a lecture for the British-Italian League, he felt more estranged than ever from his homeland and quite happy to be absent from the turmoil in Florence. As the Fascist threat heightened, he began to anticipate the real possibility that he would be forced to flee Italy. Pleased at the response to his lecture, he wrote Fernande on October 14, "When Mussolini dismisses me as professor, I will go to England and give lectures for five guineas each. But first I must learn English better."[98]

However, Salvemini was not yet resigned to such a desperate fate. While he contemplated the prospect of forced exile, he also, surprisingly, considered returning to active politics. The impetus for such a thought was the foundation of the PSU, a party so new as to be unstained by the sins of the other parties of the liberal state. From Brighton, he wrote to Zanotti-Bianco that he could support the entire PSU platform. And in the final portion of the program, he recognized his own influence, "the fruit of all my work for twenty years." The problem, predictably, was not the PSU's ideas, but its leadership, especially Turati: "The men are the same old men *in whom I have no faith.*"[99]

Compounding the problem was the realization that a return to active politics would likely mean PSU candidacy for Parliament. That would require him to give up teaching, as he would never again put himself in the position of serving "two masters." More significantly, he realized that he lacked the "supple temperament" to convert his ideas into policy. In the unscrupulous world of Italian politics, he felt frustrated. "With my mad craving for clarity, for logic, for fairness," he observed, "I am driven to stir up difficulties, not to overcome them."[100]

As he contemplated his future, depressed and alienated by the direction of Italian politics, Salvemini lectured and busied himself with a chapter for the *Cambridge Medieval History.* He wrote very little about Fascism, continuing to rely upon friends in Italy for their judgments. He hoped that Fernande would accompany him from Paris to Italy in November. He had to lecture in Brescia and meet with PSU leaders in Milan before returning to Florence. The trip would give the two an opportunity for "a true honeymoon."[101]

Still, even as Salvemini planned his return, Mussolini's aggressiveness led him to expect the political situation to become intolerable. As Mussolini increased pressure on the government, Facta hoped to bring back Giolitti, and his cabinet tendered resignations. On the night of October 27, Blackshirts seized control of cities in north and central Italy. The next morning, Fascist squads converged on Rome from the north, west, and south, each commanded by a Fascist quadrumvir: Italo Balbo, former Alpine officer; Michele Bianchi, Milanese ex-syndicalist; regular army general Emilio De Bono; and Cesare De Vecchi, Piedmontese monarchist. The Blackshirt march was primarily a psychological ploy designed to dramatize the political crisis and provoke trauma. Lack of sufficient firepower made a violent overthrow unlikely, and the military was prepared to protect Rome. At checkpoints outside the city, armed authorities halted the Blackshirts, numbering about 20,000. Mussolini remained in Milan, repeating Fascist demands for five of twelve cabinet posts.

Mussolini's bluff now forced the ruling class to try to accommodate him. As Fascist columns gathered outside Rome, under pressure from anti-Fascists in his government, Facta finally asked King Vittorio Emanuele to declare martial law. The king and the army almost certainly could have crushed the Fascist coup. However, Mussolini had assured the king that the crown was safe, and the king preferred not to test the army's loyalty because the political leadership thought it was necessary to bring Mussolini into the government. The king refused Facta's request. Two hours later, Facta resigned.[102]

Through Salandra, the king offered Mussolini four cabinet posts. By now, however, after a series of frenzied phone calls, Mussolini had simply refused to join a Salandra government. Salandra told the king that Mussolini must be made prime minister. On October 29, after two days without a government, the king summoned Mussolini and asked him to form a cabinet. He accepted. The next day, while Mussolini was assembling his coalition government, authorities allowed the Fascists to conclude their march. Their "conquest" of Rome complete, they gathered at the Palazzo Chigi to celebrate as Prime Minister Mussolini addressed them from the balcony.[103]

Salvemini followed the events from Paris, where he had returned the last week of October. The March on Rome surprised him, but he believed that the crisis would not last long. "The Fascists," he wrote to Rossi, "will break their necks on foreign policy and financial policy. Then, what will be will be." However, although Salvemini—along with most other observers—persisted in underestimating the long-range threat of Fascism, he suffered no illusion about the immediate peril. "In these conditions, what is best for me to do?" he asked

Rossi. In the next few lines of the letter, he foreshadowed the impact of Fascism on his life:

Probably I will be dismissed; it is the least that the Fascists can do with me. . . . Let them dismiss me rather than to commit an act against my conscience and against my dignity: for example, to accept the new regime, to swear loyalty, etc. But probably they will not wait until I refuse to do something. They will send me away. And goodnight and good-bye within six months.

If Italy were not in the hands of these wild madmen, I would return quietly to Florence to give my exams, resume lecturing, and await . . . dismissal. But . . . in Italy life will not be possible except for the followers of the *duce*. Given my past, as soon as I arrive in Florence, I will be thrown in the clink or sent abroad. . . . In Italy I will be, in the best scenario, reduced to silence. Outside Italy, in a setting difficult but free, I can resume . . . my propaganda.

Beginning a new life of secrecy, he asked his new friend "Esto" Rossi to consult an older friend, the University of Florence historian Niccolò Rodolico. "If the two of you believe that I should come back, wire Fernande . . . these words: *everything calm, come*. If you believe that it would be better for me to stay here, wire: *everything perfectly calm*."[104]

NOTES

1. Quoted in Yvon De Begnac, *Taccuini mussoliniani*, Francesco Perefetti, ed. (Bologna, 1990), 220.

2. GS to PS, November 12, 1918 and January 22, 1919; to Antonio Salandra, February 2, 1919; to GLR, March 13, 1919; to Z-B, April 24, 1919, *Cart 1914*, 445–464; *La questione dell'Adriatico*.

3. GS, "Il progetto della Società delle Nazione," *Opere* III (2), 490–501.

4. GS to GLR, March 13, 1919, *Cart 1914*, 452.

5. GS to GP, May 9, 1919, *Cart 1914*, 471.

6. GS to ED, February 18, 1919, 447–448; to PS, February 19, 1919, 449; to GLR, March 13, 1919, 452–453; to GP, May 1, 1919, *Cart 1914*, 464–465; "Per chiarire le idee," *Opere* IV (1), 462–465; "Intervista" *L'Italia del Popolo* (Milan), April 26, 1919, Harvard Library;

7. GS, "Il nostro primo convegno," 588–591. See also Alceo Riosa, "L'interventismo," 536.

8. GS, "Gl'incidenti di Milano," BF, *L'U*, 686. Translation from GS, *The Origins of Fascism in Italy* (New York, 1973), 179.

9. UO, entry of April 21, 1920, *I Taccuini, 1914–1923* (Florence, 1955), 28; GS, "La mia opposizione al fascismo," *Opere* VIII, 662.

10. GS, "Rivoluzionari conservatori," in BF, *L'U*, 694. Translation from GS, *Origins of Fascism*, 217.

11. S-W, *ILF*, 510–527.

12. Rene Albrecht-Carrié, *Italy*, 96–103; JB, *LMV*, 245–264.

13. Riosa, "L'interventismo," 554.

14. Quoted in Riosa, "L'interventismo," 546. See also, BM, "Richiamo alla misura," *OO* XIII, 126–127.

15. GS, "La camicia di Nesso," *Opere* III (2), 509. Translation is from Albrecht-Carrié, *Italy*, 146–147, emphasis added. See also JB, *LMV*, 278–279.

16. ET, *Sal*, 206; MLS, *Sal*, 105.

17. GS, "Le proteste," *Opere* III (2), 527.

18. JB, *LMV*, 300–303.

19. GS, "Tristezze e speranze," *L'U*, June 28, 1919.

20. "Il programma fascista," BM, *OO* XVII, 220–221; "Colloqui e commenti," BM, *OO* XVIII, 212–213; "L'Attuale momento politico," BM, *OO* XVIII, 222; "Estrema follia," BM, *OO* XVIII, 336–337.

21. GS, "L'Incidente di Fiume," *Opere* IV (1), 471–474; to Carlo Sforza, December 20, 1919, *Cart 1914*, 532.

22. S-W, *ILF*, 540–547.

23. GS, "Postilla," *Opere* IV (1), 471–475; "Il bivio," *Opere* III (2), 540–541.

24. GS, "Postilla," 474–475; speech to the Chamber of Deputies on February 6, 1920, *Opere* III (2), 557; "Il ministro Giolitti," July 2, 1920, *Opere* III (2), 581; "Disciplina militare," *Opere* IV (1), 491; and his August 7, 1920 speech to the Chamber in *Opere* III (2), 626–631.

25. GS, "Per una riforma elettorale," *L'U*, March 30, 1918; "Per la riforma elettorale," *L'U*, May 4, and November 16, 1918; "La rappresentanza proporzionale," *L'U* November 23, 1918; "La riforma elettorale," *L'U*, July 17, 1919; "La riforma elettorale," *L'U*, August 21, 1919.

26. GS, Preface, *SSQM*, xxix.

27. GS, "I combattenti," *Opere* IV (1), 466–467; MLS, *Sal*, 114–115.

28. GS to UO, August 14, 1919, *Cart 1914*, 494; to Tomasso Fiore, July 28, 1919, *Cart 1914*, 478–479; notes on Ferdinando Bernini, "Combattenti e concorsi"; GS et al., "Le elezioni del 1919 in provincia di Bari," *Opere* IV (1), 478–482.

29. ET, *Sal*, 213.

30. "La prima adunata fascista," BM, *OO*, XIV, 43.

31. GS, "Cominciamo a intenderci?" *L'U*, October 5, 1918; see also "La mia opposizione al fascismo."

32. AK to FT, November 19, 1920, *Turati-Kuliscioff Carteggio*, V, 1919–1922 (Turin, 1977), 575–576.

33. GS to Z-B, August 10, 1919, *Cart 1914*, 491–493; to UO, August 14, 1919, *Cart 1914*, 494; to Commendator Franchi, Ditta Zanichelli, Bologna, September 8, 1919, *Cart 1914*, 500.

34. GS to AGh, October 3, 1919, 502; to UO, July 31, 1919, 480; to Fiore, August 9, 1919, *Cart 1914*, 489; PS, *Chi é Gaetano Salvemini* (Rome, 1919), WL; RC, *Salvemini e Molfetta*, 20. "Una protesta contro la candidatura Salvemini," *La Stampa*, October 24, 1919; GIS, *Diary* II, 276.

35. Salandra to GS, August 30, 1919, 498; GS to Salandra, September 2, 1919, *Cart 1914*, 499–500; GS to UO, August 14, 1919, *Cart 1914*, 495.

36. GS, *La politica estera di Francesco Crispi*, *Opere* I (3), 107–135.

37. RC, *Salvemini e Molfetta*, 19–20; ET, *Sal*, 222.

38. RC, Salvemini e Molfetta, 19–20; GS, "Elezioni in Puglia," *L'U*, October 30, 1919; "Un dialogo telegrafico," BF, *LU*, 715–716; to UO, October 23, 1919, *Cart 1914*, 508–510; to LA, October 28, 1919, *Cart 1914*, 513; to Angelo Tulli, October 16, 1948 in Pasquale Minervini, ed., *Gaetano Salvemini: Corrispondenze Pugliesi* (Mezzina-Molfetta, 1989), 252 n.

39. GS to UO, October 23, 1919, 510; to LA, October 28, 1919, *Cart 1914*, 513.

40. DeG, *Italian Fascism* (Lincoln, 1989), 29–30.

41. GS to Fiore, November 27, 1919, *Cart 1914*, 521; to Fiore, July 28 and December 6 1919, *Cart 1914*, 478–479 and 525.

42. GS, Preface, *SSQM*, xxx; to Fiore, December 6, 1919, *Cart 1914*, 525.

43. In December 1919, the Combattenti parliamentary group changed its name to the Partito di Rinnovemento Nazionale. (The name Combattenti will be used both before and after December 1919.) GP to GLR, December 6, 1919, *Cart 1914*, 526.

44. GS to Fiore, November 28, 1919, *Cart 1914*, 522.

45. GS, speech to the Chamber of Deputies, December 20, 1919, *APID*, 498–504.

46. GS, *Il Ministro della mala vita* (Florence, 1910) in *Opere* IV (1), 73–141.

47. GS, "Noi rinunciatari," *APID*, 924–926.

48. Quoted in De Begnac, *Taccuini mussoliniani*, 219.

49. GS, "Le condizioni generali della nostra provincia" (Discorso pronunziato alla Camera Italiana), August 12, 1920 (Bari, 1920).

50. GS, "Un grave errore," *Opere* VIII, 553–555.

51. GS, "Una dimissione," *L'U*, February 12, 1920; UGM to GS, February 11, 1920, *Cart 1914*, 538.

52. GS to UO, June 14, 1920, *Cart 1914*, 546; to Giancinto Panunzio, December 15, 1919 in *Cart 1914*, 531.

53. GS to ED, January 27, 1920 in *Cart 1914*, 534; "Un'anonima sconcezza," January 29–February 5, 1920 and "La curiosità di Tecoppa," March 11, 1920, *L'U*.

54. ET, *Sal*, 223–226; GS, "Impotenza,"*Opere* IV (1), 485–488; to ED, July 5, 1920, *Cart 1914*, 547; to Fiore, July 8, 1920, 548.

55. ET, *Sal*, 186 n.; FT to AK, March 24, 1920, *Turati-Kuliscioff Carteggio*, V, 444, quoted in Albrecht-Carrié, *Italy*, 550 n.

56. GS speech to the Chamber of Deputies, July 2, 1920, *Opere* III (2), 579–610; to LA, July 9, 1920, *Cart 1914*, 549–550. See also Frank M. Snowden, *Violence and Great Estates in the South of Italy* (Cambridge, 1986), 136–139.

57. GS to Fiore, July 8, 1920, *Cart 1914*, 548, and December 2, 1920, *Cart 1914*, 558.

58. GS, speech to the Chamber of Deputies, *APID* III, 2771–2787; to LA, July 9, 1920, *Cart 1914*, 549–550; "Il ministero Giolitti,"*Opere* III (2), 607–610.

59. GS, speech to the Chamber of Deputies August 7, 1920, *Opere* III (2), 612–631; "Querelles d'Allemands," *L'U*, August 19, 1920.

60. ET, *Sal*, 234–236.

61. GS to Carlo Sforza, (after November 12, 1920), *Cart 1914*, 556; to Sforza, end of November 1920, *Cart 1914*, 557; "Il primo passo," *Opere* III (2), 635–637; "Il conte Sforza"; "L'eterna bugia"; "Quanti sono gl'italiani in Dalmazia?," *L'U*, November 18, 1920.

62. GS, "Il Trattato di Rapallo," speech given to the Chamber of Deputies, November 24, 1920, *Opere* III (2), 637–653; ET, *Sal*, 237–239.

63. Paolo Spriano, *L'occupazione delle fabbriche, settembre 1920* (Turin, 1964).

64. GS, "Il metodo giolittiano," *Opere* VIII, 562–565; *The Fascist Dictatorship in Italy* (New York, 1927), 25–34; Spriano, *L'occupazione*, 135–136.

65. GS, "Per un voto alla camera," BF, *L'U*, 780–784.

66. "Dopo due anni," BM, *OO*, XVI, 212. See also DeF, *il riv*, 590 ff.

67. GS to Panunzio, March 13, 1921, 10–11; April 15, 1921, 13–16; April 16, 1921, 16–17; April 20, 1921, 18; to GD, July 5, 1921, *Cart 1921*, 21–22. Preface, *SSQM*, xxxii.

68. GS to Panunzio, April 15 and 16, 1921, *Cart 1921*, 13–17; to Ettore, Rota, September 5, 1921, *Cart 1921*, 27; to Niccolò Rodolico, September 26, 1921, *Cart 1921*, 30; Preface, *SSQM*, xxxii.

69. GS to G. Panunzio, April 15, 1921, 15; to Luzzatto, July 5, 1921, *Cart 1921*, 18–19.

70. GS to GD, July 5, 1921, *Cart 1921*, 21; Preface, *SSQM*, xxxi-xxxii.

71. DeF, *il riv*, 602 ff.; S-W, *ILF*, 585–596.

72. GS, *Fascist Dictatorship*, 54–75.

73. DeF, *il fas* I, 26–35.

74. S-W, *ILF*, 603–612.

75. GS, speech to the Chamber of Deputies, August 2, 1920, *APID*.

76. UO entry of April 21, 1920, *I Taccuini*, 28.

77. GS, "Politica ambigua," *Opere* III (2), 631–634.

78. *CdS*, February 28, March 1–5, 1921; Roberto Cantagalli, *Storia del fascismo fiorentino, 1919–1925* (Florence, 1972), 147–175.

79. GS to Gino Luzzatto, March 3, 1921, *Cart 1921*, 9–10.

80. DeF, "Fascism" in PC, ed., *Historical Dictionary of Fascist Italy* (Westport, Conn., 1982), 207; DeG, *Italian Fascism*, 30.

81. GS to ER, September 24, 1922, 83; BF, *L'U*, 11–20; Lamberto Borghi, "Gaetano Salvemini e *L'Unità*" in *Educazione e Autorità nell'Italia Moderna* (Florence, 1967), 136–156; Alessandro Levi, "*L'Unità* periodico (1911–1920) del Salvemini," *Il Ponte*, November 1945; ET, "*L'Unità* di Salvemini"; Giuseppe Petraglione, *L'Unità di Salvemini* (Trani, 1945); Leonardo Sacco, "*L'Unità* e l'intenso sodalizio di Giustino Fortunato con Salvemini," *La Gazzetta del Mezzogiorno*, January 31, 1979; *La cultura italiana del'900 attraverso le riviste*, IX, *passim.*; EG, "Salvemini" in ES, *Sal*, 192–210; John M. Cammett, *Gramsci*, 31–34; Paolo Spriano, *Storia di Torino operaia e socialista* (Turin, 1972, 2nd ed.), 262–264; Rota, "Una pagina," 379.

82. GS, Introductory Essay, AWS, *IGE*, xxi.

83. ET, "Nota biografica," 230–231; Paolo Alatri *Le origini del fascismo* (Rome, 1956); RV, *Il dopoguerra, passim*.

84. DeF, *il fas* I, 252–280.

85. On Salvemini's response to early Fascism, see MLS, *Sal*, 122–127; DeC, *Sal*, 330–334.

86. GS to Oliviero Zuccarini, February 16, 1922, *Cart 1921*, 45; to GF, March 22, 1922, *Cart 1921*, 48–49.

87. GS to ED, August 19, 1921, 24–25; to Rota, September 5, 1921, 28; to ED, March 22, 1922, *Cart 1921*, 49–50.

88. GS to ER, November 6, 1921, *Cart 1921*, 31–35.

89. GS to ER, April 3, 1922, *Cart 1921*, 51.

90. AK to FT, March 12, 1922, *Turati-Kuliscioff Carteggio*, V, 848.

91. GS to FS, April 21, 1922, *Cart 1921*, 53–54; to FS, August 27, 1922, 67; August 29, 1922, 67–69; September 22, 1922, 81–82; October 14, 1922, 90–92; October 19, 1922, 96–97; October 23, 1922, *Cart 1921*, 97–99.

92. GS to ED, March 22, 1922, 49–50; to UO, May 30 and July 20, 1922, 55–56; to FS, August 5 and 29, 1922, 59–60, 68; to MB, late August, 1922, 65; to Enrico Bassi, August 31, 1922, 69–70; to ER, September 6, 1922, *Cart 1921*, 73–74.

93. GS to BB, October 6, 1922, *Cart 1921*, 86.

94. GS to FS, September 2, 6, and 22, 1922, *Cart 1921*, 70–72, 80–81; to ER, September 6, 1922, *Cart 1921*, 73; to MB, September 6 and 8, 1922, *Cart 1921*, 75–76, 78–79; "The Roman Question," *Contemporary Review*, September 1922, 297–303.

95. GS to ER, September 24, 1922, *Cart 1921*, 83. See also NT, *Carlo Rosselli dall'interventismo a "Giustizia e Libertà"* (Bari, 1968), 105.

96. "L'Attuale momento politico," BM, *OO* XVIII, 218–222; "Chiarificazioni," BM, *OO*, 252–253; "L'Ultima discorso dal banco di deputato," BM, *OO* XVIII, 289–293; "Noi e il partito popolare"; "Ai fascisti romani," BM, *OO* XVIII, 318–20, 330–331.

97. "L'Azione e la dottrina fascista dinnanzi alle necessità storiche della nazione," BM, *OO* XVIII, 416. See also "Discorso di Cremona," BM, *OO* XVIII, 423; "Dal malinconico tramonto liberale all'aurora fascista della nuova Italia," BM, *OO* XVIII, 434–435; DeF, *il fas* I, 302–309.

98. GS to FS, October 7, 1922, 87–89; to ER, October 7, 1922, 89–90; to FS, October 14, 1922, *Cart 1921*, 90–92.

99. GS to Z-B, October 16, 1922, *Cart 1921*, 93–94 (emphasis in the original); to ED, October 17, 1922, *Cart 1921*, 95–96.

100. GS to Z-B, October 16, 1922, *Cart 1921*, 93–94.

101. GS to FS, October 17 and 19, 1922, *Cart 1921*, 94–95, 96–97.

102. Antonino Répaci, *La marcia su Roma: mito e realtà* (Rome, 1963) I, 503–578; II, 76–77, 150–153, and 362–375; Efrem Ferraris, *La marcia su Roma veduta dal Viminale* (Rome, 1946), 87–123; Marcello Soleri, *Memorie* (Turin, 1949), 146–153; DeF, *il fas* I, 303–357.

103. Ferraris, *La marcia su Roma*, 119–123; Répaci, *La marcia su Roma*, I, 571–613; II, 354, 370– 71; Soleri, *Memorie*, 153–159; DeF, *il fas* I, 357–387.

104. GS, *Mem*, 5; to ER, October 29, 1922, *Cart 1921*, 100–101.

Chapter 7

The Making of an Anti-Fascist

Better Mussolini than Bonomi, Facta, Orlando, Salandra, Turati, Baldesi, D'Aragona, Nitti. Until there is a series of new leaders . . . , we must prevent a return to the old leadership and let Mussolini continue to misgovern. . . . Mussolini serves the useful function of crushing the old oligarchies. These old oligarchies must never regain power.

Gaetano Salvemini, 1922[1]

Before Salvemini could possibly become an anti-Fascist, Fascists were, from the very beginning, strongly anti-Salvemini, and when eventually Mussolini came to power, Salvemini's place in the ranks of the opposition was already well established.

Roberto Vivarelli, 1967[2]

While in Paris contemplating a return to Florence, Salvemini learned that he had become the focal point of protest within the university's faculty. Girolamo Vitelli, Professor of Greek Literature and a longtime associate with whom he had worked on an educational reform commission, had raised questions before the faculty senate about Salvemini's "anti-Italian" activities abroad. He explained to Vitelli that he had been "silent" on the Adriatic issue for two years and had neither written nor spoken on Italian politics while in England.[3]

Friends described the deteriorating political climate in Italy, and their advice reflected inherent contradictions that made his decision to return to Italy more perplexing. Umberto Morra told of being ousted from a cafe for refusing to stand at the singing of "Giovinezza," the Fascist anthem. Salvemini heard from the town of Cremona of the savage activities of Roberto Farinacci, the local Fascist *ra*. Gino Luzzatto, while warning of Mussolini's dictatorial tendencies, at the same time took comfort in the return to publication of a number of news-papers, and he encouraged his friend to return. Vitelli informed him that the faculty had unanimously approved his one-year leave of absence, and they thought that the dispute over his reappearance at the university would subside by Christ-mas. Gaetano Mosca advised that he could return without being bothered. Especially helpful was the heartfelt letter from a student reassuring his mentor that the student body stood firmly behind him.[4]

Within two weeks of the Fascist March on Rome, Salvemini made his decision. Based largely on the encouragement of friends, he planned a hasty trip to Florence, but only to administer examinations and to pick up books and papers that he needed in England. He would then leave, until political conditions favored a permanent return. In a declaration ironically echoing a past exchange, he wrote to Prezzolini: "No militant politics, but works of culture." He would write books, teach history, and leave politics to the unscrupulous.[5] This "quietist" philosophy was precisely the point on which he had criticized Prezzolini's editorship of *La Voce* more than a decade earlier.

The return to Florence proved unsettling. His reputation seemed to be in some peril because many believed that he had left out of fear and fatigue rather than as an act of political protest; others would say that he was only posing as an exile, imitating Mazzini. He told his wife that his primary reason for returning was to prove that he was not afraid. Sensitive to such allegations, he thus remained ambivalent about the brevity of his stay. Underlying all such considerations was the chilling prospect of traveling without benefit of a passport.[6]

He immediately began to feel that he should have remained abroad. Florence was becoming the most intensely Fascist of all cities. The faculty, which had granted his leave request in part to prevent local Fascists from disrupting his classes, now reversed its decision. That ruling, in turn, undercut his formal request to the Ministry of Education. "Who knows," he noted with ironic foresight, "whether at the end of this I might not be discharged as a professor and go to the United States?"[7]

Having vowed to exit active politics, Salvemini decided to record his thoughts privately. "In my desperate decision to abandon militant politics," he wrote, "perhaps this diary will permit me to discharge my electricity within myself rather than to let it explode in public." The diary thus serves as a valuable record of his responses to some of the most crucial events of his time. Most important, it fills the void created by his public silence. He felt an obligation to record the events of the day in order to understand Mussolini's rise to power, and because he hoped to use the diary as notes for a book on Fascism, it becomes a significant document in its own right. He closed his initial entry with an uncertain vow: "Absolute silence in politics. . . . I must succeed in overcoming all the impulses that continually draw me toward politics. But will my temperament prevail?"[8]

The first test of this vow of public silence came within days of the initial diary entry. He promised Piero Gobetti a letter on Fascism to be published in *Rivoluzione Liberale*. As he had feared, his temperament got the best of him. His need to remain aloof was conscious, if not entirely rational. "Fifty and tired," he sensed a new political crisis in which he would have "nothing to say, nothing to do."[9] A tone of despair frequently punctuated the diary: "This is the dreadful condition to which I am reduced: I have no faith in either Mussolini or Federzoni, nor in the adversaries of Mussolini and Federzoni."[10]

Of all the parties, only the PSU showed him promise, but he had little desire to join. He did not wish to be a minority within a minority. Twenty years had been enough. He felt strangely detached from the political struggle. "I tried to be the brakeman in 1919," he wrote, "and I thus contributed to unleashing two years of Fascist assassins. . . . I have no wish to be the brakeman a second time." After some months of confusion, he considered reopening *L'Unità*; meanwhile, he preferred to work in the British Museum, completing his history of the Triple Alliance and reading Italian newspapers four days late.[11]

Among his more important diary entries is an attempt to explain Fascism one month after the March on Rome. He interpreted the movement essentially in the context of European postwar disillusionment. In Italy, he saw evidence of unfulfilled popular expectations, of a sense of diplomatic defeat bred by nationalist propaganda, and of both hopes and fears of revolution. If Fascism originated in a spontaneous bourgeois reaction against the fear of left-wing violence, it was also buttressed by the military, police, *carabinieri*, and courts. Thus Fascism had its roots planted firmly in the moral defects of the "leadership class" that had already discredited the Constitutional system. He saw direct continuity between Giolitti and Mussolini: "The 'dictatorship' of Mussolini is not new," he wrote on November 29. "Giolitti was dictator from 1902 to 1913."[12]

Diary entries and letters written in the months following the Fascist coup reflect Salvemini's close scrutiny of the Fascist movement. By the spring of 1919, the first "Fascist coalition" had emerged: unemployed veterans, generals, and industrialists. Using the industrialists' financial support, Mussolini then took over this coalition in the name of anticommunism. Fascism had come to Florence in February 1921, and now local "Fascists of the first hour" were being challenged by new Fascists who were taking over political offices and competing for control of the movement. Mussolini, once preoccupied with D'Annunzio, no longer feared him. From an antisubversive movement, the Fascists had in 1921 and 1922 become antiparliamentary and were now moving against universal suffrage. Violence spread. Mussolini, he wrote, was merely a "bass drummer" for the military, nothing else—"an exaggerated Crispi." At some point, he expected the Fascists to initiate an international crisis and to provoke foreign intervention by ruthlessly repressing worker and peasant protests. Most remarkable in these early observations was his ability to see both complexity and change in a movement that many labeled simply anti-Bolshevik. The biggest liability was his tendency to overplay the role of the military.[13]

The return to Italy quickly brought Salvemini to his senses. After a few days in Florence, he understood his choices: preserve his job and a chance to resume political activity by remaining in Italy; or leave behind both teaching and future political options. Regardless of his yearning for the serenity of the British Museum, Salvemini decided to face the reality of at least half a year in Italy.[14]

Resigned to living in Florence through much of 1923, he resumed academic duties and some social contacts. He was assisting his sister-in-law Lidia's thesis in medieval history and was busy reading three others, including those of Ernesto Sestan and Nello Rosselli, soon to be one of his most devoted protégés.[15] Meanwhile, he practiced English with another political disciple, Marion Cave of the British Institute of Florence, who translated his lectures. Even then, in the midst of his political malaise, he responded to the French occupation of the Ruhr Basin by submitting articles to be published anonymously in *The Manchester Guardian* and in Giuseppe Donati's new journal, *Il Popolo*, which had become the organ of the PPI.[16]

The latter case was especially revealing. Donati was a left-wing Catholic activist and a former student in Florence whose politics bore Salvemini's influence. Salvemini declined Donati's request to collaborate in the writing of *Il Popolo* because he could not bring himself to affiliate with the Catholic party, even through its press. Nevertheless, he found the idea alluring, especially at the very moment he had suspended political writing. "No matter how old and tired, I am always a thoroughbred," he responded. He agreed instead to submit unsigned articles. "I am your friend," he told Donati. "I feel a duty to help you. . . . I remain always the same, uncivilized, outside all parties."[17]

The irony of Salvemini's self-imposed censorship is that controversy stalked him in spite of it. The publisher's release of his book on the Italian workers' movement produced a polemic from Turati, who denounced him for using the arguments of conservative economists and even Fascists.[18] Meanwhile, Prezzolini's *La coltura italiana* appeared, characterizing Salvemini as an example of the fusion of history and action, a writer who used current affairs to attract an audience to the past. It was a fair judgment from a former colleague who would later find such an appraisal more difficult.[19]

As Salvemini followed this newly restrained approach to political journalism, he explored its limits. His plan to publish a diplomatic history based on secret documents assured that he would not achieve the anonymity he claimed to covet.[20] An article published in April 1923 served notice that pseudonyms would not deflect attention. The article was one of those published by Donati in *Il Popolo,* criticizing the French occupation of the Ruhr and blaming French nationalists and steel industrialists for undue influence on the policy.[21] Two hours after the edition reached the newsstands, Rome was abuzz with controversy. Both the French Embassy and the Italian Foreign Ministry tried frantically to identify the author. Donati, keeping the secret, urged Salvemini to persist. Even in conforming to his new constraints, he created controversy.[22]

In April 1923, Salvemini discussed politics with a young man from Milan, a left-wing, anti-Fascist Catholic who opposed Don Sturzo as an opportunist. He advised the man to avoid any anti-Fascist bloc that would promise to topple Mussolini only to replace him with the "old *camorre* [gangsters]." Mussolini served the useful function of destroying the old oligarchy, and that group should never be allowed to regain power.[23] A month later, Salvemini suggested a coalition including Sturzo, Albertini, Amendola, and metalworkers' leader Bruno Buozzi, an extraparliamentary, anti-Giolittian alternative to a military dictatorship.[24]

Salvemini had expected Mussolini's government to fail within six months; but in the spring of 1923, it showed little sign of collapse. In his correspondence, rejecting a return of the old ruling class, he gave some impression of sympathy with Mussolini. This impression in part derives from the hyperbole Salvemini used in his letters. Responding to talk of the prospect of a military solution, he wrote that he preferred even Mussolini to a military dictatorship. He warned of the danger implicit in a parliamentary coalition of old leaders. "The country could not tolerate these people for two weeks," he wrote. "I would ask Mussolini for a new march on Rome, and I would take part."[25]

The supreme irony of this period of political inactivity is that, in early 1923, in the midst of what is considered his political hiatus, Salvemini helped to launch the Florentine anti-Fascist movement. In January, Carlo Rosselli and "Esto" Rossi approached him with the idea of chartering the "apolitical" Circolo di Cultura (Cultural Club). Actually, the group had existed informally since December 1920, when a group of about twenty friends, students, and professors, including Salvemini, had begun to meet weekly in the office of lawyer Alfredo Niccoli to discuss political, economic, and social issues. Rosselli and Rossi now hoped to expand the group. Skeptical of their ability to find enough members and to function free of Fascist interference, Salvemini nonetheless joined. In February 1923 he met the two, as well as a few university associates, to inaugurate the Circolo. The group quickly exceeded fifty members, necessitating a move to larger quarters, a fifteenth-century palace on the Borgo S. Apostoli near the Arno, where Rosselli assembled a library of political books and reviews.[26]

In the highly polarized setting of that day, the club quickly gravitated toward politics and gave Florentine anti-Fascists a kind of oasis in the midst of escalating Blackshirt brutality. Within the privacy of the palace hall, Salvemini lectured regularly on political topics.[27] On the strength of his personality, his status, and his moral influence, he quickly emerged as leader, and members began to refer to the group as the "Circolo Salvemini." As the police took notice, they employed the same name. This group of students and associates, sometimes known as the "*scuola* Salvemini [Salvemini school]," provided him with a new "family." He would later refer to Ernesto Rossi as his "eldest son" among what would be a whole generation of intellectual offspring. What he could not have anticipated was the suffering and tragedy that awaited him in these promising new relationships.[28]

Salvemini also met privately with numerous political figures and thus kept alive channels of communication. Among them was former Foreign Minister Carlo Sforza, who had resigned his post as ambassador to France in protest of Mussolini's appointment as prime minister. Sforza spoke with esteem for Amendola and Sturzo and with contempt for Mussolini, passing along numerous anecdotes to a willing listener. Salvemini was particularly pleased that Sforza praised *L'Unità* as a rare and intelligent journal.[29] While at the British Institute in early 1923, Salvemini encountered the historian Guglielmo Ferrero, who proceeded to lecture him on the need to remain "*contro corrente*" (in opposition). Salvemini's diary reflects the irony he saw in the occasion: "When was Ferrero ever *contro corrente?*" he wrote. "Nearly all I have done for twenty years is to remain *contro corrente.*"[30] The diary also records Piero Gobetti's comments praising him in a public lecture for influencing an entire young generation of Italians. "That I have had a great influence on the culture of Gobetti and another thousand young Italians seems clear to me," he wrote. "But on Italian culture, not at all."[31] Shortly thereafter, while conducting research in Rome, he was hailed by Giacomo Matteotti, socialist deputy and PSU founder, who promptly invited him to join the new party. In an implicit reference to Turati, Salvemini replied that there was no hope of his return to socialist ranks because he lacked confidence in the old leadership.[32]

The diary provided Salvemini with an unusual opportunity to express candid self-appraisal. On the fourteenth anniversary of the Messina earthquake, he found the memory so painful that he could maintain his sanity only by suppressing it. Weighing prospects for political action, he concluded that he had no base of support, even in southern Italy. Immediately after the war, he had seen the Combattenti as promising, but he quickly found them to be a group of "scoundrels." In the North he remained politically paralyzed in a hostile environment. Thus his decision to abandon organized politics seemed to him well founded. In May 1923, another reformist socialist whom he respected approached him about a return to politics. Reminding him of the continuing political support that he enjoyed among the peasants of Apulia, Giuseppe Patruno asked Salvemini to state his conditions for a return to public life. Salvemini's response was as unrealistic as it was predictable. Upon Mussolini's fall from power, a new government would have to take power, one he could trust and whose legislative candidates he could approve. He would then run as a government candidate in a propaganda-free campaign. When another Apulian friend persisted in soliciting his candidacy, he responded that he would consider the right cabinet position, but not a seat in the Chamber. Another campaign was unlikely.[33]

The day after Gobetti's lavish praise, Salvemini contemplated his political successes and failures. "My friends and my enemies attribute my failures to my temperament—sharp, resentful, intransigent, critical, instinctively adversarial." He was convinced that they were wrong, that his failures were the result not of personality conflicts but of the incompatibility of his ideas. He recalled such notable successes as universal suffrage, the Treaty of Rapallo, and the teachers' movement. However, when he had championed the cause of the South, he had run into resistance and had been forced to become polemical and uncompromising.[34] Responding to a compliment from an old friend and political supporter in Molfetta, Giacinto Panunzio, he noted the more constructive side of his personality: "If I have succeeded in influencing men like you, I owe it to my ferocious rigidity."[35] In a rare introspective mood, Salvemini pondered the burden of his own prescience. To anticipate changing political conditions excessively would lead to inertia and detachment and would render him, more than ever, an "unheeded Cassandra."[36]

In addition to passages revealing personal insight, the diary contains a wealth of commentary on Italian politics and postwar diplomacy, recorded in anticipation of a book on Fascism. In April 1923, he detected a signal that Mussolini was moving his government toward antiparliamentary violence. The occasion was a PPI Congress in Turin, the first anti-Fascist stance by a convention of a political party. Salvemini's instincts, as usual, proved reliable. This PPI provocation deepened the party's rift with the Vatican and led Mussolini to dismiss his Popolari ministers, part of an intensifying three-way contest between the prime minister, the Vatican, and the PPI.[37]

Fascism began to occupy his thoughts with increasing insistence. He recorded some early anecdotal accounts of the growing tension that began to invade everyday life in Italian cities. Donati and some of his associates had experienced incidents in theaters in which much of the audience had either refused to stand for "Giovinezza" or had demanded that the royal march be played instead, and had demonstrated for the king and against Mussolini. He also heard of anti-Fascist demonstrations in Messina, Catania, Palermo, and Calabria.[38]

Salvemini's most interesting analysis of Fascism is the theme of a diverse and changing movement. This appraisal showed some elements of the now widely accepted view that the movement was fragmented into competing groups. He observed that this internal conflict occupied more and more of Mussolini's time.[39] For example, even as Mussolini was moving toward the right, some conservative forces remained suspicious of him.[40] Salvemini maintained that although originally Fascism had been a spontaneous movement of the lower and middle bourgeoisie, now bankers and large industrial and farming interests joined them, along with the military bureaucracy and reactionaries in the civil service. The regular army, he heard, resented the Fascist militia at the very time that Mussolini was regularizing it. Salvemini now saw the Fascist government moving toward military despotism. Nationalist influence further ensured the rightward tendency as the Italian Nationalist Association merged with the Fascist Party. Although the Fascist left remained, Mussolini's reported break with revolutionary syndicalist Michele Bianchi documented this rightward trend. "The old Italy prolongs itself in the new," Salvemini observed. "And history is always the same."[41]

As the Fascist movement changed, Salvemini noted that Mussolini had been falling under the influence of the worst elements of his party. "By himself, he would not be a bad man: he has tried to surround himself with experienced men; but his followers take his hand and lead him where he does not wish to go."[42] Salvemini soon modified this appraisal, however. In rejecting a proposal to support Bonomi, he mused, "At least with Mussolini, the positions are more clear. He browbeats both Bonomi and us." To support Bonomi's reacquisition of power would only lead to his cooperation with Giolitti "against Mussolini and us."[43] His partially sympathetic treatment of Mussolini would soon end, but for the moment he mused that he might even write a biography of the man.[44]

While in Rome, he talked to De Viti de Marco and Guglielmo Zagari, colleagues at *L'Unità*, who gave Mussolini's government a mixed review, criticizing his financial administration but crediting him with disciplining the country. Recording their comments in his journal, Salvemini noted, "The trains run on time. Contributors voluntarily pay their taxes because they believe that they will help balance the budget." He then responded skeptically to his friends' assessments: "It is a pity that [these taxpayers] are destined to be deluded."[45]

Throughout 1923, Salvemini continued to record a number of incidents of repression and violence. He heard reports of local elections in which Fascists threatened castor oil and beatings to voters who refused to support the party list. He heard that Fascists had assassinated fifty-eight persons, many of whom were found in the Po River. In February, amid reports of mass arrests of communists throughout Italy, he learned of the arrest in Turin of his friend Gobetti because of the anti-Fascist views expressed in *Rivoluzione Liberale*.[46]

Salvemini's decision to avoid publication in Gobetti's journal may have temporarily deflected the scrutiny of the police. By the spring of 1923, however, he began to feel the Fascist threat closing around him. One of the first indications was an account from a friend that Mussolini had inquired directly of Giovanni Gentile, Minister of Public Instruction, about him. "One fine day, when they do not know what else to do to save the country," Salvemini reflected, "they will also put me in prison." At the same time, he read the new law empowering the cabinet to dismiss university professors for undermining public confidence in its work.[47]

The May 1923 elections brought the political pressure literally to his door. On the morning of election day, a Fascist knocked and announced that he had an automobile to transport Salvemini to the polling place. He graciously refused, announcing his intention to abstain. A few minutes later, five more Fascists appeared, demanding to know if Salvemini truly intended to abstain.

"Yes, it is true," he responded.

"For what reasons?"

"No law requires me to explain the reason for my abstention. I have the right to abstain and I abstain."

"Be careful that you understand the consequences of your abstention."

"I am being careful. And I have decided not to change my mind."

"To abstain indicates opposition to Fascism."

"You have the right to interpret my abstention as you wish. As for me, I know that if I vote, I show that I am afraid of threats and that gives proof of cowardice."

"We have not threatened you. We have only said to be careful of what you are doing."

"Precisely, these are your words; and I have understood them perfectly."

"Well, then. I will make a note on my list of your refusal to vote. We have four witnesses."

"There is no need of witnesses. There is no danger that I will betray myself."

"You are not a good Italian."

"In this moment I serve my country by refusing to perform an act that would be cowardly."

"Well, then, we understand each other."

"Good day."

Reflecting upon the incident with Carlo Rosselli and Piero Jahier, Salvemini noted that although the conversation with the Fascists had been quiet and proper, he wondered if he had been targeted for singular treatment.

As accounts of the elections reached him, he heard that many voters were driven like frightened animals to the voting places and that the Fascists voted for large numbers who were absent or dead. He recognized these as "southern elections."[48]

Two weeks after the elections, Fernande informed her husband of a disquieting incident in Paris. The day after visiting Count Sforza, her son Jean was called by the Italian ambassador and interrogated about Sforza. During the interview, the ambassador also asked about Salvemini. Jean, his mother said, told the ambassador only what he wished to tell him. Nonetheless, it was clear that government authorities, both local and national, were beginning to focus on Salvemini.[49]

Further cause for concern came in early June when he heard that when authorities had searched Gobetti's house, they had seized a letter in which Salvemini had predicted Mussolini's imminent downfall. That same week he learned that Gentile, his ultimate boss at the centralized Ministry of Public Instruction, had formally joined the Fascist Party.[50]

Mussolini's campaign for electoral reform provided the context for further political crisis through the spring and early summer. His electoral bill, named after its Fascist sponsor, Giacomo Acerbo, proposed to alter the system of proportional representation by awarding the largest party two-thirds of the 535 seats in the Chamber of Deputies, provided that the party won at least 25 percent of the votes. The law was designed ostensibly to overcome the deadlock between the PSI and the PPI. Because it furnished the Fascist Party with a convenient tool for controlling Parliament, the Acerbo law also threatened the other parties. Salvemini believed that the law would enable the Fascist regime to entrench itself for an extended period in an atmosphere of cowardice.[51] It would make the elections a farce; thus, if the law passed, the best recourse would be abstention.[52]

At the end of June, Mussolini brought the campaign for the Acerbo law to Florence, where, at an official reception, Cardinal Alfonso Maria Mistrangelo embraced the prime minister. Salvemini, alarmed at the incident, understood that the posturing over the election law was part of a larger process.[53] The Vatican had begun to accommodate itself to Mussolini in January when Cardinal Pietro Gasparri, the Vatican Secretary of State, had reached an agreement with Mussolini to improve relations. Now the Acerbo law had become the focal point of the new collaboration, as Fascist pressure influenced the Vatican to stop Sturzo from obstructing the bill's progress. A special commission, chaired by Giolitti, overwhelmingly endorsed the bill. In July, the Vatican forced Sturzo's resignation as secretary of the PPI, which Salvemini saw as Mussolini's triumph and the pope's abandonment of the party.[54] That same month, the Chamber of Deputies passed the Acerbo law by 100 votes; within one year, Mussolini would employ it to take control of that body.[55]

In the summer of 1923, Salvemini desperately searched for a way to leave Italy to deliver a scheduled series of foreign policy lectures at King's College in London. When the police headquarters in Florence denied his July passport application, he suspected Michelangelo Zimolo, head of the Florence *fascio*. However, once he had been rejected in Milan as well, he concluded that the decision had come from Rome. His appeal to the Ministry of Interior also failed, and at this point friends in Rome related a disturbing story: the final determination had come from Mussolini himself. Acting under the policy of denying documents to anyone who would criticize the government while abroad, the prime minister had refused Salvemini, telling Giovanni Gentile that the decision was "absolute and categorical."[56] His friends were correct.[57]

Thwarted on one front but determined to find a way to England, Salvemini contacted Jahier, a member of the Circolo di Cultura who had offered to lend him his passport. They considered forging a document by changing the photo. Then he discovered that the PSI operated an Office of Humanitarian Emigration to assist Italian laborers in traveling abroad. After a friend in the Milan office arranged his surreptitious departure, he traveled to Bardonecchia, near the border, where he met a Frenchman in the cafe at the train station. The man escorted Salvemini onto a train to Modane, across the French border, where the two warily exited. They passed two French customs agents, greeted them, and continued alongside the tracks. The mysterious guide gave Salvemini a ticket for Paris and the name of a Parisian who would help him get to England. Once in Paris, Salvemini gave a photo and seventy-five francs to his new contact. Within twenty-four hours he had a passport, acquired on the black market, signed by the Italian Consul, valid for travel in France and England for one year. The next day he departed for England.[58]

He spent the rest of the summer and most of the fall abroad, living with the realization that he still traveled at considerable risk. Although he had a temporary Italian passport that appeared authentic, the Italian government knew that they had never issued one. Thus, while he could move from England to France, when he returned to Italy he would be in some jeopardy. He knew that Florentine Fascists had learned of his illegal departure the day after he left Italy, probably by intercepting his mail. In fact, he heard that Mussolini had shown Gentile copies of his letters to English friends; as a result, Salvemini had to resort to a secret address in Paris where letters would be sent to him. Worse yet, he heard from Rossi that local Fascists were planning to charge him with illegal departure as soon as he returned, hoping to put him in jail.[59]

The fact that Mussolini had taken a personal interest in his travels proved unsettling. Anxiety now set in. Salvemini feared that when the British press published a report of his first lecture, some Fascist official would instruct the Italian ambassador in London, the Marchese Della Torretta, to have him expelled. He knew that this had already happened to a young economist who had been deported for criticizing Mussolini's banking policy.[60]

His anxiety intensified as he heard about Blackshirt violence and forced conformity in Tuscany. Unable to follow day-to-day Italian politics, and dependent on letters from Rossi and other friends, he was reduced to imagining a return to a more repressive Italy. He heard that rumors circulated of his disappearance and that nationalists were pressuring Gentile to take action against him. When the nationalists learned of his lecture series on foreign policy, they denounced him in *L'Idea Nazionale* as anti-Italian, a familiar theme. Rossi wrote him that a nationalist lawyer from Florence claimed that Salvemini had maligned Italy while traveling in France the previous year. He knew that two professors were in the process of being dismissed for failure to perform, because Fascists had kept them from lecturing.[61] He anticipated that growing official repression would soon saturate the higher education system, leading to purges and conformity, enforced ultimately by a loyalty oath to *Il Duce*. "Naturally I will not swear [the oath]," he wrote to Rossi, "and then *crack*." It was further evidence of the prescience that he knew to be part gift, part curse.[62]

In early October, Rossi and Nello Rosselli sent him a copy of the Florentine newspaper *La Nazione*, which printed an official manifesto from the directory of the local *fascio* denouncing Salvemini. The Fascists laid out an elaborate case against him, replaying all the old themes: anti-Italian, wartime deserter, traitor who gave away Dalmatia. To this they added that he would now further defame his country in the lectures at King's College, and they now asked Fascist students and faculty at the university to assist the directory in punishing him. His friends Jahier and Gobetti came to his defense in *Rivoluzione Liberale*. Gobetti declared that the Salvemini case was an example of "collective lunacy" and of "persecution" of a man of "foresight" and "moral heroism," and thus it constituted an insult to the Italian people. Gobetti's endorsement, however, was small consolation, as tension mounted. That same week Rossi sent Salvemini an article calling for the expulsion from foreign states of any left-wing Italian who defamed the government while abroad.[63]

"Nostalgia for the sky, the sun, the light of Italy" and for his Italian students called him. Yet lingering doubt about his request for leave from the university forced him to face the most fundamental personal issue of this period: Did Italy afford him a future? By the fall of 1923, spreading repression nudged him toward accepting his fate. He lashed out in frustration at Fascists who "read my letters, . . . drive me in an automobile to vote, . . . deny my passport, . . . treat me as a special subject of surveillance. All this disgusts me," he wrote to Rossi. "I ask only to be left alone." The free English political environment was becoming ever more appealing.[64]

Rossi made impassioned appeals on several occasions for his mentor to return, advising him that many young Italians depended on his teaching and his inspiration to lift their hopes. He was not the type, Rossi wrote, to become the indifferent, cosmopolitan sage. "Your deepest spiritual roots are in . . . our soil," he pled. "Your loves and hates are here among us." Salvemini acknowledged this point, admitting to Rossi that his English students would not share with him the same intellectual relationship. "With you, my rapport is also moral," he wrote of his Italian students. "And my entire life has a tone common with yours."[65]

Salvemini's correspondence indicates a temporary reconciliation to the rapidly worsening environment. Hoping to obtain a legitimate passport, he wrote to Ugo Ojetti, who had connections with the Fascist government, reassuring

Ojetti that he had no intention of producing propaganda about the government, only of lecturing on foreign policy. However, he did not intend to renounce "any particle of my freedom or my rights."[66] To Ernesto Rossi he wrote in August, "We must renounce active politics. But this is not to say that we must renounce real life." They would have to avoid organized partisan politics; but in everyday life—Rossi in his Agrarian Society, Salvemini at the university—they must remain "always faithful to our ideals of life. The field of activity is more limited, but we must remain always who we are."[67]

Concerned about the twenty-one-year-old Gobetti, who had already been arrested several times and was under constant surveillance, Salvemini warned the brilliant journalist that one of his articles was "*too* violent."[68] He gave similar advice to Carlo Rosselli. This caution to avoid trouble by refraining from verbal excess was not without irony, given Salvemini's past penchant for provocative rhetoric. Within two months of Salvemini's warning, *squadristi* raided Gobetti's house, and in 1925 they beat him so severely that he died the next year from the injuries. That Salvemini barely avoided similar fate can be attributed partly to his temperate conduct in the two years after the March on Rome.

Salvemini's second visit to England proved productive. Carlo Rosselli joined him at Hindhead for three weeks at the Fabian Society Summer School. Though disappointed to find that the English Labourites supported a protectionist trade policy, he shared their commitment to democratic socialism and individual liberties. More importantly, he won the respect of a number of them, including Sidney and Beatrice Webb, John Maynard Keynes, and George Bernard Shaw; their support would soon prove invaluable.[69]

He and Rosselli managed to find some entertainment in the Summer School's musical review and several Gilbert and Sullivan operettas, which he found at the same time amusing and juvenile. A story he playfully told Rossi captured a lightheartedness seldom detected in this troubling era. He and Rosselli had met a beautiful Irish widow who charmed them with her vocals at the piano. The young Rosselli, irresistible to women, admired her; so did Salvemini. Their last evening in town, the two took a moonlit walk with her. "Rosselli was aggressive," Salvemini wrote boastfully, "I taciturn. At the end of the evening, the beauty declared that I pleased her more. Irreparable disaster!"[70]

In mid-September Salvemini rented a flat in London, where he learned that he had been granted his request for a leave. He had five weeks to learn the language. While memorizing his presentation, he learned a few hundred English words in the process. The night before the first lecture, he wrote to Rossi: "Tomorrow . . . will be my English exam!"[71]

The King's College lecture series examined Italian foreign policy and helped to establish Salvemini as a serious diplomatic historian, especially abroad. He explained the Triple Alliance as an effective instrument of Italian policy when carefully balanced by stable relations with Britain, France, and Russia. Thus he praised the work of former diplomats Costantino Nigra, Visconti Venosta, and Robilant, while rendering harsh judgment of the policies of Crispi, Giolitti, and particularly Sonnino. The emphasis he placed on balanced and thoughtful statecraft, and the accompanying condemnation of mindless bluster and nationalist adventurism, would stand as implicit criticism of Mussolini's foreign policy, even as Italian troops occupied Corfu in September.

The tone, however, was more objective and balanced—even consciously so—than his more polemical treatment of the same subjects in the political press during the war, and his methodology was solid, especially his use of unpublished documents.[72] The Genoa newspaper *Il Lavoro* published the eleven lectures throughout the fall and into the winter. In a tribute to Salvemini published after his death, his former student Ernesto Sestan praised his diplomatic history of this era for its "rigor of method and absolute serenity of judgment."[73] These are not terms often used to characterize Salvemini's historical writings after World War I, even by his disciples.

On the advice of Placci and Berenson, Salvemini made a gesture toward the Italian government by delivering a lecture ticket to the Embassy. He heard that Ambassador Della Torretta considered it an "honor" for Italy that such an "illustrious" historian was lecturing in England. Although he did not attend, Della Torretta did send a representative from the Embassy, giving Salvemini some hope that the Italian government was not all Fascist thugs. He followed the King's College lectures with a similar series at Oxford, published in both England and Italy.

The first week of December 1923, his English lecture series complete, Salvemini took the train from Paris to Florence with some trepidation about the worsening political climate. He left his black market passport in Paris, to assure himself that it would be safe in case he needed it again. His wife had similar apprehensions. He expected Fernande to join him in about one week, and her "only fear," she told him, was that if she needed to return to Paris to attend to her children or her mother, the Italian authorities would refuse her permission to enter France. He found a modest *pensione* and in spite of having returned to his job, his meager salary would support him for only twenty days each month.[74]

On December 6, the day he arrived in Florence, he delivered without incident his first lecture at the university. As he had anticipated, his students provided him with psychological support and refuge. This relationship would give Salvemini a wellspring of strength throughout the Fascist era and would serve as the source of the heroic view—perhaps enhanced by his long absence—of Salvemini as great "maestro."[75]

While resuming his teaching, Salvemini wrote untiringly about a broadening range of subjects but avoided overtly political topics, because, he explained, to write about those would me "not healthy."[76] He had been warned to proceed carefully upon his return because the Prefect of Florence would be monitoring his every move, prepared to take punitive action. He knew that he was under surveillance. He had heard repeatedly that Florentine Fascists were trying to find a way to deprive him of his job by introducing legal proceedings against him, although he knew of no basis for such action. He had some expectation that they might not pursue him, because he did not intend to occupy himself with active politics again in his life. "It appears that the orders are to leave me alone with my head in one piece."[77]

Salvemini's assumption about his own physical safety, if he really believed it, was a risky one. At the very time he returned to Florence, Italy was becoming a much more dangerous place. In November 1923, Blackshirts had sacked the home of former Prime Minister Nitti, who, in spite of voting against the Fascists, had not been a vocal opponent. Giovanni Amendola, a much more intransigent opponent and leader of the Liberal Party, had been beaten severely by Fascists in December 1923. In January 1924, just weeks after Salvemini's return, Mussolini had dissolved Parliament and called for April elections. Although the prime minister maintained a public facade of respectability, he privately began to organize a campaign of violence. In February he placed gangster and Blackshirt Amerigo Dumini in charge of a special enforcement unit. As the April elections approached, Fascists assaulted hundreds of political opponents. All the while, Mussolini maintained his distance.[78]

In early 1924, Salvemini began to give some consideration to affiliating with the PSU, just as his friend Matteotti had asked him to do nearly a year before. He felt some sense of responsibility to join a party because he knew that some young people were waiting for him to make such a move, but he wanted to see how the PSU would perform in the April elections, and he doubted the ability of some of their old socialist leaders to stand up to the Fascists.[79]

On election day, April 6, Mussolini achieved the majority for which he had worked. His "national list," including non-Fascists, won 66 percent of the votes and 374 of the 535 seats in the Chamber of Deputies—results gained through rampant violence and fraud and in spite of strong opposition, particularly among the working class in the northern cities. In addition, in order to win, Mussolini had turned to financial and industrial elites to forge an effective coalition, and that combination would orient the Fascist movement in the conservative direction that Salvemini had long predicted.

Matteotti, the PSU leader and a member of Parliament, repeatedly denounced the violence. When Dumini's squad met in an effort to intimidate parliamentary opponents, it focused on Matteotti. On May 30, Matteotti made one of many bold speeches on the floor of the Chamber, condemning the election as fraudulent and documenting incidents of Fascist brutality. Fascists shouted interruptions to his speech, Mussolini joining in. The next day, under orders from Cesare Rossi, Mussolini's press secretary, the Fascist press attacked Matteotti.

On several occasions, Mussolini remarked that leading opponents should be shot in the back, and he was overheard privately saying that someone should "get rid of" Matteotti.

On June 10, while Matteotti was on his way to Parliament, five men attacked him and forced him into a car driven by Dumini. As Matteotti struggled with his kidnappers, he was stabbed to death. The assailants then buried him in a ditch outside Rome. Dumini then drove the car to the Ministry of Interior, where he left it for the night. The next day, one of the accomplices, Giovanni Marinelli, delivered Matteotti's briefcase to Mussolini's office.

Mussolini knew the details of the crime, but when Matteotti's wife reported him missing and his fate became a matter of intense public concern, Mussolini denied all knowledge. On June 12, Mussolini addressed Parliament, saying that although he suspected foul play, the police had turned up no evidence. A number of leading Fascists, including Giuseppe Bottai and Chief of Police Emilio De Bono, believed that Mussolini was involved. He vacillated, then took more decisive measures designed to counter any appearance of impropriety. He dismissed Parliament, ordered Dumini's arrest, mobilized the Fascist militia, and dismissed Cesare Rossi, for whom Dumini worked. De Bono ordered the arrests of Rossi, Dumini, and Marinelli while refusing to honor his obligation to relinquish the case to the magistrates. During De Bono's investigation, evidence vanished, Marinelli and Rossi were released, and Rossi fled to France. Subsequent public pressure forced Mussolini to fire De Bono, but otherwise the prime minister held his ground.[80]

Opposition mounted in both houses of Parliament. In the Senate, Albertini led the anti-Fascist campaign. Salvemini wrote to Albertini, encouraging him to support a vote of "no confidence" in Mussolini.[81] Senators debated the issue, but the vote failed by 225 to 21. Albertini maintained steady pressure on Mussolini, eventually resulting in the government's removal of the Albertini brothers from *Il Corriere* and its conversion to a Fascist newspaper. Salvemini also encouraged Giuseppe Donati, publisher of *Il Popolo*, in his effort to denounce De Bono.[82]

In the Chamber of Deputies, the anti-Fascist parties pursued a bolder approach. On June 13, about 150 socialists, Popolari, liberals, republicans, and communists walked out in protest of Matteotti's death. They announced that they would boycott the Chamber until Mussolini's government resigned, a strategy they labeled the "Aventine Secession," named after an attempt by Roman plebeians in 494 B.C. to force concessions from patricians. The moderate Aventine leadership appealed unsuccessfully to the king to dismiss Mussolini.

Matteotti's murder shocked Salvemini into the most momentous decision of his life; having advised his friends not to avoid real life, real life had now hit him in the face. Five weeks after Matteotti's disappearance, Salvemini joined the public protest against Fascism. Convinced that his passivity had lent support to the regime, he made a conscious decision to join the anti-Fascist movement in spite of his reservations about its leadership. In his *Memoirs*, written more than thirty-five years later, he recalled the decision: "Even if it meant standing alone, I had to say a resolute 'no' to this regime; to do what I must, come what may."[83]

He even joined the PSU, a clear departure from his long-standing condemnation of organized parties. He emphasized that joining the party did not indicate his return to public life, and thus his friends could not expect him to announce his candidacy; instead, it was a matter of stepping forward in a time of danger.[84]

The specific occasion was a rally commemorating the death of Cesare Battisti in late July 1924. As several hundred demonstrators gathered at a movie theater near the train station, they circulated a memorial pamphlet with a feature article by Salvemini. In it, he demanded that Mussolini explain his role in Matteotti's murder: either he had ordered the assassination and should go to prison, or one of his close subordinates had ordered it and Mussolini should resign. Piero Jahier gave an inspirational tribute to Battisti, and as soon as he finished, the crowd began to chant: "*Viva* Matteotti!" Salvemini joined in the cry. The protesters then marched through the streets along Via Cavour to the Piazza San Marco. Marion Cave led the processional, carrying a wreath that she placed on the bust of Battisti in honor of Matteotti. Fascists watched but did not retaliate. Salvemini had a sense that his article and his participation in the protest would bring retribution. If, as one recent historian has written, the Fascists were already anti-Salvemini, they now understood that he was unequivocally and openly an anti-Fascist.[85]

Salvemini quickly took a place of prominence in the ranks of Florentine anti-Fascism. A number of those who would become well known for their resistance—"Esto" Rossi and the Rosselli brothers, for example—were at this time quite young and still unknown. Once Salvemini emerged as an anti-Fascist, his prominence as an academician and writer made him virtually the only mature and established leader of the local movement, and thus a special target of Blackshirts and police.

Gaetano and Fernande left Florence at the end of July for a resort on the Ligurian Sea. There they spent the summer, resting and allowing her to recuperate from an extended illness. When the vacation ended, she visited friends in Cannes to avoid the chill that winter would bring to Florence. Authorities still blocked their efforts to secure passports.[86] While they were on vacation, Salvemini learned that Matteotti's body had been found, confirming long-held assumptions and intensifying pressure on Mussolini to take action against the killers. As criticism of Mussolini grew, Fascists began to strike back at the critics; in Florence they targeted the Circolo di Cultura.[87]

By the time Salvemini returned to Florence at the end of September 1924, local Fascists had now focused on him as a leader of the Florentine opposition.

On November 2, while participating in a Matteotti protest rally sponsored by
Italia Libera, a republican anti-Fascist organization, Salvemini was arrested,
then released.[88] When the University of Florence reopened in November, the
reprisals sharpened. Fascists threatened him personally to the point that he
never knew when he left for class whether he would return safely. Once he
reached campus, he found that controversy permeated the students and faculty
as well. When Giovanni Ansaldo accused a Fascist Latin professor of identify-
ing certain anti-Fascist students to the local Blackshirts, Salvemini, convinced
that his colleague was not responsible, published a strong defense of the professor in Gobetti's *Rivoluzione Liberale*. Ansaldo retracted his accusation.[89] However, the publicity brought Salvemini even closer scrutiny. The same week, the
local Fascist paper, *Battaglie Fasciste*, made the now familiar charge of treason
and labeled him a "perverter of youth" who had proselytized his students to the
anti-Fascist campaign "in the corridors of his own home."[90]

The previous summer, when Mussolini had realigned his government to include more conservatives, the king, the Vatican, and the military had supported
him. As a result, rumors spread throughout the summer and fall that Mussolini
planned to abandon the old Fascists in favor of this conservative alliance. In late
December, intransigent Fascists such as Farinacci and local *squadristi* pres-
sured Mussolini to accept responsibility for Blackshirt violence, including the
death of Matteotti, and to lead a second Fascist revolution. Some Fascist militia
leaders conspired to oust *Il Duce*. On the last day of the year, thirty-three of
them burst into Mussolini's office, surrounded his desk, and demanded that he
put an end to anti-Fascist criticism and lead them in a revolutionary seizure of
power. After a heated exchange, he agreed to silence anti-Fascists.

On the same day they made their demands of Mussolini, Tullio Tamburini,
one of the most recalcitrant militia leaders, orchestrated an armed assault by
about 10,000 *squadristi* against Florentine anti-Fascists. The day began with
demonstrations in the Piazza Santa Maria Novella and the Piazza della
Signoria, and then evolved into assaults targeted at the offices of newspapers,
organizations, and lawyers suspected of anti-Fascism. Officials—from the
mayor to the prefect, the chief of police, and the military commander—did not
interfere. Later in the day, about ten young Fascists were seen ransacking the
office of the Circolo di Cultura, throwing furniture, books, and reviews out the
window onto the Piazza S. Trinità.[91]

The first week of 1925 proved to be a turning point in Mussolini's career, a
phase some have called the "second coup d'etat." On January 3, after weeks of
Fascist violence, Mussolini delivered a defiant speech to Parliament:

I, and I alone, assume the political, moral, and historical responsibility for everything
that has happened. . . . Italy, my friends, demands peace, tranquility, and constructive
calm. We will give you these things, if possible with love, but if necessary with force.

You may be sure that within forty-eight hours of this speech, the situation will be clarified in every way.[92]

In the days that followed, *squadristi* struck anti-Fascists around the country. Florentine Fascists had called a "general mobilization" for all of Tuscany. On January 5, the Prefect of Florence issued a decree dissolving the Circolo di Cultura in the interest of public order.[93] Later that month, while discussing Mussolini's speech of January 3, Salvemini, the Rosselli brothers, Rossi, and some friends agreed that the Aventine strategy was flawed and that anti-Fascists needed to prepare for a lengthy resistance. Interior Minister Luigi Federzoni had given prefects full power to control the press. It was this attack on freedom of the press that convinced Salvemini of the Fascist threat against all political liberties. He said to the group, "Now that the freedom of press has been abolished, the underground press must arise." A few days later, when Salvemini returned from Rome, Rossi handed him a modest two-page tabloid entitled *Non Mollare* ("Don't Give In"). It was Italy's first underground anti-Fascist newspaper.[94]

Over the first ten months of 1925, twenty-two issues of *Non Mollare* appeared, dominated by Salvemini's writing. Normally they printed a few thousand copies under cover of night at one of several local presses and then turned them over to Italia Libera, whose members distributed them among students and faculty in Florence, Padua, Milan, Rome, and elsewhere. *Non Mollare*'s hardest-hitting articles were exposés by Fascists, each trying to prepare a defense for violent crimes by blaming superiors. In February, the paper featured the Filippelli memorandum naming Matteotti's murderers, heretofore unpublished, because no paper would dare; in March, an allegation by a Fascist militia chief that De Bono had ordered the 1923 beating of Amendola, and a charge by a former Fascist official in Turin that Mussolini had directly ordered that Gobetti be taught a "severe Fascist lesson"; and in June, a 1924 letter from Cesare Rossi to Mussolini, directly tying the prime minister to Matteotti's murder.[95]

In March, *Non Mollare* rallied to the cause of freedom of the press and blamed the king for allowing Mussolini to violate Italy's free press law. Salvemini and his associates then urged Italians to oppose Vittorio Emanuele on his tour by striking when he visited Milan and to boycott his visit to Florence, declaring in April, "Whoever participates in the [celebration] will become an accomplice of the Fascists." Salvemini abided by his own boycott request but could not resist asking a friend to observe. She gleefully reported that the king's contingent had marched through streets and *piazze* that were vacant except for Blackshirts and a few tourists. Salvemini's opposition to the king would only harden over the duration of the Fascist era.[96]

That spring, Fascists unleashed a more malicious offensive against Salvemini. The university environment itself was becoming more hostile. Piero Calamandrei remembered the dramatic events that interrupted his own lecture one afternoon in March. A column of Fascists marched into the College of Letters, looking for Salvemini's class. They found the door to the history lecture hall and tried to force their way through it. The door held, however, apparently because Salvemini's students successfully blocked their entry. Calamandrei, in an attempt to persuade the Fascists to leave, told one of them that the university must remain free of such party demonstrations.

"That would be true if Fascism were a party," the young man responded. "But we Fascists are the state."

In the midst of the shouting and threatening, Salvemini's class ended. The door opened, and the professor emerged, stoic, his hat shoved down over his head, escorted by students. No one touched him. Behind him, concealed in a hallway, two prominent Fascist professors watched in silence. Giovanni Brunetti was president of the faculty; Antonio Garbasso was mayor of Florence.

The next week, Salvemini was scheduled to give the keynote address at the university commemorating his former professor Pasquale Villari. The day before, the local Fascist press condemned Salvemini, adding "anti-Fascist and standard-bearer for the Aventine" to the usual list of invectives. They argued that since the Academic Senate would not stop Salvemini's speech, Florentine Fascists would. "Salvemini Must Not Speak," the headlines read. The university rector, a respected scholar, showed little interest in confronting the Fascists, and thus he agreed to cancel the ceremony to avoid a disturbance.[97]

The following day, when Salvemini walked into the history lecture hall, he halted briefly, surprised to see that the first few rows were filled with faculty members from various departments. It was a dramatic gesture of support for a beleaguered colleague and a statement on behalf of academic freedom. Salvemini, pale with emotion, sat in his chair, gathered himself, and launched an emphatic lecture on the Congress of Berlin, showing no further sign of being distracted by this exceptional event. As he finished and walked toward the exit, the students and visitors hailed him with enthusiastic applause.[98]

Throughout the spring he managed to write for the legitimate press, continuing to emphasize diplomatic issues and historical themes. Gobetti published Salvemini's book *Dal Patto di Londra alla pace di Roma*, and new editions of his *Mazzini* and *Rivoluzione francese* appeared as well. At the same time, he emerged as a more open anti-Fascist. He signed Benedetto Croce's anti-Fascist manifesto, and his writing in the periodical press became more critical of Mussolini's policies, in some cases provoking censorship.[99]

In April, authorities began to focus more earnestly on *Non Mollare*. A new prefect was assigned to Florence, and soon police arrested one of the distributors. Then on April 29 police raided a law office and seized copies of the newspaper. Most disturbing was Salvemini's suspicion that police had infiltrated their circle. One month later, his apprehension proved justified when the spy turned up with a police officer at the door of Ernesto Rossi. The spy, a printer named Renzo Pinzi, then made blackmail demands against Salvemini and Rossi, which the two ignored. However, Rossi, directly involved in distributing the papers, fled to the homes of friends and then to France; Salvemini, less culpable, remained in Florence. At the trial of the lawyer Gustavo Consolo, correspondent for *Avanti!*, Pinzi testified, tying him to the publication of *Non Mollare*. During the trial, Pinzi named Rossi and Salvemini. Two days later, on June 8, 1925, authorities arrested Salvemini in Rome and transported him to the Regina Coeli prison.[100]

Salvemini spent one week in the Roman prison. A young communist prisoner, assigned to clean his cell, befriended him, bringing him news and books from other political prisoners. Otherwise, he found the routine monotonous. To lighten their burden, he and the other prisoners sang arias from *Rigoletto* and *Aida* while they paced the corridor. He worked about six hours each day and slept about ten. Authorities allowed him neither pencil nor paper except to write his wife one four-page letter.

While Salvemini was in Rome, a court in Florence sentenced one of the lawyers to nineteen months and acquitted Consolo for lack of evidence. As Salvemini was preparing to leave for his own trial in Florence, his young friend whispered to him, "Let us hope that in purgatory the blessed soul of Lenin will pray for us." Salvemini never forgot the irony of this religious syncretism.[101]

As he left the prison in handcuffs, Salvemini saw his friend Emanuele Modigliani, who provided a taxi to transport him to the train station along with the two *carabinieri* who were assigned to guard him. When they arrived, he heard the ovation of a number of well-wishers, confronted by a group of jeering Fascists. They slept most of the way, awakened by the conductor's cry, "Florence! Florence!" Groggy, they left the train, only to realize that they had gotten off at the wrong Florence station. The *carabinieri*, unfamiliar with Florence, agreed to follow Salvemini, who, still handcuffed, led his guards to the converted convent on Via Ghibellina called the Murate prison, where they found the gates closed. After a wait, prison officials conducted him to his cell.[102]

By mid-June, letters of support began to arrive from John Maynard Keynes, the historian George Macaulay Trevelyan, Prezzolini, and other English and Italian friends. In his replies, Salvemini consistently asked family and friends not to exaggerate his plight. He was no martyr, no Mazzini, he told them. Aside from the boredom of the regimentation, he had few complaints. He was treated with respect during his entire incarceration, and he remembered the singing and conversations with some fondness. Friends recalled hearing his infectious laughter from the street as they approached the prison. In fact, in his recollections, Salvemini referred to the "guaranteed security" that his weeks in prison afforded him, a welcomed respite from the previous months of growing tension. Hundreds of friends supported him with a petition of sympathy published in *Il Corriere della Sera* and reprinted in the anti-Fascist press. Meanwhile,

Carlo Rosselli assured that new issues of *Non Mollare* circulated so that authorities would know that Salvemini and Rossi were not exclusively responsible for the anti-Fascist "libel."[103]

After a month at the Murate prison, Salvemini was brought to trial on July 13. A large crowd filled the courtroom as Salvemini, in a cage, consulted his attorneys. Most were his friends and colleagues, including Carlo Rosselli, who approached the cage and warmly extended a hand toward his mentor. "What are you doing here?" Salvemini demanded. "Get out. . . . Do you want to fall into a trap? Get out, I implore you. I command you." Rosselli lowered his head, turned, and left the courtroom. Salvemini's trepidation for his student was warranted. A number of *squadristi* were seen among the crowd, and a larger number waited outside.[104]

Anticipation mounted among the rival groups as they watched the judge emerge from his chamber. His proclamation satisfied neither side. Salvemini's trial would be postponed to await the testimony of the prosecution's main witness. The delay granted Salvemini provisional freedom. As the pro-Salvemini crowd left the courtroom, walking from the Piazza San Firenze toward the Bargello, a group of Fascist thugs leaped from behind a newspaper kiosk and brutally attacked them with clubs, seriously injuring World War I hero Raffaele Rossetti, Professor Alessandro Levi, and lawyer Nino Levi. Among the victims was Ferruccio Delaini, one of Salvemini's attorneys, who died from the injuries a few months later. That same week in Siena, another of Salvemini's defense attorneys, Ferruccio Marchetti, was beaten to death.[105]

An officer of the *carabinieri* escorted Salvemini to safety in a cellar in the Palace of Justice until the disturbance had ended, then called for help to escort him back to the prison. Around midnight, four guards escorted Salvemini out of the Murate by carriage to his house on the Piazza d'Azeglio. They left him in the middle of the street, and as they drove away he became suspicious. He turned and headed down the Via Giusti toward the Rosselli house, where he spent the night. At dawn he departed, looking for safer quarters. His suspicions were well founded. That same night, Fascists waited for him at Berenson's Villa I Tatti at Settignano on the outskirts of the city. The next day, Fascists sacked the Rosselli house and riddled the outside walls with bullets. The prefect, rather than investigating the break-in, castigated Amelia Rosselli for allowing her sons to study with Salvemini.

Ironically, the judge had restricted Salvemini to Florence as a condition of his release, whereas local Fascists had banished him from the city. He thought of staying with the Berensons, but he knew that the Fascists had tapped Berenson's telephone and were watching I Tatti. Ugo Ojetti now intervened for him. Ojetti personally contacted the prefect, who assigned two police agents to escort Salvemini to Rome under protective custody. When he reached the Rome train station, his old friend Niccolò Rodolico very discreetly put him on a train for Naples in the company of two new police guards. In Naples, he spent several days at the house of Giustino Fortunato, where Croce visited him. Then he joined the Benzoni family at Capo di Sorrento—along with the ever-present guards.[106]

The week he spent in the Naples area afforded time to consider his situation and to write friends. Frustrated by the trial, certain that he could have won the case and thus taught the Fascists a lesson, he considered his immediate future. The rector of the university had already informed him that, under Fascist-era laws, he was obligated to repay the institution his wages from the period of his incarceration. He suspected that government employees, including university professors, would be among the first fired for anti-Fascist activities. In that case, he would have to leave Italy in order to support his family. While in Sorrento, he learned that once again Giovanni Amendola had been attacked, this time suffering life-threatening injuries at the hands of *squadristi* in Montecatini.[107]

By mid-July, speculation had begun to spread that Mussolini would issue an amnesty in order to free Matteotti's murderers, and on that basis Salvemini had begun to weigh his options. He left Naples on July 27 to stay with Rossetti near Portofino, the two agents in tow. It was at Rossetti's house near the Ligurian Sea on July 31 that Salvemini heard that Mussolini had published the anticipated amnesty. He now knew that he was free.[108]

Late on the night of August 1, he left Genoa on a train, the guards beside him. As the train pulled into the station in Milan at about 3:00 A.M., he saw that the guards were sleeping soundly. Quickly, he left the train with his small overnight bag and a 350-page government document, dashed through the station, and hailed a taxi, giving the driver false directions. He then took a second taxi to his destination. He spent several days in Milan with Fausto Pagliari, Ferruccio Parri, and their anti-Fascist friends, assuming that the authorities would soon forget about him.

When he felt the time had arrived for his ultimate flight, he took a train to Modane, familiar from his previous escape. Apprehensive about the police trailing him, he doubled back to Novara, then to Aosta. There he contacted Federico Chabod, a university student who housed him for a night. On August 16, 1925, Chabod and a few friends drove Salvemini through the Little St. Bernard Pass. It was slightly past noon, and neither Italian nor French customs agents bothered to interrupt lunch to ask for a passport. His friends dropped him at the first French train station, where he began two decades of exile.[109]

NOTES

1. GS, entry of April 3, 1922, "MeS," 163.
2. RV, *The Origins of Fascism in Italy*, I (Naples, 1967), viii.

3. GS to Girolamo Vitelli, November 9, 1922, *Cart 1921*, 116–121; entry of November 20, 1922, "MeS," 6.

4. Umberto Morra to GS, November 13, 1922, 124; Gino Luzzatto to GS, November 13, 1922, 124–127; Vitelli to GS, November 14, 1922, 131–132; Gaetano Mosca to GS, November 16, 1922, 135; Virgilio Procacci to GS, November 16, 1922; Ida Ghislaberti to GS, December 21, 1922, *Cart 1921*, 161–162.

5. GS to GP, November 14, 1922, *Cart 1921*, 128–129.

6. GS to FS, November 22, 1922, *Cart 1921*, 148.

7. GS to ER, November 12, 1922, 121–123; to FS, November 18, 1922, 141–142; to ED, November 20, 1922, 144–145; to Mosca, November 22, 1922, *Cart 1921*, 145.

8. GS, entry of November 18 1922, "MeS," 3–6; RV, "Salvemini e il fascismo" in ES *ACGS*, 143.

9. GS to Giacinto Panunzio, November 22, 1922, *Cart 1921*, 151.

10. GS entry of November 21, 1922, "MeS," 9; entry of January 6, 1923, "MeS," 67.

11. GS to Mosca, November 22, 1922, 145–147; GS to FS, November 22, 1922, 148; to G. Panunzio, November 22, 1922, *Cart 1921*, 150–152.

12. GS entries of November 18, 24, 27, and 29, 1922, "MeS," 4, 10–15, 17–19, 20; Luigi Lotti, "Salvemini e il Fascismo," *Nuova Antologia* (Rome), July 1973, 321–323 and RV, "Salvemini e il fascismo," 142–143.

13. GS to Mosca, November 22, 1922, 145–147; GS to Panunzio, November 22, 1922, 150; Tommaso Fiore to GS, January 19, 1923, *Cart 1921*, 169–170; GS entries of November 24, 27, December 4, 10, 23, and 26, 1922, "MeS," 13–14, 17–19, 24, 41–43, 51–54.

14. GS to FS, November 22, 1922, *Cart 1921*, 149.

15. GS to FS, December 20, 1922, 160–161; to UO, June 21, 1923, *Cart 1921*, 212–213.

16. GS to Carlo Sforza, February 3 and 20, 1923, 173–175; to GD, March 29 and Easter, 1923, *Cart 1921*, 182–183. The articles were "Sintomi di profonda crisi in Francia," *Opere* III (2), 692–698; "La Germania e le riparazioni," *Opere* III (2), 698–702; "Reparations Problem: Cross Purposes in France—The Views of a European Statesman," *MG*, April 20, 1923.

17. GS to GD, March 29, 1923, *Cart 1921*, 182–183; to MB, October 25, 1924, *Cart 1921*, 317.

18. GS, *Tendenze vecchie e necessità nuove del movimento operaio italiano* (Bologna, 1922); Roberto Veratti (with a long note by FT), "Tendenze vecchie e necessità nuove del nostro movimento," *CS*, April 16, 1923; to PG, April 28, 1923, *Cart 1921*, 193.

19. GP, *La coltura italiana* (Florence, 1923), 341.

20. GS to Editore Zanichelli, June 28, 1923, *Cart 1921*, 215.

21. GS, "Sintomi di profonda crisi in Francia," *Opere* III (2), 692–698.

22. GS entry of April 11, 1923, "MeS," 185.

23. GS, entry of April 3, 1923, "MeS," 163; entry of May 27, 1923, "Memorie e soliloqui," in *Opere* VI (2), 212.

24. GS entry of May 1, 1923, "MeS," 201.

25. GS to Panunzio, May 2, 1923, *Cart 1921*, 195–196.

26. GS entry of January 18, 1923, "MeS," 2, 88; to ER, November 6, 1921 in *Cart 1921*, 32. According to Piero Calamandrei, Salvemini had been participating since 1920. PiC, "IlM," 71–112. See also NT, *Carlo Rosselli*, 113, n. 34, and 120–121; Stanlislao Pugliese, *Carlo Rosselli* (Cambridge, MA, 1999).

27. PiC, "IlM," 75–76.

28. See also AG, *VCR*, I, 27–34; ET, *Sal*, 58; DeC, *Sal*, 335; Simonetta Tombaccini, *Storia dei fuorusciti italiani in Francia* (Milan, 1988), 53.

29. GS, entry of January 19, 1923, "MeS," 88–91.

30. GS, entry of February 4, 1923, "MeS," 88–91.

31. GS entry of January 25, 1923, "MeS," 94.

32. GS entry of May 3, 1923, "MeS," 204.

33. GS entries of December 29, 1922, January 25, and May 1, 1923 in "MeS," 61, 94–95, 201–202; Panunzio to GS, June 6 and July 6, 1923, *Cart 1921*, 205–206, 220–221; GS to Panunzio, July 9, 1923 and February 17, 1924, *Cart 1921*, 221–222, 290.

34. GS entry of January 25, 1923, "MeS," 95–96.

35. GS to G. Panunzio, July 9, 1923, *Cart 1921*, 222.

36. GS entry of January 26, 1923, "MeS," 99–100.

37. GS entries of April 13, 15, and 18, "MeS," 187–190.

38. GS entry of April 30 and May 14, 1923, "MeS," 198 and 207.

39. GS entry of April 29, 1923, "MeS," 196.

40. GS entries of January 6 and 10, 1923, "MeS," 67, 78, and 83.

41. GS entries of February 14 and 22 and April 6, 7, and 9, 1923, "MeS," 135, 138, 170, 171, 175.

42. GS entry of January 30, 1923, "MeS," 109–110.

43. GS to Luzzatto, June 14, 1923, *Cart 1921*, 209.

44. GS entry of April 18, 1923, "MeS," 189.

45. GS entry of April 9, 1923, "MeS," 184.

46. GS entries of February 12 and April 24, 1923, "MeS," 132 and 192.

47. GS entries of March 8 and 9, 1923, "MeS," 149.

48. GS entries of May 13, 15, and 16, 1923, "MeS," 206–210.

49. GS entry of May 24, 1923, "MeS," 211.

50. GS entries of June 3 and July 7, 1923, "MeS," 215, 223; GF to GS, June 3, 1923, *Cart 1921*, 203.

51. GS entries of June 5 and 11, 1923, "MeS," 216–217.

52. GS to Panunzio, July 9, 1923, *Cart 1921*, 221.

53. GS entry of June 21, 1923, "MeS," 219.

54. GS entry of July 11, 1923, "MeS," 223.

55. On the Acerbo law, see DeF, *il fas* I, 518–618; Alberto Aquarone, *L'organizzazione dello stato totalitario* (Turin, 1965), 37–39; Adrian Lyttleton, *Seizure of Power* (New York, 1973), 125–129.

56. GS to UO, July 15, 1923, *Cart 1921*, 225; to ER, July 19, 1923, *Cart 1921*, 226; to UO, July 28, 1923, *Cart 1921*, 231; entries of July 13 and August 23, 1923, "MeS," 224–225.

57. Emilio De Bono, Director of Public Safety, telegramed the Prefect of Florence in July: "The President of the Council [BM] absolutely does not want a passport to be granted to Professor Salvemini." MI to Prefetto di Firenze, July 1, 1923, *CPC*"S" ACS. See also Prefetto di Firenze (Garzaroli) to MI, June 30, 1923, *CPC*"S" ACS; "Passaporto per l'estero," *Pd'I*, September 27, 1923.

58. GS to ER, July 19, 1923, *Cart 1921*, 226; entry of August 28, 1923, "MeS," 225; *Memorie*, 7.

59. GS to ER, September 13, 1923, *Cart 1921*, 244; ER to GS, September 16, 1923, *Cart 1921*, 250; Mayor of Lucca to BM, October 8, 1923, *SPD*, *CR*"S."

60. GS to ER, July 19, 1923, *Cart 1921*, 229–230; to UO, July 28, 1923, *Cart 1921*, 230–233; entry of August 28, 1923, "MeS," 225.

61. ER to GS, September 16, 1923, *Cart 1921*, 250; ER to GS, October 3, 1923, *Cart 1921*, 262.

62. GS to ER, July 19, September 3, 21, and 26, 1923, *Cart 1921*, 229, 241, 253, and 259; to UO, July 28, 1923, *Cart 1921*, 231–232; entry of September 13, 1923, "MeS," 230; ER to GS, August 21 and September 26, 1923, *Cart 1921*, 236, 260.

63. "Il Direttorio del Fascio di Firenze"; "Ordine del giorno," *La Nazione* (Florence), October 4, 1923; ER and Nello Rosselli to GS, October 4, 1923, *Cart 1921*, 263, n. 1; ER to GS, October 5, 1923, *Cart 1921*, 266; GS, *Mem*, 7–9; Piero Gobetti, "Commento quotidiano: il case Salvemini," *Rivoluzione Liberale*, October 16, 1923.

64. GS to ER, July 19, August 28, September 3 and 21, 1923, *Cart 1921*, 229, 240–242, 253; to Sforza, September 21, 1923, *Cart 1921*, 257; to ED, December 15, 1923, *Cart 1921*, 283; to G. Panunzio, December 29, 1923, *Cart 1921*, 285; ER to GS, October 5, 1923, *Cart 1921*, 266–267.

65. ER to GS, September 4 and 16, 1923, *Cart 1921*, 242–243, 251; GS to ER, September 21, 1923, *Cart 1921*, 255.

66. GS to UO, July 28, 1923, *Cart 1921*, 232–233.

67. GS to ER, August 28 and September 13, 1923, *Cart 1921*, 239, 246.

68. GS to PG, April 23, 1924, *Cart 1921*, 298.

69. GS, entry of September 1, 1923, "MeS," 227; to Z-B, August 15, 1924, *Cart 1921*, 307; Nicky Mariano, *Forty Years*, 89–90.

70. GS to ER, August 28, 1923, *Cart 1921*, 240.

71. GS to ER, October 8, 1923, *Cart 1921*, 267. See also ET, *Sal*, 54.

72. *La politica estera dell'Italia dal 1871 al 1914* (Florence), revised 1950 as *La politica estera dell'Italia dal 1871 al 1915* (Florence), *Opere* III (4), 291–451. See also Ernesto Ragionieri, "Gaetano Salvemini, storico e politico," *Belfagor* V (1950), 532–535; ES, "Lo storico," in ES, *ACGS*, 26–35; Piero Pieri, "Gaetano Salvemini, Storico dell'età moderna e contemporanea," *Rassegna Storica Toscana* IV (1958), 115–120.

73. ES, "Lo storico," in ES, *ACGS*, 31.

74. GS to ER, October 8, 1923, *Cart 1921*, 268; Fernande Dauriac to GS, October 12, 1923, *Cart 1921*, 268–270; GS to Sforza, December 7, 1923, 277; to PG, February 3, 1924, 288, *Cart 1921*; G. P. Gooch, "Professor Salvemini and the Fascists," *Contemporary Review*, 129 (February 1926), 181.

75. GS to ED, December 15, 1923, *Cart 1921*, 283. See also Morra, "Carteggio Salvemini-Rossi," *Il Mondo*, January 26, 1960; ES, "Salvemini storico e maestro,"

Rivista Storico Italiano LXX (December 1958), 5–43; Lidia Minervini, "Ricordi di Salvemini: Amico e Maestro," *Il Mondo*, October 22, 1957, 11–12.

76. GS to ED, December 15, 1923, *Cart 1921*, 284; to LA, December 29, 1923, *Cart 1921*, 284; to PG, January 24 and February 3, 1924, *Cart 1921*, 286–288; *Dal Patto di Londra alla Pace di Roma* (Turin, 1925); "Un esame critico delle *Memorie* di Giolitti," *Opere* IV (1), 501–511.

77. GS to Sforza, September 21 and December 7, 1923, and February 23, 1924, *Cart 1921*, 257– 258, 277–278, and 294; to ED, December 15, 1923, *Cart 1921*, 283; entry of September 21, 1923, "MeS," in *Opere* VI (2), 231; *Mem*, 29–41.

78. DeF, *il fas* I, 518–618.

79. GS to G. Panunzio, February 17, 1924, *Cart 1921*, 292; to Sforza, April 12, 1924, *Cart 1921*, 297.

80. DeF *il fas* I, 518–618; PC and Brian R. Sullivan, *Il Duce's Other Woman* (New York, 1993), 286–298; DeG, *Italian Fascism*, 50–54.

81. GS to LA, June 24, 1924, *Cart 1921*, 299.

82. GS to MB, October 25, 1924, *Cart 1921*, 317; "Donati e Berneri," *Opere* VIII, 97–99.

83. GS, *Mem*, 10–11.

84. GS to ER, July 20, 1924, *Cart 1921*, 302 n. 2.; to Enrico Bassi, September 12, 1924, *Cart 1921*, 312.

85. RV, *Origins of Fascism in Italy*, I, viii; NT, *Carlo Rosselli*, 193.

86. Prefetto di Firenze (Garzaroli) to MI, June 9, 1924; Ministro dell'Interno to Prefetto di Firenze, June 20 (?), 1924, *CPC*"S," ACS; Il Sottosegretario di stato to MI, June 22, 1924; Prefetto di Firenze (Garzaroli) to MI, June 24, 1924, *CPC*"S," ACS.

87. GS to ER, July 20, 1924, *Cart 1921*, 302; to FT, July 28, 1924, *Cart 1921*, 303; to MB, August 28, 1924, *Cart 1921*, 310–311; to ER, September 3, 1924, *Cart 1921*, 312.

88. GS, Piero Jahier, Z-B a vari, October 24, 1924, *Cart 1921*, 315–316; ET, *Gaetano Salvemini: Un profilo biografico* (Rome, 1963), 59.

89. GS, "Rettifica alla *Pistola ad Omero*," *La Rivoluzione Liberale*, February 15, 1925; to PG, February 11, 15, and 18, and April 19, 1925, *Cart 1921*, 322–324, 327; to Ermenegildo Pistelli, May 25, 1925, *Cart 1921*, 330–331. See also PiC, "IlM," 95–97.

90. Lodovico di Caporiacco, "Università e apoliticà," *Battaglie Fasciste* (Florence), February 14, 1925; Gooch, "Professor Salvemini and the Fascists," 184–185.

91. PiC, "IlM," 76–81; Pugliese, *Rosselli*, 29–34; NT, *Carlo Rosselli*, 193–194.

92. DeF, *il fas* I, 711–722. Mussolini's speech is found in *OO*, XXI, 235–241. Translation is from PC and Sullivan, *Il Duce's Other Woman*, 297.

93. PiC, "IlM," 79.

94. GS, "*NM*," 3–10, *Opere* III (3), 465–473; to LA, May 25, 1925, *Cart 1921*, 331–332; AG, *VCR*, I, 42; ET, *Salvemini: Un profilo biografico*, 60; Pugliese, *Rosselli*; NT, *Carlo Rosselli*, 193–194.

95. GS, ER, and PiC, *Non Mollare* (Florence, 1955); to LA, April 1, 1925, *Cart 1921*, 326–327; GS, "*NM*," 5–21 and "Tavole," and ix–x and xxx–xxxi; "Il *Non Mollare*" in Rossi, ed. *No al Fascismo* (Turin, 1963), 29–33. Pugliese, *Rosselli*, 38–43; NT, *Carlo Rosselli*, 195.

96. GS, "Il *Non Mollare*," in Rossi, ed. *No al fascismo*, 38–39; AG, *VCR*, I, 42–43.

97. PiC, "IlM," 100–101 and "Tavole," xx; GS, *Mem*, 12–13; to Rector, University of Florence, December 2, 1925 in Gooch, "Professor Salvemini and the Fascists," 183–185; "*Slav*emini è servito: sotto per gli altri!," *L'Impero* (Rome), December 3, 1925, *SPD, CR*"S."

98. PiC, "IlM," 100–102.

99. GS to Benedetto Croce, April 30, 1925; Croce to GS, after April 30, 1925, *Cart 1921*, 327–328.

100. Salvemini was arrested at 4:00 P.M. on June 8, 1925, at the National Economic Ministry in Rome, where he was attending a ceremony for the promotion of a friend. Il Questore di Roma (Pirilli) to Capo Gabinetto Ministro and DGPS, June 8, 1925, *CPC*"S," ACS; BM to Cesare Nava, June 10, 1925, *SPD, CR*"S"; "Salvemini, jugoslavo di razza!" 1925, *SPD, CR*"S"; GS, "*NM*," 14–15; AG, *VCR*, I, 44; FT to AK, June 8 and 10, 1925 in Turati-Kuliscioff *Carteggio*, VI, 672 and 680–681.

101. GS, "*NM*," 16; *Mem*, 14–15; to FS, June 18, 1925, *Cart 1921*, 335–338; to Piera Albertini Giacosa, July 19, 1925, *Cart 1921*, 349–352.

102. GS, *Mem*, 16–17.

103. "Un indirizzo di simpatia a Gaetano Salvemini," *CdS* June 27, 1925, *SPD, CR*"S"; GP to GS, June 11, 1925, *Cart 1921*, 334–335; Ray Strachey to GS, June 17, 1925, *Cart 1921*, 335; GS to FS, June 18, 1925, *Cart 1921*, 335–338; to his brother (Mauretto), June 18, 1925, *Cart 1921*, 338–340; *Mem*, 14; "*NM*," 16; Henry Bolton King to GS, June 22, 1925, *Cart 1921*, 340; John Maynard Keynes to GS, June 22, 1925, *Cart 1921*, 340; George M. Trevelyan to GS, June 25, 1925, *Cart 1921*, 341; T. Okey to GS, June 26, 1925, *Cart 1921*, 341; AG, *VCR*, 45; Mariano, *Forty Years*, 123; UO, "La visita a Salvemini in carcere," in *Salvemini: Alcuni significanti tributi*, special Salvemini edition of *Controcorrente* (Boston), 1958. The petition, "Un indirizzo di simpatia a Gaetano Salvemini," appeared with 163 signatures in *CdS*, *La Voce Repubblicana*, and *Rivoluzione Liberale*, June 27, 1925.

104. Prefetto di Firenze (Palmieri) to MI, July 13, 1925, *SPD, CR*"S"; AG, *VCR*, 45–46; "Il prof. Salvemini in libertà provvisoria," *Il Giornale d'Italia*, July 14, 1925, *SPD, CR*"S."

105. PiC, "IlM," 102–105; GS, *Mem*, 26; AG, *VCR*, 46.

106. Prefetto da Firenze (Palmieri) to MI, DGPS, July 7, 1925; Questore di Roma (Pirilli) to DGPS, July 16, 1925; Prefetto di Napoli (Castelli) to MI, July 16, 1925; Prefetto di Napoli to MI, July 20, 1925, *CPC*"S" ACS; GS to Gina Lombroso Ferrero, July 14, 1925, *Cart 1921*, 344; to UO, July 14, 1925, *Cart 1921*, 344–345; to PG, July 18, 1925, *Cart 1921*, 347; "*NM*," 18–19; *Mem*, 24–26; AG, *VCR*, 46.

107. GS to Giacosa, July 19, 1925, *Cart 1921*, 351–352; Rector, University of Florence to GS, July 15, 1925, *Cart 1921*, 345; GS to Ferrero, July 23, 1925, *Cart 1921*, 353.

108. Prefetto di Napoli to MI, July 27, 1925; Prefetto di Napoli (Castelli) to MI, July 28, 1925; Prefetto di Genoa (Darbesio) to MI, DGPS, July 30, 1925, *CPC*"S" ACS; Angelo Crespi to GS, July 20, 1925, *Cart 1921*, 353; GS to Giacosa, July 30, 1925, *Cart 1921*, 359–363; *Mem*, 24–26; Nello Rosselli to GS, August 6, 1925, *Cart 1921*, 369–370.

Salvemini was amnestied by Regio Decreto n. 1277, July 31, 1925 ("Amnistia e indulto per reati communi e militari"), published in the *Gazzetta ufficiale del Regno d'Italia*, 1 agosto 1925, n. 177. Biographical summary, Prefetto (Florence), February 20, 1927, *CPC*"S" ACS.

109. GS, *Mem*, 27–28.

Chapter 8

The Making of an Exile

This was one of Mussolini's gravest errors: he let slip through his hands his most decisive and intelligent adversary.

Ernesto Rossi, 1957[1]

On the night of October 4, 1925, death squads of Florentine Fascists set in motion a calculated campaign to eliminate local opposition. The raids were also an attempt by the intransigent Fascist Tullio Tamburini and his militia to recapture the fervor of the *squadrismo* that had characterized the Fascist movement in its earliest phase. When Florentines awoke the next morning, they learned that the victims of the "pogrom" included the socialists Gaetano Pilati and Gustavo Consolo, both linked to *Non Mollare*. Pilati was shot in bed and Consolo was killed in front of his wife. Rumor had it that the Blackshirts had also assassinated Salvemini.[2]

Salvemini was actually staying with Fernande in Paris, safely out of reach of the squads. Had Salvemini not escaped two months earlier, Rossi believed that he certainly would have been a victim of the violence. His name had been among the first on the proscription list.[3]

A few days after the "Fatti di Firenze," Lina Waterfield, a reporter for the London *Observer*, traveled to Florence. While there, she arranged an interview with Italo Balbo, one of the original quadrumvirs of the March on Rome and now a top Fascist leader, recently dispatched to Florence by Mussolini to reestablish order. *Il Duce* saw the Florentine violence as a challenge to his attempt to gain control over the Fascist Party, and at an October 5 Fascist Grand Council meeting demanded an end to *squadrismo*. He was also preparing for the Locarno Conference and found the violence an international embarrassment.[4]

Balbo issued orders restoring discipline and condemning the enemies of Fascism. When Waterfield met Balbo, he politely handed her a written policy statement. Then he remembered that she numbered Gaetano Salvemini among her friends. Suddenly Balbo's demeanor turned ugly, and he launched a verbal assault on Salvemini, accusing him of poisoning the minds of Italian youth and insisting that he should be stripped of his chair at the university. When Waterfield defended her friend as a disciple of Mazzini, Balbo furiously retaliated, "Salvemini ought to be put up against a wall and shot!"[5]

By the time Salvemini reached safety in France in August 1925, he was already planning a long-term exile in England or the United States. That plan, still vague, was contingent on the Fascist regime remaining in power. Within a year, Salvemini would embark upon his "third life," the life of an exile, or *fuoruscito*,[6] exploring opportunities for a professional career while mounting an anti-Fascist campaign. He soon dedicated himself to this task with such intensity that he became the acknowledged leader of the anti-Fascist exiles and one of Mussolini's most formidable adversaries. In fact, this "third life" would consume so much of his creative energy that it would redefine his identity, and his career as historian and anti-Giolittian political activist would be largely forgotten.

In the late summer of 1925, however, he was not yet convinced that he would lose his job or that the regime would survive another year. Because he had no source of income, he still hoped to return to Italy to reclaim his job. He wrote to the rector of the University of Florence requesting a reinstatement on the basis of the amnesty,[7] but lingering uncertainty about his status forced him to consider more expedient alternatives. He tried unsuccessfully to contact the mysterious Frenchman who had sold him the black market passport in 1923, asked French and English friends to help him find a job, and made inquiries in the United States.[8]

The news from Italy was appalling. In fear of the authorities, the Florentine woman to whom he had entrusted his papers—diaries, documents, and a complete collection of *Non Mollare*—had burned them. Yet he believed that these same authorities were anxious to protect him: "If they kill me," he wrote, "it will become a second Matteotti case; if they assault me it will become a third Amendola case." Another assurance was his notoriety in England, where a number of prominent Liberals and Labourites continued to protest his treatment, even in the House of Commons. Mussolini's sensitivity to Fascism's image abroad seemed to offer some hope that he would be safe. On the other hand, there was a serious question as to Mussolini's ability to control local *squadristi*.[9]

The first week of September, Salvemini arrived in Paris to join his wife. Paris was already a refuge for Italian anti-Fascists, including Amendola and Donati, who welcomed Salvemini as a major asset to the cause.[10] Once Salvemini arrived, he began to contact the other *fuorusciti* and to reunite with "Esto" Rossi in their campaign of anti-Fascist protest. All that Salvemini had taken with him into exile, except for his small personal bag, was the Santoro file: a large packet of prosecutor's charges against Fascists, especially those related to Matteotti's murder. He and Rossi sent them to Florence, where Carlo Rosselli published them in *Non Mollare*, frustrating the authorities.[11] This technique of secretly mailing information back to Italy, discovered in desperation during his first weeks in exile, would become a favored tactic of the nascent anti-Fascist movement.[12]

Salvemini felt a desperate need to return home,[13] but in Italy the regime was consolidating its power and conditions were becoming more menacing. One friend wrote in mid-September, "The battle by all the opposition [groups] is lost." Salvemini's fate now seemed clear. In view of his anti-Fascist activities, there seemed no hope of him returning while the Fascists held power.[14]

Advice from friends conflicted. While pro-Fascist Ugo Ojetti advised him to avoid interviews or articles critical of the government, Carlo Rosselli made an ardent plea for his mentor to return to provide intellectual force and to build a new leadership class among the young generation. "This man is you," Rosselli wrote. "There is no one else in Italy."[15]

The first week in October, as classes were to begin, Salvemini learned that the rector rescinded the July order and restored his faculty status, but it was at that same moment that the Blackshirt violence had erupted. Now he heard that soldiers always watched his house and that he had been blacklisted.[16] It was up to Piero Calamandrei, law professor and close adviser, to give his friend the heartbreaking news: "Given the state of mind of the Florentine Fascists, it is mathematically certain that your return to the university would produce turmoil and devastation."[17]

Similar warnings came in rapid succession. Nitti, Berenson, and Sestan advised him against returning, and Marion Cave wrote from Florence that local Fascists had sworn that Salvemini would never again teach in the city.[18] In contrast, Carlo Rosselli held out hope, admitting that local Fascists were out of control but suggesting that Salvemini join him in Milan, where he could organize an elite among the dispirited anti-Fascists. Rosselli anticipated a period when Mussolini would normalize his regime and thus would have to accommodate political expression.[19] Salvemini's sister-in-law and student, Lidia Minervini, having heard that he planned to resign, pled on behalf of faculty and students that he instead request a leave of absence.[20]

The Florence "pogrom" provided the catalyst for Salvemini's decision. In October, he wrote to Nicky Mariano that he had decided to live abroad: "My revulsion for a government of assassins is stronger than my attachment to my students."[21] He explained that he would use the freedom afforded in exile to tell the world the truth about the Fascist regime. To return to Florence, abandon anti-Fascism, and remain silent would be the ultimate cowardice. Fernande was in full sympathy; they had calculated that they could support themselves by his publications and lectures and her French language lessons to tourists visiting Paris.[22]

On November 5, Salvemini submitted his now famous letter of resignation to the rector of the University of Florence: "The Fascist dictatorship has suppressed in our country those conditions of liberty without which the teaching of history in the university—at least as I understand it—loses all its independence and, therefore, all its dignity."[23]

"I am starting life over for the third time," he observed. "I began it at seventeen when I arrived in Florence; I started over at thirty-five after losing everything at Messina; I begin [life] again at fifty-two."[24] His decision to commit to the life of a *fuoruscito* was filled with implications, not the least of which was the choice of a new home. His wife's home in Paris was, for several reasons, less appealing than other alternatives. On the pragmatic level, England offered more immediate possibilities for earning a living, and he had established many more contacts among the intellectual community there than in France. Just as important was his growing belief that his anti-Fascist campaign must concentrate on English and American opinion, anticipating the day when Mussolini's government ran into international problems. Furthermore, he felt at home in London, "free among the free, a man among men," a reflection of his strong affinity with English political culture; in France, he felt more like an exile. Copies of his letter of resignation appeared in the British press, reinforcing the reservoir of good will that English Liberals and Labourites held for him since his lectures and subsequent reports of his arrest and imprisonment.[25]

It soon became clear that he might not have to make a material sacrifice at all. In return for a series of articles, a Czech journal had offered him a sum that paid a year's rent, and in three days he had written an article that paid the equivalent of an additional two months' rent. Similar projects in England and France led him to calculate that by April he would have earned enough to support his family for the entire year of 1927. That year he had earmarked for a lecture tour in the United States, a prospect that excited him. Having already delivered more than sixty lectures since fleeing Italy, while publishing about fifty articles in six countries and completing his first book on Fascism, he would now be able to earn a living by lecturing.[26]

The anticipated American tour was part of a plan to launch an anti-Fascist movement in exile. Propaganda would play an essential role not only in shaping English and American opinion but, by smuggling anti-Fascist journals into Italy, Italian opinion as well. Moreover, now that *Non Mollare* had suspended publication, he hoped to publish a similar journal in England or France. Relying on Italian newspapers and whatever books and clippings Italian friends made available, he devised the ingenious method of using Fascist sources to demonstrate the government's failures. By the end of 1925, Marion Cave and others were regularly mailing him periodicals, and the regime worried about the potential impact of his revelations.[27]

In a dialogue with Salvemini over the propaganda campaign, Ernesto Rossi identified a crucial problem: a vast majority of Italians living abroad were laborers who read very little and certainly had little appetite for a review of the *Non Mollare* type. Salvemini had greater hope than Rossi in the potential of mounting an effective anti-Fascist movement abroad and had already begun to publish in the labor press and the Italian-language press in England, France, and the United States. The necessity of mobilizing one million Italian emigrants, most of them blue-collar workers in the United States, would remain a major challenge for years to come. In the meantime, Salvemini was committed to creating a review that would clarify the ideas of the anti-Fascist movement while preparing a vanguard of a few thousand Italians who could work independently, not relying on the old parties. Published abroad, this journal would enjoy greater freedom than did Italian reviews such as the Milanese *Quarto Stato*, in which Carlo Rosselli and Pietro Nenni had to veil their message. A point on which Rossi and Salvemini agreed was the need for a clandestine tabloid that would be circulated in Italy to keep alive an underground anti-Fascist network.[28]

Attempts on Mussolini's life led the regime to institute more repressive legislation at the end of 1925. When police arrested former PSU Deputy Tito Zaniboni, the government took away from Parliament its ultimate power, making the prime minister responsible only to the king. In the process, they passed laws that outlawed secret societies, Zaniboni's party, and its newspaper, *La Giustizia*, a step toward silencing all opposition. Included in the new round of repressive laws were those enabling the government to dismiss its employees for "political incompatibility" and deprive of citizenship and property any Italian abroad who disturbed public order in Italy. All punishment could now be accomplished by administrative order without judicial recourse. At the end of November, Salvemini heard that the government was targeting him under the new laws.[29]

Fascists immediately challenged the minor propaganda victory that Salvemini had won with his letter of resignation. First, when the Academic Senate of the University of Florence voted unanimously to reprimand him for injuring the Italian government in the foreign press, the Fascists publicized the results as widely as they could. Then, on December 4, the rector informed him that the Minister of Public Instruction (ignoring his resignation) had dismissed him for abandoning his position, retroactive to October 16, and had billed him for all subsequent pay.[30]

By the end of 1925, reports were reaching Salvemini that confirmed his dread of the loss of academic freedom. Marion Cave wrote that schoolchildren were now being required to give the Fascist salute and that Fascist librarians at the university were recording student requests. In the process, they had begun to limit the circulation of Salvemini's works.[31]

Traveling between France and England in 1926, Salvemini maintained his propaganda assault on the Fascist regime.[32] He quickly encountered opposition. First, an Italian professor at Oxford, demanding that he not criticize the government, tried to block his lectures. Undaunted, Salvemini delivered the lectures on "The Rise of Fascism" in February 1926. His initiation came while addressing the National Liberal Club of London, when he was challenged by Luigi Villari, son of Salvemini's beloved former professor and a leading defender of Fascist policies. Villari directed the Italian propaganda effort in England, and through his work, Salvemini complained, "the Fascist version reached an immense public in all countries and became daily bread of any college professor who wanted . . . to become an 'expert' in recent Italian history."[33]

Opposing Villari was initially anguishing because of the great admiration he had held for Villari's father:

I was always convinced that Pasquale Villari, . . . if he were living, would have sided with me and not with his son. But the pain of writing this surname always disturbed me. Finally, after much distress, I discovered the means to overcome this uneasiness: I wrote Luigi XXX.[34]

Villari would become Salvemini's nemesis in England as the two engaged in a running polemic in the British press and in lecture halls.[35]

Salvemini's propaganda campaign was complicated by the considerable support that Mussolini commanded in England, particularly among Conservatives. Winston Churchill had praised the Fascist government, and Austen and Neville Chamberlain and Rudyard Kipling had joined the chorus, along with George Bernard Shaw and a number of British newspapers. In 1926, Sir Oswald Mosley was still a Labourite, but by 1932 he would found the British Union of Fascists.[36]

In Italy, the Fascist press responded to Salvemini's lectures and articles by intensifying the verbal barrage. In February 1926, the Roman Fascist-Futurist paper *L'Impero* wrote, "It would not be surprising if some Fascist, with guts and a heart, lost his temper and sent [Salvemini] to reflect about his affairs in a quieter and more peaceful world." *Il Popolo d'Italia* implored its readers to "make life difficult" for the exiles, while the Milanese Fascist paper *Il Torchio* spelled out its message less equivocally: "Go ahead, you Fascists who love *Il Duce*. . . . Cross the borders. . . . kill!"[37]

While the level of threats escalated, so did the legal campaign to punish Salvemini and other *fuorusciti*. On September 30, the government issued a royal decree, based on his activities as a *rinunciatario*, a publisher of *Non Mollare*, and a critic of the Fascist regime, depriving Salvemini of his citizenship and his pension. To dramatize the point, Admiral Costanzo Ciano, a member of Mussolini's cabinet, travelled to Molfetta to be made an honorary citizen in a ceremony in which he officially replaced Salvemini in his hometown citizenry. According to the January law under which the decree was issued, Salvemini could now also be deprived of all his property, including royalties from his books.[38]

In October 1926, a New York promoter introduced to him by F. S. Nitti proposed a series of American lectures on Fascism. Salvemini accepted, and with the aid of Berenson and Walter Lippmann—and over the opposition of the Italian Embassy in Washington—he obtained a visa. He set lofty goals: lecturing on Fascism for six months from New York to San Francisco, and earning enough money to support his family for the next year. In the last days of 1926, Salvemini left Le Havre on his first trans-Atlantic voyage.[39]

The years 1927–1933 marked a period of transition in Salvemini's life. They were years of near frantic activity during which he made round-trip crossings of the Atlantic on four occasions, delivered scores of lectures, taught at several American universities, published numerous articles and two books on Fascism, and helped to organize two major political groups of anti-Fascist Italian exiles. This period of prolific work and extensive travel was also one of intellectual transition—in his understanding of Italian Fascism, in his development of an anti-Fascist campaign, and in his view of America.

Propaganda—or informing the world of the truth about the Fascist regime, as he saw it—was the primary tactic of Salvemini's campaign. In an era when Mussolini was at his peak of popularity in the United States and Western Europe, this was a daunting task indeed.[40] To discredit the Duce was only the beginning, however.

In September 1926, in a letter entitled "Fascism without Mussolini," he had stated another axiom: in spite of the fact that much of the world identified Fascism with Mussolini, the real power in Fascist Italy lay in a coalition of generals and industrialists. A more stable, moderate man, such as Luigi Federzoni, could thus succeed Mussolini with little loss of Fascist power. In a remarkably farsighted analysis, Salvemini made the case that ridding Italy of Mussolini was not enough. When he fell, the forces behind him must be removed from power as well.[41] At every opportunity, Salvemini would broadcast this argument throughout the next two decades.

If, at the end of 1926, Salvemini already knew the Fascists too well, he knew very little about Americans. He hoped to explain the realities of Fascist Italy to the American public, "not to speak to the converted."[42] He would quickly discover how few Italian Americans had themselves "converted" to anti-Fascism, and how many found Mussolini's Italy a source of pride, especially because of the effectiveness of Fascist propaganda. The sobering comprehension of these truths quickly deflated his hopes that the United States might readily be transformed into an anti-Fascist force.

On January 5, 1927, the day he arrived in New York, Salvemini gave the press several lessons, one in interviewing and at least two in Italian history. His impatience rendered him the most unlikely of candidates for the kind of human-interest feature story that American newspapers preferred. He quickly directed the questioning to Fascism, bitterly attacked the regime, and labeled the March on Rome a "military coup" and the Fascist Party "an unscrupulous armed minority."[43]

The next morning, he discovered that his agent had scheduled two major appearances, the first sign of a rigorous schedule. First he spoke at a luncheon meeting of the board of directors of the Foreign Policy Association. In his introduction to the American banquet circuit, he disliked the idle chatter even more than the badly prepared food. Nonetheless, he quickly won his audience with forthright answers. Questioned about the intent of his tour, he explained that he had come to make speeches in order to earn a living; at the same time, he hoped to inform the American public about conditions in Fascist Italy.[44]

Then a *New York Times* editor, an apparent admirer of Mussolini, asked him if in fact unemployment had not decreased. Salvemini responded, "How do you know that there is not unemployment?"

"Statistics tell me."

"Do you not know," Salvemini replied, "that statistics are the height of deception?"

The luncheon guests roared their approval, and at that point Salvemini knew that he had passed his first test. He also learned the lesson that humor was a valuable commodity at such affairs, where Americans "combined lectures and digestion."[45]

That same evening he was escorted across town to face a second test, this time an audience of journalists, university professors, and businessmen at one of New York's exclusive clubs. Lippmann presided, and after a speech on Fascism Salvemini was confronted by Thomas Lamont, a partner in the Bank of Morgan. The most ardent of all the American financiers who patronized Mussolini, Lamont had just returned from negotiating a $100 million loan to Italy on extremely favorable terms.[46]

At issue was the economic credibility of Fascist Italy. Lamont asked Salvemini if the loans that Mussolini had secured in America did not prove that he had won America's confidence. In answering, Salvemini launched his campaign to undercut Fascist claims of economic progress. First, the Italian economy had begun to improve by 1920, and thus Mussolini had merely reaped the benefits of the policies of the pre-Fascist governments; second, he had squandered the benefits of that recovery by rewarding his private backers. In fact, Salvemini concluded, any reputation for economic success that Mussolini had won had been the result of Fascist propaganda and American loans.

Salvemini believed that he won the final exchange with Lamont, but his buoyancy was tempered by the realization of the awesome proportions of the battle that lay ahead. Particularly discouraging was the influence that Fascist propaganda had already won among the sophisticated audience of New York businessmen and professionals, but, as was frequently the case on this tour, the demanding itinerary left him little time for reflection. At the end of an exhausting day, his agent boarded him on a train for Columbus, Ohio, where he was scheduled to speak the next afternoon.[47]

Salvemini made the 1,400-mile trip from New York to Columbus to Portland, Maine, in little more than two days. In the process he had delivered four lectures. Later in the tour he wrote to his wife in Paris that he had seen little of America except "telegraph poles and conference rooms." What he did see made a strong impression on him, particularly the vast geographical expanses. Americans seemed to travel great distances—the equivalent of Lisbon to Berlin, for example—as if they were merely traveling across town. Traveling at night, regularly deprived of his preferred ten hours of sleep, he usually felt like a "wet rag" the next day.[48]

On January 15, Salvemini arrived in Boston, barely ahead of the winter's bitterest storm. Harvard professor William Y. Elliott presided at the 1:00 P.M. Saturday luncheon meeting of the local Foreign Policy Association for a debate on Mussolini's policies. What Salvemini soon discovered, but the press did not report, was that he was confronting two Fascist propaganda agents, part of a comprehensive plan of Italian Ambassador Giacomo De Martino. De Martino won the approval of his government to counter Salvemini's campaign with one of his own: avoiding violence that might win sympathy for Salvemini as victim, ignoring him as much as possible in the Fascist press, and providing Fascists to debate him at his lectures. Bruno Roselli and James P. Roe were two who would shadow him. He knew Roselli from the previous Saturday's debate in Portland, Maine, and he was familiar with Roe's work.[49]

A professor of Italian literature at Vassar College and a former attaché of the Italian Embassy, Roselli presented a challenge to Salvemini because of his poise, Oxford accent, and impressive physical bearing. Roe represented another kind of challenge altogether. He was an admirer of Fascism and a supporter of the Fascist League of North America (FLNA) who had spent considerable time traveling in Italy. However, he was introduced simply as a New York lawyer and editor and therefore appeared as an American who, like many others, had been greatly impressed with the achievements of Fascist Italy.[50]

The three men delivered their presentations. Salvemini made his case of Fascist repression and its inherent dangers. Roselli lauded the discipline, order, and prosperity that he claimed Mussolini had brought to Italy, following the Fascist line that the *Il Duce* had saved the country from economic chaos and Bolshevik revolution. Roe praised Italian industrial and economic progress and argued that such strength was the best guarantee against war.

Salvemini presented a contrast to the dapper Roselli. He was older and paunchy in his one, ill-fitting suit that seemed to be taking the travel as hard as he. Nevertheless, his enormous energy and his reputation for courage in the face of Fascist threats and imprisonment won the respect of much of the audience.

As would often be the case, questions turned to Mussolini's leadership. Salvemini knew that to destroy Mussolini's respectability, he would have to discredit him as well as his policies. Mussolini was a master of illusions, he declared, who was taking Italians down the road to ultimate disaster. Anti-Fascists in the audience believed that Salvemini had again prevailed, but newspaper accounts were inconclusive. The Fascist government, recording the reports of agents in attendance, was satisfied that Salvemini had been "effectively refuted."[51]

Before leaving Boston, Salvemini made the acquaintance of two men who were to become valuable allies in the long campaign that lay ahead. One was Michele Cantarella, a young Sicilian veteran of the Alpine Corps who was completing his graduate work at Boston University and was destined to become—along with his wife, Hélène—a trusted friend and an anti-Fascist colleague. The other was Felix Frankfurter, respected Harvard Law professor and confidant of many leading American liberals. In later years, Frankfurter's intimacy with New Dealers would provide Salvemini with a potential link to policy makers.[52]

After speeches in Cleveland and Montreal, Salvemini returned to New York for four days of activities. The first major engagement was a return to the Hotel Astor for a luncheon meeting of the Foreign Policy Association. The publicity from his previous appearance helped to produce a crowd of 1,200 diners and an additional overflow audience in the balcony of the large ballroom, this time including a sizable Italian-American contingent. In some respects it was a repeat of the previous Saturday's meeting, with Salvemini and the ubiquitous Roselli in turn rendering contrasting evaluations of Fascist Italy. "Italy no longer has free, representative institutions, but a dictatorship," Salvemini charged. "Italy no longer has a king, but a prisoner of war with the title of king."[53]

Then he turned to Mussolini: "In recent years, Italy has produced two marvelous actors of the cinema: Mussolini and [Rudolph] Valentino. If you want to understand the hold Mussolini has on the Blackshirts, remember the demonstration over Valentino when he died."[54]

As the crowd's excitement grew, someone shouted from the balcony behind him: "You're a liar!" When the man repeated the remark, city detectives hustled him from the auditorium. Salvemini kept his poise at this first hint of disorder. But the exchange intensified when he was confronted by Count Ignazio Thaon di Revel, president of the FLNA. Thaon di Revel waved a book that he claimed listed "Fascists assassinated by Bolsheviks, your friends."

Salvemini denied the allegation and countered with charges of Fascist violence. Thaon di Revel retaliated with the all too familiar attack on Salvemini's patriotism. The crowd maintained its interest for more than three hours. Sophisticated audiences had never before heard such an impassioned and powerful anti-Fascist plea, simply because Italian-American anti-Fascists had not talked to them.

Reviews were mixed. Fascist authorities noted that Salvemini had painted a most dismal situation in Italy. The Fascist-leaning New York Italian language daily *Il Progresso Italo-Americano* scored a victory for Thaon di Revel and Roselli, whereas the *Herald Tribune* reported that Salvemini seemed to win more applause. He agreed, but now he realized that Fascists would exploit two themes in particular, those of communism by association and *anti-italianità*. The former was designed to play to a general American audience, which unfamiliar with the subtleties of the European Left, might be led to assume that Salvemini's socialism was communism. The attack on Salvemini's patriotism was one that Fascists had used before and would use quite effectively in Italian-American communities.[55]

Two nights after the affair at the Hotel Astor, Salvemini addressed a smaller but no less eager audience at the Society for Ethical Culture on West Sixty-fourth Street in Manhattan. Fascist authorities described the Society membership as "predominantly Masons and Jews," several hundred of whom turned out to hear Salvemini speak. The appearance also drew a sizable group of Italian Americans, more polarized and raucous than any American audience he had yet witnessed Among them were a number of Fascists, including Thaon di Revel, Giacomo Bonavita, and Domenico Trombetta, publisher and editor of *Il Grido della Stirpe* ("The Cry of the Race"), which he called the "most faithful voice of Fascism in America."[56]

As Salvemini began his criticism of *Il Duce* and his policies, hecklers in the gallery began to interrupt. When the noise increased, members of the bomb squad and detectives, alerted after disturbances at the Astor, began to hustle the Fascist hecklers from the hall. Before Salvemini had finished his presentation, police had evicted more than fifty spectators. Joined by other Fascists, they gathered outside the hall to continue shouting. The police captain at the local precinct station then dispatched reserves, who established police lines a block from the Society hall. As they moved on the crowd to drive them from the building's entrance, Bonavita, referred to as a Fascist "triumvir," was stabbed by an unidentified assailant.[57]

The increasingly hostile response from Italian-American Fascists indicated that Salvemini's campaign was hitting home and that he would find heated opposition at every turn. His combative instincts were strong, however, and, having been driven by thugs and by official harassment from a nation where he felt the laws had been made a mockery of, he was eager to test the freedoms of the press and public expression in America.

Between speaking engagements, Salvemini often added informal presentations organized by local anti-Fascists. While in New York, he accepted the invitation of Oswald Villard to meet with the editorial staff of *The Nation*. Villard became a friend, supporting anti-Fascist causes and soliciting Salvemini's articles for publication. The pace of his political activities kept Salvemini occupied. He wrote to Villard: "I belong to an agricultural, old, slow civilization, and I am bewildered by this new environment."[58]

At the end of his first week in the United States, *The Nation* published his article "Mussolini Chokes the Press." He had written it in London, using Fascist sources—decrees, circulars to prefects, memoranda, statements from the semiofficial press, and the press law of December 1925—to document the demise of the free press in Italy.[59]

He participated in a symposium with Roselli before 1,000 members of the Economic Club of New York before traveling again to the Midwest. In Chicago, in late February, while addressing a crowd at the LaSalle Hotel, he was challenged by Federica Blankner, an admirer of the Fascist education system. After contesting his message, she vitriolically attacked him as a "traitor" and a "charlatan" who was selling out his country for "two hundred dollars a lecture."[60]

Returning to the East Coast, Salvemini sustained the same pace, addressing 300 members and guests at a Foreign Policy Association luncheon in Philadelphia in mid-March, then appearing at an "open forum" at the Hippodrome Theater in Baltimore. The next day he spoke at the weekly Town Hall series in Manhattan, and the following night he attended a banquet in his honor in Hoboken, New Jersey. Here 1,500 guests joined in the celebration, among them a number of leading American anti-Fascists, including members of the Anti-Fascist Alliance of North America (AFANA), a New York labor-leftist coalition, and a number of anti-Fascist immigrants from Molfetta.

At the speakers' table was his old friend Raffaele Rossetti, who had founded the Italia Libera group in Italy; Vincenzo Vacirca, former Italian socialist deputy and an editor of the New York anti-Fascist newspaper *Il Nuovo Mondo*; and the colorful anarcho- syndicalist leader Carlo Tresca, publisher and editor of *Il Martello*. Rossetti introduced his friend with lavish praise, stressing the moral qualities he had brought to America. This partisan audience provided relief from the usual barrage of opposition and one of only three opportunities to address his audience in Italian.[61]

On a Sunday afternoon in April, *Il Nuovo Mondo* sponsored a gathering of 2,000 Italian Americans at the Cooper Union hall at Fourth Avenue and Eighth Street in the East Village. It was to be Salvemini's last appearance on the tour. Tresca and Rossetti spoke, as did Carlo Fama, a prominent physician and an anti-Fascist activist. Fittingly, this last meeting focused on a major theme of the emerging American anti-Fascist program. Fama claimed that Ambassador De Martino had asked the Italian Chamber of Commerce to assist him in fighting anti-Fascists in the United States. Because the Italian Embassy was generating Fascist propaganda, Fama demanded the recall of De Martino. Fama opposed the propaganda on the basis that it was socially divisive and unpatriotic and thereby represented a national security risk to the United States. This attempt to counter Fascist propaganda activities would become a focus of Salvemini's campaign.[62]

As he concluded his tour, it was becoming clear to Salvemini that the key to the success of the anti-Fascist movement would be the battle for the hearts and minds of Italian America. Although the great majority of Italian Americans had been considered at least nominally patriotic American citizens, they also held strong emotional ties to the country of their birth. During the four months of his lecture tour, Salvemini had seen enough to know that the task would not be easy, but the experience of the last few weeks had led him to believe that a mass Italian-American anti-Fascist movement was possible.[63]

It was with mixed feelings that Salvemini boarded the steamer *Republic* for his return voyage to England on April 29, 1927. The pace had proved tiring, largely because of what he saw as unreasonable scheduling by his manager. He had found New York overwhelming and had not even found time to visit the Metropolitan Museum of Art. Nevertheless, the experience had given him hope. The Italian Embassy was sure that he had failed, but he knew that the struggle had barely begun, and he looked forward to his next American campaign. Meanwhile, he could enjoy the material success of the tour, which had produced enough income, especially given his frugal lifestyle, to support his family for three years without other employment.[64]

Out of the tensions between the New and Old Worlds, beginning with his first American lecture tour, Salvemini generated his campaign of anti-Fascism in exile. He arrived in England in early May. After a day's delay, during which British officials scrutinized his surreptitious passport, they permitted him to enter the country. For the next five months he resided in London and Manchester, speaking and writing about Fascist Italy.[65]

At about the same time that Salvemini returned to England, an article of his appeared in an American publication that, he later recalled, summarized his evaluation of Italian politics. In "Mussolini, the Pope and the King," he wrote that Fascist repression of political freedom had made any opposition short of revolution impossible. The parties were incapable, the leadership elites were pro-Fascist, and the king was unwilling to challenge Mussolini. Only the new "liberal-republican" groups, particularly through their clandestine press, showed promise. This was his first real attempt to explain why he thought that an indigenous uprising was impossible, and thus to justify the necessity of an international campaign.[66]

Salvemini's growing belief in the need for just such a campaign redoubled the significance of his American tour; in turn, the successes of the tour encouraged him to continue exposing the faults of Fascism to American, British, and French audiences. In his articles and speeches over the next several years, before his first book on the subject appeared, several themes persist that illustrate his interpretation of early Fascist history.

Repeatedly he demythologized Mussolini's rise to power, arguing that the March on Rome was a coup d'état and refuting Fascist claims to have saved Italy from political and economic ruin.[67] Once in power, he wrote, the Fascists consolidated their position by a series of Constitutional changes that had destroyed Italian democracy: suppression of parliamentary opposition; transfer of executive power to a perpetual head of government who ruled by arbitrary royal decree; and the establishment of the elitist corporate state and the Fascist Grand Council.[68]

Salvemini explained the demise of democracy in the loss of traditional freedoms. The government had "fascistized" the two greatest Italian newspapers, *Il Corriere della Sera* and *La Stampa*. They had also fined printers, blacklisted journalists, and organized official boycotts, with the effect of drastically reducing the number of opposition papers. After Anteo Zamboni's failed attempt to assassinate *Il Duce*, the third such attempt of 1926, the government suspended the rest of the papers. Furthermore, Mussolini took over as Minister of Interior with sweeping new legal authority. New "Exceptional Decrees" of November 1926 dissolved all parties other than the PNF and established *confino* (domestic exile), OVRA (secret police), and the Special Tribunal for the Defense of the State to conduct political trials.[69]

Convinced of the need to convey the reality of Fascist repression to the world, Salvemini sketched the outlines of a comprehensive anti-Fascist program. He believed that an armed anti-Fascist invasion would be "absurd" from both a political and technical point of view and that no "revolutionary committee" of exiles could direct a successful internal revolt from outside the country.[70] Because he understood the strength of the sources of Fascist power, Salvemini had never been optimistic about the fall of the Fascist regime. "This is a very long illness," he had told a friend as he fled Italy, "and it will end in a war." At his age, he doubted that he would live to see the return of liberty to his native land. Growing up in the South had not been conducive to optimism (one of his pseudonyms, it will be remembered, was "il pessimista"). Nor had his audiences made him optimistic. Since he was convinced that the Fascist regime could be toppled only by external force, he turned with determination to the task at hand: to build an anti-Fascist movement and a climate of opinion outside Italy that would throw its weight against Mussolini when *Il Duce*'s international adventurism left him vulnerable.[71]

Based on his first lecture tour, he elaborated on his propaganda initiative in July 1927. Because of Italy's economic dependence on the outside world, most evident in recent U.S. loans to the regime, the most effective contribution the exiles could make would be a propaganda effort extending beyond the English-speaking world to encompass the ten million Italians living outside Italy. Among the politically active Italians abroad, he estimated that the anti-Fascists held a four-to-one advantage. He knew that his success would be determined in large measure by his ability to win the loyalties of the less receptive Italian-American working class.[72]

In addition to spreading anti-Fascist propaganda, his strategy was to prepare Italians living abroad to accept a democratic agenda. The anti-Fascist movement must be prepared for the "day after" the inevitable crisis of the Fascist regime, when Italians would finally turn against Mussolini. Italian communists would be waiting with a plan, he wrote, but, left alone, they would establish a dictatorship worse than Mussolini's. The old political leaders of the liberal state also had their plan, whose ideas had already been proven bankrupt. The test of Salvemini's anti-Fascist movement would be its ability to prepare a third group, especially the youth, who were committed neither to Marxism nor to the existing Constitution. Such an appeal would have to be based on concrete reforms, immediately restoring individual freedoms, decentralizing power, and providing land, housing, and justice for peasants and workers.[73]

Throughout the Fascist era, Salvemini would reinforce these major themes—the first designed to undercut Mussolini and his supporters in the battle for foreign opinion, the second to prepare the world for the fall of Fascism, the third to enlist Italians abroad to support a program of democracy and justice.[74] The focal point for all elements of the campaign was neither Italy nor France, he wrote. "The key is in England and the United States."[75]

In lamenting the loss of Italian freedoms, Salvemini began in 1929 a modest defense of pre-Fascist Italy. "We did not have in Italy complete democracy," he wrote in Donati's *L'Italia del Popolo*. "But we had continually extended the area of democracy." This is the earliest evidence that Salvemini had begun to reevaluate the Giolittian era. Fascist repression had so violated his sensibilities that he began to see Italian democracy, in retrospect, as more meritorious.[76]

The most abhorrent aspects of the loss of Italian democracy were the injustice and violence of the Fascist system. He set out to pierce the veil of respectability in which Mussolini had shrouded his government. Using Italian newspapers, semiofficial publications like Farinacci's *Cremona Nuova*, and eyewitness accounts smuggled out of Italy, Salvemini documented a pattern of abuses inflicted with impunity against anti-Fascists. In the *Atlantic Monthly* he reported that Fascists under the notorious Augusto Ragazzi had attacked agricultural workers of Molinella, a stronghold of socialist opposition.[77] Later, in *The Nation*, he documented the judicial favoritism afforded the perpetrators of the Fatti di Firenze and the contrasting harsh sentences given to Ferruccio Parri and Carlo Rosselli for helping Turati to escape.[78] Using such case studies, Salvemini explained how Mussolini had "fascistized" the bench and the bar, imposed the death penalty for political offenses, and deported anti-Fascists to penal islands.[79]

Salvemini's propaganda campaign in the English press met formidable opposition, including a rejoinder from George Bernard Shaw. When the noted Irish dramatist published a letter in the London *Daily News* defending Mussolini and Fascism, Italian anti-Fascists and English leftists protested in an extended letter-writing campaign.[80] Salvemini joined the fray in October, eagerly engaging this new adversary in a polemic that *The Manchester Guardian* would sympathetically label that "The Taming of the Shaw."[81] Understanding that Shaw brought vast prestige to the battle, Salvemini charged that Shaw had been duped by Fascists and had lost his intellectual and moral bearing. He succeeded in putting Shaw on the defensive and winning considerable editorial support.[82]

Salvemini had begun his association with the Concentrazione Antifascista when it was founded in the spring of 1927. The Concentration was a confederation of Italian anti-Fascist political parties that had been reconstituted in France. After several months of negotiations, the party leaders had met in April 1927 at Nerac, France, where they had forged a fundamental agreement to organize anti-Fascists outside Italy while encouraging clandestine opposition within the country. The founders guaranteed the autonomy of the member parties, virtually assuring sectarian fragmentation.[83]

Support for the Concentration required patience and moderation, qualities for which Salvemini was not known. Of greater difficulty for him were the members' allegiances to the pre-Fascist and Aventinian parties, which he had criticized for facilitating Mussolini's rise to power.[84] Although Salvemini was not a member of the Concentration, he supported its efforts to forge an anti-Fascist organization. He frequently debated its leaders and contributed regularly to its newspaper, *La Libertà*.[85] In a series of 1927 articles, he warned against reviving the old party structures and ideologies. One of the most vivid lessons he brought back from his American tour, he wrote, was a demand that the leaders of the democratic parties "reach agreement on a common tactic and program."[86]

In the Concentration, Salvemini began to assume the role he would play in the anti-Fascist movement throughout the Fascist period, that of intellectual leader among the exiles. One historian has described this relationship as "external participation."[87] In this role, he persistently advocated his ideas—advising against dissension, romanticized notions of the imminent collapse of the Fascist regime, and the anticipation of post-Fascist politics. He thus became the "conscience" of the movement, sometimes regarded as moralistic, sometimes resented, but never ignored. In fact, he fit the role so well that eventually groups of anti-Fascist exiles, in his absence, often found themselves asking, "What would Salvemini say?"[88]

In 1927, an American publisher issued *The Fascist Dictatorship in Italy*, Salvemini's first book-length treatment of the subject, and the genesis of his trilogy on Fascism. His first book since the rise of Fascism brought to the anti-Fascist campaign the full range of his professional skills. The detailed reconstruction of events gave credence and power to his attacks against the regime and rendered his political message unique. Thus the debate begins in earnest over one of the important questions of Salvemini's three major books on Fascism: Are they history or propaganda?[89]

Although the books have been regarded as products of the *fuoruscito* experience, that is not entirely true. He was able to write a detailed account of the early movement largely because he had been preparing notes during his final three years in Italy; thus the work retains an immediacy that is invaluable. Because the book was formulated between 1922 and 1925, when sources were scarce, its accuracy and durability are all the more remarkable. When he fled, he first presented his interpretations in periodicals and lectures in England in late 1925 and 1926. When the book appeared in 1927, no scholarly works on Fascism existed. With the possible exception of Luigi Salvatorelli's insightful essay, *Nazionalfascismo* (1923), the earliest works on Fascism were either anti-Fascist critiques or Fascist propaganda.[90]

Salvemini's book differed from other early writings on Fascism by virtue of its methodology: succinct, "concrete" analysis that incorporated detailed documentation, including Fascist sources, and thus made *The Fascist Dictatorship* a lasting resource for scholars.[91] The larger issue is not Salvemini's accuracy, but whether he selected and ordered the evidence in such a way as to serve his anti-Fascist bias and whether he delivered his interpretations with a polemical tone, thereby distorting the totality of the regime.

Salvemini wrote *The Fascist Dictatorship* at a time when he believed that the greatest threat to his anti-Fascist campaign was Mussolini's appeal to the English-speaking public. To counter *Il Duce*'s image and Luigi Villari's efforts, Salvemini revealed a Mussolini largely unknown outside Italy. He was viewed as a "man of order" when, Salvemini believed, the historical record would show that Mussolini was just the opposite.[92] Thus, a major theme of the book is Mussolini's early career as a revolutionary socialist. The young Mussolini had been a serious revolutionary who accepted the Leninist position of neutrality in World War I. The "man of order" had been a man of revolution. In October 1914, Mussolini had come out in support of the war, viewing it as a means to social upheaval. As a result, rather than preventing the outbreak of a Bolshevik revolution in Italy, Mussolini had contributed to the social disorder of 1919–1920. Once he became convinced of the impossibility of revolution, however, he made a calculated move to the right. Here Salvemini was clearly using the tools of the historian to achieve a propaganda goal—the debunking of Mussolini's image—and he selected his evidence accordingly. Nevertheless, in documenting Mussolini's revolutionary socialism, Salvemini made a durable historical contribution as well.[93]

Although Salvemini focused on Mussolini, he also treated Fascism as a movement not simply to be identified with its most famous leader, as much of the world tended to do. Using the historical method to trace the roots of Fascism, he found them in the politics of the liberal state. He introduced the concept of "parliamentary paralysis" to explain the inability of successive cabinets to govern.[94] In a primarily political explanation, he emphasized the reactionary nature of Fascism, with its violent methods and antidemocratic values. Conservatives, reactionaries, nationalists, and militarists supported the Fascists as a counterforce to Bolshevism; career soldiers provided valuable organization and training, and in a time of crisis the army, the king, and the courts refused to stop Fascist lawlessness. In looking to the pre-Fascist era and in emphasizing the roles played by the army and the crown, Salvemini provided original contributions to the historical study of Fascism.[95]

In addition to the political interpretation, Salvemini explored a wide spectrum of causation—including the social, economic, and psychological crises of the postwar era, factors that had been largely ignored in the existing literature. In this respect he influenced subsequent writers such as Angelo Tasca and Federico Chabod, and he established a periodization of Fascism still widely accepted.[96]

One of the book's more notable contributions to the serious study of Fascism was Salvemini's portrayal of its complexity and dynamism. He depicted the early Fascist movement as "ultrarevolutionary," a position only recently accepted by scholars. However, he observed, the movement became more heterogeneous and more conservative in 1921, when Mussolini brought widely divergent groups under the banner of the PNF. Thus Salvemini identified the changing and divergent factions of the Fascist movement as no one else had done.[97]

As for polemicism, the issue is insignificant. For a man of such passions, Salvemini wrote *Fascist Dictatorship* with remarkable restraint. For example, on the question of whether French subsidies to *Il Popolo d'Italia* explain Mussolini's conversion to a prowar stance, Salvemini writes only that Mussolini was "publicly accused" of receiving the funds—now accepted as fact—and documents the accusations with four separate sources.[98] A polemical tone does invade the book occasionally, and especially near the end as he describes the murder of Giacomo Matteotti. In a later edition, he moderated the account of the Matteotti crisis, especially the role of Cesare Rossi, head of Mussolini's press office. After Rossi twice visited him in Paris to plead his case, Salvemini backed off from his accusation that Rossi had given the order for the murder, but he stopped short of accepting his plea of innocence.[99] Even so, given the impact of the Matteotti crisis on Salvemini's life and the fact that he was documenting the murder to the outside world for the first time, the original emotional tone is at least understandable.[100] Any antagonistic shading is also offset by the value of the historical documentation. It must be remembered that Salvemini was not writing for the ages. He was, as one observer has noted, a "historian of the present."[101] The enduring historical worth of his work is all the more exceptional when measured against his purpose: to unmask the regime.

Except for taking several summer trips abroad, Salvemini lived in England through 1928. He spent the remainder of this transitional period in Paris, punctuated by ventures back to the United States and England. While in London, he advised the Concentration, expanded his relationships with the British Left, and solicited support from the Trades Union Council. All the while, he waged the propaganda battle with Fascists and their British sympathizers.[102]

In opposing Luigi Villari and others, Salvemini's method of concrete analysis required that he obtain detailed, fresh information. He relied upon the British Museum's collection of *Il Corriere della Sera*, upon information sent to him from Paris by its former editor-in- chief, Alberto Tarchiani, and upon friends in Italy. Parri, Zanotti-Bianco, Nello Traquandi, and Riccardo Bauer, all members of the clandestine resistance movement, sent him books, pamphlets, newspapers, official statistics, and various other documents with which to build his case against the Fascist regime.[103]

In order to strengthen his campaign, Salvemini launched two new initiatives in 1928. Among his supporters in England he organized the Friends of Italian Freedom, which amplified the English-language effort against the regime, particularly in their own publication, *Italy To-Day*.[104] A second new venture was an international exposition of the anti-Fascist press that opened in Cologne, Germany, in June 1928. Salvemini raised enough money in England to finance the show and meticulously collected the materials. As a result of his campaign, he had by 1928 earned the reputation within Italian diplomatic circles as "the principal exponent of anti-Fascism in Great Britain."[105]

Despite the frugality of his life in London and Paris, Salvemini had virtually exhausted his funds by the end of 1928. Dependent on the irregular income he could generate from lectures, books, and university courses, he gratefully accepted in late 1928 an invitation to teach a course in Italian foreign policy at the New School for Social Research in New York.[106]

This second trans-Atlantic venture surpassed the first in both duration and variety. He traveled for five months, meeting a broad range of Italian Americans and discovering among them an *Italianità*—a pride in things Italian—so strong and widespread that it forced him to reevaluate his plans. He also met several Americans who would later offer him university positions.

Salvemini arrived in New York aboard the Cunard liner *Berengaria* from Southampton on the morning of January 3, 1929. Four days later he delivered the first of twelve weekly lectures to a class of twenty to twenty-five students at the "London Terrace" campus of the New School on West Twenty-third Street in Manhattan. The Italian consul general in New York, whose agents observed the class with interest, happily reported to Rome a modest response to Salvemini's first academic venture in the United States.[107]

The course at the New School was less than a week old when Salvemini addressed the Foreign Policy Association of Worcester, Massachusetts, marking the beginning of an ambitious schedule of speeches. By the end of March, he had delivered more than thirty lectures to civic groups and college audiences in the Northeast. He returned most frequently to Philadelphia and the greater Boston area, lecturing at each stop on one of five topics. The speech he presented most frequently on campus was entitled simply "Fascism."[108]

On February 11, when Salvemini had reached the midpoint of his lecture series at the New School, the Italian government announced the Lateran Pact and the accompanying Papal Concordat, by which church and state reached reconciliation after half a century. The arrangement, widely accepted as a victory for Mussolini, promised to be a valuable issue for Fascist propagandists in the United States. Salvemini, his anticlerical instincts flaring, incorporated the subject into his speeches. Appearing at Swarthmore College in the suburbs of Philadelphia on February 19, he interpreted the treaty as a concession by the government.[109] What Salvemini did not know as he addressed the group of fifty-seven at Swarthmore was that the Italian government had interfered with his presentation. The consul general had used influential persons to persuade the president of the college not to send invitations to the speech, and he took credit for the reserved tone as well as the small size of the group.[110]

In the East Coast speeches, Salvemini emphasized several themes. At the University of Pennsylvania department of history, he articulated a continuing revision of his views on pre-Fascist Italy: Italians had suffered political and economic regression under Mussolini. He repeated the point often; for example, in May at an outdoor debate with former *New York Post* Rome correspondent Percy Winner, before a large and intense group of Italians at Irving Plaza in New York City.[111]

In April 1929 Salvemini left New York for the West Coast. As he made his way by rail, he scrutinized the Italian communities that were to be a main constituent of the American anti-Fascist organization he planned. On Sunday morning, April 7, he arrived in Los Angeles aboard the Union Pacific. The fatigue of his journey was quickly forgotten when a spirited delegation of about fifty workers greeted him in a red-and-white-bannered motorcade that announced, "WELCOME SALVEMINI." It was his first direct contact with Italian-American laborers. They escorted him through the city's blue-collar neighborhoods, then allowed him to relax before his Sunday night speech.[112]

Salvemini's host in California was Joseph Ettor, the former syndicalist labor leader famous for his role in the 1912 Lawrence, Massachusetts, strike. Ettor coordinated the tour on behalf of such local anti-Fascist groups as Libertà and the Garibaldi Association and introduced Salvemini to the Italian-American working class. Arrangements tensed when Professor Constantine Panunzio requested that, in addressing an influential audience in San Diego, Salvemini deliver a moderate message. The need to reconcile Italian Americans and other Americans to the anti-Fascist campaign would continually challenge Salvemini.[113]

For the moment, he could approach the groups separately. After addressing the Los Angeles chapter of the American Civil Liberties Union on the night of his arrival, Salvemini spoke the next evening to a group of 500 Italian Americans at Symphony Hall. Speaking in Italian, he denounced the Fascist regime, pleasing his host with his "bubbling" eagerness and clarity.[114] His excitement energized the crowd, which included Fascist sympathizers, and disturbances ensued. A socialist reporter attributed the near riot to prior attacks on Salvemini by the Fascist press.[115]

His English-language appearances presented a different challenge. When he read his lectures, the audiences had difficulty understanding him. Practice improved his formal presentations, and he found greater success in spontaneously responding to questions, forgetting about pronunciation and charming his audiences with his passion.[116]

On April 17, Ettor escorted Salvemini to San Francisco for a week of lectures in the Bay Area. During this final week in California, he spoke repeatedly to packed houses. Press coverage was good, partly because of the attention given his visit by *Il Corriere del Popolo*. Under the guiding hand of Ettor, Salvemini spoke to a wide range of campus meetings, civic clubs, unions, and private groups.[117]

Exposure to notable Italian Americans in California made Salvemini acutely aware of a substantial problem confronting his anti-Fascist campaign. Many of the most wealthy and powerful Italian Americans—the *prominenti*—

were either conservative or sympathetic to Fascism. Professor Panunzio had made this point in asking for assurances of Salvemini's moderation, and both he and Ettor had difficulty raising money to sponsor the tour because of concern among the *prominenti* about Salvemini's politics.[118]

Addressing a convention of labor leaders in San Francisco, Salvemini learned another lesson in American politics. Presenting the case against Fascist unions, he explained that union officials, with the sanction of the government, had the authority to conscript members, withhold dues, and negotiate contracts without rank-and-file approval. To his disbelief, his audience eagerly approved these authoritarian methods. After fifteen minutes, he felt that he was "giving a lecture of Fascist propaganda, to the honor and glory of *Il Duce*."[119]

The return voyage by rail across the continent in the spring of 1929 offered Salvemini time to reflect on his West Coast venture. Despite difficulties, he had generated an auspicious response and good press coverage. He had made new friends who would become allies in the anti-Fascist cause, and he had forged a new facility with the English language.[120]

Above all, he understood for the first time the difficulty he faced in recruiting anti-Fascists from Italian-American communities, where an attraction to Mussolini was much stronger than he had anticipated. In his memoirs, written forty years later, he recalled the following:

They were almost all tireless workers, bound to their immediate and distant families by heroic deeds of sacrifice. Arriving in America illiterate, barefoot, and with sacks on their backs, they silently bore difficulties and pain, despised by all because they were Italians. And now you could hear repeated—even by Americans—that Mussolini had made Italy into a country where there was no unemployment, where everyone had baths in their homes, and the trains ran on time, and that Italy was respected and feared in the world. Whoever said that this was not so destroyed not only their ideal fatherland, but wounded their personal dignity. Italy, the Italian government, and Mussolini represented an indivisible unity in their minds; to criticize Mussolini was to fight against Italy and to offend them personally.[121]

Back from California, Salvemini stopped in the Boston area to visit friends and to lecture in Cambridge and Somerville. At Harvard he made several new acquaintances among the faculty. The noted Church historian Giorgio La Piana in turn introduced him to such prominent historians as Arthur Schlesinger, Sr., William L. Langer, and Samuel Eliot Morison. Their assistance would soon prove valuable.[122]

While completing his lecture obligations and preparing to return to Europe, Salvemini received a perplexing inquiry from a young poet. Lauro De Bosis was the twenty-eight-year-old son of a well-known Roman lyrical poet and an aristocratic American mother. He had taught Italian language and literature at Harvard and had published translations of a number of literary works. Yet when he requested a conference, Salvemini first thought of his Fascist sympathies. The young writer had supported the first phase of the movement, and in 1929 he held the position of secretary of the Italy-America Society of New York, an organization for the promotion of cultural relations between Italy and the United States. Knowing that the organization had perpetuated Fascist propaganda, Salvemini accepted De Bosis's request only reluctantly.[123]

De Bosis quickly won Salvemini's sympathy with his youthful directness. He explained his naive response to Fascism, his attraction to Crocean liberal politics, and his growing dislike of Fascist propaganda. He also said that he had tried to eliminate propaganda from the Italy-America Society in favor of a more traditional cultural program.[124]

Once he had earned Salvemini's confidence, De Bosis presented an audacious proposal. What did he think, the young poet asked, of a plan to fly an airplane over Rome, dropping leaflets that would exhort the Italian people to put an end to the shame of the Fascist regime? The older man attempted to regain his equanimity, neither wishing to encourage such a dangerous proposal nor to discourage such a useful one. He explained the difficulties and the potential consequences. Then Salvemini told him that if the flight were technically possible, he applauded from the heart.

"It is possible," De Bosis responded.[125]

Soon after his meeting with Lauro De Bosis in New York, Salvemini returned to Europe to rejoin his wife. When he reached Paris, he met with Alberto Tarchiani, who informed him of a bold plan for the imminent rescue of Carlo Rosselli, whom he had not seen since he left Florence four years before. Tarchiani had first proposed a rescue in the summer of 1927, when Rosselli was in prison awaiting trial in Savona. He had then been sentenced to five years' confinement on Lipari Island, where he had written *Socialismo liberale* and had further developed his political ideas in discussions with other anti-Fascists.[126]

Two of them—F. Fausto Nitti, nephew of the former premier, and Emilio Lussu, the militant Sardinian Action Party leader—joined Rosselli in an escape from Lipari on the night of July 27, 1929. Tarchiani had arranged the motorboat and pilot and awaited the escapees in Tunisia. There he joined them and accompanied them across the Mediterranean to Marseilles, where they landed and prepared to rejoin friends and family in Paris.[127]

Salvemini learned the details of the rescue plan from Tarchiani's telegram. Tarchiani asked that he join Turati and the anti-Fascist journalist Alberto Cianca to meet the fugitives in the Lyon station: "We are arriving tonight," it read. Salvemini could not avoid the chilling thought that the escapees might arrive in chains. Outside a cafe near the Lyon Station, the three waited "with our hearts in our mouths." In the shadows, their shapes distorted by the streetlight, appeared the tall form of Tarchiani accompanied by two others. Salvemini remembered the reunion as "one of the greatest joys of my life."[128]

The return of Rosselli and Lussu spurred plans for a new anti-Fascist organization, Giustizia e Libertà (GL). They joined other exiles at Salvemini's home in the suburb of St. Germain-en-lay for "animated discussions." As they organized, they maintained contact with several leaders of the clandestine movement in Italy, including Rossi, Parri, Bauer, and Giovanni Mira. They shared a political perspective of the democratic Left that was anticlerical and distrustful of existing anti-Fascist groups. Eight years later, Salvemini recalled that GL was to have been a "third alternative" to Fascism and communism: "a democratic, active, militant, aggressive movement, of the sort that existed in the first half of the nineteenth century, when political liberty had to be and was won by revolutionary methods."[129]

Although GL included members of the pre-Fascist parties, one of its tenets was to reject the parties themselves in favor of a "supraparty" movement of individuals. Salvemini and Rosselli developed this position as well as the rest of the GL political program: rejection of Marxism as well as the liberal state; pursuit of a free, democratic republic based on social justice. In committing to both *interclassismo* and "social justice," the GL leaders were hoping to appeal to the democratic Left while avoiding the terms *socialism* and *communism*, both of which were laden with partisan meanings.[130]

Initially more important than its ultimate political objectives was the attempt to establish GL as a "revolutionary movement," more flexible and less prone to doctrinal dispute than the old parties, organized inside Italy, and committed to terrorist deeds. GL's support for revolutionary deeds was intended to publicize anti-Fascism, embarrass Mussolini's government, and give hope to its opponents. Salvemini would support such actions only if they occurred outside Italy, and even then his enthusiasm was limited by political realism. Nonetheless he "applauded from the heart" the naive, passionate plans of De Bosis, was quick to defend exiles accused of such deeds, and readily exploited the publicity for anti-Fascist purposes. As a result, four incidents that brought notoriety to GL also linked him, fairly or not, to the principal participants: Fernando De Rosa, Camillo Berneri, Giovanni Bassanesi, and Lauro De Bosis.[131]

In October 1929 at a Brussels train station, De Rosa fired a shot at Crown Prince Umberto as he arrived to visit his fiancée, the Belgian princess Maria José. De Rosa, a young maximalist socialist from Turin, had reportedly been encouraged by several GL members. Salvemini believed that De Rosa had intended not murder but a protest against the Fascist regime. He based this conclusion on statements De Rosa had made to Giuseppe Modigliani and on circumstantial evidence—in particular, that the small-caliber pistol was ineffective from the distance from which De Rosa fired.

When De Rosa went on trial in September 1930, Salvemini and a number of Giellisti (GL members) traveled to Brussels to testify in his defense. He recalled that they "tried to make the jurors aware of the tears and blood spilled by the Fascist dictatorship in Italy." Their testimony amplified De Rosa's propaganda but failed to sway the jury. The court found him guilty and sentenced him to five years.[132]

Closely related was a Fascist counterinitiative to harass and discredit GL. It surfaced three months after De Rosa's trial, when Brussels police arrested Berneri, an anarchist professor, and French authorities apprehended Rosselli, Tarchiani, and Cianca. Berneri was charged with carrying a pistol and five photographs of Mussolini's Minister of Justice, Alfredo Rocco, who was attending a conference in Brussels; seven packages of dynamite caps were discovered in Cianca's apartment, along with a note from Berneri, linking the two cases.

Although not immediately obvious, both incidents were the work of one man, the agent provocateur Ermanno Menapace, a Fascist spy who had infiltrated anti-Fascist ranks. He had conspired with Berneri in his plot against Rocco and in another against the Belgian royal family, and he had "planted" the explosives in Cianca's apartment. He had then tipped off authorities in both capitals. Because Paris and Brussels had been regularly subjected to violent incidents, a climate of apprehension existed that rendered believable the rumors of enormous anti-Fascist conspiracies. Word quickly spread of a GL effort to assassinate the Italian delegation to the League of Nations and to murder Fascist Foreign Minister Dino Grandi.[133]

Salvemini soon found that Fascist propagandists had tied him to both incidents. Berneri was a disciple and former student of Salvemini who had worked on *L'Unità* and *Non Mollare* before both had fled Italy. Menapace accused Salvemini of paying Berneri for bombs to be used in the rumored League of Nations plot. Berneri was convicted in both Belgium and France.

Although the charges against Salvemini were patently false, the message was clear: Fascists would be tenacious adversaries in the battle for world opinion. They would not hesitate to attack his character or to conspire to harm him. By creating an aura of suspicion around the *fuorusciti*, Fascist authorities could convince the French and Belgian governments to conduct police surveillance, which would in turn inhibit anti-Fascist activities. Salvemini had learned that the Italian government was ruthless in suppressing opposition, and they now had let him know that they would pursue him wherever he went. "Berneri fell into the nets of Ermanno Menapace," he wrote later. "There were few *fuorusciti* who did not stumble sooner or later in some net of espionage."[134]

Although Salvemini had been a charter member of GL, had contributed to its design, and felt more comfortable in GL than he ever had in the Concentration, he still remained outside its organizational core. Eventually, he would disagree with Rosselli about the direction of the organization and would distance himself even more, retaining his role as intellectual, more committed to ideas than to organized politics. Fifteen years later, in a letter to Lussu, he recalled that he had participated as well as he could in GL's early phase. After 1929, he would not resume an active leadership role until he moved to the United States.[135]

In the years 1930–1933, Salvemini accepted a series of university lectureships at Harvard and Yale, with the result that he spent more time in the United States than in previous years and continued what he called his "discovery of America."[136] The Italian government responded to his American activities by interfering each time he was extended a teaching offer.

In the spring semester of 1930, Salvemini taught his first Harvard course. While the Berneri trial continued in Brussels, Salvemini left on his third trip to the United States. La Piana, with the support of William Langer, had arranged with the history department for Salvemini to teach a course on Italian foreign policy. Shortly after the course began in February, the Italian consul general in Boston reported to the ambassador that the professor had "refrained scrupulously" from making references to modern Italy because, in response to indirect pressure from the Embassy, the Harvard administration had "read him the riot act."

It is not clear whether Harvard had actually warned Salvemini in 1930 to avoid contemporary politics, or whether the consul's report was a product of wishful thinking. Salvemini may not have discussed the Fascist era in his course, but by his own account, he pursued his political activities, both on and off college campuses. He must not have "embarrassed" the administration, as the consul reported, because Harvard subsequently hired him twice. Nonetheless, the Italian government expressed growing concern about Salvemini's presence at such a prestigious institution and conducted surveillance of his activities.[137]

Salvemini spent "five happy months" at Harvard. His colleagues received him warmly, and La Piana and the Cantarellas befriended him. It was in 1930 that Hélène Cantarella began to translate into English a number of articles that Salvemini drafted in Italian, a practice that enabled him to publish in the American press.[138]

During this first semester at Harvard, Salvemini began to acquaint himself with the peculiarities of American campus life, such as dormitories and American-style written examinations administered on the "honor system." He found the highlight of the campus to be the Widener Library, one of the best in the world, with its rich collection of Italian works. He was especially impressed with the accessibility of its open stacks, its long hours of operation, and the cubicle where he could work. When he returned to Harvard in 1933, he would make the Widener Library his "second home."[139]

After speaking tours of the southeastern and midwestern United States, punctuated by visits to the New York area, he left New York on August 25 for

Paris. In four months of teaching one course, he had made $5,000, which, he calculated, was "enough to live for two years; a true godsend." In rejoining Fernande, he began his final protracted residency in Europe.[140]

When Salvemini resumed his GL activities in France, he found that, as a result of a number of arrests, the movement had been forced into a defensive phase. An informer had revealed to the Italian police the code name of Ernesto Rossi ("The Puppet"), and they were searching for him in Florence and Bergamo. Salvemini tearfully implored Rossi to stay in France for his safety, but Rossi was determined to return.

After De Rosa's conviction, Rosselli and Tarchiani were convicted in Lugano along with Giovanni Bassanesi for assisting the young Catholic liberal in his audacious 1930 midday propaganda flight over Milan.[141] Salvemini considered both trials to have been strategic "triumphs," in that sentences were minimal and both cases publicized opposition to the Fascist regime. The same could not be said for the arrest by Italian police of twenty-four GL members in Italy. The arrests marked the beginning of what he later called "a year of disaster, of which I cannot think without horror."[142]

Salvemini was bedridden, recovering from an asthma attack, when he heard the news in early September. Arrested were GL's entire clandestine command, including his close friends Rossi and Bauer. Fearing the death penalty, Salvemini organized a newspaper campaign in Europe and the United States on behalf of the Giellisti. Response was enthusiastic and widespread, and as a result Salvemini was able to focus attention on the Special Tribunal and thus to pressure Mussolini. The twenty-year sentences represented a relative victory; however, the exiles understood the great loss to the movement of two important leaders. For Salvemini, the thought of Rossi's confinement would remain until 1943 a gnawing and very personal reminder of the repression of the Fascist regime.[143]

The "year of disaster" seemed endless. In October 1930 several arrests in Rome touched off a series of events that provoked the young poet Lauro De Bosis to put into action the plan he had discussed with Salvemini the previous year. While De Bosis was in transit to New York, Rome police arrested his mother and two friends, Mario Vinciguerra and Renzo Rendi, along with members of the conservative anti-Fascist Alleanza Nazionale. The Special Tribunal in December 1930 sentenced Rendi and Vinciguerra to fifteen years imprisonment each.[144]

De Bosis now accelerated his plan. Concerned by his lack of credibility among anti-Fascists, frustrated and penniless in Paris, he recruited sponsors and began pilot training. Inspired by Bassanesi and by his own lyrical poem *Icaro* (Icarus), he persisted, despite crashing one plane during a training flight. On the afternoon of October 3, De Bosis took off from the French coast in his plane *Pegasus*. He reached Rome at about 8:00 P.M. and swooped daringly low over the Carso, Piazza Venezia, and other crowded squares, dropping pamphlets that urged the Italian people and the king to join forces in order to rid themselves of their Fascist oppressors. After almost half an hour, De Bosis left Rome, pursued by fighter planes of the Italian Air Force. Apparently out of fuel, he crashed to his death in the Tyrrhenian Sea. Once again Salvemini had lost a young friend to the campaign against Fascism.[145]

Beleaguered by this succession of emotionally draining losses, and recovering from his bouts with asthma, Salvemini was relieved to note the end of this "cursed year." In the spring he visited London, where he was joyfully reunited with Nello Rosselli. Nello, engaged in research at the Public Record Office, offered support to his former mentor: "He made me promise," wrote Salvemini, "that in case of need I would turn to Carlo for assistance, and he would reimburse his brother. I would never again see this beloved student."[146]

On September 1, 1932, Salvemini once again left France for the United States, this time to teach at Yale University. After a stop in New York, he proceeded to New Haven at the end of the month. He taught graduate students as a visiting professor in international relations in the fall term and planned to remain through the spring. Once again he was impressed by the "stupendous" campus library, the generosity of his colleagues, and the dedication of his students. The American universities pleased him, and he gradually began to consider the idea of settling in the United States.[147]

By the time he had completed his stay at Yale, Harvard, Princeton, and the University of California had offered visiting lectureships. Because the Italian government knew that he was a candidate for permanent employment, they stepped up pressure in the form of surveillance, attempts to discredit him, the use of informants, interception of his mail, and by provoking a series of public incidents. Part of the general offensive against the exiles, this campaign did create a kind of notoriety that accompanied him as he settled in the United States. This effort by the regime also was an acknowledgment that Mussolini considered the anti-Fascist campaign to be significant for the same reason that Salvemini did: it made *Il Duce*'s image vulnerable in the English-speaking world.[148]

Salvemini's combativeness sometimes accommodated their campaign. In January 1932, he began a polemic in the British press, engaging British intellectuals and rectors of Italian universities in a three-way debate over the Fascist university professors' loyalty oath of 1931. For six months he succeeded in putting the Fascist regime on the defensive and forced them to explain their educational policies.[149]

Salvemini initiated a second confrontation in response to Mussolini's amnesty of seventeen exiles, including Salvemini, in commemoration of the

March on Rome.[150] When he read in *Il Popolo d'Italia* the government's boast of generosity, he produced a flurry of interviews, letters, and articles to expose it as a cynical propaganda ploy.[151] In the process, he exchanged letters with Fascist Grand Council member Giuseppe Bottai, demanding that the government show good faith by restoring to him the royalties from his books.[152]

At the same time he was challenging Bottai, Salvemini asked the Italian consul in New Haven to issue him a passport.[153] He got neither a passport nor his royalties. Instead, the Italian government reaffirmed his status as a fugitive from justice. On November 29, the Special Tribunal informed the Ministry of Interior that the arrest warrant for Salvemini was still in effect. The warrant, dated December 23, 1930, had listed Salvemini among thirty-one anti-Fascists wanted for committing "insurrections against the powers of the State."[154]

When he completed the course at Yale in February 1933, Salvemini had earned "another $5,000; another two years of life."[155] He decided to settle in Cambridge, Massachusetts, a prospect that he had been considering for at least three years. There he would be able to write and lecture and thus generate enough income to support himself and Fernande, who, for reasons he never explained publicly, would remain in Paris. He moved into a room on Berkeley Street and immediately began to make use of the vast resources of the Widener Library. At the same time he registered with a speakers bureau and began to deliver speeches in a number of New England locations, primarily New Haven and the Boston and New York metropolitan areas.[156]

When Salvemini boarded the steamer *Champlain* on June 24 for a return to Paris for the summer of 1933, he had no reason to anticipate a teaching offer. However, rumors had already begun to circulate within Italian government circles.[157] On April 20, the consul in Boston had telegramed his government that Salvemini had been offered a "chair of history" at Harvard; the following week the Minister of Foreign Affairs asked the Ministry of Interior to furnish information for the purpose of blocking Harvard's appointment of Salvemini.[158] By the time the Italian government had discovered that its information was erroneous, it had been assured by an informant at Harvard that President A. Lawrence Lowell would never hire such an "unworthy pseudo-professor."[159]

NOTES

1. ER, "Il nonconformista."

2. GS, "*NM*," 26–31.

3. GS, *Cart 1921*, 419n; "The Civilization of Italy" [letter to the Editor], *New Statesman*, November 7, 1925, 106; ER, "Il nonconformista"; ET, "Nota biografica," 254.

4. DeF, *il fas* II, 131–138; Claudio Segrè, *Italo Balbo* (Berkeley, 1990), 138–140; Adrian Lyttleton, *Seizure of Power,* 281–288.

5. Lina Waterfield, *A Castle in Italy* (London, 1961), 220–221. See also Segrè, *Balbo*, 139–140.

6. The term *fuoruscito*, of medieval origin, was reintroduced by the Fascists to refer to the political exiles. In turn, the exiles adopted the term as a badge of pride, and Salvemini entitled his memoirs *Memorie di un fuoruscito*. He wrote, "I did not play the part of 'the exile.' . . . Neither did I like the term 'refugee.' . . . I have always preferred to call myself '*fuoruscito*,' taking for myself a term that the Fascists used with opprobrium: *fuoruscito*, that is to say, I left my country to continue by means at my disposal the resistance that had become impossible at home." GS, *Mem*, 88–89.

7. GS to Rector, University of Florence, August 27, 1925, *Cart 1921*, 396.

8. GS to ER, August 16 and 24, 1925, 379 and 390–392; to PiC, August 17, 1925, 380–383; to Z-B, August 26, 1925, 395; ER to GS, August 22, 1925, 385–386; Wickham Steed to GS, August 24, 1925, 389–390; PiC to GS, September 12, 1925, *Cart 1921*, 412–413.

9. Waterfield to GS, August 15, 1925, 377–378; F. S. Nitti to GS, August 16, 1925, *Cart 1921*, 380; Ambassador (London) to BM, June 24 and July 7, 1925, *DDI*, settima serie, IV, 36 and 45; Dino Grandi to Ambassador (London), November 18, 1926, *DDI*, settima serie, IV, 378–379; GS to ER, August 16 and 20, 1925, 379, 384; to PiC, *Cart 1921*, 380–383.

10. Copy of report, Ambassador (Paris), December 29, 1925, *CPC*"S"; Novello Papafava to GS, October 31, 1925, *Cart 1921*, 461.

11. Copy of report, Prefecture of Florence, January 4, 1926, *CPC*"S"; copy of report, Consulate (Zurich), March 24, 1926, *CPC*"S"; GS to ER, August 29, 1925, *Cart 1921*, 397.

12. GS, "*NM*," 19–21; ET, "Nota biografica," 253; Giovanni Mira to GS, October 27, 1925, *Cart 1921*, 452.

13. GS to ER, August 24, 1925, *Cart 1921*, 391; Waterfield to GS, August 15, 1925, *Cart 1921*, 377–378; UO, entry of November 15, 1925, *I Taccuini*, 205–206.

14. Rodolfo Savelli to GS, September 17, 1925, *Cart 1921*, 416.

15. F. S. Nitti to GS, September 25 and 30 and October 4, 1925, 418, 423–424, and 425; CR to GS, September 29, 1925, 419–423; Raffaele Ciasca to GS, October 12, 1925, *Cart 1921*, 434; UO, entry of October 4, 1925, *I Taccuini*, 187–188.

16. GS to Nicky Mariano, October 11, 1925, *Cart 1921*, 431.

17. Rector of the University of Florence to GS, October 2, 1925, 425; PiC to GS, October 5 and 14, 1925, *Cart 1921*, 426, 437.

18. Biancafiore (Marion Cave) to GS, October 20 and November 7, 1925, 443 and 476–478; GS to UO, October 1925, 461–462; Cave to GS, November 7, 1925, 476–478; F. S. Nitti to GS, October 10, 1925, 430; ES to GS, October 6, 1925, 426–427; PiC to GS, October 5 and 20, 1925, *Cart 1921*, 426, 442.

19. CR to GS, October 21, 1925, *Cart 1921*, 447–449.

20. Lidia Minervini to GS, November 2 and 6, 1925, 465–466 and 471–472; GF to FS, November 5, 1925, *Cart 1921*, 471.

21. GS to Mariano, October 11, 1925, *Cart 1921*, 431.

22. GS to PiC, October 15, 1925, 440; to MB, October 14 and November 11, 1925, *Cart 1921*, 436 and 481–482.

23. GS to Rector, University of Florence, November 5, 1925, *MCP*; GS, "The Teachers' Oath in Fascist Italy," *Massachusetts Law Quarterly*, n.d., "Salvemini Reprints," Pusey; Prefect of Parma to DGPS, December 17, 1925, *CPC*"S."

24. GS to MB, October 14, 1925, *Cart 1921*, 436–437; RV, "Salvemini e il fascismo" in ES, *ACGS*, 139.

25. GS to MB, November 11, 1925, *Cart 1921*, 482; G. P. Gooch, "Professor Salvemini and the Fascists," 181–185; "L'Enseignement de l'histoire et le Fascism," *Europe* (Paris), December 15, 1925; *Il Corriere degli Italiani* (Dijon), December 20, 1925; *Le Journal des Debats* (Paris), December 30, 1925; *Volonté* (Paris), December 1925, 3; Janet Trevelyan to GS, November 7, 1925, *Cart 1921*, 478.

26. Jean Borovička to GS, November 16, 1925, 487–488; GS to Tomasso Fiore, November 22, 1925, 491; to Z-B, December 14, 1926, *Cart 1921*, 543; memorandum, October 9, 1927, *SPD*, *CR*"S."

27. GS to Z-B, November 25, 1925, 493–494; "The 'Plot' against Mussolini," *The Labour Magazine* (London), December 31, 1925, 239–245; *La dittatura fascista in Italia*, 269–270; Cave to GS, December 6, 1925, *Cart 1921*, 514–516; ET, "Nota biografica," 254; Chief of Police to Ambassador (Paris), September 19, 1927, *CPC* "S"; DeF, *il riv*, 580–587.

28. ER to GS, December 28, 1925, April 26 and August 26, 1926, 528–530 and 532–535, 536– 539; GS to ER, September 14, 1926, 539–543; to Z-B, December 14, 1926, *Cart 1921*, 544.

29. "The 'Plot' against Mussolini," *Opere* VI (2), 239–243; DeF, *il fas I*, 600–609; CD, *ME*, 33–37; CR to GS, November 7 and 11, 1925, 473–474; Raffaelle Rossetti to GS, November 30, 1925, 499–500; Cave to GS, November 7, 1925, *Cart 1921*, 477. The laws were probably the citizenship law of June 13, 1912, n. 555, and the law of January 31, 1926, n. 108, both of which were later used against him. See also "Oggi il senato discuterà la legge sui fuorusciti," *Il Tevere*, January 25, 1926, *SPD*, *CR*"S" and GS, *Cart 1921*, 354 n. 1; See also "La Commissione per i fuorusciti," *La Tribuna* (Rome), September 23, 1926, *SPD*, *CR*"S"; Il Segretario federale di Roma (Maraini) to BM, November 2, 1925 and Segretario politico di Molfetta (Maggialetti) to BM, November 29, 1925, *SPD*, *CR*"S"; copy of telegram, Olga Mezzono to BM, January 23, 1926; "L'opera dei fuorusciti è un'arma nelle mani degli stranieri," *Il Tevere*, January 26, 1926; press release, Agenzia Stefani, June 25, 1926, *SPD*, *CR*"S."

30. Rector of the University of Florence to GS, November 25 and December 4, 1925, *Cart 1921*, 494 and 514; Prefect of Florence (Maggioni) to MI, May 2, 1933, *SPD*, *CR*"S"; "Deliberazione del Senato accademico dell'Università di Firenze," *Pd'I*, November 27, 1925; GS to Rector, December 2 and 19, 1925, *Cart 1921*, 506–510 and 519.

31. Cave to GS, December 6 and 22, 1925, *Cart 1921*, 515 and 522.

32. GS, "English Views of Italy," 236–238; "The Civilization of Italy," 234–236; "Italian Diplomacy during the War," 294–310; "O il bastone o la discussione," 244–245; "Mussolini and the Bombs," 245–246, *Opere* VI (2).

33. GS, *Origins of Fascism*, 44; *Mem*, 105–107.

34. GS, *Mem*, 105–107.

35. Cesare Foligno to GS, October 29 and November 2, 1925, *Cart 1921*, 459–460 and 466; copy of letter, Div. AGR to Ambassador (London), May 1, 1926; copy of letter, Ambassador (London), May 10, 1926, *CPC*"S"; Luigi Villari, letter, *Westminster Gazette* (London), January 22, 1926; GS, Letter to the editor, *Review of Reviews*, March–April 1926, 244–247; letter, "Is Italy Prosperous," *The Westminster Gazette*, August 2, 1926; *Mem*, 42–45; Fontana to CG (Liverpool), October 7, 1926, *CPC*"S"; MAE to MI, November 6, 20, and 24, 1926, *CPC*"S."

36. Denis Mack Smith, *Mussolini's Roman Empire* (New York, 1977), 12, 254; Alastair Hamilton, *The Appeal of Fascism* (New York, 1971), 291; R. J. B. Bosworth, "The British Press, Conservatives and Mussolini, 1920–1934," *The Journal of Contemporary History*, 5 (1970), 163–182.

37. GS, *Mem*, 45–47 (translation from Iris Origo, *A Need to Testify*, 155); "Abuse of Professor Salvemini," London *Times*, January 26, 1926.

38. GS, *Mem*, 47–50; *Cart 1921*, 354n.; Regio Decreto n. 1753, September 30, 1926 ("Inflizione della peredita della cittadinanza con la confisca dei beni al Professore SALVEMINI"), *Gazetta Ufficiale del Regno d'Italia*, October 10, 1926, n. 243, *CPC*"S." The Regio Decreto was issued under the citizenship law of June 13, 1912, n. 555, and the law of January 31, 1926, n. 108.

39. GS to Oswald Garrison Villard, September 24, 1926, GSL; F. S. Nitti to GS, May 15, 1926, cited in DeC, *Sal*, 449; GS to Z-B, December 14, 1926, *Cart 1921*, 544. See also Under- Secretary of State to Ministry of Interior, July 21, 1926, *CPC*"S"; Ambassador (Washington) to MI, August 11 and December 28, 1926, *CPC*"S"; CG (New York) to Ambassador (Washington), November 2 and December 13, 1926, *CPC*"S"; Prefect (Rome) to MI, December 12, 1926, *CPC*"S"; "Campagna Antifascista all'Estero," October 30, 1926, *CPC*"S"; MAE to MI, October 23, 1926, *CPC*"S"; Giacomo De Martino to BM, October 16, 1926, *DDI*, settima serie, IV, 359–360.

40. For a discussion of Mussolini's American popularity, see JD, *MFas*, 22–73.

41. GS, "Fascism without Mussolini," *Opere* VI (2), 246–248.

42. Copy of intercepted letter, GS to Giuseppe Ranieri, November 7, 1926, *CPC*"S"; CG (New York) to MI, December 4, 1926, *CPC*"S."

43. *NYT*, January 6, 1927. Salvemini's arrival was also reported in *L'Italia del Popolo* (Buenos Aires), January 7, 1927, *SPD*, *CR*"S."

44. ER, "Il nonconformista"; MC interview.

45. GS, *Mem*, 59–61.

46. Gian Giacomo Migone, "Aspetti internazionali della stabilizzazione della lira: il piano Leffingwell" in *Problemi di storia nei rapporti tra Italia e Stati Uniti* (Turin, 1971), 43–93; and "La stabilizzazione della lira: La finanza americana e Mussolini," *Rivista di storia Contemporanea*, 2 (1973), 145–185; JD, *MFas*, 145–156; GS, *IFAUS*, 137, and "Twelve Years of Fascist Finance," *Foreign Affairs*, 13 (April 1935), 473–482.

47. GS, *Mem*, 61–62; ET, "Nota biografica," 257; JD, *MFas*, 148; PC, Introduction, GS *IFAUS*, xv.

48. ET, "Nota biografica," 258; GS, *Mem*, 63; MC interview; GS to Villard, January 16, 1927, HoL.

49. Copy of telegram, Ambassador (Washington) to MAE, January 12, 1927, *CPC*"S"; *Christian Science Monitor*, January 15, 1927; MC interview; entry of January 8, 1927, *CPC*"S."

50. MC interview; GS, *IFAUS*, 55–56, 142; memorandum from Bruno Roselli, November 19, 1926, *CPC*"S"; MAE to MI, November 20 and December 28, 1926, *CPC*"S"; CG (New York) to MI, November 22 and December 13, 1926, *CPC*"S"; copy of telegram, Ambassador (Washington) to MAE, November 26, 1926, *CPC*"S."

51. GS, *Mem*, 63–64; entry of January 15, 1927, *CPC*"S."

52. Frances Keene, ed., *Neither Liberty nor Bread* (New York, 1940), 360–361; MC interview; MS, "Antifascisti italiani negli Stati Uniti," *Atti del congresso internazionale di storia americana* (Genoa, 1978), 275.

53. "L'Italia sotto il Fascismo," transcript of debate, Salvemini and Roselli (New York, n.d.), Center for Migration Studies (Staten Island); *Il Progresso Italo-Americano*, January 23, 1927.

54. GS, *Opere* VI (2), 249–250.

55. *NYHT*, January 23, 1927; GS, *Mem*, 65; *Il Progresso Italo-Americano*, January 23, 1927; *MC interview, December 1979; entry of January 22, 1927, CPC*"S"; GS, *Opere* VI (2), 248–270.

56. Entry of January 24, 1927, *CPC* "S"; JD, *MFas*, 84.

57. *NYT*, January 25, 1927; *Il Progresso Italo-Americano*, January 25, 1927.

58. GS to Villard, January 8 and 16, 1927; Villard to GS, January 17, 1927, GSL.

59. GS, "Mussolini Chokes the Press," *The Nation*, 124 (January 12, 1927), 34–36; GS to Villard, November 24, 1926, and January 16, 1927, GSL; GS, *Mem*, 6.

60. *NYT*, February 5, 1927. Entry of February 15, 1927; entry of February 5, 1929; MAE to MI, February 6 and March 31, 1927, *CPC*"S"; JD, *MFas*, 253–254.

61. CG (New York) to MI, December 4, 1926, *CPC*"S." Entry of March 18, 1927, *CPC*"S"; "Una lettera di Salvemini," *Opere* VI (2), 303.

62. *NYT*, April 25, 1927; *Giustizia*, April 23, 1927; entry of April 24, 1927, *CPC* "S."

63. GS, "L'opera degli emigrati," *Opere* VI (2), 295–297; ET, "Nota biografica," 258; PC, Introduction, GS, *IFAUS*, xvii.

64. GS to Villard, April 28 and June 30, 1927, GSL; *Mem*, 63; telegrams, De Martino to MAE, September 27, 1926; De Martino to MAE, November 22, 1926; Ambassador (Washington) to BM, December 6, 1926; Marchetti to MAE, October 17, 1927, ASMAE, *SAP*, f. 7931, "Passaporti"; Ambassador (Washington) to BM, March 8, 1927, *DDI*, settima serie, IX, 72.

65. Entries of May through July 7, *CPC*"S"; GS, *Mem*, 90.

66. GS, "Mussolini, the Pope and the King" trans. *Opere* VI (2), 274–285.

67. GS, "March on Rome," *Current History*, 19 (October 1932), 38–43; "L'Italia e il regime fascists," *Corriere degli Italiani*, February 28, 1926; W. Henderson Pringle, ed., *Economic Problems in Europe Today*, (London, 1928); GS, "Debiti esteri e responsabilità interne," *Opere* VI (2), 306; letter to the editor, *Opere* VI (2), 361–363.

68. GS, "Parliamentary Reform in Italy," *Contemporary Review*, 63 (April 1928), 447–454; "The Grand Council of Fascism," *Foreign Affairs* VII (January 1929), 292–300.

69. GS, "Mussolini Chokes the Press," 34–36; "The Treatment of the Press in Fascist Italy," *The New Statesman* (London), January 15, 1927, 412–413; Alberto Aquarone, *L'organizzazione,* 98–102; DeF, *il fas* II, 210 ff.; DeG, *Italian Fascism,* 55–56.

70. GS, "L'opera degli emigrati, I," *Opere* VI (2), 290–293.

71. GS, *Mem,* 59–61.

72. "L'opera degli emigrati, II," *Opere* VI (2), 293–297.

73. GS to Z-B, December 14, 1926, *Cart 1921,* 543–549.

74. GS, "English Views of Italy," 236–238; "Fascism without Mussolini," 246–248; "Abstractions and Reality in International Politics," 48–54; "Mussolini and the Bombs," in *Opere* VI (2), 245– 246.

75. GS to Z-B, December 14, 1926, *Cart 1921,* 543–549.

76. GS letter, "Che cosa è stata la 'democrazia' in Italia," *L'Italia del Popolo,* May 31, 1929; 'Problemi della crisi italiana," *L'Italia del Popolo,* June 20, 1929.

77. GS, "The Simple Annals of Fascism," *Atlantic Monthly,* 134 (June 1927), 820–828.

78. GS, "Murder by 'Persons Unknown,'" *The Nation,* 125 (July 13, 1927), 34–35; "An Episode of Fascism," *The Nation,* 125 (November 16, 1927), 556–557.

79. GS, "Justice in Italy," *Opere* VI (2), 310–312; letter, *MG,* June 22, 1928; "Mussolini Hölle," reproduced in *Italy To-Day,* July 1929, *AGS.*

80. Shaw letter, "Bernard Shaw on Mussolini," *Daily News* (London), January 24, 1927; GS, *Opere* VI (2), 315–318 and *G. B. Shaw e il fascismo* (Parma, 1955).

81. "What does G. B. Shaw Know about Italy?," editorial, *MG,* October 19, 1927.

82. Friedreich Adler, "An Aberration," GS, *Opere* VI (2), 318–319; Shaw to Adler, "Mr. Shaw and Mussolini," *MG,* October 19, 1927; "Life and Politics," *The Nation and Athenaeum,* 21 (November 5, 1927), 179–180.

83. Santi Fedele, *Storia della concentrazione antifascista, 1927–1934* (Milan, 1976), 22–27; Simonetta Tombaccini, *Storia dei fuorusciti,* 64–71.

84. GS, "L'opera degli emigrati"; "Astrattismi e semplicismi," *Opere* VI (2), 298, 309.

85. Frank Rosengarten, *The Italian anti-Fascist Press, 1919–1945* (Cleveland, 1968), 50–54; AG, *VCR,* 163–164; Elena Aga Rossi, *Il movimento repubblicano, Giustizia e libertà e il partito d'Azione* (Bologna, n.d.), 14; Gaetano Arfé, "Salvemini nella concentrazione antifascista," *Il Ponte* XIII (1957), 1168–1171; Fedele, *Storia della concentrazione antifascista,* 38.

86. GS, "Per una piu forte Concentrazione"; "L'opera degli emigrati: I"; "L'opera degli emigrati: II"; "Gli antifascisti all'estero: III"; *Opere* VI (2), 285, 290–293, 293–297, 297–302.

87. RV, "Salvemini e il fascismo" in ES, *ACGS,* 145.

88. MC interview, December 1979.

89. GS, *The Fascist Dictatorship in Italy,* I (New York, 1927). The revised edition appeared in England the next year as *The Fascist Dictatorship in Italy,* I (London, 1928) and in translation as *La dittatura fascista in Italia* (New York, 1929), *La terreur Fasciste* (Paris, 1930), and into Chinese (Shanghai, 1929). Memoranda (Paris), April 12, 1930 and April 25, 1931, *SPD, CR*"S." See also GS, *Mem,* 93–94, and NT,

"Gaetano Salvemini storico del fascismo," *Studi Storici*, October-December 1988, 904. On the compatibility of Salvemini's style with his English-language readers, see GS, *Mem*, 42, and RV, introduction to *Opere* VI (1), viii. *The Origins of Fascism in Italy*, published posthumously in 1961, could been considered a fourth in this series, as could *The Prelude to World War II*, essentially a revision of *Mussolini Diplomatico*. See NT, "Salvemini storico," 907.

90. LS, *Nazionalfascismo* (Turin, 1923). Anti-Fascist interpretations from the left included Giovanni Zibordi's *Critica socialista del fascismo* (Bologna, 1922), Pietro Nenni's *Storia di quattro anni, 1919–1922* (Rome, 1946). In English, Carleton Beals, *Rome and Death* (New York, 1923) and William Bolitho, *Italy under Mussolini* (New York, 1926) offered firsthand critical accounts of Fascism. Luigi Villari's *The Awakening of Italy* (London, 1924) and Margherita Sarfatti's *The Life of Benito Mussolini* (London, 1925) were the most influential of all works published abroad at the time.

91. GS, *Mem*, 42; *FDI*, 208–219; DeF, *il fas* II, 131; MLS, *Sal*, 224–225.

92. GS, *FDI*, 60–61.

93. GS, *FDI*, 10–16, 42–43, 52. The French subsidy has now been established as fact, although it came after Mussolini had changed his position on the war. Charles Delzell, "Mussolini's Italy Twenty Years After," *Journal of Modern History* XXXVII (March 1966), 54, citing DeF, *il riv*, 285–287.

94. GS, *FDI*, 8, 103; RV, Introduction to GS, *Origins of Fascism in Italy* (New York, 1973), xi.

95. GS, *FDI*, 14, 50–53, 61–62, 87–97, 114–120. In arguing the reactionary nature of the movement, Salvemini cited Umberto Bianchelli's 1922 book, *Memorie*, and Mario Missiroli's *Il fascismo e i partiti politici italiani* (Bologna, 1934), 36. See also RV, introduction to GS, *Origins of Fascism in Italy*, x-xi; DeF, *Interpretations of Fascism*, 143, 152; Lyttleton, *Seizure of Power*, 39–41, 101–120; Francis L. Carsten, "Interpretations of Fascism," in Walter Laquer, ed., *Fascism: A Reader's Guide* (Berkeley, 1976), 427–431.

96. Salvemini called the psychological factor by the Freudian term *neurasthenia*—a kind of social neurosis or malaise—not confined to a single class, and focused on the government, the bourgeoisie, and the capitalists. GS, *FDI*, 3–9. DeF, *Interpretations of Fascism* (Cambridge, 1977), 112. See especially Angelo Tasca ("A. Rossi"), *The Rise of Italian Fascism* (London, 1938). For a comparison, see RV, introduction to GS, *The Origins of Fascism*, x-xi.

97. Michael Ledeen, "De Felice"; GS, *FDI*, 3–60, 97–102; DeF, *il riv*, xxii and 662; DeG, *Italian Fascism*, 34–35; Edward R. Tannenbaum, "The Goals of Italian Fascism," *AHR*, LXXIV (April 1969), 1183–1204.

98. GS, *FDI*, 12.

99. Compare GS, *FDI*, 231–296 to the British edition, 317–386. In the latter work he wrote, "There is no doubt whatever that the gang captained by Dumini acted under superior orders. . . . The complicity of Cesare Rossi is not so irrefragably proved as that of Marinelli." See also *Mem*, 93–94; RV, Preface to GS, *Opere* VII (1), ix; NT, "Salvemini storico," 904.

100. On the Matteotti crisis, see GS, *FDI*, 294–296. DeF, *Interpretations of Fascism*, 152, points out that Salvemini provided "previously unpublished material" to re-

veal the Matteotti crisis. For a judgment that Salvemini was polemical, see HSH, "Gaetano Salvemini tra scienza storica e polemica" in *Archivio Trimestrale* 8 (July-December 1982), 834. Salvemini made editorial changes of both substance and tone in the 1928 English edition. Because of lengthy discussions with Cesare Rossi in Paris in 1927, Salvemini altered his account of the Matteotti murder. He also softened some polemical phrases from the American edition. See GS, *Mem*, 93–94 and NT, "Salvemini storico," 904.

101. Elio Apih, "Salvemini storico" in *ACGS*, 93.

102. Entries of March 19 and 23, 1928, *CPC*"S." GS, *Mem*, 105ff; Alberto Merola, preface to GS, *Opere* VI (2), xix.

103. GS, *Mem*, 106; entries of January 2 and March 5, 1928, *CPC*"S."

104. "Residui dolorosi nella scuola italiana," memorandum, November 4, 1928, *SPD*, *CR*"S," "Borgese, G.A."; *Mem*, 107; *Italy To-Day*, April 1931, November–December 1931, February 1932; ET, "Ricordi di Salvemini," 193.

105. Entry of March 23, 1928, *CPC*"S"; Chief of Political Police (Bocchini) to Prefects, October 1, 1927, and entry of November 11, 1927, *CPC*"S"; memorandum, September 1927, *SPD*, *CR*"S"; Undersecretary of Foreign Affairs, Grandi, to Ambassador (Berlin), October 26, 1927, *DDI*, settima serie, V, 475; GS, *Mem*, 102; Adriano Dal Pont, Alfonso Leonetti and Massimo Massara, *Giornali fuori legge* (Rome, 1964), 226–227.

106. GS, *Mem*, 107; entry of March 7, 1929, *CPC*"S."

107. Entries of January 19, 1929, and March 7, 1929, *CPC*"S"; *NYT*, January 3, 1929.

108. Entry of March 7, 1929, *CPC*"S."

109. Philadelphia *Public Ledger*, February 20, 1929.

110. CG (Philadelphia) to Ambassador (Washington), February 20, 1929; Ambassador (Washington) to MAE, February 26, 1929, *CPC*"S."

111. "Fascism Denounced by Noted Italian in Phila.," *The Trades Union News* (Philadelphia), February 14, 1929; "Fascism Is Debated," *NYT*, May 27, 1929.

112. GS, *Mem*, 109; Joseph Ettor to CPa, April 9, 1929, *PaP*; Nino Valeri and Alberto Merola, Preface to GS, *Opere* VI (2), xx; PC, Introduction, GS, *IFAUS*, xvix.

113. Ettor to CPa, March 13, 18, and April 9, 1929; CPa to Ettor, March 21, 1929; George M. Day to CPa, April 9, 1929; Iva Ettor to CPa, May 1, 1929, *PaP*; Telegram, CPa to MacDonald, March 22, 1929; Foreign Policy Association to CPa, March 23, 1929.

114. Ettor to CPa, April 9, 1929, *PaP*.

115. "Cronaca Cittadina," *Il Corriere del Popolo* (San Francisco), April 18, 1929; "Denunciation of Il Duce Almost Brings a Riot," *Los Angeles Times*, April 9, 1929.

116. George M. Day to CPa, April 9 and 19, 1929, *PaP*.

117. Iva Ettor to CPa, May 1, 1929, *PaP*.

118. CPa to Ettor, March 15 and 21, 1929; Ettor to CPa, March 13, 18, and 22, April 2, May 12, 1929; Iva Ettor to CPa, May 1, 1929, *PaP*.

119. GS, *Mem*, 111–112.

120. Ettor to CPa, April 9, 1929, *PaP*; PC, Introduction, GS, *IFAUS*, xix-xx.

121. PC, Introduction, GS, *IFAUS*, xx, translated from GS, *Mem*, 110.

122. GS, *Mem*, 112; ET, "L'Opera di Gaetano Salvemini," 24; PC, Introduction, GS, *IFAUS*, xx.

123. GS, introduction to Lauro De Bosis, *Storia della mia morte e ultimi scritti* (Turin, 1948), reprinted in GS, *Opere* VI (2), 434 ff.; Mollie Della Terza, "Lauro De Bosis (1901–1931)," *Harvard Library Bulletin*, 30 (July 1928), 253–281; GS, *Mem*, 113.

124. GS, *Mem*, 113–114.

125. GS, *Mem*, 114.

126. AG, *VCR*, 141–142.

127. AT, "L'Impresa di Lipari," in ER, ed., *No al fascismo*, 165–166; F. Fausto Nitti, *Escape* (New York, 1930); Emilio Lussu, "The Flight from Lipari," *Atlantic Monthly*, vol. CL (July 1930); Emilio Lussu, *La catena* (Paris, 1929; Rome, 1945); CR, *Scritti politici e autobiografici* (Naples, 1944); Prefect of Savona to MI, February 27, 1940, *CPC*"S."

128. GS, *Mem*, 115–116; Alessandro Schiavi, *Esilio e morte di Filippo Turati (1926–1932)* (Rome, 1956).

129. GS, "Carlo and Nello Rosselli," 693; AG, *VCR*, 170ff.

130. Carlo Rosselli led the "Giellisti," as they called themselves, by resigning from the PSU in November 1929. *Interclassismo* is the rejection of the Marxist principle of class struggle in favor of interclass cooperation, in this case excluding no classes from the anti-Fascist movement. See also GS to CPa, October 20, 1930, *PaP*; "Carlo e Nello Rosselli," 693–697; Valeri and Merola in GS, *Opere* VII (2), xx; AT to RP, January 18, 1932, quoted in Fedele, *Storia della concentrazione*, 76; AG, *VCR*, 176–178; Stanislao Pugliese, *Rosselli*, 129–134; ET, "Nota biografica," 260 and "Ricordo di Salvemini," 193; RV, "Carlo Rosselli e Gaetano Salvemini" in *Giustizia e Libertà nella lotta antifascista*, 80–82.

131. GS, "Per un piu forte Concentrazione," 285; "Astrattismi e semplicismi," 310; "Avere idee nuove," *Opere* VI (2), 298.

132. CD, *ME*, 64; LS and Giovanni Mira, *Storia del fascismo*, 500ff.; AG, "L'attentato di Bruxelles," in ER, ed., *No al fascismo*, 171–199; *Mem*, 153.

133. GS, *Mem*, 126–128; CD, *ME*, 66; AG, *VCR*, 186–187.

134. GS, "Donati e Berneri," *Opere* VIII, 101.

135. GS to Emilio Lussu, January 18, 1945, *Ld'A 44*, 82–83.

136. GS, *Mem*, 136.

137. Entry of April 2, 1930, *CPC*"S."

138. GS, *Mem*, 136; MC interview.

139. GS, *Mem*, 136–147.

140. Entry of August 26, 1930, *CPC*"S"; GS, *Mem*, 136.

141. Egidio Reale, "Il volo su Milano," in ER, ed., *No al fascismo*, 159–175; AG, *VCR*, 189–193; GS, "Carlo e Nello Rosselli," 697; Pugliese, *Rosselli*, 136, 137, 172, 206; CD, *ME*, 66.

142. GS, "Carlo e Nello Rosselli," *Opere* VIII, 679–701; *Mem*, 154.

143. GS, *Mem*, 156–157; CD, *ME*, 71–75; ER, ed., *No al fascismo*, 193–214; AG, *VCR*, 193–200; ET, "Nota biografica," 262.

144. Della Terza, "Lauro De Bosis," 269–270.

145. Lauro De Bosis, *The Story of My Death* (New York, 1933); CD, *ME*, 67–71; GS, *Mem*, 156–163; LS and Mira, *Storia del fascismo*, 519–521; Della Terza, "Lauro De Bosis," 269–278.

146. GS, *Mem*, 156–169.

147. New Haven *Journal-Courier*, November 18, 1932; New Haven *Register*, November 18, 1932; GS, *Mem*, 169–175; ET, "Nota biografica," 264.

148. CG (New York) to Ambassador (Washington), February 6, 1933, *CPC*"S."

149. GS letters, *Italy To-Day*, March-August 1932; "Teachers' Oath," 69–71.

150. Regio decreto, November 17, 1932, "Revoca di precedenti decreti con i quali si era inflitta la perdita della cittadinanza italiana a diciasette persone," n. 1753, "Salvemini," reported in *Gazetta Ufficiale*, December 2, 1932, *CPC*"S" and *Il Messaggero*, November 17, 1932, *SPD*, *CR*"S."

151. Memorandum, "Sempre a proposito dell'amnestia," December 7, 1932, *SPD*, *CR*"S"; GS, *Mem*, 169; to AT, November 4, 1932, *AGL*, "Salvemini."

152. GS to Giuseppe Bottai, November 23, 1932, and January 17, 1933; Bottai to GS, December 28, 1932, *Mem*, 171–174; GS to Bottai, December 19, 1932; Bottai to BM, December 19, 1932; Bottai (?) to GS, December 28, 1932, *SPD*, *CR*"S"; "Un insegnante replica all'attacco contro Mussolini" and "Sempre a proposito dell'amnistia," *SPD*, *CR*"S."

153. Telegram, MAE to MI, November 24, 1932, *CPC*"S"; Chief of Political Police (Bocchini) to prefects, January 5, 1933, *SPD*, *CR*"S."

154. Vice Attorney General, STDS, to MI, November 29, 1932, *CPC*"S"; Arrest Warrant (dated December 23, 1930), STDS, November 29, 1932, *CPC*"S"; Office of Judicial Police, STDS, to MI, July 6, 1927, *CPC*"S."

155. GS, *Mem*, 169, 175; to AT, March 5, 1930, *TP*.

156. CG (Boston) to MI, April 29, 1933, *CPC*"S."

157. GS, *Mem*, 175; CG (New York) to Ambassador (Washington), June 26, 1933, *CPC*"S."

158. CG (Boston) to MAE, April 20, 1933, *CPC*"S"; MAE to MI, April 29, 1933, *CPC*"S."

159. MAE to MI, April 29, 193[3?], *CPC*"S."

Chapter 9

The Harvard Years: In the Eye of the Storm

In the British Museum I thought I had found paradise. . . . But the true paradise I discovered at Harvard. . . . I understood that [the] desire to make the library serve the needs of the students is a curious hobby of almost all American librarians. The libraries are one of the finest flowers of American civilization.

Gaetano Salvemini, 1935[1]

After spending the first eight and a half years of exile in a state of almost constant mobility, Gaetano Salvemini settled in Cambridge, Massachusetts. With the start of the spring semester at Harvard in February 1934, he began a new teaching career that would span the Great Depression and World War II and last until his retirement, at age 74, in the spring of 1948. This final era of his professional life has been largely neglected. In fact, because so little is known of the Harvard years, they have produced a mythological imagery: Cambridge as "enchanted island"; Salvemini as "medieval monk," living in austere quarters and spending his waking hours in the library; Salvemini as "outsider," a nonentity in faculty matters and an alien to American politics. Although a thin thread of truth runs through these images, they have served to distort his life more than to elucidate it.

Late in 1933 Ruth Draper presented Harvard with a proposal for funding a lectureship in Italian culture in honor of Lauro De Bosis.[2] Draper, a wealthy actress known for her dramatic monologues, had been the devoted companion of the young poet before his tragic death.[3] As if to perpetuate the legacy of his anti-Fascism, she endorsed Salvemini for the lectureship.[4] Returning from

Paris in September, he discovered this "pleasant surprise"; after negotiations between Draper and the Harvard administration were completed, Salvemini accepted a half-year appointment to deliver six public lectures and a seminar for a salary of $2,000.[5]

Harvard would renew Salvemini's appointment as the Lauro De Bosis Lecturer for fourteen years and would thereby provide him, for the first time in almost a decade, a reliable means of support.[6] A stable position afforded him a dormitory apartment and an office where he could assemble his collection of newspaper clippings and files; capable students out of whose midst might emerge a band of disciples like those he had known at the University of Florence in the 1920s; a carrel in the Widener Library adjacent to its superb collection of Italian historical volumes; and, thereby, a base of operations for writing, speaking, corresponding, and organizing—indeed, for all phases of his anti-Fascist campaign. Harvard would thus provide Salvemini with an anchor against the political storms that battered so many refugee scholars.[7] In another sense, Harvard's prestige would prove to be a real advantage. The affiliation would earn him immediate credibility in American liberal circles, no small asset in the new American phase of the battle to be waged.

In appointing Salvemini to the Lauro De Bosis chair, Harvard gave an unintentional boost to the fortunes of Italian anti-Fascism. His reputation as a European historian at several of the great Italian universities had undoubtedly appealed to Harvard, just as its reputation appealed to him. If the administration and history faculty had not known of his anti-Fascist activities before 1933, they learned about them from the Italian Embassy in the months before he was hired. The decision to appoint him lecturer may have signified a choice to ignore political considerations, but the effect was the same. Harvard had provided Salvemini with a refuge.

Salvemini's campaign against Fascism actually preceded him to the Harvard campus. Five years before, while Arthur Schlesinger, Sr. was completing his term as chair of the history department, only his boldness in the face of an "untoward incident" ensured Salvemini an opportunity. Schlesinger had cabled Salvemini in London, extending an invitation to teach for a semester. Before Salvemini could accept, Harvard President A. Lawrence Lowell asked Schlesinger to withdraw the invitation because of the objections of a member of the Corporation (Harvard's governing board). When Schlesinger objected, the president dropped the matter. Schlesinger assumed that Salvemini's reputation as an outspoken anti-Fascist had made him unacceptable to someone of influence in Boston who was, like many Americans, a Mussolini enthusiast.[8] In any event, without Schlesinger's decisive action, Harvard may never have considered hiring Salvemini.

By the time Harvard offered him the Lauro De Bosis chair in 1933, faculty members affiliated with both Fascist and anti-Fascist camps had organized to apply pressure on the university. Salvemini's friend Giorgio La Piana, an authority on Church history, used his influence to secure the position.[9] La Piana's foe in this power struggle was the chairman of the Department of Romance Languages, Jeremiah D. M. Ford, a native of Cambridge who held three Harvard degrees. More important, "Jerry" Ford was an admirer of Fascism who collaborated with the Italian Embassy and aligned himself with the "Brahmin" establishment on campus, of which President Lowell was the personification.[10] While chairing the committee that reexamined the Sacco and Vanzetti case, Lowell had "engaged in vitriolic correspondence" with one of Salvemini's strongest supporters, Harvard Law School professor Felix Frankfurter. This simply reinforced the weakness of Salvemini's position within Harvard circles.[11]

When the Harvard Corporation selected James B. Conant to replace Lowell in 1933, Salvemini's prospects improved. More liberal and internationalist in his values, Conant was committed to academic freedom and determined to withstand coercion from outside the university.[12] Nonetheless, Ford persisted. He reported the Italian consul general's complaints to Dean Kenneth Murdock, expressed his "utter contempt" for Salvemini in a vitriolic letter to Conant, and propagated the vicious rumor that Salvemini had made an attempt on the life of the Italian crown prince at Brussels. The next week, Ford pressed the issue with Conant, requesting a private meeting and calling Salvemini "dangerous" and a "turbulent Republican with anarchistic tendencies."[13] Ford's efforts came too late, as Conant informed him in his polite but cool response: "The appointment has been made and cannot be changed."[14] Consequently, the Italian government was confronted with a fait accompli, even though it had been guarding against just such an eventuality for more than three years.[15]

Nevertheless, the Fascist government was able to secure one concession from Harvard: Salvemini was hired on the condition that he not propagandize in his lectures. This restriction was a product of the caution employed by all parties in securing the appointment, including Murdock and La Piana, who, in an effort to short-circuit Ford's campaign, had suggested this stipulation, almost certainly with Salvemini's approval.[16] In his response to Conant's greeting, Salvemini acknowledged the point:

You may be assured that never my lectures or my seminar will be used for political propaganda. The wishes of the donor who made possible my appointment are sacred to me. But even if this reason was not existent, my loyalty to Harvard University and the respect I owe myself as a scholar would alone be sufficient to prevent me from using the classroom for any other but scholarly purposes.[17]

In expressing his gratitude to Ruth Draper, Salvemini took delight that the lectureship had infuriated the Fascist regime by striking a double blow: Salvemini in the Lauro De Bosis chair. He noted that the Fascists' real motive was to deprive him of income so that they could stop his anti-Fascist campaign "*outside the school*"—and that they would not rest.[18]

Harvard's injunction against propaganda did not inhibit Salvemini. He knew that those students who came to understand Italian history—especially from a Mazzini-Salvemini perspective—would understand the tyranny of the Fascist state. In addition, he infused all his lectures with contemporary references. To make an analogy to Fascist Italy was not propaganda, it was simply an extension of the realization that "all history is contemporary history." Frankfurter once advised a student, "Whatever Salvemini teaches will be *current*."[19] Thus Salvemini pragmatically accepted Harvard's limitation because it meant no real sacrifice at all. His off-campus lectures went on as before and, in time, he began to address controversial contemporary issues on campus as well.[20]

In launching the inaugural Lauro De Bosis lectures, Salvemini cautiously postponed his tribute to the poet until the end of the series so as to win the confidence of his audience before making a political statement. However, such caution did nothing to defuse the Fascist campaign. On Sunday, March 4, 1934, the day before the first lecture, *The New York Times* printed a story that the Fascist regime had planted a few days earlier in its continuing effort to discredit Salvemini. Just when he had overcome the hiring crisis, he recalled, the story hit like "a thunderbolt from the sky."[21] The *Times* picked up the story from the Associated Press wire service in Rome, placed it prominently, and gave it the following headline: "BOMB IN ST. PETER's LAID TO PROF. SALVEMINI; IN EXILE HERE, HE IS ACCUSED WITH SIX OTHERS." The *Times* reported that the Italian government also charged Salvemini with conspiring against Mussolini's life. Salvemini, they concluded "has been called 'the man most hated in Italy' because of his opposition to Fascism."[22]

Disturbed by the story and convinced that it was designed to deprive him of the De Bosis chair, Salvemini took the advice of the placid La Piana and went directly to President Conant to refute it. Conant, likewise unruffled, advised Salvemini simply to wait and defend himself if necessary; U.S. authorities would have to convene an extradition hearing only if the Italian government pursued the charges. Meanwhile, Conant assured him, Harvard would also wait.[23]

However, after further consultation with La Piana, Salvemini decided to push more actively to clear his name. He telegramed Mussolini, demanding that *Il Duce* have him sentenced and then request extradition.[24] Although the *Times* had printed the press release uncritically, several philo-Fascist Italian-language dailies reported the charges as if they had been proven. *Il Progresso Italo-Americano* reported in its headline, "The Double Crime Was Plotted at Paris—Was Financed and Instigated by the Well-Known Anti-Fascists Alberto Cianca, Carlo Rosselli and Gaetano Salvemini."[25] After dropping the idea of libel action against the press, Salvemini was relieved to read, several weeks later, that the *Times* admitted his innocence.[26] Yet the Fascist regime had succeeded once again in distracting him, and once again they had shown that his presence in the United States, and particularly on the faculty at Harvard, was a matter of grave concern to them. "The Fascists have not been able to prevent my appointment this year," he wrote to Draper. "They will start a new fight next time."[27]

The move to Harvard marked a turning point in Salvemini's life. For some critics, Cambridge has become a metaphor for his semiretirement, an escape from reality and responsibility to the "enchanted island" of academia; in the words of one writer, it was a "refuge after the final shipwreck."[28] It was actually Salvemini who supplied the "enchanted island" metaphor in a letter to Mary Berenson:

My life here, dear Mary, is happy, as far as a man can be happy. Basically, I do not live in America, I live in Widener Library from 8:30 A.M. until 12:30 P.M.; and from 3:00 P.M. until 7:30 P.M. When to these hours of work I add ten hours of sleep, which I cannot do without, there remain for me very few hours to live in America. And in these few hours my America is Cambridge, an enchanted island, where all are generous and gentle with me and where life passes quietly like the Charles River. . . . I am the richest man in America because I am the proprietor of Widener and do not pay taxes.[29]

Compared to London and Paris, where he had spent the eight preceding years, this college community of about 100,000 clearly represented a deceleration in the pace of his political activity. It removed him from the center of Italian-exile organization to a sheltered setting, remote and insulated from the European capitals. The "barrier" of the Ivy League campus lent an additional sense of escape.

Further reinforcing the image of escape was the impression of personal isolation he projected and the pessimism he sometimes expressed. To many he seemed preoccupied with Italian matters. A friend recalled waking Salvemini when he fell asleep during a lecture on South America. He opened one eye and uttered in a stage whisper, "I amma notta interested in Venezuela."[30] H. Stuart Hughes recalled "seeing him from a distance, walking as if in a trance. His heart must have been in Italy—certainly not in Cambridge."[31] Max Ascoli noted that, although Salvemini had friends, "on the whole he was isolated and bitter."[32] The austerity of his personal life reinforced these images, suggesting that within the "enchanted isle" he had actually retreated further into his own cloister.

To be understood, however, the issue of Salvemini's state of mind must be applied to his performance, not only in academics at Harvard but in political affairs beyond the ivory tower. When that test is applied, it is clear that the move to Cambridge inhibited neither his professional nor his political life.

If the monkish metaphors used to describe Salvemini are deceptive and the allegations of escapism are inaccurate, there is an explanation: he lived his life at Harvard on two levels. In part, he was the *"wissenschaftlich* professor,"[33] lecturing on medieval communes or on the Risorgimento. It was in this role that he generated the well-known images. To many he remained a curiosity on campus, an "exotic and an eccentric," an alien presumably estranged from the outside world as well. In fact, his life in this professorial role was sharply limited, much more than his teaching function had been in Florence, where it had been openly integrated with politics in his grand scheme. There his students had joined him in the political activities of the Circolo di Cultura, and there the Fascists would not tolerate an independent voice. In Cambridge, he merely taught classes; his students were part of his academic world, more than many imagined, but never became comrades in his passionate political campaigns.

The key to understanding Salvemini at Harvard is to know that he operated on a second level, related to the first but more exhausting of his time and energy. This was the role of anti-Fascist intellectual, relentlessly attacking the Fascist regime. In this capacity, he conducted research on Fascist Italy, which produced a seemingly endless flow of publications; he maintained an extensive correspondence with friends and anti-Fascist colleagues in the United States and in Europe; he lectured widely; and he organized a tenacious anti-Fascist campaign. Ironically, it was this role that connected him with the world beyond the campus. The loneliness and tragedy of his personal life and his alienation from campus activity were real, but they did not inhibit him.[34]

The reality of Salvemini's personal life in Cambridge was that although he worked in the midst of friendly colleagues and admirers, he lived his day-to-day life largely without them. His was a kind of personal, psychological isolation, largely but not entirely by choice. "He led the life of a voluntary recluse," wrote Enzo Tagliacozzo, who was his assistant at Harvard.[35] Although he won friendship and esteem from his colleagues, he remained on the periphery, a nontenured lecturer, an outsider in the history department. Hughes remembers that Salvemini played no role in faculty politics and was somewhat a "second-class citizen" on a campus still largely monopolized by WASPs.[36] As a lecturer and not a department member, Salvemini was excluded from the business of the history department, a status he probably preferred. On the other hand, the department supported him at each critical juncture in his Harvard career, and, while not ideal, the relationship was mutually acceptable. Most expatriate scholars faced institutional hostility, but few adjusted as well as he.[37]

Tagliacozzo's reference to his mentor as a "voluntary recluse" in part reflects Salvemini's enthusiastic acceptance of the role of intellectual. Just as his steady criticism of Italian politics had set him apart from an ordinary existence in Italy, so he remained largely estranged from life in his new country. It was the classic Socratic role, the scholar as "critical conscience" whose perspective automatically alienated him from society.[38] The significant difference was that whereas in Italy the Fascist regime had revoked his citizenship and stripped him of the incumbent rights, in the United States he would be able to maintain his identity as *homo politicus* with immunity.

The cultural element of Salvemini's alienation proves more elusive. To some extent, although he was a good candidate for assimilation into American life, he simply showed little interest in becoming an American at any time during the 1930s. It was not that he was "deracinated," as social scientists claim so many refugee scholars were.[39] In fact, he consciously chose the United States as his new home. Once in Massachusetts, he certainly did not withdraw. He was, instead, a selective participant in American life. When American politics focused on Italy, education, or another of his favorite issues, his interests soared, but his curiosity about American life never broadened. His friend Bernard Berenson noted, "Salvemini taught at Harvard for years and never heard of [Nathaniel] Hawthorne. Indeed . . . he never ceased to be absorbed by purely Italian problems."[40] He never left Giacomo Puccini to discover Aaron Copeland or Alessandro Manzoni to find Walt Whitman.

Another factor distancing Salvemini from life in his new country was the difficulty faced by all refugee intellectuals in adapting to new surroundings. Unlike most, however, Salvemini avoided the extremes of either debilitating trauma or elevated productivity.[41] As a result, his work continued uninterrupted and the tenets of Salveminian independent radicalism remained unshaken: universal suffrage, democratic socialism, Mazzinian republicanism, tariff and electoral reform, and opposition to northern Italian economic interests. If anything, remoteness of time and place strengthened his commitment. Equally unaltered were his anticlericalism and personal religious skepticism.

It was the relative ease of Salvemini's transition that spared him the jolt experienced by so many exiled European scholars. This successful adaptation is largely attributable to his compatibility with the English-language world. He had been learning English since 1922, when he had listened at length to political harangues in Hyde Park and sung from the hymnals in the parish churches around Brighton. Although he spoke with an accent, he now possessed an exceptional mastery of the language. Just as important, he far exceeded most expatriates in his ability to "think in English."[42]

In Salvemini's case, the language issue was primarily cultural. His ideas were compatible with the American intellectual tradition, particularly his pragmatism and his penchant for factual empiricism. In fact, Salvemini's ideas were more suitable to expression in the English language than in Italian. He shared an "affinity" with the Anglo-Saxon mind and a "predilection for logically ordered facts."[43] His direct, simple style and his distrust for abstractions rendered his prose readily translatable.

It was Salvemini's great fondness for the Widener Library that provided the symbol of alleged escape to the monastic life. There he was known to spend entire days, month after month.[44] In Paris he had found using the Bibliothèque Nationale to be an ordeal; but at Harvard, he was amazed to find that the library was "made for scholars and not for its staff."[45] Several times each day he would walk from his apartment in Leverett House through the tranquil Harvard Yard to the Widener and up the stairs to his carrel, just across the aisle from the Italian history section. Here he could browse the open stacks, in contrast to European libraries. In his carrel he kept his books, including those he ordered on loan, free of charge, even from England. Here he could resume his work without interruption. This "second home" provided him the solitude that was the primary need of most refugee scholars.[46]

Beyond the image of Salvemini disappearing into the stacks of the Widener Library were his solitary physical presence and his proclivity to read and write for lengthy, concentrated periods. His voracious appetite for work became legendary. It seemed to his friends that he never rested until, fatigued from excessive work, he became ill. Guido Ferrando remembered Salvemini's visits to Poughkeepsie. Upon arrival, after exchanging pleasantries, he would go immediately to his room and start to work. "It was formidable work: ten hours a day at the table."[47] The spartan simplicity of his life also contributed to the monastic imagery. He lived in a two-room "faculty suite" in Leverett House, a student dormitory. The small room contained his bed, the larger one his study; both were filled with newspapers, books, and documents.[48]

The austerity was real. On his modest income of $2,000 per year, he supported his wife in Paris and sent money to families of his imprisoned anti-Fascist friends and to various anti-Fascist organizations. Ferrando recalls that "Salvemini was not afraid of poverty."

One time he said to me: "You will see, I will end up in a hospice for the poor"; and he smiled, without bitterness. I believe basically he liked poverty, because he felt that only in [poverty] could man be completely free. Wealth creates responsibility, commitments and preoccupations of all sorts. The rich are never free. . . . Salvemini, like all truly great men, lived and died poor. His was a dignified and decorous poverty that did not brutalize but ennobled. . . . His spiritual inner riches he communicated and gave to all, without hoarding. In a certain sense, Salvemini's poverty can be considered Franciscan: to have nothing and to possess everything in a spirit of charity.[49]

Then there was the basic reality of his personal solitude. Having lost his wife and five children a quarter century earlier, he now left behind Fernande, whose failing health kept her in Paris with her two children.[50] He had regularly returned to Paris during eight years of forced travel in exile, but return trips would now be less frequent. His letters continued to show great affection for her, and he supported her financially and planned for her future,[51] but acceptance of the Harvard chair implied a permanent departure from his second family.

This separation was compounded by the tragic rift with his beloved stepson, whom he had known since Jean's youth in prewar Florence. In January 1934 news broke of a scandal brought on by French swindler Alexandre Stavisky. The Stavisky affair polarized French politics, produced riots, and forced French Premier Camille Chautempts to resign and President Edouard Daladier to form a new government. Soon Salvemini received an appeal for help from his stepson, who, he had learned, was involved in the affair. The profound dilemma then unveiled itself. Jean was suspected by Parisian GL members to have been operating under the pay of the Italian Embassy, which in turn was believed to be in collaboration with right wing factions to undermine the Daladier government. Salvemini made the agonizing decision of principle: he refused any attempt to intervene on behalf of one who had chosen to conspire with the Fascists.[52]

Clearly Salvemini suffered from loneliness. The question of isolation and bitterness, however, is another matter. Hélène Cantarella emphatically disagrees: "Bitter Salvemini *never* was," she writes.[53] Max Salvadori remembered him as consistently "energetic and combative."[54] Arthur M. Schlesinger, Jr., then a teenager, recalls Salvemini's warmth, his humor, and his love for young people.[55]

Having lost the intimacy of family by 1934, Salvemini relied upon new friends to fill the void. A tightly knit group of Italian anti-Fascists in the Northeast provided camaraderie: La Piana at Harvard, the Cantarellas at Smith College, Guido Ferrando at Vassar, and Roberto and Maritza Bolaffio in New York.[56] His friends also included Italian-American leaders, New Deal liberals, and public figures such as Helen Keller and Walter Lippmann. It was this solid support system in the larger community that enabled him to adjust. His magnetism and the sympathy he evoked as a victim of Fascism always attracted friends and disciples. His friends, in turn, provided a safety net to protect him against the worst abuses of refugee life suffered by many of the exiled scholars.[57]

There were also new colleagues at Harvard, including Frankfurter, Murdock, and Donald McKay, who provided companionship and intellectual stimulation. Gregarious and entertaining, he found himself in demand socially, a regular guest in the homes of Schlesinger and others. Samuel Eliot Morison, the tall and aloof Boston Brahmin, already completing his second decade in Harvard's history department, "melted" in Salvemini's presence and frequently invited him to dinner. "I was not only his friend," Morison recalled, "I loved him."[58]

Even the circumstances of his daily life are deceiving. He ate most of his meals at the campus refectory or the faculty dining room, which, for a man who had an acute appreciation for good food, required a daily sacrifice. Nonetheless, he reconciled himself to the realities of campus life and found a certain social pleasure. Dean Murdock remembered that Salvemini seemed happiest in the common room in Leverett House,

silent with closed eyes, apparently asleep, while the talk went on around him. But when an ill-considered or foolish remark was made, his eyes would open and the room would ring with his "Nonsense!" And if something that really interested him was said, he would sit bolt upright, or jumping to his feet and pacing to and fro, would burst into excited and exciting eloquence.[59]

Because he committed enormous energy to the anti-Fascist cause, he was, in the Harvard years, anything but isolated from the world. In fact, he spent most of his waking hours building bridges to that world. Any isolation he suffered was neither political nor geographical, because Harvard's ivory tower linked him to his other world, providing the resources for his campaign, including connections with Americans. This outward thrust from Cambridge was not a romantic escape but a continuing engagement in the struggle for the future of Italy. In his memoirs, he claimed that he had left in order to continue the campaign of resistance that had become impossible in Italy:

I did not suffer from nostalgia. I lived always with my spirit in Italy: I subscribed under fictitious names to a half dozen daily papers of different shades of opinion, and I avidly read all the Italian reviews I could find in the libraries or in the houses of friends. . . . This was to live in Italy, and not to be an exile in America, or in England, or in France.[60]

This singlemindedness did not mean that he lived in the past. He never looked back, except in an occasional quiet moment or in a letter to an old friend. His Italian world was a very real one, one of Fascist repression, economic deception, and growing international adventurism. The more he investigated and contemplated Italian politics and global affairs, the greater his realization that his two worlds, Italian and American, were merging.

Hence, the physical image of the old professor disappearing into the library becomes too facile a caricature. For unlike the monks of the cloistered orders, Salvemini did not retreat. His life on the "enchanted island" is actually a paradox. When he seemed to be turning inward, he was turning outward. When he worked ten hours a day while visiting Ferrando, "his mind was always concentrating on the social and political problems close to his heart."[61] When he climbed the massive marble stairway to his carrel in Widener Library, it was not to investigate medieval Florence but the Florence of the Fascist era. He was more likely poring over Fascist press releases from a copy of the previous week's *Il Corriere della Sera* than one of the volumes from Harvard's

Risorgimento collection. The library, his carrel, his humble quarters were his connections with Italy and with the outside world of his own day.[62]

The physical appearance of Salvemini crossing Harvard Yard, head bent reflectively, was deceptive in another sense. It hid his innermost qualities. Although he was at least part moralist, in spirit and temperament he was anything but monastic. He ventured outside Harvard to speak in public at every opportunity. Although he maintained a professional decorum in the classroom, on the public rostrum he became the aggressor, and when interviewed by the press he was a tiger. A newspaper writer who anticipated a conventional, human-interest biographical sketch of Salvemini quickly discovered the illusion of his subject's appearance. When the reporter asked for some biographical background instead of asking for his assessment of Italian issues, Salvemini exploded furiously:

I don't like to talk about myself. No, no, no. I don't talk about myself with anybody. I don't even talk about myself to myself. Why don't you ask me what I think about Churchill's speech in the House of Commons? It was disgusting. Why don't you ask me what I think about the State Department, the House of Savoy, Roosevelt, the Church? That is important. What do you think I am, a Hollywood actress? You are wasting your time. Go, go, go.

Then the reporter asked Salvemini why, since he was educated in clerical schools, he became "unruly," and "what makes an anti-Fascist?"

"Why, why, why? You ask why, why," Salvemini roared, slamming himself angrily back into the cushions of the sofa. "I do not know why I am an anti-Fascist. My mother and father made me, just like Mussolini's mother and father made him. I was born this way. I don't know why."

"Gaetano Salvemini is one of democracy's angry men," the reporter wrote: "He has many enemies and most of his friends are afraid of him."[63] The story in *P.M.* effectively conveys Salvemini's combativeness and his fiery spirit. Appearances aside, he was more the prophet than the monk, more Jeremiah than Augustine.

When Salvemini began his Harvard career, he had ambitions to write purely historical works. He failed to achieve that goal, but not because he "atrophied" or suffered the "arrested development" experienced by many refugee scholars. Instead, it was the exigencies of his anti-Fascist campaign that distracted him from this task.[64] Consequently, he wrote nothing about medieval communes or the Risorgimento; instead, he produced four books and countless articles on the Fascist regime. And although the books became at times polemical in tone, his research was as meticulous as limited documentation would permit. He used historical analysis, but his primary purpose was often didactic.[65] The product of the Harvard years is a body of literature written by a fully engaged intellectual who made a singular contribution to the study of the Fascist era.

Before he left Europe, Salvemini had come to believe that foreign policy represented the Fascist regime's greatest vulnerability. Convinced that Mussolini's adventurism would lead to crisis, Salvemini set out to prepare Americans for the denouement. *Mussolini Diplomatico* (1932), the first book Salvemini produced during his American career, was one of the earliest full-length accounts of Fascist foreign policy.[66] Although it has since drawn substantial criticism, some have considered the second part of his trilogy on Fascism to be his finest work.[67] It was a natural successor to *The Fascist Dictatorship* because Salvemini persisted in emphasizing the primacy of Mussolini's domestic politics. Accordingly, *Il Duce*'s otherwise confusing behavior in foreign affairs could be explained in terms of his need to create the appearance of success in order to stabilize the regime.[68]

For this reason, Mussolini's instincts and experience paid enormous benefits. "The man is a journalist," Salvemini wrote.[69] By a combination of censorship, rewards, and punishments, he used *The New York Times*, the *Chicago Tribune*, and other newspapers to manipulate international opinion. The results were conspicuous. The world press nurtured the mythology of *Il Duce*, invoking the loftiest of comparisons—Cromwell, Machiavelli, Napoleon, Mazzini, Dante, and even St. Francis. In fact, Salvemini noted, many Americans had so embraced this mythology that they now believed that the difficulties of the Great Depression demanded an "American Mussolini."[70] Salvemini was determined to expose such fabrication; not only did it distort conditions in Italy, but it imperiled his American campaign.

Salvemini's rendition of Mussolini as propagandist led him to downplay *Il Duce*'s diplomatic skills. Quoting Fascist sources, he described a policy whose only plan was to prevent the stabilization of Europe, thus allowing Mussolini, sooner or later, "to grab something here or there."[71] Most important, Mussolini tried to destabilize Franco-German relations—for example, by supporting German nationalists in their opposition to the Versailles status quo.[72] Salvemini portrayed this behavior as reckless gamesmanship, the antithesis of adroit diplomacy. A number of historians accepted at least a modified form of Salvemini's thesis that Mussolini's foreign policy was propagandistic, demagogic, and virtually incoherent.[73]

Salvemini believed that by the summer of 1928, Mussolini had found a formula that reconciled his domestic and international needs. *Il Duce* would allow Dino Grandi, named foreign minister in 1929, to issue peaceful declarations in diplomatic language designed to placate the Western democracies; while at home he would play the "double game" of delivering bellicose speeches designed to maintain political support, justifying the great sacrifices demanded of the Italian people as necessary to win "grandeur" for the nation.[74]

This view of Mussolini as opportunistic exploiter of foreign policy lent itself to polemical tone. Salvemini labeled Mussolini the "maestro of the art of bluff" who repeated chauvinistic phrases every day, boasting that the Italian people were prepared to march to war as soon as he gave the signal.[75] He faulted *Il Duce* for "playing Napoleon" in North Africa and "playing on the map of folly" in the Balkans.

Nonetheless, Salvemini generally wrote with restraint in this 1932 edition.[76] With the exception of the seizure of Corfu in 1923, Mussolini had not yet committed aggression. The rise of Hitler (rendering Mussolini "really dangerous") and *Il Duce*'s militant move into Ethiopia would require a series of reassessments over two decades in which Salvemini would place much blame on the British and French for accommodating Mussolini.[77] His 1932 rendition of Mussolini as menacing, improvisational propagandist helped to set the stage for *Il Duce*'s decline in international prestige once his open confrontation of the Western democracies made him the object of critical scrutiny.[78]

Even by the summer of 1931, as he wrote the book, Salvemini anticipated the international problems of the next decade. He was troubled by the warming relationship between Italy and Britain, especially Austen Chamberlain, the Tories, and the Foreign Office. He noted with alarm the Fascist praise for the success of Hitler and the Nazi party in 1930 and the enthusiastic response of the German nationalist press.[79]

Salvemini believed that the Italian government should lead the "Small Powers" toward a European peace within the League of Nations framework. He measured Mussolini's diplomacy against his own vision of an Italy that would someday give power to good and moral men, faithful to the principles of the Risorgimento, who would pursue peace over their personal ambitions and scorn imperial glory.[80] This ideal, always implicit in Salvemini's work, is often obscured by his well-known pessimism; it is a standard, at the same time both lofty and simple, that explains why so many men would fail him throughout his life.

If Salvemini made a mistake in his 1932 interpretation, it was to characterize Fascist diplomacy as more monolithic a product than historians now believe it to have been in this era, before Mussolini took over as foreign minister. Throughout the book, though attributing individual public statements to Balbo, Grandi, legislators, Futurists, and other Fascists, Salvemini referred to them as "Mussolini and his friends." Although he distinguished between "moderate," "extremist," and "intellectual" Fascists, he failed to identify any divergent elements of foreign policy making, such as professional diplomats and ardent nationalists.[81] Thus, for example, when Grandi in 1930 made a conciliatory gesture toward peace and international economic recovery, it was a disingenuous part of Mussolini's "double game," and Grandi was a mere "functionary" of Mussolini.[82]

Repeatedly, Salvemini lamented the unavailability of documents that would have made his job easier and more accurate. In the absence of such archival documentation that has since shed light on the internal conflicts of the Italian diplomatic process of this era, Salvemini's one-dimensional treatment of the subject is understandable. Notwithstanding these shortcomings, *Mussolini Diplomatico* is a remarkable achievement. It remains today both a primary source in itself and a point of departure when evaluating Fascist foreign policy. Virtually all research conducted since 1945 on Fascist foreign policy has made use of *Mussolini Diplomatico*.[83]

Shortly after publication, Salvemini mailed a copy to *Il Duce* with the sarcastic inscription "in admiration and gratitude" to his "infallible and inexorable collaborator." Curiously, Mussolini read the book in February 1932 and made marginal notes throughout it. After the war, when Salvemini finally saw his book filled with *Il Duce*'s comments, he noted that in fewer than ten places did Mussolini express either disagreement or equivocation. He felt that he had passed this former schoolteacher's "history examination."[84]

Much more has been written about Salvemini's publications than about his teaching. Those students and colleagues who have reflected on Salvemini as maestro, both Italian and American, have universally admired him. One student remembered the "scientific rigor"of a humble, patient, young Salvemini at the University of Pisa.[85] Another recalled from the University of Florence the Socratic dialogues, the scrutiny of documents, and "the force of his logic."[86] Ernesto Rossi lauded his commitment to nurturing the "critical spirit," teaching his students always to question even the most venerated institutions. "He taught us," Rossi concluded, "to be nonconformists."[87]

In his teaching career at Italian universities, Salvemini had won a reputation as master teacher as well as virtuoso practitioner. His friends often added a third dimension to their tribute, praising him as a man whose model life of "thought and action" distinguished him from the traditional professor and assured him of substantial influence on his students.[88] What they seemed to admire most was a simple integrity that unified the various phases of his life.

It was the influence of his ideas as well as his personality that enabled Salvemini to become a friendly mentor to his students, "always discreet, never meddlesome."[89] In Florence, in the combative years when Fascism swept Tuscany, his influence on students had been most notable. The shared danger of publishing the first anti-Fascist journal had strengthened their ties, and in the process he had become known affectionately to the students of the Circolo as *lo zio* (uncle).[90] It was, he remembered, a group "founded on faith and courage in the hour of distress."[91]

The camaraderie, spirit and valor of the Circolo group set the standard for his rapport with students, particularly the bond with Carlo Rosselli, which would provide the basis for the GL group until 1935. Several other Salvemini protégés, like Aldo Garosci, emerged as anti-Fascist activists and historians of the period and won a place in the heroic mythology of the resistance movement. Paying tribute to Rossi and the Rosselli brothers in a speech in 1951, he could remember no young people "more noble than these three." It was to them that he owed "the most beautiful experiences that have enriched my spirit as a teacher and as a man."[92] Too often, as in the case of the Rosselli brothers, his praise took the form of eulogies to young victims of Fascist violence.

At Harvard, Salvemini failed to find another group of students like the Florence Circolo, a fact that Garosci believed left him "a little morose."[93] Clearly he found students who followed his intellectual lead, but according to Morra he found no "filial friends," no one with whom he felt "moral solidarity."[94] Such expectations were hardly realistic. In fact, his initial exposure to Harvard had led him to anticipate differences: friendly students, dedicated, demanding the full value of teaching for the tuition they paid.[95]

Salvemini did develop social relationships with some of his Harvard students, however. Living at Leverett House, he was part of Harvard's experiment, emulating Oxford and Cambridge, to create an integrated learning-living environment, including a tutorial study in the master's suite and a library in each residential building.[96] He regularly "held court" with undergraduates in the Leverett common room, and he accepted dinner invitations from them on a fairly regular basis, reciprocating by inviting them to the university club.[97] Salvemini developed a rapport with a number of them, some of whom began to refer to him, just as his students in Florence had done, as "Uncle Gaetano." Occasionally, the friendships proved lasting. "I have made some good friends here," he wrote to Mary Berenson in 1935, noting his lifelong good fortune "to make friends, to grow fond of them and to be beloved by them."[98] These personal relationships with his students reveal a dimension of his Harvard experience that has been overlooked.

In his fourteen years at Harvard, Salvemini usually taught a graduate course every other year and an undergraduate course in each spring semester, rotating surveys of Italian history with courses in Renaissance Italy, the Risorgimento, and Italian diplomacy.[99] His light teaching load afforded him time to write and lecture on contemporary Italian affairs and to travel as a visiting professor in the summer and fall.

It would be a serious mistake to evaluate Salvemini's impact at Harvard merely on the basis of his production of books; for while he was writing them, he was at the same time creating a new interest in the Italian past. In this sense, Harvard acquired a real bargain in landing Salvemini. He immediately established himself as America's "premier authority on Italian politics and history."[100] In turn, Harvard's prestige enhanced his own reputation, and Harvard became, for many years, a recognized center for the study of Italian history.[101] Harvard had already built strong programs in art history and Renaissance studies, and the Widener Library held a superb collection on the Risorgimento, numbering 40,000 volumes.[102] Before 1930, Italian studies at American universities (Harvard included) had focused on language, arts, and literature. The critical, systematic inquiry into modern Italy began only in the Fascist era, a phenomenon that H. Stuart Hughes attributes largely to Salvemini.[103]

Salvemini's influence was more inspirational than organizational, in the sense that the Harvard curriculum reflected no structured Italian history program. Instead, he exercised his influence primarily by example. Whom did he inspire? Many were undergraduates like Harry Marks, who was studying German history at the time.[104] According to Hughes, the "beloved master" influenced even those who did not take his courses.[105] Jerre Mangione, who later wrote poignant descriptions of the Italian-American experience (*Mount Allegro*, *An Ethnic at Large*), writes that he first fell under Salvemini's influence when the professor spoke at his high school in Rochester, New York.[106]

In addition to the students who took classes from him, Salvemini nurtured a number of American protégés, especially Hughes, Norman Kogan, and A. William Salomone.[107] Interestingly, none experienced a conventional student-mentor relationship with him. What he did for all three was to assist in revising their doctoral dissertations for publication, Hughes's *United States and Italy* and Kogan's *Italy and the Allies*. Salomone learned from Salvemini's earlier research on pre-Fascist Italy but in the process arrived at a contradictory interpretation. To his surprise, he found that when Salvemini returned the final draft of *Italy in the Giolittian Era*, the older scholar now accepted his basic thesis. In addition to these notable successes, Salvemini also contributed to the work of other students, such as Reinhold Schumann and Catherine Boyd.[108]

Salvemini's influence is impressive, especially in the absence of the conventional seminars and dissertations. The books of Hughes, Kogan, and Salomone contributed to an American, English-language scholarship of modern Italy, just as those of Schumann and Boyd added to the American literature on medieval Italian communes. Moreover, as had been the case in Florence, Salvemini's influence transcended the production of historical works. His students taught Italian history to the next generation of Americans: Hughes at Brown, Princeton, Stanford, and Harvard; Kogan at Connecticut; Salomone at Haverford, Temple, the University of Pennsylvania, and New York University; Boyd at Carleton College in Minnesota; and Schumann at Brandeis and Boston Universities.

All of these American protégés also testify in their own way to being inspired by Salvemini's courage. Schumann, who took his daughters to an American military cemetery in Europe to impress them with the cost of protecting freedom, said that Salvemini's commitment to the same cause qualified him to join "the company of these white crosses."[109] Kogan praised Salvemini for "[communicating] to his disciples his love for academic research and [spreading] the warmth of his moral conscience."[110] Hughes acknowledged a "debt" to

Salvemini: "His books stimulated my thought; his words encouraged me; his example acted as a tonic."[111] For Salomone, what had been a professional relationship gradually became a bond of "near filial" affection for his "maestro," whose "disciple" he became:

> Whatever the heights of moral indignation or the depths of despair his contemplation of men's errors and failures, not excluding his own, had sometimes involved, Gaetano Salvemini, this anti-Machiavelli stamped with deep Socratic features, had never despaired of human intelligence and of courage and integrity nor of their capacity to help him in the ceaseless search for truth.[112]

Indeed, he created a *scuola Salvemini* (Salvemini School), not in the sense that his students and friends uncritically accepted his political views, but that he developed at Harvard nothing less than the American study of modern Italian history.[113]

Salvemini left tangible evidence to document his teaching. He compiled his Harvard notes and research into a manuscript, two versions of which were discovered and later published. The book represented one of eight manuscripts he intended to write or revise while at Harvard. In this instance, he was successful, if only posthumously. It would remain his final work on Fascist Italy. More a synthesis than an original work, *The Harvard Lectures* nonetheless proves that Salvemini's ideas were evolving remarkably all the while he taught at Harvard in the 1930s, his seventh decade of life. The most extraordinary change is his reassessment of pre-Fascist Italy. Although it has long been assumed that this revision occurred only later, in response to Salomone's *Italy in the Giolittian Era*, the process had actually been underway for almost two decades.[114]

Salvemini had first established his anti-Giolittian critique in 1910 in his accusatory pamphlet *Il Ministro della mala vita*, a view he had maintained throughout his Italian career. Then in 1927, after almost two years in exile, he had published in the Parisian journal of the PRI a letter indicating that he had begun to rethink the entire era. Some Italian Republicans had alleged that, since Italian democracy had never existed, Mussolini could not have suppressed it. Salvemini responded, "In Italy we did not have *all* of democracy. We had less democracy than Switzerland, England, the United States, even France; but we were continually enlarging the area of democracy."[115]

Salvemini made this reference to American democracy just after returning from his initial American voyage, exposed for the first time to the reality of a system he had idealized. He had found a political culture not without its own intolerance, some of it directed at Italian Americans; and he had observed a system so imperfect as to execute Nicola Sacco and Bartolomeo Vanzetti on the basis of an unfair trial conducted in an outrageously prejudicial setting. During Salvemini's visit the campaign for pardon had peaked, and he had supported the demonstrations.[116] He then returned to Paris and London, which, he found, also fell short of the standard of democratic perfection. It was then, in the late 1920s, that Salvemini began to re-examine the Giolittian era. He did so in response to several factors: the rise of Fascism; Fascist claims to have upheld the traditions of the Italian liberal state; and his own observations of the imperfections of democracy abroad.

In his Harvard lectures, Salvemini elaborated on his reassessment of pre-Fascist Italy, again using his American experience as a point of reference. During the Great War, the U.S. government had more severely repressed dissent than had its Italian equivalent: long prison sentences for pacifists, dismissal of teachers, a ban on teaching the German language, and suppression of newspapers. He recalled that in Italy he had opposed the government's policies throughout the war without ever fearing dismissal from his teaching post. "If this is not democracy," he wrote, "imperfect democracy, to be sure, . . . nobody will ever know what democracy really is." It had been, in a phrase Salomone would popularize several years later, "democracy in the making."[117]

Hardly the demon who had menaced freedom throughout Salvemini's earlier polemics, the Giolitti of the Harvard lectures is given a more balanced treatment within the broader framework of the liberal state. Salvemini credits Giolitti as a parliamentarian and blames him for using that very skill to enact universal suffrage as a trick to weaken the PSI and to build support for his campaign to conquer Libya. In his long career, he had legalized trade unions, accepted the right to strike, and sensibly administered public finances. Giolitti's culpability was in undermining parliamentary institutions and public confidence through his manipulation of elections in the South. It was a system he had not invented but had perfected and applied unscrupulously to three successive national elections.[118]

In refocusing on the prewar era, Salvemini reproached the Vatican and the House of Savoy for their support of Fascism. Avoiding the overt anticlericalism of which he was sometimes accused, Salvemini explained the failure of the PPI to capitalize on its 1919 electoral success. Most significantly, he attributed its weakness to the domination of a democratic rank-and-file by an orthodox and reactionary leadership.[119] Finally, Salvemini warned his readers to avoid the assumption that the Vatican spoke for the Italian people. "The Holy See holds a far greater influence upon England and the United States than upon Italy," he claimed. This was part of a broadening claim that the vast majority of the Italian people supported neither the Fascist government nor the institutions upon which it rested.[120]

The Harvard Lectures' estimate of Giolitti's place in history would have been less an issue except for two factors: To an entire generation of readers, Salvemini had been known for his condemnations of the prime minister as his *bête noire* and as the corrupter of Italian democracy; and the historiography of the liberal state would reemerge as a contentious political issue in the "battle of the books" about Giolitti. In this way, the *Harvard Lectures*, when eventually published, would take center stage in a high-stakes political debate.[121]

In December 1938, Salvemini delivered a series of four lectures at the University of Chicago that were published the following year as *Historian and Scientist*.[122] Remarkable in several ways, they provide a rare statement of methodology and an even rarer attempt to define the field of historical study. Indirectly, they serve to justify his life as intellectual and political activist.

Salvemini contrasted history with the social sciences: the newer field deduces laws of human behavior, while historians subjectively reconstruct the facts. As examples of subjectivity, he offered Karl Marx and Vilfredo Pareto, whose passions, he said, undermined their claims to scientific detachment. To reconcile himself with scientific research, the historian must openly confess his biases. In a mea culpa destined for notoriety, he admitted the following:

I, for my part, declare that my mind is carpeted with biases—religious, philosophical, scientific, social, political, national and even personal—and that I constantly make use of my biases in my studies. I am not ashamed of this fact, because biases are not irreconcilable with scientific research.[123]

The premise of innate bias led Salvemini to the theme of the lectures. Historical interpretation requires "ethical judgments," the necessity of which justify the scholar's political advocacy of his ideas. Thus, the historian should be a man of action, overcoming the "moral indifference" that seemed to be in vogue in academia. Ultimately, both historian and social scientist should be judged by a utilitarian standard: Did their work offer the community greater opportunity for justice, well-being, and happiness?[124]

In presenting this defense of political activism, Salvemini gave the ultimate apologia for his life. Aware that historical research provided him neither absolute truth nor clairvoyance, he made the existential choice to perform a moral act. "To live means to act," he declared. Neither history nor the social sciences give moral guidance, only mere hints. A decision to act comes not from scholarly inquiry, but from a moral commitment.[125]

Salvemini's lectures captured the essence of a life in which scholarship and politics had often intertwined. In a review of the Italian edition of *Historian and Scientist*, Croce would later challenge his position. Undaunted, Salvemini persisted in asking "all those questions no one else dares to ask," believing that he was fulfilling the ideal social role of the intellectual.[126]

Salvemini's commitment to the pressing issues of his anti-Fascist campaign was so intense that it led him to sacrifice scholarly production. By creating a steady stream of criticism of Fascism, Salvemini provided Americans—particularly liberals—a specific anti-Fascist, independent, pro-Italian agenda. This effort drained his considerable energy and cost him the opportunity to elevate his reputation as a scholar. Yet even though he never completed his magnum opus on Italian diplomacy, he did earn a reputation not only as a dauntless anti-Fascist activist but also as an authority on Fascism. The paradox is that although the demands of exile disrupted his scholarship, those very demands gave him the opportunity to build a more enduring reputation and to make a more significant contribution.

The view of Cambridge as "enchanted island" misses the mark, for among the most striking characteristics of his life were its consistency and continuity. In 1933, he simply transferred his campaign to New England and New York, which, by the end of the decade, would become the hub of all anti-Fascism among the Italian exiles. Far from an "enchanted island" of withdrawal from the world, Cambridge became his operational base. Its apparent quiet belied the fury of the activity he produced: four books, plans and manuscripts for eight others, scores of articles and speeches, and a new anti-Fascist political organization. For Salvemini, Cambridge was the quiet eye of a storm center.

NOTES

1. GS, "The Nelson Gay Risorgimento Collection in the Harvard College Library," *Harvard Alumni Bulletin*, February 22, 1935, reprint, "Salvemini" file, WL.

2. Kenneth B. Murdock, Dean of the Faculty of Arts and Sciences, to James B. Conant, President, November 13, 1933, *CoP*. The Conant Papers are considered the official Harvard Corporation records of this era. Barbara S. Meloni, Curatorial Assistant, HA, to CK, February 3, 1984.

3. Neilla Warren, ed., *The Letters of Ruth Draper* (New York, 1979). See also Iris Origo, *A Need to Testify*, 79–127.

4. Murdock to Conant, November 13, 1933, *CoP*; LaP(?), "To the President and Fellows of Harvard College," late November(?) 1933, *CoP*; GS, *Mem*, 175.

5. GS, *Mem*, 175; CG (Boston) to CG (New York) November 23, 1933, *CPC*"S"; Conant to GS, December 16, 1933; GS to Conant, December 18, 1933; press release, December 20, 1933, Harvard University News Office, 1933, 238; Henry James, Board of Overseers, to Francis W. Hunnewell, Secretary to the Corporation, January 2, 1934; Hunnewell to Henry L. Shattuck, Treasurer, Harvard College, January 3, 1934; Clarence Henry Haring, Chairman, Department of History, to GS, January 19, 1934; Ruth Draper to President and Fellows of Harvard College, May 1, 1939, *CoP*.

6. GS to CPa, February 5, 1936, *PaP*. Salvemini was appointed De Bosis Lecturer by a vote of the Harvard Corporation on December 11, 1933. On June 2, 1934, the History Department voted to recommend Salvemini as the 1934–1935 De Bosis Lecturer. "He appears to have been reappointed to the Lectureship each year." Meloni to CK, February 3, 1984. However, Salvemini wrote in 1936 that "my appointment

ends in 1939. Thus my life is insured for four more years." GS to CPa, February 5, 1936, *PaP*; GS, *Mem*, 175.

7. Anthony Heilbut, *Exiled in Paradise* (New York, 1983), vii.

8. Arthur M. Schlesinger, *In Retrospect* (New York, 1963), 92–93, 131. Arthur M. Schlesinger, Jr. believes that Lowell's appeal to his father to reconsider the invitation was probably a pro forma request made to satisfy the Overseer. SI.

9. Memorandum, CG (New York) to MI and Ambassador (Washington), January 6, 1934, *CPC*"S."

10. "Ford, Jeremiah Denis Matthias," *Harvard University Gazette*, April 25, 1959, HA; Samuel Eliot Morison, *Three Centuries of Harvard, 1636–1936* (Cambridge, 1936), 440; *CPC*"S," *passim*; Reinhold Schumann to CK, July 4, 1993; SI.

11. Roberta Feuerlicht, *Justice Crucified* (New York, 1977), 358–361; Gardner Jackson, *Reminiscences* (Glen Rock, N.J., 1972), 280.

12. Conant, *My Several Lives* (New York, 1970), 89, 446ff.

13. J. D. M. Ford to Murdock, December 11, 1933, *CoP;* to Conant, December 15 and 22, 1933, *CoP*; Copy of telegram, Ambassador (Washington) to Minister of Foreign Affairs, January 11, 1934, *CPC*"S."

14. Conant to Ford, December 16, 1933, *CoP*.

15. Hunnewell to GS, December 14, 1933; Conant to Haring, December 14, 1933; to LaP, December 15 and 23, 1933; LaP to Conant, December 16, 1933, *CoP*; press release, December 20, 1933, Harvard University News Service, 1933–238, *CoP*; *Boston Herald,* December 20, 1933.

16. Murdock to Conant, November 13, 1933; LaP(?) to President and Fellows of Harvard College, late November(?) 1933; LaP to Conant, December 16, 1933; Conant to LaP, December 23, 1933; Conant to GS, December 16, 1933, *CoP*.

17. GS to Conant, December 18, 1933, *CoP*.

18. GS to Draper, January 21, 1934, Autograph file, *DeBC*; "Teachers' Oath," 523.

19. Louis Lyons, "Gaetano Salvemini and the Nieman Fellows of Harvard," in *Controcorrente* (Boston), December, 1958.

20. GS to Draper, January 21, 1934, autograph file, *DeBC*; *Stampa Libera*, November 2 and 3, 1933; "Salvemini to Speak at Forum," Harvard *Crimson*, October 16, 1945.

21. Salvemini, *Mem*, 176.

22. *NYT*, March 4, 1934.

23. GS, *Mem*, 176; to AT, June 17, 1934, *TP*.

24. Telegram, GS to Capo del Governo, Rome, March 5, 1934, *SPD, CR*"S."

25. *NYT*, March 4 and 6, 1934; Boston *Evening Transcript*, March 5, 1934; GS, "Saint Peter, Mussolini and Salvemini," manuscript, GSS. *Il Corriere d'America* reported Salvemini's complicity as proven fact.

26. V. Veeder, Attorney, to GS, May 24, 1934, GSS.

27. Telegram, Ambassador (Washington) to Minister of Foreign Affairs, March 8, 1934, *CPC*"S"; SI; GS to Draper, January 21, 1934, Autograph file, *DeBC*.

28. DeC, *Sal*, 388; GGM, *Problemi di storia nei rapporti tra l'Italia e Stati Uniti* (Turin, 1971), 116–118; HSH, *The Sea Change* (New York, 1975), 94–95.

29. GS to MB, March 15, 1935, in Morra, ed., "L'esperienza inglese," *Il Mondo*, September 13, 1960.

30. Lyons, "Salvemini," 77.

31. HSH to CK, August 3, 1983.

32. MA, "Salvemini negli Stati Uniti," 16.

33. HSH to CK, October 2, 1983.

34. GS to AT, August 19, 1949, *TP*; Vincent Carosso to CK, September 19, 1983; MS to CK, July 30, 1983; NK to CK, August 1, 1983.

35. ET, "Nota biografica," 265; NK to CK, August 1, 1983; MS to CK, August 1983.

36. HSH to CK, October 2, 1983; see also HSH, "Doing Italian History," *Journal of Modern Italian Studies*, I (Fall 1995), 94–95.

37. See, for example, Lewis Coser, *Refugee Scholars in America* (New Haven, 1984); Jarrell C. Jackman and Carla M. Borden, eds., *The Muses Flee Hitler* (Washington, 1983); John R. Taylor, *Strangers in Paradise* (New York, 1983); Donald Fleming and Bernard Bailyn, eds., *The Intellectual Migration, Europe and America, 1930–1960* (Cambridge, MA, 1969); and Donald P. Kent, *The Refugee Intellectual* (New York, 1953).

38. Franz Neumann, "The Social Sciences" in Neumann, ed., *The Cultural Migration* (Philadelphia, 1953), 4–13.

39. Kent, *Refugee Intellectual* , 239–242.

40. BB, *Sunset and Twilight* , ed. Nicky Mariano (New York, 1963), 421.

41. Laura Fermi, *Illustrious Immigrants* (Chicago, 1968); Heilbut, *Exiled in Paradise* .

42. Kent, *Refugee Intellectual*, 50; HSH, *Sea Change*, 95; Henri Peyre, "The Study of Literature" in Neumann, ed., *The Cultural Migration, passim*.

43. RV, Prefazione, GS, *Opere* VI (1), viii; Gian Luigi Falabrino, "Anticommunismo e anticlericalismo nelle lettere di Salvemini," *CS* August 5, 1968, 413–414.

44. HSH to CK, August 3, 1983.

45. GS, *Mem*, 338.

46. RB, "Salvemini and his Widener Library," unpublished manuscript, quoted in Origo, *A Need*, 169; Peyre, "Study of Literature," 42.

47. Guido Ferrando, "Ritratto di Salvemini," *Rassegna storia Toscana*, IV (April-June 1958), 200; MS, "Giellisti e loro amici," 281; ET, "Nota biografica," 265.

48. Gino Luzzatto, "Il Merito di Salvemini," *Il Mondo*, June 28, 1955; NK to CK, August 1, 1983; ET, "Nota biografica," 265; Carosso to CK, September 19, 1983.

49. Ferrando, "Ritratto di Salvemini," 203. By comparison, Columbia University paid Béla Bartok $3,000 and Enrico Fermi $9,000 per year. See also Fermi, *Illustrious Immigrants*, 5–8; Peyre, "Study of Literature," 47–49.

50. ET, "Nota biografica," 265; DeC, *Sal*, 389.

51. GS to MB, March 15, 1935, in Umberto Morra, ed., "L'esperienza inglese"; MC interview, June 1984.

52. MC interview, December 1979; DeC, *Sal*, 389.

53. MC to CK, June 1984.

54. MS to CK, July 30, 1983; Vincent Carosso, who was Salvemini's assistant when he visited the University of California and knew him at Harvard, remembers that he appeared to be alone and preoccupied with Italian matters. Carosso to CK, September 19, 1983.

55. SI.

56. HC to CK, June 1984.

57. HSH in Jackman and Borden, eds., *The Muses*, 113–114.

58. Origo, *A Need*, 171.

59. Quoted in Origo, *A Need*, 171.

60. GS, *Mem*, 88–89. Clearly Salvemini was preoccupied with Italian matters, particularly in the early years of exile. MS to CK, July 30, 1983; GGM, *Problemi*, 97.

61. Ferrando, *Ritratto di Salvemini*, 200.

62. ET "Interventi" in ES, *ACGS*, 187; MS to CK, July 30, 1983; telegram, Ambassador (Washington) to MAE, March 5, 1940, *CPC*"S." Norman Kogan writes emphatically: "He was not cut off from the external world." NK to CK, August 1, 1983.

63. Arnold Beichman, "We Go Calling on Gaetano Salvemini," *P.M.*, October 10, 1943, *CaP*, Box 7, "Miscellaneous Clippings."

64. GS to MB, March 15, 1935, *Il Mondo*, September 13, 1960.

65. GS to AT, November 7, 1933, *TP*.

66. The first edition was published in French as *Mussolini Diplomate* (Paris, 1932), then in Italian as *Mussolini Diplomatico* (Paris, 1932), cited as GS, *MD*. See MC, *Bibliografia, passim*.

67. ES, "Lo storico," in ES, *ACGS*, 33–35.

68. GS, *MD*, 318ff., 385 ff., 406; Jens Petersen, "La politica estera del fascismo come problema storiografico," *Storia contemporanea*, 3 (1972), 664–665; NT, "Salvemini storico," 919.

69. GS, *MD*, 318.

70. GS, *MD*, 399–402, 413–418, 428. On the influence of the Mussolini myth in the United States, Salvemini cites a survey published in the November 1934 issue of *Harper's Magazine*.

71. GS, *Mussolini Diplomate*, 214.

72. GS, *Mussolini Diplomate*, 119, 193, 227, 231–236, 292–293.

73. LS and Giovanni Mira, *Storia dell'Italia nel periodo fascista* (Turin, 1957), 657ff.; HSH, "The Early Diplomacy of Italian Fascism, 1922–1932," in Gordon Craig and Felix Gilbert, eds., *The Diplomats, 1919–1932* (New York, 1963), 225ff; Denis Mack Smith, *Mussolini's Roman Empire* (New York, 1977), viii, and *Italy* (Ann Arbor, 1969), 445ff.

74. GS, *Mussolini Diplomate*, 236–239, 282–285, 312–325, 332–333.

75. GS, *Mussolini Diplomate*, 338.

76. GS, *Mussolini Diplomate*, 127, 176.

77. GS, *Prelude*, 134. Salvemini believed in 1953 that Mussolini would have accepted some face- saving compromise in Ethiopia in August 1935, and thus was not a driven ideologue or megalomaniac (*Prelude*, 259). He wrote in the 1949 preface that his opinion of Mussolini had not changed since the era before his rise to power (*Prelude*, 8).

78. GS, *Mussolini Diplomate*, 142–151.

79. GS, *Mussolini Diplomate*, 111–112, 132–135, 187–188, 197–212, 219, 253–254, 296–302, 326–328.

80. GS, *Mussolini Diplomate*, 100–101, 180–183.

81. GS, *Mussolini Diplomate*, 68, 81, 86, 89, 119–120, 123, 127, 128–129, 148–150, 225, 248, 270; DeG, *Italian Fascism*, 92–97.

82. GS, *Mussolini Diplomate*, 282–283, 330.

83. Petersen, "La politica estera," 661; see Giampiero Carocci, "Salvemini e la politica estera del fascismo," *Scritti Storici* (January–March 1968), 218–224.

84. GS, *Mussolini Diplomatico (1922–1932)* (Bari, 1952), 497–512.

85. Lamberto Naldini, "Salvemini Maestro a Pisa," 697–700.

86. Carlo Schiffrer, "Salvemini Maestro," *Trieste Rivista politica giuliana*, 4 (1957), 34–35.

87. ER, "Il nonconformista."

88. Giuseppe Galasso, "Un maestro di moralità," *La Voce Repubblicana*, December 20–21, 1967.

89. Naldini, "Salvemini Maestro a Pisa," 698.

90. GS, "Carlo e Nello Rosselli," *Opere* VIII, 676 ff; AG, *VCR*, 31 ff; Stanislao Pugliese, *Rosselli*, 29–34; RV, "Carlo Rosselli e Gaetano Salvemini," 78n.

91. GS, Preface to NR, *Saggi sul Risorgimento e altri scritti* (Turin, 1946), 10.

92. GS, "Carlo e Nello Rosselli," 723.

93. AG, *Pensiero politico e storiografia moderna* (Pisa, 1954), 173.

94. Morra, "L'amico dei giovani."

95. GS, *Mem*, 137 ff.; to AT, March 5, 1930, *TP*.

96. Reinhold Schumann to CK, July 4, 1993.

97. Carosso, Harry J. Marks, and others recall that Salvemini knew his students outside the classroom. Marks and Kogan hosted Salvemini for dinner and, according to the latter, this practice was rather commonplace. Carosso to CK, September 19, 1983; Marks to CK, November 13, 1983; NK to CK, August 1, 1983; NK, "Gaetano Salvemini in America," *Il Mondo*, October 8, 1957.

98. GS to MB, March 15, 1935, in Morra, ed., "L'esperienza inglese"; NK, "Salvemini in America."

99. Recollections of Salvemini as teacher at Harvard indicate that he retained many of the qualities that had attracted students to his classes in Italy. ET, "L'Opera di Gaetano Salvemini," 25; HSH to CK, August 3, 1983; Carosso to CK, September 19, 1983; Marks to CK, November 13, 1984. H. Stuart Hughes remembered that the "humor and pungency of his Italian style" carried over easily into English. HSH, *The Sea Change*, 95.

100. NK to CK, August 1, 1983.

101. ET, "Nota biografica," 265.

102. GS, "The Nelson Gay Risorgimento Collection."

103. HSH, "Gli studi di storia moderna italiana in America," *Rassegna Storica del Risorgimento*, 45 (1958), 273–274.

104. Marks to CK, November 13, 1984.

105. HSH, *Sea Change*, 95; HSH, "Doing Italian History," 94–95.

106. Jerre Mangione to CK, November 22, 1983.

107. ET, "interventi," in ES, *ACGS*, 187; MS, "Antifascisti italiani negli Stati Uniti," 275.

108. HSH to CK, August 3 and October 2, 1983; NK to CK, August 1, 1983; AWS, "Momenti di storia, frammenti di ricordi con Salvemini tra Stati uniti e italia," *Archivio Trimestrale* VIII (July–December 1982), 797; Meloni to CK, November 17, 1983 and February 3, 1984; GS to CPa, February 5, 1936, *PaP*; Schumann to CK, July 4, 1993; Boyd, *Tithes and Parishes in Medieval Italy* (Ithaca, 1952), x.

109. Schumann to CK, July 4, 1993.

110. NK, "Salvemini in America."

111. HSH to CK, August 3, 1983.

112. AWS, *IGE*, 168–169.

113. HSH, "Gli studi di storia," 273–274.

114. GS, "*Lezioni di Harvard,*'" *Opere* VI (1), 299–655, published originally as *The Origins of Fascism in Italy* (New York, 1973).

115. GS, "Pre-Fascist Democracy and the Tasks of Anti-Fascism," from AWS, *Italy from the Risorgimento to Fascism* (Garden City, NY, 1970), 370; trans. from GS, "Che cosa è stata la democrazia in Italia," letter to *L'Italia del Popolo* (Paris), May 31, 1927.

116. GS to Camillo Berneri, February 29, 1927, *AGS*.

117. GS, *Origins of Fascism*, 60. Roberto Vivarelli noted this change: "the judgment he now passed on Giolitti's work was quite moderate both in form and in substance." Introduction, *Origins of Fascism*, x. This fact does not diminish Salomone's influence on his maestro, but it does indicate that Salvemini had reevaluated Giolitti prior to reading Salomone's manuscript for the first time in the spring of 1943. AWS, *IGE*, 126.

118. GS, *Origins of Fascism*, 77–85.

119. GS, *Origins of Fascism*, 143.

120. GS, *Origins of Fascism*, 137–149.

121. AWS, *IGE*, 133–169.

122. GS, *Historian and Scientist* (Cambridge, 1939).

123. GS, *Historian and Scientist*, 75.

124. GS, *Historian and Scientist*, 25, 153–160.

125. GS, *Historian and Scientist*, 83, 157–158.

126. EG, *Sal*, 209; Benedetto Croce, review of GS' *Storia e scienza* in *Quaderni della "Critica,"* 13 (March 1949), 93–95; HSH, *Sea Change*, 88; Jacques Barzun, "The Uses of History," *The Saturday Review of the Arts*, December 23, 1939, 8; Carl Becker, *AHR*, 45 (April 1940), 45; ET, "L'opere di Gaetano Salvemini," 30.

Chapter 10

Anti-Fascism in America

> [Italian immigrants] had never felt themselves to be Italians as long as they
> had been living in the old country. . . . National consciousness awoke in
> them when they came in touch (which often meant to blows) with groups
> of different national origins in America. Italy now seemed to them no lon-
> ger a land from which they had been forced to leave.
>
> Gaetano Salvemini, c. 1940[1]

At age sixty, Salvemini now took his campaign against Fascism to the United
States. When he began teaching at Harvard, the Fascist regime had entered its
second decade. Three months after his first Lauro De Bosis lecture, Mussolini
attacked Ethiopia, and within two years he sent Italian "volunteer" troops to
support Franco's army in Spain. These initiatives, which tested the global security system, also challenged Salvemini by providing anti-Fascism its first opening since the Matteotti crisis. Ironically, these very opportunities also exposed
new fissures within the campaign against Mussolini. As "conscience" of the
movement and self-appointed prosecutor of Mussolini's regime, Salvemini
resolutely maintained his course—at the cost of membership in political organizations and even friendships. He provided for some a moral rudder in a movement buffeted by shifting winds, for others an inflexible obstacle to political
compromise.

In launching his anti-Fascist campaign in the United States, Salvemini faced
a daunting challenge. He hoped to find Italian-American leaders and organizations able to provide him with grassroots support that he could then mobilize
within a broader international movement against Mussolini and his regime. Al-

though Salvemini would pursue other avenues, his success rested substantially on this effort, especially because he knew that mobilizing Italian America promised the most likely route to President Roosevelt and thereby to American policy.

In his earlier travels to the United States, Salvemini had contacted Italian-American anti-Fascists, especially the radicals who led AFANA and published *Il Nuovo Mondo*. AFANA included anarchists, syndicalists, socialists, left-wing labor groups, the radical press, republicans, more moderate socialists, and mainstream labor organizations such as the New York Federation of Labor, the International Ladies Garment Workers Union (ILGWU) and the Amalgamated Clothing Workers of America (ACWA). One of his greatest challenges was to tap this source of established Italian-American radicalism, hardened by decades of labor conflict and anti-immigrant, anti-Left hysteria. However, the anti-Fascist front had begun to disintegrate before Salvemini's arrival, and although he spoke at their rallies and supported their activities, he did not fit comfortably into their world.

His hope was to combine the resources of both the Italian-American Left and the Paris-based GL, the most promising international movement, but this would prove increasingly difficult. At an anti-Fascist rally in the spring of 1930, he had announced the formation of a North American Federation of GL in New York under the leadership of Roberto Bolaffio, an engineer whom he met at the New School and who became a trusted friend and ally.[2] He wrote to Carlo Rosselli that GL should avoid repeating the mistake of bad alliances; by associating with first the Concentration and then the PSI, GL had "bound life to death."[3] This exchange also indicated a growing dispute with Rosselli, but Salvemini continued to make speeches and collect funds on GL's behalf and supported its program through 1932. By 1933, he had pulled away to resume his customary independence.

By consolidating his New York operation under Bolaffio, Salvemini exhibited his continuing mistrust of established groups. He had found the various components of Italian American anti-Fascism badly fragmented, especially the socialists.[4] The dominant group aligned with the American Socialist Party and Luigi Antonini's Local 89 of the ILGWU. Girolamo Valenti led a dissident socialist faction; a smaller contingent included Vincenzo Vacirca and Giuseppe Lupis. Meanwhile, the more radical August Bellanca of the ACWA fought Antonini for influence over the city's Italian workers.[5]

The one common denominator of the New York socialists was their reformist socialism. The New Deal's social democracy drew them into the American political culture, and their pragmatism and their Americanization set them apart from the more radical, libertarian, and anarchist leaders like Carlo Tresca, and, for different reasons, from Salvemini as well.[6]

Salvemini became increasingly frustrated with socialist factionalism and classism and with their connection to what he viewed as the discredited parties of the past. As an alternative to the socialists, Salvemini and Bolaffio started GL groups in Hoboken, Brooklyn, the Bronx, and Greenwich Village, as well as in Boston and Philadelphia. Frustrated by financial and organizational problems, Salvemini expressed an attitude of resignation toward these "good children" of New York.[7] Throughout the tribulations, he raised money for GL. In a December 1933 speech in memory of the anarchist Errico Malatesta, Salvemini guaranteed his audiences that every "last cent" collected would go directly to Paris.[8] As he distanced himself from the Italian-American Left, he abandoned their resources in favor of a small group of confidants, more trustworthy and more focused but less likely to succeed.

Salvemini's initial difficulties with the New York socialists, the union leadership, and other Italian-American anti-Fascists reflected several broader aspects of his new American career. First there was the ever present shortage of resources. Salvemini found himself constantly searching for funds—during the Great Depression, among a poor population—and for a journal to serve his campaign.[9]

Second, the New York organizational campaign introduced Salvemini directly to American politics. Most of the union leaders and socialists Salvemini met were poorly educated, tough veterans of labor warfare and organizational battles who had climbed out of the rank and file. He generally found them to be unsavory characters and "vulgar troublemakers." Few were men of ideas. The most extreme radicals had been deported during the Palmer raids, and the survivors had been conditioned by the conservative American labor environment of the 1920s. Salvemini's past encounters with Bissolati, Amendola, and Turati had not prepared him to deal with Antonini, Valenti or Lupis.[10]

Those Italian Americans who had succeeded had become adept at negotiation and political compromise, focused on the material concerns of their union membership. In short, they had become Americanized. In contrast, Salvemini was a European intellectual who disdained political compromise and the *pateracchi* (corrupt bargains) of political parties. He had condemned Giolitti, then the parties that enabled Mussolini to achieve power, then the Concentration and GL, all for their insidious bargaining. Now convinced that the New York anti-Fascists were driven by similar political instincts more than by principle, he once again became disillusioned.

Nonetheless, Salvemini persisted, speaking to anti-Fascist groups at every opportunity. In spite of the tension, the New York labor leaders, socialists and anarchists generally maintained a respect for *il professore*, as they called him. They regarded him as a prestigious figure, as an arbiter of anti-Fascist disputes and as a mentor—but always as an outsider, a European.

Salvemini's lack of confidence in the New York labor and socialist leadership led him to separate GL, further dividing American anti-Fascism. Max Salvadori did not exaggerate when he wrote that, in America, "Salvemini *was* GL."[11] Consequently, when he withdrew, his departure ended the American presence of this important anti-Fascist organization. It was shortly after assuming the chair at Harvard in 1933 that Salvemini began to distance himself from Giustizia e Libertà in disagreement with Carlo Rosselli. The split has been the subject of some debate.

According to Rosselli, the breach originated in an earlier, fundamental difference in political views and from Salvemini's excessive idealism and moralism.[12] If Rosselli's rendition is accurate, it is difficult to explain his cooperation with Salvemini for two subsequent decades. Salvemini, on the other hand, explained that the rift opened only in 1934, when Rosselli began converting GL to a political party and when the organization "suffered profoundly [under] the philo-Communist influence of Magrini [Aldo Garosci]."[13]

Salvemini's anti-Communism was born of both principle and empiricism. Axiomatic was his inability to reconcile the communist state with his Enlightenment-based values. His aversion to ideological abstractions led him away from challenging Marxist theory; instead, he concentrated on current Marxist practices, distinguishing between "independents" who simply "accepted Communist economic doctrine" and "Stalinists" whom he fervently denounced. Although he conceded that communism may not have fully evolved, he perceived wartime Stalinism as a dictatorship of the Left, as abusive of individual freedom as was Fascism. Among the totalitarian states he found striking continuity: repression of political opposition by secret police; censorship of ideas; Mussolini's confinement of political prisoners on the penal islands, and Stalin's exiling of opponents to Siberia.[14]

Most ominous to Salvemini was communism's potential impact on Italy. It was not that he feared an Italian Bolshevik revolution in Italy in the 1930s—he saw that as unlikely, for much the same reason that he had viewed Fascist warnings of impending Bolshevik revolution to be unfounded in 1919. He was convinced that an Italian society dominated by small proprietors and agricultural workers, small businessmen, professionals, and artisans would doom any proletarian revolution to failure. "Communism is not made for these people," he wrote.[15] Now his traditional anticommunism was hardened by the Popular Front strategy, by which, he believed, communists cynically cooperated with socialists and thereby undermined his own democratic left, the "*terza via* [third way]" between communism and fascism. GL, originally committed to that path, had now lost its bearing.

Whatever the origin of their differences, when Rosselli began to recast GL as "a movement of socialist renewal" in the spring of 1934, Salvemini wrote that he would offer his resignation rather than make concessions to "Marxist demagoguery."[16] Salvemini tenaciously opposed linking anti-Fascism either to Marxism or to the pre-Fascist political parties, and he also opposed the GL strategy of attempting to start a revolution within Italy. The differences were both ideological and strategic, intensified by Salvemini's sense of losing a protégé.[17] In September 1935, when Rosselli issued the new GL leftist program in a "Manifesto to the Italians," Salvemini made his final exit. Returning from a trip to Paris, he wrote to Tarchiani that although he would remain Carlo's personal friend, he would no longer support him politically or financially.[18]

Salvemini was still very much the European, as Tarchiani reminded him; but he had severed his ties with the major European anti-Fascist organization. Nothing else remained to be done, he wrote to Tarchiani in October 1935: "I will not bother any more with Italy except as a historian." Nor would he again look to Paris to gain credibility and support for the anti-Fascist cause. However, the despair was only temporary. His perennial pessimism had never inhibited his political activism, and this departure from GL would not dull his commitment to the cause.[19]

In fact, he quickly recovered from the new challenges presented by Rosselli's leftward movement and the Popular Front strategy that Rosselli began to embrace. In response, Salvemini reaffirmed his own political program. In a lengthy letter to Tarchiani, he laid out the agenda that he was prepared to present to the Italian people: republican government, political liberties, and nationalization of large capital while protecting medium and small property. This Salveminian program remained virtually unchanged.[20]

The GL era now behind him, Salvemini embarked on his own independent American campaign against Fascism. If he no longer agreed with Rosselli and could not trust the New York socialists, he could rely on a small network of committed anti-Fascists in America: the Cantarellas, the Bolaffios, La Piana, Giuseppe Borgese, and a few others. In agreement with Salvemini's program and energized by his integrity and personal magnetism, they provided a loyal cadre that enabled him to carry on the battle.

Even before his first American lecture tour, Salvemini had written that Italy's ultimate fate lay largely in the hands of the United States. As that prophecy fulfilled itself, he knew the importance of convincing Italian Americans, whose views would be a crucial consideration of the Roosevelt administration, always sensitive to ethnic opinion. By 1933, convinced that he could not work with the leaders of the Italian-American Left, he had to recruit his own leadership.

The battle he began to wage for the hearts and minds of the Italian-American community presented enormous cultural, psychological, and political barriers. Fascists had been working in the United States for more than a decade. Italian Americans had founded the first American *fascio* in New York City, eighteen months before the March on Rome, and numerous *fasci* in other American cities thereafter. Once Mussolini came to power he attempted to control these American *fasci*. Intent on improving relations with the United States, he took the advice of Ambassador Gelasio Caetani and restricted the public activities of American Fascists that were beginning by 1923 to provoke criticism from the American press and politicians. Nonetheless, Mussolini continued to win thunderous support from such pro-Fascist publications as Agostino de Biasi's *Il Carroccio* and Domenico Trombetta's *Il Grido della Stirpe*. Then, in 1924, Mussolini replaced the cautious Caetani with Giacomo De Martino and seven months later inserted Dino Grandi as Undersecretary of Foreign Affairs as part of a reorganization of the Foreign Ministry. Grandi was intent on bringing the *fasci* abroad under control. Mussolini instructed De Martino to distance himself from the American *fasci* and dispatched Count Ignazio Thaon di Revel to New York to create the Fascist League of North America (FLNA). The *fasci* grew to about seventy, claiming more than 6,000 members.[21]

AFANA and the anti-Fascist Left, reacting to a series of public provocations by American Blackshirts, revitalized their activities. The unions, AFANA's *Il Nuovo Mondo,* and Tresca's *Il Martello* counterattacked in an escalating war of words and weapons in the streets. Even cautious Italian-American political figures, including Fiorello La Guardia, began to complain of public confrontations. The American press continued to alert readers to the spread of Fascism in Italian-American communities.

In 1928, partly in response to negative publicity, Mussolini decreed stricter controls on Fascists abroad in the face of increasing public opposition in the United States. Grandi, now foreign minister, directed De Martino to take action, and Thaon di Revel announced the dissolution of the FLNA. No longer would American Fascists enjoy a bold, high-profile organization, and no longer would American Blackshirts march. Instead, Mussolini would rely on propaganda, routed largely by the Italian Foreign Ministry through Italian consulates to more innocuous civic, cultural, and social groups such as the Sons of Italy and the Dante Alighieri Society and via radio, newspapers, pamphlets, and books. In response, Salvemini took the challenge to identify Fascist "transmission belts," embarking on a collision course with Italian-American community leaders, or *prominenti*.[22]

Salvemini found the new policy vulnerable because, if they knew, Americans would resent such manipulation by a foreign government, just as they had resented American Blackshirt parades; accordingly, he set out to inform Americans of Fascist activities. Because the Italian government had cultivated a sense of *Italianità* in the "Little Italies" of America, he would have to proceed cautiously or risk being labeled "anti-Italian," just as had happened at home.

Originally, Salvemini had misjudged the political sympathies of Italian Americans. Returning to Europe after his first American tour, he had estimated that about 80 percent of the politicized Italians living outside Italy were anti-Fascists. He had met few Italian Americans on that first trip, however, and after broadening his exposure, he developed a more realistic appraisal.[23] By the time he settled in Cambridge he had been speaking in Italian-American communities for six years, usually at the invitation of local anti-Fascist groups. By then he came to appreciate the many factors that shaped the immigrant experience, including socioeconomic status and assimilation.

He found class to be a key to understanding Italian-American politics. Among the largely apathetic working class, he wrote, "Fascist propaganda acts like a spark in a dynamo." Notable also was a lower middle class of "parasites," who, as *padroni* (labor bosses), had exploited poor immigrants. When immigration had virtually ceased, the Italian consuls used them in their capacities as newspaper writers, radio announcers, and party operatives to spread Fascist propaganda. Likewise, the Italian-American upper middle class gave Fascism solid support. By 1940, Salvemini concluded that although only 5 percent of the Italian-American population was Fascist, Fascism enjoyed majority backing among successful businessmen and professionals.[24]

The leadership, or *prominenti*, had adjusted to American life. These professionals and leaders of business, labor, and politics had broken the confines of immigrant life after World War I. Fascist propagandists now targeted them because of their influence. With the exception of Congressman Vito Marcantonio, Italian-American political leaders readily lent their names and prestige in public support of Mussolini's achievements.[25] By maintaining patronage machines in Italian neighborhoods, these leaders became a valuable commodity, not only to the Fascists but also to American political leaders, and particularly to the administration of Franklin Roosevelt. None of them, including La Guardia, criticized Fascism after 1925.

Equally influential were the Italian-American labor leaders Luigi Antonini (AFL) and August Bellanca (CIO). Socialists and opponents of Fascism, they competed for control of the workforce. Their ability to deliver the votes of the rank and file gave them political power, but they could not deliver their workers to the anti-Fascist cause. To the extent that Salvemini turned to them as political allies, he would inherit the internal quarrels of union politics; knowing that, he continued to steer a very careful course among the labor leaders and radicals.

As American political parties exploited them for partisan purposes, Italian Americans developed political assumptions that exacerbated Salvemini's task. First was the belief that electing an Italian to office would benefit the ethnic community. Since most politically successful Italian Americans were hostile to the exiles' dogmatic anti-Fascism, Salvemini and the others faced an immense task of political education.

A second and more onerous challenge was to overcome the belief that the proper role of Italian Americans was to support Italy in the international arena. *Prominenti* used political connections in an attempt to influence FDR to act in

favor of Fascist Italy on such matters as the Ethiopian War and neutrality laws.[26]
This effort would resurface after Roosevelt's "stab in the back" remark about
the Italian invasion of France threatened to drive Italian wards into the open
arms of Republicans in the 1940 election.[27]

This relationship between Italian communities and American politics was a
key issue in Salvemini's campaign. It has been argued that he failed to grasp either.[28] In fact, he understood both; he simply refused to accept the status quo or
to work within its confines. In his visits to Italian-American communities,
Salvemini learned of the devastating impact of discrimination on political attitudes. "Most Italian immigrants," he wrote, "know only the hardships of America where they have been looked down upon as 'dagoes' and 'wops.'" In
addressing such issues, he predated most scholars of his day, who overlooked
the psychological impact of alienation. He believed that the Americanization of
Italian immigrants had been superficial, in that the working class had retained
strong sympathies for the country of their birth. For these reasons he was relatively tolerant of their philo-Fascism, blaming Fascist propagandists and the
Italian-American leadership.[29]

His admiration for the social reform agenda of the New Deal had been tempered by his realization that FDR was more a pragmatic political operative than
a Wilsonian-Mazzinian idealist. In part, Salvemini's rejection of the American
system resulted from Salvemini's long-standing distaste for power politics.
Ettore Rota had in 1919 christened him "the anti-Machiavelli of contemporary
society." Half a century later, Ascoli called him "the greatest enemy of politics
of all the men I have ever known."[30]

The thread that runs through Salvemini's public life is not dogmatism—for
he espoused no ideology—but the idealist's refusal to compromise his democratic values. Given the realities of modern democratic pluralism and his unwillingness to work through existing political structures, he was unlikely to
find a system, under Giolitti or Roosevelt, in which he could do more than state
his case from a distance.

As an independent agent, Salvemini severely limited his options. He could
wage the battle of public opinion through speeches and articles; and he could
organize his own movement, free from Marxists, ideological quarreling, and
"corrupt bargains" with American unions and political parties. The latter approach was restricted to an intellectual elite. The former could be more broadly
framed if he chose to diversify his appeal.

The most serious problem facing Salvemini's campaign was the success of
Fascist propaganda among Italian Americans. Their unique experience made
Italian immigrants vulnerable. In confronting other American groups, they had
developed a new sense of ethnic identity. In the process, sympathy for their native land magnified, and they forgot the hardships that had driven them from
home. "Italy became in their minds," he wrote, "a land from which they felt ex-

iled, of whose past glories they felt proud, and for whose present fortunes or misfortunes they felt glad or miserable."[31]

Salvemini's approach to Little Italy compounded his difficulties. When he spoke in the Italian community, he usually spoke to committed anti-Fascists. His articles seldom appeared in the mainstream Italian-language press. Consequently, his impact was limited. Had he been able to cooperate with the socialists and labor leaders, he might have had regular access to their journals. Isolated from them, as well as from the *prominenti*, did he sacrifice too large an audience of potential "converts"? Would he be able to reach the mutual aid societies and religious and fraternal groups whose leaders were the targets of his attacks? Moreover, how successfully could he answer charges that anti-Fascists were anti-Italian?

Writing and lecturing in the early 1930s, Salvemini focused on the familiar themes of the repression, injustice, and economic failure of the Fascist regime in a series of articles directed primarily at English-speaking audiences.[32] By the time he settled in Cambridge, he had expanded his approach from narrow, vitriolic attacks to a more comprehensive assessment of Fascism. In criticizing the economy, he cited party and government sources to point out contradictions between Fascist claims and reality. No theoretical economic interpretation emerges from these articles; instead each employs the discrete "problemistic" analysis for which he was known.[33]

At the same time, he was drafting a more formidable study of the centerpiece of Fascist economics, the corporate state. When *Under the Axe of Fascism* appeared in 1936, it completed his trilogy.[34] In the ongoing battle over Fascist propaganda, Mussolini's claims of social and economic innovation rested largely on his ambitious attempt to reorganize Italian production into new institutional components called corporations. Established in 1926, this scheme promised to solve industrial conflict by creating syndicates of capital and labor under the beneficent control of the Minister of Corporations, who would theoretically operate in the public interest.

The ideological moderation of the corporate state broadened Fascism's appeal, helping Mussolini to consolidate his dictatorship by recruiting new elements of the middle class while isolating radical Fascists such as the syndicalist Edmondo Rossoni. Corporativism promised to rationalize the capitalist economy through planning and to overcome class divisions, thereby attracting technocrats and managers, many of whom had shied away from Fascism because of its radicalism and violence.[35] Its moderation and emphasis on planning also appealed to some Americans. At a time when the Great Depression forced a reevaluation of the economic system, a number of American businessmen and journals applauded Mussolini's innovative theme. Journalists, supplied with a steady diet of official statistics and free use of the Atlantic cable, perpetuated the mythology of progress. As a result, the corporate state achieved a certain prestige that contributed to Italy's international credibility as a nation of enlightened leadership, moving purposefully in a period of widespread economic confusion. Although its economic benefits were negligible, the corporate state yielded a propaganda triumph that served Mussolini's international designs.[36]

Salvemini countered Fascist claims with "accurate information," a task ideally suited to his methodology. Ideological attacks had made little impression on mainstream Western opinion; in contrast, a Salveminian point-by-point examination promised to reach middle-road British and American readers who had applauded Mussolini for achieving economic progress while controlling social conflict.[37]

Salvemini claimed to expose the reality of the corporate state: an elite group of businessmen and industrialists controlled the employers' organizations, whereas party bureaucrats dominated the Fascist labor associations. The 1927 Charter of Labor was a collection of "meaningless words." Citing Fascist sources, he concluded that the much-heralded corporate state was a sham.[38]

Against this background, Salvemini deflated the economic "triumphs" of the Fascist state: the highly publicized "battles" against tuberculosis, illiteracy, and malaria; the elimination of beggars; the rising standard of living. Using sources he had collected since leaving Italy in 1925, he argued that real wages had fallen; that unemployment had risen; that Fascist policies had undermined the eight-hour day and the minimum wage; that food consumption had decreased in a period of population expansion; and that the failure of Fascist unions to protect workers had contributed to a general decline in the standard of living, more pronounced in the South. Finally, the regime had achieved "social peace," not by economic planning but by coercion, not by the corporate state but by the police state.[39]

Under the Axe of Fascism, part scholarship and part propaganda, typifies Salvemini's American work. He is, as he had always been, both positivist historian and passionate advocate, the Mazzinian in action. His instinct for expressing history in poignantly human terms never more acute, he put corporativism to the same test he had applied to medieval Florence and turn-of-the-century Apulia: What was the lot of the peasant and the worker, and what was their measure of freedom? Amid the reality of life in Fascist Italy, Salvemini found striking anecdotal evidence. Illegal child labor meant eleven-year-old boys carrying ore out of the sulphur mines. Employing women to undercut wages in brick factories meant that each carried one and a half tons of bricks in eight hours. After laying bare the Fascist economy on a case-by-case basis, Salvemini concluded, with characteristic passion and moral certainty, that Fascist claims of progress were spurious.[40]

In his conclusion, Salvemini offered a sweeping characterization of the Fascist economy. Painting with a broader stroke, he reconciled the contradictory elements of the regime—its syndicalism and its reputation as a capitalist mono-lith. The latter, according to Salvemini, was the real Fascism. Although syndicalists had supported early Fascism, Mussolini had purged this left wing through a series of actions culminating in the Ethiopian War, when he had sent many of them to Africa as "volunteers."[41]

If not a movement of the Left, was Fascism a "capitalist dictatorship?" Salvemini thought not. What he found was a form of elite pluralism. In spite of the support given to Fascism by industrialists, they were forced to compete for power with what he labeled the "three bureaucracies" of Fascism: the civil service, the regular army, and the Fascist Party. In their midst, Mussolini acted as a power broker, moving cautiously, making compromises, "now sacrificing the big business man to the high civil servant, now the civil servant to the big business man . . . never sacrificing the military chiefs," ultimately acquiescing in the face of pressure or necessity.[42]

This was not Mussolini the absolute autocrat, the dictatorial *Duce* of a totalitarian state. In presenting this alternate interpretation, Salvemini contributed to a broader understanding of Fascism. Particularly useful was his rendition of a heterogeneous, changing state. Shunning theory, he nonetheless helped to lay the historical foundations on which others would build more abstract analyses of Fascism.[43] Salvemini's greater concern, of course, was his impact not on the writing of history but on public opinion in Great Britain and the United States.

The clash of Italian and Ethiopian troops at the oasis of Walwal in December 1934 turned Salvemini's focus from economics to diplomacy. In fact, no single event more severely damaged Salvemini's rhetorical campaign against Mussolini than *Il Duce*'s success in Ethiopia. Diplomatic realities soon sobered Salvemini's response. Convinced that Mussolini could be stopped by a British or French demonstration of force under League of Nations auspices, he was equally certain that neither European power nor the League would intervene. The futility of the League's limited sanctions further assured Salvemini of the paralysis of European diplomacy and reaffirmed his earlier view that the United States would ultimately play a key role in the European conflict. In this respect, and because of Mussolini's growing popularity in Little Italy, the Ethiopian War underscored the significance of Salvemini's anti-Fascist efforts in the United States.[44]

The manifest importance of the conflict led Salvemini to broaden his campaign. Because he held so little confidence in the French commitment to oppose Fascism, he advised the Giellisti in Paris to move to England or the United States. At the same time, he began to contemplate the post-Fascist era and to attempt to influence public opinion on the future of Italy. Fearing that world opinion would rally behind a pro-Fascist successor in order to preempt a communist government, Salvemini published in 1936 a manifesto, signed by leading anti-Fascists, asserting that neither a communist revolution nor a conservative counterrevolution would succeed; and that a secular republic, based on individual liberty and fundamental social-economic reform, provided a more workable alternative. It was the first volley in a war of words that would culminate in a book nearly a decade later.[45]

In May 1936, after the infamous Italian bombing and gassing of Ethiopian troops, Italian armies under Generals Pietro Badoglio and Rodolfo Graziani captured Addis Ababa and Harrar, ending the war. Mussolini triumphantly proclaimed Ethiopia to be part of the Italian Empire, ascending to the pinnacle of his popularity among Italians at home and abroad. At the same time, his aggression damaged his support among the Western powers and created for Salvemini a long-awaited opportunity.[46]

Within two months of the fall of Addis Ababa, a revolt of nationalist military officers touched off a civil war in Spain that would soon polarize world opinion. Hitler and Mussolini separately supplied military power to assist General Franco's insurgents in their conquest of southern and western Spain. The French—after briefly supplying the republican government—and the British followed a course of nonintervention. Meanwhile, Russian "advisers" and various anti-Fascist groups arrived to fight Franco. In the midst of this momentous ideological struggle, Italian anti-Fascists never questioned *whether* they should intervene, but on whose behalf. Most supporters backed either the legitimate republican government or an anarchist faction in Barcelona.[47]

The one exile who most ardently embraced the Spanish Civil War was Carlo Rosselli. Viewing the war as an ideological Armageddon, Rosselli threw GL's support to the anarchists of Catalonia, organizing and then commanding a column of Italian volunteers. Other exiles participated as well, most notably Randolfo Pacciardi. Under Pacciardi's command, the Comintern's Garibaldi Battalion won a notable victory over Mussolini's troops at Guadalajara, defending the Madrid government and reaping a propaganda coup. International attention quickly made the war the cause célèbre of the Left.[48]

In the midst of anti-Fascist triumph, Salvemini remained largely silent.[49] He collected money for the Giellisti in Spain, but advised Rosselli against GL's large-scale intervention. Neither an idealogue nor a romantic, he did not view the conflict as an epic struggle of Left against Right. He had opposed militant gestures in the past and, convinced that only the major powers were capable of toppling Mussolini, he saw no evidence that GL's military intervention was more than a quixotic venture. The real question, as Salvemini saw it, was not whether Franco won or lost in Spain, but whether the British and French opposed Mussolini. Their refusal to intervene revealed their failure to realize that a Fascist victory in Spain weakened their own national security. Salvemini's failure was to recognize the possibility that GL's intervention in Spain, even a military failure, might generate sympathy from the Western powers. He soon admitted that he had erred, noting the Garibaldi Battalion's success in igniting political enthusiasm. The international crisis he had hoped for failed to develop. He argued that anti-Fascists would have to wait until *Il Duce*, in his recklessness, initiated a campaign so threatening to world stability that he would give the democracies no choice but to retaliate with military force.[50]

In June 1937, Salvemini heard tragic news of the Rosselli brothers. Carlo, who had persisted in vocal opposition to the Fascist regime, was convalescing at a health spa in Normandy when Nello and Carlo's wife, Marion, visited him. After Marion's departure, French fascist Cagoulards ambushed the brothers on a lonely road and stabbed them repeatedly. Salvemini saw Mussolini's hand in the killings.

The deaths of the Rosselli brothers, whom he had loved as his own children, dealt Salvemini a severe blow. In a life filled with sorrow, he had outlived his own children and now, sadly, he had outlived his intellectual progeny. Of his three "sons," the young men he cherished most, Ernesto Rossi languished in a Fascist prison, and Carlo and Nello were martyred by the same brutal forces.[51]

As Salvemini's conviction grew that the French and British governments were appeasing Fascism, he sharpened his assault against Fascist activities in the United States. He was now particularly intent on destroying the notion that all Italians and all Italian Americans were Fascists, an assumption that he feared could produce tragic results.[52] He aimed the first salvo of his renewed campaign at the Casa Italiana of Columbia University and its director, Giuseppe Prezzolini, Salvemini's former associate at *La Voce*. Designed as a cultural link with Italy, the Casa sometimes functioned as a propaganda forum for supporters of the Fascist regime.[53]

Salvemini initiated his offensive in January 1935, shortly after *The Nation* exposed Fascism at Columbia and called on President Nicholas Murray Butler to investigate. One of *The Nation*'s charges was that the Casa had refused to invite anti-Fascists to speak.[54] When two student groups invited Salvemini to appear at the Casa, he demanded an invitation from Prezzolini.[55] *The Nation* published the correspondence, including the Casa's withdrawal of the student invitation. Salvemini continued through 1942 to charge Prezzolini and the Casa with Fascist propaganda, and what had been a friendship two decades earlier now disintegrated into the bitterest animosity.[56]

Begun as a piecemeal attempt to collect information on Fascist activities, Salvemini's project culminated in a full manuscript. Since the U.S. government had begun to examine subversive activities, he hoped his text would persuade them to investigate Fascists. The House of Representatives had created in 1930 a Special Committee to Investigate Communist Activities, chaired by New York Democrat Hamilton Fish.[57] After Hitler seized power, Congress began to scrutinize the radical Right, investigating such groups as the Bundists and Coughlinites. With support of liberals and the Roosevelt administration, the House in 1934 created the Un-American Activities Committee, chaired by Democrat John McCormack of Massachusetts.[58]

Salvemini, however, held little hope for investigations of right-wing subversion because of the conservative climate in which Congress worked. A greater problem was Samuel J. Dickstein, who directed the committee's activities. A New York Democrat with connections to Tammany Hall and the *prominenti*, Dickstein avoided investigations of Fascist activities that might lead to his supporters.[59]

While Salvemini attacked the Fascist regime in the press, Girolamo Valenti, editor of *La Stampa Libera*, tried to convince the McCormack Committee to investigate Fascism in America. Salvemini and Valenti had their differences, but on this they agreed. Valenti submitted his report to Dickstein, but the committee declined to call him as a witness. In February 1935 the committee issued a report on Nazi, Fascist, and Communist organizations in the United States. They also recommended modest legislation, including the registration of foreign propaganda agents, which became the McCormack Act of 1938.[60]

Valenti persisted, and when the committee was revived in 1938, he won his chance to testify. This time the committee was chaired by Martin Dies, an anti-union, anti-New Deal, anti-immigrant Congressman from Texas. A protégé of powerful House Speaker Sam Rayburn, Dies used the committee to attack communists and, in the process, generated considerable publicity.

On October 3, 1938, Valenti gave detailed testimony about Fascist activities, and a year later the committee heard Giuseppe Borgese of the University of Chicago on the same topic. Even though the American press covered the hearings, the anti-Fascists' testimony was buried amid thousands of pages of transcripts. Frustrated, Salvemini followed Valenti's model and began to compile detailed notes of individuals and organizations engaged in promoting Fascism in the United States, hoping to supply this information to the Dies Committee.[61] At the same time, he planned a new anti-Fascist organization against a background of mounting Nazi aggression. Hitler's armies occupied Czechoslovakia and assaulted Poland, the Nazi-Soviet nonaggression pact was signed, and Britain and France declared war on Germany. World War II had begun.

Since breaking his formal ties with GL—and particularly since the assassination of Carlo Rosselli—Salvemini had not worked closely with the *fuorusciti* in Paris. Now the war in Europe necessitated closer cooperation. In February 1939, the Paris headquarters of GL dispatched journalist Alberto Cianca to the United States to strengthen ties, and another GL activist, Max Salvadori, arrived in New York to assume a position at St. Lawrence University. On February 25, Cianca and Salvadori met with Salvemini and several New York anti-Fascists to discuss a new political initiative. The product was the American

Committee for Italian Liberty, which would recruit prominent Americans to help divulge Fascist activities in the Americas. Salvemini agreed to coordinate the initiative.[62]

The Cianca mission rallied support for GL and interested the State Department. In a meeting with Secretary of State Cordell Hull and Assistant Secretary Sumner Welles, Cianca and Bolaffio sounded an important Salveminian theme: most Italians did not support Fascism and would revolt when conditions were right. Hull reportedly promised to convey their comments to Roosevelt.[63]

Hitler's invasion of Poland on September 1, 1939 infused the American exiles with a sense of urgency. Within three weeks, Salvemini and his associates founded the Mazzini Society. He joined Bolaffio, Lionello Venturi, Renato Poggioli, and Michele Cantarella at the Cantarella home on the Smith College campus in Northampton, Massachusetts, to create the new anti-Fascist organization. They agreed to mount a new campaign to mobilize the American public and American policy makers against totalitarianism, monarchism, and clericalism, with a particular eye toward the postwar reconstruction of a democratic Italy.

It was Salvemini who suggested the name of the Italian republican patriot he revered. He hoped that the Mazzini Society could avoid the mistakes of the Concentration and GL by refraining from party allegiances and ideological squabbles. The group was to include democrats of the Left and center, Italian exiles committed to a republican and anti-clerical position—in short, very much a Salveminian consensus.[64]

During the winter of 1939–1940, as Europe braced for war, the society's founders struggled to organize. At a December 28 New York session, Mazzini members named Salvemini, Borgese, and Venturi to an executive council, with the first two responsible for drafting a charter.[65] At this juncture, Salvemini encountered an ominous challenge from Max Ascoli of the New School. An anti-Fascist exile who had come to the United States on a Rockefeller grant in 1931, Ascoli maintained ties to American liberals, the Roosevelt administration, and the State Department. He opposed limiting Mazzini Society membership to exiles and argued that the group had to be unequivocally committed to the interests of the United States. When Salvemini prevailed, Ascoli departed, creating the unique opportunity for the intellectual to function as political leader.[66]

Events in the late spring of 1940 rapidly overtook the efforts of this small band of exiles, and in the process altered Salvemini's role. In April, German naval and airborne forces invaded Denmark and Norway, and by the end of the month they had broken Norwegian resistance. Ten days later, without warning, German armies invaded the Netherlands, Belgium, and Luxembourg. By mid-May, German mechanized divisions had driven deeply into northern France, dividing the British, Belgian, and French forces. Anticipating Mussolini's entry into the war, the Mazzini Society on May 26 issued its first manifesto, which appeared in a number of American dailies. With a new urgency, Salvemini implored readers to distinguish between "love of Italy and support of Fascism." Already expecting the United States to influence the shape of a post-Mussolini government, he believed it more crucial than ever to discredit Fascism and Fascists.[67]

On June 10, after the Germans had renewed their offensive campaign, Italy declared war on France and Great Britain, and Italian troops invaded southern France. More than any event since the Matteotti crisis, Mussolini's entry into the war sent a shock wave through the anti-Fascist movement. The next day, President Roosevelt publicly characterized the invasion as a "stab in the back" of France. The immediacy and bitterness of this official response imperiled Italian citizens living in the United States, who now faced the daunting prospect of being identified with the enemy if the United States entered the conflict. At the same time, the Mazzini Society now held the distinction of being the only organized anti-Fascist group in the United States. Four days after Italy's invasion, with Salvemini unable to attend, the Mazzini Society met in emergency session and added to their charter an oath to "the ideals of liberty and democracy that inspire the constitution of the United States." They then expanded the executive committee to eight, dropped Salvemini, and added Ascoli. One week later, the executive committee named Ascoli president.[68]

Ascoli promptly began to reshape the group from a band of "transplanted intellectuals" to an American popular movement. Although Salvemini did not disagree in principle, Ascoli's pursuit of these goals would drive the two further apart. Now limited in his official capacity, Salvemini seemed content in his roles as leader of Massachusetts anti-Fascists and intellectual authority figure for the entire movement. His tenure as active political leader had lasted six months.[69]

As German forces moved quickly to drive France out of the war, Paris was evacuated, Verdun fell, Marshall Petain replaced Reynaud as head of the Third Republic and, on June 22, signed an armistice. In the attendant confusion, Italian exiles fled the Nazi-Fascist effort to take political prisoners, while Salvemini and other Mazzini Society members scrambled to provide an American refuge. The British, initially unhelpful, changed policy with the fall of France and escorted Sforza and Tarchiani to England. The two then continued to New York and soon joined the Mazzini Society.[70]

The harrowing stories told by Sforza and Tarchiani inspired a renewed effort. Salvemini joined the Italian Emergency Rescue Committee (IERC), which attempted to raise transportation money for the refugees and convince the American government to admit them. The IERC succeeded in assisting hundreds of Italian anti-Fascists to escape France. Many moved to New York, transplanting the core of the external resistance movement across the Atlantic. Among the new arrivals were Sturzo, Cianca, and Pacciardi.[71]

For Salvemini and his colleagues, this migration of political leaders to New York presented opportunities as well as liabilities. They were men of proven ability whose narrow escape from Axis forces and tales of less fortunate countrymen sharpened the focus of anti-Fascism in America. Since many were European intellectuals, they brought no American patriotic commitment, thereby strengthening Salvemini's position vis-à-vis Ascoli.

Buoyed by their arrival, Salvemini realized that they also bore certain limitations. Men without a country, they would live in fear of internment, particularly if the United States entered the war. That insecurity might induce attitudes of deference toward American policy, bolstering Ascoli's influence. In addition, their allegiances to Italian parties might further complicate an already contentious political environment. Most significantly, a number of the new refugees aspired to positions in a post-Fascist government, an ambition Salvemini deemed to discredit their advocacy of a government-in-exile. As intellectual leader and moralist, he believed he should protect the movement from such contamination.

In the midst of the migration of anti-Fascists from Europe, Salvemini took an oath of American citizenship. The decision was the culmination of more than five years of disquietude, during which he was forced to decide in which capacity, Italian or American, he could best serve his campaign. As early as 1934, he had recognized that the ultimate outcome of the Franco-German struggle would rest with England and the United States; and by the fall of 1935, he had begun wrestling with the citizenship question, which he weighed in this global context. In the midst of the Ethiopian conflict, he wrote Tarchiani with disgust that he had begun to think the unthinkable. If Mussolini were successful in defying the League of Nations, Salvemini would ask for American citizenship, an idea that he was finding less repulsive each month. "I am truly becoming," he continued, "a 'man without a country.'" Tarchiani admonished him to be more concerned with the destiny of Italy and less with "noble pride" and "spiritual integrity."[72]

The final decision came in response to Mussolini's October 1939 attack on Greece. Ultimately, Salvemini chose American citizenship for several reasons. First, he believed that American political institutions, imperfect as they were, came closest to his ideals. Second, he was convinced that American citizenship would not destroy his lifelong ties to Italy. In the United States, because of its immigrant traditions, "the citizen has the right to have two souls: that of his country of origin and that of his country of adoption." What he was rejecting, he wrote to Felix Frankfurter, was not his Italian heritage but the outrages Mussolini had committed in Ethiopia, Albania, Spain, and now Greece. Frankfurter found Salvemini's praise for the oath of American citizenship so moving that he sent a copy to Roosevelt and later used a quote in a Supreme Court case.[73]

A third factor was more practical: American citizenship would prove useful in his anti-Fascist campaign. Inhibited by his alien status, he had been forced to exercise caution. Particularly after the outbreak of war, he found many Americans growing intolerant of exiles. However, as an American citizen, he felt he could openly challenge U.S. policy and "demand justice for the Italian people."[74] Later he would be enjoined to defend the decision, but in proclaiming his new status, he expressed only exuberance: "I have become an American citizen. . . . I am no longer an exile."[75]

This choice changed not only Salvemini's legal standing, but the way he thought of himself and of the anti-Fascist movement. He never became an American in the fullest sense. Especially after becoming a U.S. citizen, he exercised his right to criticize American politics and felt reluctant to plunge headlong into the politics of Italy.[76] Nonetheless, he held a deep affection for his adopted country, as he wrote to anarchist Armando Borghi, whom he had just helped to free from Ellis Island: "With all its immense defects, [American democracy] is, on the whole, preferable to any other regime."[77]

By the time Italy entered the war, he was quicker to criticize his colleagues for their ambitions to play a political role in post-Fascist Italy and more adamant in rejecting his own. Moreover, he abandoned his earlier demand that the Mazzini Society remain an organization of exiles in favor of Ascoli's attempt to broaden it to an American group.

The arrival of the new wave of refugees reinvigorated the anti-Fascist movement. In line with Tarchiani's expansion of the Mazzini Society, Salvemini made the Massachusetts section the most robust outside New York. This aggressive growth alarmed Fascist officials.[78]

Salvemini's work on behalf of the Mazzini Society burdened his crowded schedule. Until the fall of France, he had returned to Paris regularly to see his wife and friends. Each spring semester he taught at Harvard, and during the idle months he pieced together lectures, primarily in the Northeast, but ranging from Pennsylvania, Ohio, and West Virginia to the University of Georgia and Tulane University, to Los Angeles, San Francisco, Minneapolis, Chicago, Cincinnati, and Montreal. His schedule intensified with the advent of war, at one point reaching sixteen lectures in one month. During the war he published more than 500 articles, or an average of two per week. The view that in Cambridge Salvemini lived in a state of semiretirement rings hollow in the face of such evidence.[79]

Salvemini's wartime lectures and articles were designed to drive a wedge between Italian Americans and the pro-Fascist leaders in their communities. Typical were a series of public meetings coordinated with the Mazzini Society in 1941. In February he joined Ascoli, Sforza, and Borgese at a Greenwich Village rally at Cooper Union, summoning support for the British against the Axis powers. "We have always affirmed that Mussolini was not Italy," he exhorted the crowd of 1,500. "The recent defeats are *not* defeats for the Italian people."[80]

The following month Salvemini organized a rally that drew 700 to Faneuil Hall in Boston. In a speech broadcast to Italy, he employed apocalyptic rhetoric to divide the philo-Fascist "gang of conspirators and profiteers" from ordinary, "honest and sincere" Italian Americans. He made a patriotic appeal to his American audience to turn their backs on the "paid Fascist agents," and he implored American authorities to strike the Fascists "without pity" while sparing the deceived to allow them to repent.[81]

His June recruiting tour of nearly twenty cities proved disappointing. However, rapidly changing conditions boosted anti-Fascist efforts. Roosevelt's drive to abandon neutrality, his "arsenal of democracy" policy, and his public condemnation of Italy's entry into the war coalesced to produce a more receptive American climate.[82]

In the summer of 1940, Salvemini found a publisher for a pamphlet on "Italian Fascist Activities in the United States," a synthesis of the card file he was compiling for the Dies Committee. He documented in detail a pervasive network of propaganda "transmission belts," explaining their success in a social-cultural context. He listed radio stations that featured Fascist programming; pro-Fascist newspapers; Italian-American fraternal clubs; afterschool clubs ("Doposcuole") and sporting clubs; Columbia University's Department of Italian language and Casa Italiana and others, including American priests and reporters, particularly those of *The New York Times*. He hoped that such a "concrete analysis" would convince readers of the dangers of ignoring the "anti-democratic activities of a foreign government," and he urged the American government to restrict diplomats and deport propagandists.[83]

Shortly after Italy declared war, an FBI agent first contacted Salvemini while he was visiting a friend in New Jersey. This and subsequent interviews were conducted within the context of an expanding domestic intelligence operation, developed under what J. Edgar Hoover later called a "secret oral directive" from Roosevelt.[84] In the sixteen-month period between the initial contact and American belligerency, the FBI contacted Salvemini numerous times, and by the end of 1940 the agency considered him a reliable informant. Intelligence agencies circulated his pamphlet and investigated some of the groups he identified.[85]

In March 1941, an FBI agent visited Salvemini in his carrel at the Widener Library to conduct the first of a series of interviews on Fascist activities. Salvemini acknowledged that he knew nothing of espionage and that he had also been in touch with the Dies Committee and the Immigration and Naturalization Bureau. At Salvemini's suggestion, the FBI solicited copies of the *Bolletino* of the Italian Ministry of Foreign Affairs as a source of propaganda activities. Otherwise, they gave his interviews routine consideration.[86]

The more thoroughly Salvemini investigated Fascist activities, the more he became convinced that one man dominated Italian-American support for Mussolini: Generoso Pope. Pope's success in the building supply business had made him a millionaire, and he had subsequently purchased, with Mussolini's specific approval, four Italian-language newspapers. The largest, *Il Progresso Italo-Americano*, had a circulation of about 100,000. Throughout the 1930s, Pope's newspapers provided favorable coverage to the Fascist regime while taking advantage of Mussolini's news service and, after 1939, free use of the Atlantic cable.[87]

In addition to his propaganda, Pope personified the pro-Fascist attitudes of many of the *prominenti*. He had traveled to Rome to be honored by Mussolini, and he had praised *Il Duce* at numerous public events. His power in New York's Tammany political organization made him a key figure in "delivering" Italian wards to the Democratic Party. Having supported Roosevelt in 1932 and 1936, he was rewarded in 1940 with the chair of the Italian Division of the Democratic National Committee. In his bid to influence Italian-American opinion and U.S. policy, Salvemini would inevitably confront Pope.[88]

In battling Pope, the Mazzini Society in 1939 approached Lupis, publisher of the socialist monthly *Il Mondo*. Salvemini reluctantly endorsed this decision, recalling problems with New York socialists and believing Lupis to be overly ambitious. More important, Salvemini preferred that the Mazzini Society control its own press. Nonetheless, the parties struck an agreement: Lupis shared editorial policy with the Mazzini Society, joined the group, and promised financial assistance.[89]

In spite of his misgivings, Salvemini wrote regularly for *Il Mondo* for two years, most notably a fifteen-part series on the diplomacy of World War I and a continuing barrage of criticism of *New York Times* coverage of Fascist Italy. He hounded American pro-Fascists for facilitating propaganda, directly attacking his major antagonists: Prezzolini, James P. Roe, and Bruno Roselli.[90] As the war progressed, Salvemini modified his pre-Pearl harbor anti-Fascism, deprecating Italian generals, stepping up his reproach of Winston Churchill, challenging the policies of the State Department, and scrutinizing the administration's relationship with the Vatican.[91] The *New York Times*, despite Salvemini's criticism of its reporting, editorially endorsed his positions.[92]

Not satisfied with the use of *Il Mondo*, the Mazzini Society developed a bold strategy to seize *Il Progresso* or, failing, to convert it to their cause. Sforza and Ascoli pressed the Roosevelt administration to investigate Pope and to support an anti-Fascist Italian-language newspaper. As pressure mounted against Pope by late 1940, Salvemini and Lupis fired volleys from the pages of *Il Mondo*.[93]

Pressure from Roosevelt convinced Pope to negotiate with Ascoli, but Salvemini would settle for nothing less than an "*uncompromising surrender*" from the anti-Fascists' "worst enemy." "We shall go on hammering at Pope," he wrote Ascoli. But by the end of the summer, Pope had retaliated, carrying to the final meeting with Ascoli a letter from Roosevelt asking that Pope fire only the most pro-Fascist of his writers. Ascoli found Salvemini perplexing. In contrast, Salvemini harbored few regrets over the failure of Ascoli's negotiations, as he had put little faith in them. He was simply continuing to play the role of intellectual, holding anti-Fascism accountable to his high standards.[94]

At the same time, Salvemini distanced himself from Lupis. When Antonini cut off the ILGWU subsidy to *Il Mondo* because of the attacks on Pope, Lupis found another sponsor and decided to detach his paper from the Mazzini. Realizing the implications of the loss, Salvemini advised Lupis against this "colossal blunder" and threatened to end his collaboration. Nonetheless, with no other forum for Mazzini Society views, Salvemini advocated cooperation with Lupis's new sponsor. Negotiations failed, and in October 1941, after reopening briefly as a daily, *Il Mondo* collapsed.[95]

A key factor distancing Salvemini from Lupis was the latter's efforts to form a government in exile. Italian exiles in a number of cities around the globe, modeling General Charles De Gaulle's "Free French" movement, formed "Italia Libera" groups and solicited British and American recognition. When Italy entered the war, the British, initially diffident, began to embrace moderate anti-Fascist groups.[96]

Sforza's July 1940 arrival in New York had directly confronted Salvemini with the Free Italy prospect. Within two weeks, Sforza had met with Roosevelt, and from that point he doggedly lobbied the administration to recognize a government in exile. Salvemini supported the idea for a year, urging the *fuorusciti* to prepare in the event that the British presented the opportunity. He disqualified himself and endorsed a committee of Sforza, Tarchiani, and the Republican Carlo a Prato. At this juncture, Italian authorities were convinced of Salvemini's support of both a government in exile and an invasion force.[97]

However, by early 1941 Salvemini became apprehensive because of the machinations of a London Free Italy group, headed by the Catholic monarchist Carlo Petrone, that was negotiating with the British for recognition and for support of an invasion of Italy. Salvemini objected to Petrone's conservatism and to his conspiratorial efforts to advance his own career at the expense of the Mazzini Society, which had similar plans. In May, a republican faction including Paolo and Piero Treves, sons of the former socialist leader Claudio, ousted Petrone, and by June the British had withdrawn their subsidy. The Free Italy movement now gravitated to New York.[98]

By August, these events led Salvemini to reevaluate not only his stand on Free Italy but on the entire anti-Fascist battle. He moved closer to Ascoli's position, suggesting a Mazzini Society with an American citizenship requirement that would insulate it from fifth-column charges. It would lobby on behalf of a

Free Italy made up of exiles, who could both aspire to postwar positions and maintain their party ties.[99]

Early in the war, Salvemini held high hopes that U.S. policy would reflect New Deal liberalism and American democratic ideals. Enthusiastic about his new country, he broadcast to Italy on behalf of two Boston radio stations and the Committee to Defend America by Aiding the Allies, and he wrote a testimonial entry for the semiofficial *I Am an American*, an anthology of statements by naturalized citizens.[100]

However, even as he sounded these American patriotic themes, Salvemini expressed misgivings about British policy. His deep-seated distrust of Tory influence in the Foreign Office derived from his Labour and liberal ties in England and his own radical republican worldview. He intensified his assault on British policy in response to Churchill's May 1940 BBC address in which the prime minister told the Italian people that "one man and one man alone" had led Italy to war against the crown and the Vatican. He characterized Churchill's implicit support for continuing Fascism without Mussolini as a futile attempt to offer Italians hope for a separate peace.[101]

At the same time, Salvemini was infuriated by the "Churchill-Simovich deal," by which the British had reportedly promised Trieste to a postwar Yugoslav state. He protested that the British had appropriated Italian territory through a private deal with generals and nationalists and had recognized a Yugoslav government in exile while refusing to recognize its Italian equivalent. He urged Ascoli and Sforza to convince Roosevelt to denounce the "Simovich deal" and to mobilize the Mazzini Society against British policy: "If Churchill wants to dismember Italy he must not reckon on our cooperation. We have to speak every day on the radio from Boston to Italy." And with a burst of indignation he blasted nationalists: "Italian and Yugoslav nationalists have to quarrel among themselves and thus dishonor their own countries. They all have the mentality of horsedealers. We are not horsedealers," he wrote. "We are honest men."[102]

The Japanese attack on Pearl Harbor, and Italy's declaration of war against the United States four days later, radically transformed the anti-Fascist movement in the United States, forcing Salvemini once again to contemplate his own role. Suddenly, Italian aliens living in the United States found themselves in the spotlight, as did the pro-Fascist *prominenti*. For years Salvemini had expected the United States ultimately to influence Italy's future; now that possibility had materialized. The Mazzini Society was now fully engaged in a high-stakes contest with newly converted "pre–Pearl Harbor Fascists" to shape American policy.

Citizen Salvemini wasted little time in criticizing his new government, focusing first on the administration's position on Free Italy. Three days after Pearl Harbor, the State Department issued a cautious statement on "Free Movements," expressing sympathy but stopping short of recognition. Attached was a mandate that American citizens be excluded, a confirmation of the Ascoli-Salvemini position. When the State Department asked Salvemini to submit a list of potential Free Italy leaders, he endorsed Sforza, Tarchiani, a Prato, Pacciardi, and the Republican journalist Aurelio Natoli. However, his enthusiasm for this policy was dashed in early 1942 when Roosevelt, accepting the recommendation of the War Department and his British allies over the State Department position, rejected the request to recognize a Free Italy movement. Although Sforza persisted, Salvemini, much less committed to the idea, re-treated.[103]

Immediately after Pearl Harbor, a second issue surfaced to compound Salvemini's disenchantment with American policy: the classification of the 600,000 Italian citizens residing in the United States as "enemy aliens," which made many Italians fear that they would suffer the same punishment given the Japanese. When the Justice Department arrested some suspected Fascist agents, Salvemini warned against a generalized anti-Italian hysteria; and when he learned that one of the leading *prominenti*, Edward Corsi, had been appointed chairman of the New York Enemy Alien Board, he labeled Corsi "A Wolf Guardian of the Sheep."[104]

In the spring of 1942, in response to pressure from influential Italian Americans, a movement surfaced in the newly created Office of Facts and Figures to rescind the Enemy Alien status of all Italians. Roosevelt eventually agreed, and on Columbus Day, Attorney General Francis Biddle announced the new policy deleting Italians from the list. Three weeks later, Salvemini responded in *The Nation*, labeling the policy "Good, But Not Good Enough." While he applauded the decision, he called on the administration to revoke the citizenship of Italians who had participated in Fascist activities.[105]

This tenacious anti-Fascist campaign began to pay dividends in 1942. Hearing from the Office of Naval Intelligence that Salvemini had compiled a list of some 8,000 persons actively supporting Fascism in the United States, FBI director J. Edgar Hoover ordered a reassessment of Salvemini and his information. When an agent from the Boston Field Office visited him, Salvemini explained that over a period of many months, he had paid Italian refugees in New York fifty cents an hour to search old newspapers for the names of those who had participated in pro-Fascist events. He had spent about $800 in compiling the list, which he would sell to the government for $500. Hoover's office, concluding that Salvemini's list was a more valuable source than he himself, procured a copy and in August began to investigate selected individuals.[106]

In the months after Pearl Harbor, Salvemini became more disillusioned by signs that conservative forces were leading the Roosevelt administration toward a mistake of epic proportions. The "nightmare scenario" began to seem all too likely: Roosevelt's special envoy to the Vatican, Myron Taylor, was conspiring with British Tories and certain English and American diplomats to control Italian policy; and the administration, eager to solidify Italian-American support for the war effort and for the Democratic Party, had begun to rely on *prominenti* of philo-Fascist inclination. The tragic consequences might well produce the ultimate continuation of Fascism without Mussolini.[107]

Salvemini's attempt to counter conservative forces in the formulation of Allied diplomacy toward Italy became his last passionate political cause. By late 1942, he began to refer to "British and American Tories" whose emerging commitment to counterrevolution was blinding them. At the center of this effort he saw Churchill, committed to protecting both Italy's traditional institutions and Britain's "spheres of influence."[108]

In this final campaign, Salvemini came to believe he could no longer trust two of his most influential associates, who, he believed, had lost their independence of action for different reasons: Sforza, because of his ambitions for postwar Italian politics, and Ascoli, because he had accepted a position at the State Department.[109] Salvemini remained the conscience of the movement. But by 1942 his moralism and fierce independence had become less tolerant. He wrote Ascoli in response to a meeting that Sforza held with La Guardia and Antonini: "I was terrorized. . . . I could not write one simple word in any paper without publicly deploring this terrible blunder which has made Sforza the prisoner of war of La Guardia and Pope."[110]

Believing that many of his anti-Fascist associates had failed to maintain an unsullied commitment to the future of a secular, democratic Italian republic, Salvemini began to operate even more independently, relying now on only a small circle of trusted friends. Refusing to mellow at age seventy, he fought this last campaign with all the ferocity of his battles against Giolitti. Knowing that the Roosevelt administration directly intervened in Italian affairs, he often lost sight of the president's pragmatism and of the complexities of wartime diplomacy, and too often assumed that Churchill and Roosevelt were in agreement about postwar Italy. Some of his assumptions have been proven inaccurate. He saw conspiracies where none existed and lost faith in the integrity of his foes. However, he understood remarkably well the fundamental logic of Allied diplomacy toward Italy. In his eagerness to accentuate impurities in the politics of Ascoli, Sforza, and Antonini, he became increasingly personal, and in the zeal of his criticism of their leadership, he drifted away from his last important political organization.[111]

By early 1942, Salvemini's departure from the Mazzini Society had become a near certainty. He threatened to resign, terminated his contributions to the Society's newspaper, and refused to attend its convention. However, upon Bolaffio's urging, Salvemini dispatched to the June meeting a "declaration of principles," updated to advocate a Wilsonian peace, the punishment of ranking Fascists and their collaborators, and the exclusion of royalists and communists from the Mazzini Society's campaign. He had now become even more wary of Stalin's international intrigues and of the prospect of a Communist Party acting as Stalin's agent. This was not an obsession. He thought that if he continued to work for a democratic Italy, he had no choice but to oppose Stalin, because of his influence on both Allied diplomacy and Italian communists. He framed his anti-Stalinism in tactical terms, arguing that cooperation would discredit anti-Fascists as communist puppets: "[Let us] strike together, but march separately," he advised.[112]

Salvemini's anticommunist position, presented to the 600 delegates as part of the report of the political committee, sparked the liveliest debate at the convention. After a spirited exchange between two of anti-Fascism's most colorful personalities, the war hero Pacciardi and the anarchist Tresca, the delegates endorsed the plank by nearly three to one.[113]

Despite his apparent victory in absentia, Salvemini was growing more adamantly opposed to Ascoli's pro-ally position, and now amplified his protest against the growing influence of the ILGWU's Antonini. Salvemini criticized the labor leader's ties to Generoso Pope, but Antonini's real strength was his mass base and his New Deal connections. Ascoli was willing to work with the union to strengthen the hand of the Mazzini Society, whereas Salvemini insisted that incorporating the AFL's right wing would weaken the Society's ability to produce a secular republic after the war. Salvemini believed that Antonini threatened to deliver the Society to the enemy—not to Fascists, but to more insidious Italian-American conservatives and Fascist sympathizers.[114]

Salvemini admonished Ascoli, Sforza, and Tarchiani, more flexible politicos, for losing their bearing. He had become, more than ever, the conscience of anti-Fascism. To some of his colleagues, his irascibility and rigid moralism were now magnified beyond reason, and they began to view him as the "mother-in-law" of the movement. He wrote to Ascoli in early 1942, convinced that British and American diplomats were scheming to hand Italy a "weakly diluted Fascism" and that La Guardia, Ed Flynn of the Democratic Party, Corsi, Antonini, and Pope were scheming to control Italian affairs in the United States. Ascoli disputed the existence of a pact between Roosevelt's advisers and the *prominenti*, and he cautioned Salvemini against conspiracy theories. He did not, however, deny the ascendancy of Antonini.[115]

In the spring of 1942, Ascoli invited Salvemini to preside over a large "Victory for America, Freedom for Italy" rally in Washington. In response to what would be his last opportunity to take a public leadership role in the Mazzini Society, Salvemini penned a firm rejection. He explained that he could not participate without referring to "insensate" British and American policies, based on "treacherous information" from the Vatican, that were bound to lead to "dark hours for Europe and a terrible isolationist and Fascist awakening for America."[116]

Antonini presided in Salvemini's place, sharing the rostrum with Alan Cranston and Dean Acheson, two diplomats supportive of the anti-Fascist position. The occasion proved another success for the labor leader, and it marked the transition of the Mazzini Society from an elite group of European exiles to a more diversified organization. Once again, Salvemini's insistence on principle over politics diminished his influence.

In June, when Antonini sent Salvemini an invitation to an Italian American Labor Committee banquet, he received a stern reprimand in which Salvemini professed to being "deeply disturbed" by Antonini's attitude toward the likes of Pope and Corsi. Since they had converted it was no longer necessary to fight them, Salvemini argued, but it was essential to block them from leadership positions: "The Mazzini Society ought not to act as a transmission belt of the Administration."[117]

If any doubt remained about Salvemini's association with the Mazzini Society, he laid the issue to rest. "What will happen now to the Society I do not know," he wrote to Ascoli in July, "and I confess that I do not care to know." The next week he told Panunzio: "I am through with the Mazzini Society."[118]

When in August the State Department sponsored a Pan-American anti-Fascist conference in Montevideo, Uruguay, Cordell Hull backed Sforza and dispatched a close Antonini aide to organize the meeting. The 1,500 delegates endorsed Pacciardi's Italian Legion and Sforza's Free Italy, and their commitment to a "democratic and social republic" demonstrated the lingering vitality of Salvemini's ideas. However, Sforza's abandonment of that very program in deference to Churchill's monarchism—along with Antonini's growing leverage—indicated a further decline in Salvemini's political fortunes.[119]

Salvemini's mounting skepticism about American policy was corroborated by the late 1942 Washington visit of Dino Gentili, leader of the London-based Italian exiles. Before going to Washington to lobby, Gentili stopped at Harvard. When he sought advice on territorial issues, explaining that he had lost confidence in the British, Salvemini advised him against relying on Washington. Shortly thereafter, when Gentili met with American officials, he enjoyed only limited success, further convincing Salvemini of the futility of relying on the American government to counterbalance the Tories.[120]

Still, Salvemini pressed American intelligence agents to pursue "pre–Pearl Harbor Fascists" who were, in his eyes, a continuing threat to Italy's interests. Partly in response to his complaints, the Immigration and Naturalization Bureau initiated denaturalization proceedings against Francesco Galluci for making Fascist propaganda broadcasts in the Boston area, and called Salvemini to testify. This zealous campaign nearly backfired when, in December 1942, New York investment banker Luigi Criscuolo, another subject of Salvemini's pamphlet, filed a complaint with the Bureau, demanding Salvemini's denaturalization on the basis of alleged "mental reservations" during the application process. As a result, the Bureau ironically opened against Salvemini in early 1943 the same proceedings he had urged them to use against Galluci.[121]

It was not Criscuolo's complaint, but Salvemini's own outspoken opposition to Allied policy that convinced American authorities to scrutinize his activities. In the spring of 1944 the Justice Department called off the denaturalization investigation, and intelligence agencies lost interest in his information on Fascist activities. By then the Office of Censorship was intercepting his mail, and intelligence agencies monitored his ideas on postwar Italy.[122]

On July 10, 1943, the Allied armies invaded Sicily, and within two weeks the Fascist Grand Council had voted no confidence in Mussolini, who had then been arrested by the king. In the ensuing "Forty Five Days," Italians found themselves suspended between Fascism and freedom, enemy and ally. Had Sforza and the Free Italy advocates succeeded in winning recognition from the Atlantic powers, they could have seized the moment; having failed, they could only press desperately for concessions. Their hopes for a provisional government were finally destroyed when, on September 8, Marshall Pietro Badoglio announced that he and King Victor Emmanuel III had signed an armistice with the Allies. Although the decision was one of expediency, the anti-Fascist exiles felt betrayed by the Allied commitment to forces they viewed as tarnished by two decades of collaboration with Fascism. Meanwhile, as the Germans attacked, Badoglio gave no orders; instead he and the king abandoned the capital and the army for the safety of Allied-occupied Brindisi. On September 12, German commandos boldly rescued Mussolini from his mountain prison and transported him to the shores of Lake Garda, where they established the puppet Salò Republic.[123]

For Salvemini, the fall of Fascism was a cruel irony. It should have provided the occasion for celebration; instead, this cause to which he had dedicated the previous twenty years of his life ended in futility, apparently fulfilling his worst fears by prolonging Fascism without Mussolini. When Roosevelt declared in his "Fireside Chat" of July 1943 that the United States would "have no truck with Fascism," Salvemini asked if the president included in his definition of Fascism "those Fascist leaders who for twenty years had been accessories to all of Mussolini's crimes. The King is one of them. Badoglio is one of them."[124] The one remaining hope was that the Allied governments would commit to suspending the monarchy and leaving the permanent institutional questions to the Italian people, or, failing that, would back away from any commitment to the Vatican and the House of Savoy. By mid-1943, Salvemini began to form new political associations with several factions, especially republicans and dissident labor leaders, while he worked with an ever-shrinking group of loyal confidants.

More politically isolated than ever, Salvemini turned to an individualistic tactic, and in late 1943 published, together with his friend La Piana, *What to Do with Italy*. The book would be his last, and it signified a permanent departure from his Mazzinian pursuit of "thought and action." His influence was now relegated exclusively to the realm of ideas.[125]

What to Do with Italy was the culmination of Salvemini's extended effort to influence American opinion. His uncanny foresight enabled him to address key post-Mussolini issues in a book that appeared several weeks before the Fascist Grand Council overthrew *Il Duce*. He had expected the king to survive alongside an "Italian Darlan or Pétain," not Badoglio, but former Foreign Minister Dino Grandi. This issue of the monarchy's future embodied one of the two major themes of the book. A resolute republican all his life, Salvemini argued that the House of Savoy had thoroughly discredited itself for two decades—blocking the use of military force against the "March on Rome," asking Mussolini to form a cabinet, signing decrees establishing the dictatorship, and working in concert with the Fascist regime. Once again, Salvemini found himself in the rare position of defending his former nemesis, the liberal state, this time against criticism that Italy was ill-prepared for a republican system. Furthermore, he made a strong theoretical case to abolish the monarchy based on the concept of "popular legitimacy," whereby the Italian people would best be served by a republic.[126]

The public debate on the future of the Savoy dynasty heated by the end of 1943. Salvemini published his views and found support in the American press from such writers as William Shirer and I. F. Stone, while Walter Lippmann, *Collier's,* and *Saturday Evening Post* backed the monarchy.[127] However, this issue was overshadowed for the moment by Salvemini's opposition to the Vatican, the dominant thesis. La Piana, an authority on Church history, lent credibility. The two Harvard scholars argued that, like Victor Emmanuel III, Popes Pius XI and XII had discredited themselves by supporting the regime. For two decades, the Vatican had ignored abuses of its lofty doctrines, choosing instead to praise the moral and religious climate of the Fascist State. Furthermore, Salvemini found widespread support for Mussolini among American Catholic clergy, and an increasingly friendly relationship between the Vatican and the Roosevelt administration. He noted that F.D.R. had broken a seventy-year tradition by appointing a personal ambassador to the pope.[128]

The book touched off a furor among American Catholic intellectuals. Leading the outcry was PPI founder Luigi Sturzo, now convalescing in a Jacksonville, Florida, hospital. Sturzo published a series of responses in *Commonweal*, arguing that the authors had intentionally diminished the papacy's criticisms of totalitarianism and anti-Semitism while overemphasizing the Lateran Treaty. Sturzo's review evoked public rejoinders that were softened by a respectful exchange of letters. Sturzo chided the professor for being "more severe than the prophet Ezekiel"; Salvemini addressed the priest in confessional tones, beseeching "counsel and moral comfort in this moment of anguishing responsibility for each of us"—a rare instance in which Salvemini relinquished higher moral ground.[129]

Beyond the institutional questions of monarchy and Church, the authors proposed a comprehensive postwar settlement. The process would begin with a "cooling period" in which Italians would choose a democratic republic, followed by a program of fundamental political and economic "reconstruction."[130]

At about the same time that *What to Do with Italy* appeared, the American Catholic hierarchy was thrown into a panic by rumors that the State Department had awakened Salvemini in the early morning hours and had flown him to London to establish a new Italian government. The persistence of such a fantasy illustrates the extent to which some American Catholics considered Salvemini a pariah. His severe anticlericalism also undercut his influence with a presidential administration that favored the Vatican.

Salvemini had a penchant for provoking rumors, some of which began to trouble the anti-Fascist community. Ascoli wrote the following in late 1943:

Scarcely a week passes when I do not have somebody coming to see me and reporting something terrible that Salvemini has said or done (Salvemini has given *P. M.* the names of those Italians of Giustizia e Libertà who are now risking their lives in Italy, and has called them British agents; Salvemini has said that he wished the Germans had sunk the ship on which Sforza and Tarchiani came here).[131]

Ascoli assured Salvemini that he did not believe what he heard, but the rumors persisted. Salvemini kept them alive with occasional harangues, and his confidential opinions confirm a growing bitterness toward former colleagues. In 1944, for example, after Sforza accepted a position in the Badoglio cabinet, Salvemini described Sforza to the FBI as a "senile, vain individual who places vanity above his love for the Italian people."[132] Salvemini's bitterness was recognized by American authorities as well as by associates, and by late 1943 some fellow anti-Fascists had begun to return the barbs. In a November letter to Tarchiani, referring sarcastically to his former friend as "Don Gaetano," a professional extremist and a "Father Divine to himself and the members of his cult," Ascoli proclaimed that "the disintegration of the small anti-Fascist world" was complete.[133]

The splintering of the exile community created a vacuum in anti-Fascist organization. Antonini moved aggressively to consolidate the New York labor movement, the *prominenti* and anticommunist forces into the American Committee for Italian Democracy; Bellanca and others countered with a rival labor organization whose Carnegie Hall Columbus Day rostrum Salvemini shared with La Guardia and Pacciardi.[134]

The next month, at the Mazzini Society's annual meeting, Antonini attempted to capture control of the group, a move Salvemini had long anticipated. Salvemini supporters forged a coalition to block Antonini, but the veteran labor leader wielded proxy votes and a host of new Mazzini initiates to foil the challenge. Led by Pacciardi, Bellanca, and Panunzio, fifty members marched out of the raucous meeting in protest, in effect abandoning the anti-Fascist organization to Antonini.[135]

The Antonini majority first condemned the dissenters as communists, then consoled them with a Salvemini-like criticism of the king, Badoglio, and Fascist sympathizers. Ascoli, who now worked for an Antonini aide in the Office of Inter-American Affairs, followed with an endorsement of the new leadership. Salvemini's nightmare had now materialized. His group had become a community agency to sponsor war bond drives, a lever for the ILGWU, and a channel for State Department policy.[136]

Vindicated in his prognosis, Salvemini now found himself even more alone. Ascoli thought that "Don Gaetano" was "locked into the most efficient axis" with Pacciardi and Bellanca. In fact, in the aftermath of Antonini's power play, Salvemini's following was much less formidable than Ascoli believed.

Although isolated and weakened, Salvemini was not finished.[137] With La Piana he enlisted Mazzini dissidents and American liberals in Friends of Italian Freedom for a rally at Faneuil Hall in Boston in January 1944. At about the same time, he and a few associates recruited maestro Arturo Toscanini to Italia Libera, another group they formed to influence Allied policy, and utilized Pacciardi's newspaper of the same name to publicize their cause. In June 1944 their "American Manifesto" created a major splash in *Life* Magazine, warning readers against Allied preferences for a reactionary "demofascist government." *Life* published Ascoli's rebuttal, objecting to the manifesto's portrayal of Sforza and Croce as "quislings" of the Allies for serving in the Badoglio government. A month after the *Life* manifesto, the Friends of Italian Freedom dissolved, leading the OSS to record "the break-up of the Salvemini front."[138]

Salvemini now operated as an anti-Fascist committee of one. He retained his inner band of close friends but was finally freed from any obligation to compromise with others on political issues. He embarked on a speaking tour, a lone figure carrying his message for three weeks through the East and Midwest, then to California. At each of the twenty stops he delivered variations on the same "What to Do with Italy" lecture, then fielded questions. The OSS reported that he was "well received" and "remarkably good-humored in answering hostile questions." He ended his tour in San Francisco in time to begin a guest lectureship during the spring of 1944 at the University of California.[139]

As he began the spring semester at Berkeley, major forces maneuvered for power in postwar Italy. For Salvemini, as for the Italian parties of the Left, no cause was greater than the abolition of the monarchy, preferably as a precondition to any peace treaty. Their major adversary was Churchill, who championed the House of Savoy to the point of ignoring a compromise, hammered out in part by Sforza, for abdication of the king and postponement of the "institutional question" until the end of the war. Then in March, the Soviets suddenly altered the course of events by recognizing the Badoglio cabinet and returning Palmiro Togliatti to Italy from Moscow. At Salerno, the PCI leader endorsed postponing the question of the monarchy's fate in favor of a Badoglio government of national unity.[140]

Togliatti's "conversion" at Salerno pleased the Allies by deferring a divisive issue. At the same time, it weakened the Left, damaged the likelihood of a republic, and infuriated Salvemini. On April 6, he published a scathing condemnation of Togliatti as "Stalin's tool . . . rented to Churchill and Roosevelt" by the Kremlin to split Italian anti-Fascists.[141] Two weeks later, Salvemini delivered a speech on the UCLA campus criticizing Allied European policy and thereby provoked with local Stalinists a polemic that launched his last American battle. At a press conference, he advised reporters to keep an eye on Togliatti. When a reporter asked about Togliatti's ideology, Salvemini retorted: "Doesn't everybody know that a Communist is not left or not right, but always a Communist? He receives his orders [from Stalin] and obeys them."[142]

Although recent evidence justifies Salvemini's observation of the Kremlin's influence on Togliatti,[143] American communists and fellow travelers retaliated against these blunt allegations. The afternoon that the story appeared in the Los Angeles papers, Salvemini received a telegram from the chairman of the Hollywood Writers' Mobilization, a Stalinist organization, withdrawing its invitation to him to speak unless he would promise to refrain from attacking Allied policy. The telegram was couched in patriotic terms, but the intent was clearly to disavow Stalinist hegemony. When the group's chairman called for a response, Salvemini fired back: "You keep your money. I'll keep my soul. Go to hell." The wire services picked up the exchange, and *Time*, *Nation*, and *New Republic* all published accounts. In response, American communists criticized him for opposing the new Bonomi government, formed in June 1944 with communist support, and called for the formation of an anti-Salvemini coalition outside the Mazzini Society.[144]

In response to the Allied armistice and the German seizure of northern Italy, the Italian armed resistance movement emerged. Italian partisans employed guerilla warfare against German forces and by 1944 had formalized clandestine Committees of National Liberation. Although Communists dominated the armed resistance, the Partito d'Azione (PdA), advocating a Salveminian political agenda, constituted perhaps the second largest contingent. Many of

Salvemini's former colleagues and protégés, including a number of Giellisti, were leaders of the PdA, whose legions bore names that reflected the same tradition: "Rosselli," "GL," and "Italia Libera." An American who accompanied the Fifth Army described to Salvemini the valor of his friends who, during the worst days of the conflict, actually lived in hiding in the GL headquarters. In Florence, he wrote, GL had become the PdA.[145] Because of his direct link to the PdA, Salvemini took a paternalistic interest in its decisions, urging his comrades within the movement to counter Sforza, Tarchiani, and Cianca.[146] When the PdA joined the six-party coalition after the Allied liberation of Rome in June 1944, Salvemini lost confidence in its leadership.[147]

Because of the heroism of his friends in the resistance movement and his own growing frustration, Salvemini began to express more radical views in the final months of the war. In a letter that reflects the secrecy, the militancy, and the millennial expectations of the underground, he wrote the following to the PdA partisan leader Emilio Lussu in February 1945:

I continue to hope against hope that our friend from [Lipari], "the one of the three medals" [Ferruccio Parri] will enter Milan at the head of his partisans . . . and that you and our friends who are in Switzerland will immediately join him there and proclaim at once the Italian Federal Republic . . . ; and that you will shoot at once Archbishop Schuster, and that you will proclaim yourselves at once the provisional government . . . and ask for the resignation of Bonomi and Company and that you will be ready to fight in the streets of Milan. . . . I would like to be there myself, thus to end my life fighting.[148]

As illusory as the letter seems, its rational message rang clear: Italy's best hope lay with the partisans. Because both Lussu and Parri were leaders in the PdA component of the dominant northern Italian Committee of National Liberation (CLNAI), their presence offered a democratic alternative to the communists. Through Lussu and Parri, he hoped to encourage the democratic Left to seize the moment for radical change—although he preferred that they leave the PdA, now distracted by ideological concerns, for a coalition of republicans and independent socialists. Their coalition could position itself between clericals and monarchists on the right and Stalinists on the left in anticipation of a future constituent assembly.[149] This opportunity would otherwise be lost, not only to outflank the English and the House of Savoy, but the PCI as well.[150]

Organized anti-Fascism now only a memory, Salvemini admitted the failure of his campaign.[151] Had the exiles convinced Roosevelt to confront Churchill on the "Italian question," Salvemini could have harbored some realistic hope that the Allies would eradicate Fascist influences. In retrospect, a series of factors militated against the anti-Fascists from the start. American liberals were overwhelmed by the combined conservative clout of the U.S. Army, the U.S. Department of State, English Tories, and the Roman Catholic Church. Given conservative Italian-American influence on a president preoccupied with military questions, there was little incentive for Roosevelt to defy Tory leadership, to press for abolition of the monarchy, or to confront the Vatican. By Salvemini's lofty standards, the anti-Fascist exiles were doomed.

It is now clear, however, that Salvemini should have been more pleased with his successes. He helped to provoke a serious debate, both in the press and within the Roosevelt administration, about the future of Italy, and even though their efforts damaged their organizations and their own relationships, Salvemini and the American anti-Fascists altered the parameters of American policy on postwar Italy. They had made it more difficult for American *prominenti* to remain openly pro-Fascist and thus less likely that the administration would tolerate a form of Fascism without Mussolini. As Salvemini had been insisting all along, the United States would, in the critical months of occupation, demand a democratic system in which the Italian people would determine their own political future. Unconvinced, Salvemini knew only that as the United States began to implement its policies, continuing vigilance would be imperative.[152]

In September 1944, in the midst of devastation produced by the fighting that liberated Florence the previous month, the newly appointed rector of the University, Piero Calamandrei, invited Salvemini to resume his chair of history.[153] The previous spring, Ernesto Rossi had written his old friend a heartfelt plea, imploring him to return: "Consider that we no longer have Carlo [Rosselli]. . . . We have a need for you, an enormous need for you."[154] In June 1945, when Salvemini heard that the Bonomi government was bending under pressure from the CLNAI, improving the prospects of the PdA, he wrote to Rossi's wife, Ada, "When I opened [Ernesto's letter] I cried like a baby." Others had echoed Ernesto's plea, he explained, but he had great doubts about returning. Wouldn't he make a greater contribution to Italy's future by finishing his many incomplete manuscripts than by teaching in Florence? "I would make one exception," he concluded: "If Ferruccio Parri became prime minister and needed me to help him in Rome . . . I would leave immediately."[155]

NOTES

1. GS, *IFAUS*, 4.

2. "La Voce di Giustizia e Libertà Echeggia a New York," *Il Nuovo Mondo*, May 7, 1930; GS to AT, January 23, 1932, *TP*.

3. GS to CR, January 16, 1933, quoted in RV, "Carlo Rosselli e Gaetano Salvemini," 83.

4. GS to AT, November 4, 1932, May 7 and June 5, 1933, *TP*.

5. Vanni B. Montana, *Amarostico* (Livorno, 1975), 99–100, 128–131, 189–190; Gabriella Facondo, *Socialismo italiani esule negli USA (1930–1942)* (Foggia, 1993).

6. PC, "Luigi Antonini and the Italian Anti-Fascist Movement in the United States, 1940–1943," *Journal of American Ethnic History* V, 1, 21–40; Ernesto Ragionieri, "Italiani all'estero ed emigrazione dei lavoratori italiani, in tema di storia del movimento operaio," *Belfagor*, XV (1962), 640–669, and *Italia giudicata* (Bari, 1969); Valerio Agostinone, "Sindacati americani e italiani al tempo delle scissioni" in *Italia e America dalla grande guerra a oggi*, 223; Grazia Dore, *La democrazia italiana e l'emigrazione in America* (Brescia, 1964), 341.

7. "La Voce di Giustizia e Libertà Echeggia a New York"; RB to GS, January 10, 1932; GS to AT, January 16, May 7, November 27, and December 1, 1933, *TP*.

8. GS speech, December 18, 1933, published in *La Libertà*, n.d., GSS.

9. GS to AT, May 7 and June 5, 1933, *TP*.

10. GS to AT, December 1, 1932, January 16, 1933, June 5, 1933 and October 3, 1933, *TP*.

11. MS, "Antifascisti italiani negli Stati Uniti," 274.

12. Carlo Rosselli identified the roots of the disagreement in Salvemini's rhetorical campaign against northern Italian workers and cooperatives dating back to the pre-war period. CR, "Filippo Turati e il socialismo italiano," *QGL*, June, 1932, in CR, *Scritti dell'esilio*, I (Turin, 1988), 114–115. See also Pugliese, *Rosselli*, 209.

13. GS to Emilio Lussu, January 18 and February 27, 1945, in *Ld'A 44*, 82, 117.

14. GS, "Dittatura e democrazia," *Opere* IV (2), 453–459; "Il mito dell'uomo-Dio,"*Giustizia e Libertà* (Paris), July 20, 1934 GSS; "La difesa della Cultura," *Opere* VIII, 668–670.

15. GS, "Dittatura e democrazia,"; "Il governo degli 'esperti,'" *Giustizia e Libertà*, September 21, 1934, GSS; "Carlo e Nello Rosselli," *Opere* VIII, 693; MLS, *Sal*, 130–132; DeC, *Sal*, 371–388; AG, "Salvemini radicale americano" in *Politica e storiografica moderna* (Pisa, 1954), 176–177; Falabrino, "Anticommunismo," 413–414.

16. GS to CR, April 4, 1934, *AGL*, "Salvemini"; *Mem*, 119ff; "Carlo e Nello Rosselli," *Opere* VIII, 700–701; DeC, *Sal*, 387; Leo Valiani, "Tavola rotonda," ES, *ACGS*, 367.

17. Joel Blatt, "The Battle of Turin," *Journal of Modern Italian Studies* (Fall 1995), 22–57.

18. GS to AT, October 4, 1935, *TP*.

19. GS to AT, October 4, 1935, *TP*.

20. GS to AT, September 28, 1935, *TP*.

21. PC, "Per una storia dei Fasci negli Stati Uniti, 1921–1929," *Storia Contemporanea*, XXVI, 1 (December 1995), 1061–1144; GS, *IFAUS* (PC, ed); JD, *Mfas*, 88–90.

22. PC, "Per una storia dei Fasci" and "Fascism and Italian-Americans in Detroit," 39; PC and Theodore P. Kovaleff, "Father Coughlin and Mussolini," *Journal of Church and State* XIII (Autumn 1971), 429; "Italian Fascist Activities," 6ff.

23. GS, "L'Opera degli emigrati," *Opere* VI (2), 295–296; to MC, February 17, 1927, quoted in MC to CK, December 7, 1981; *Mem*, 109.

24. GS, "Italian Fascist Activities," 4–7, 18; "The Italians at Their Best," *The Nation*, September 26, 1942, 271–272; *IFAUS*, 244–245; "Salvemini Says 5 P.C. of Italo-Americans Are Fascists, Attacks Priests as Agents," *Boston Herald* (?), October 13, 1940, Pusey.

25. See Salvatore La Gumina, *Vito Marcantonio* (Dubuque, 1969); Gerald Meyer, *Vito Marcantonio* (Albany, 1989).

26. Letter of August 19, 1936, Jack Ingegnieros, President, Italian-American Democratic Organizations of New York, cited in Louis Gerson, *The Hyphenate in Recent American Politics and Diplomacy* (Lawrence, Kansas, 1964), 123.

27. MA to Don Sturzo, November 29, 1943, *AsP*.

28. GGM, *Problemi*, 103; DiS, "Salvemini in the United States" in DiS, ed. *Italian Socialism* (Amherst, Mass., 1996), 172. For a contrasting view, see PC, "Understanding America" in the same book.

29. GS, "Italian Fascist Activities," 3–7, 24; to Egidio Reale, July 25, 1945, quoted in GGM, *Problemi*, 101; CD, *ME*, 198–202; Dadà, "Contributo metodologico," 197–218; Ronald H. Bayor, *Neighbors in Conflict* (Baltimore, 1978), 78–79.

30. Ettore Rota, "Una pagina," 322; MA, "Salvemini negli Stati Uniti"; GGM, *Problemi*, 95, 154; Antonio Donno, "Gli stati uniti visti da Salvemini" in GC, *Sal*, 406–409.

31. GS, *IFAUS*, 1–4; Ralph Della Cava, "The Italian Immigrant Experience" in Silvio Tomasi, ed., *Perspectives*, 200; PC, "Fascism and Italian Americans," 134, has suggested that "fascist propaganda was more successful among Italian Americans in the United States than it was . . . in Italy."

32. GS, "Democracy and Dictatorship," *The Harvard Graduates' Magazine*, June 1934, 280–305; "What Is Freedom?" *Annals of the American Academy of Political and Social Science*, July 1935, 1–8; "Il mito dell' Uomo-Dio," *Giustizia e Libertà*, July 20, 1935, GSS.

33. For example, GS, "Capitale e lavoro nell'Italia fascista," *Opere* VI (2), 498–541; "Twelve Years of Fascist Finance," *Foreign Affairs*, 13 (April 1935), 473–482; "Economic Forces in Italy," *Yale Review*, 25 (March 1936), 553–572.

34. GS, *Under the Axe of Fascism* (New York, 1936). Subsequent references are to the British edition (London, 1936).

35. Adrian Lyttleton, "Fascism in Italy" in Walter Laquer and George L. Mosse, eds., *International Fascism, 1920–1945* (New York, 1966), 75–100.

36. JD, *Mfas*, 160–166, 225–232; Herman Finer, *Mussolini's Italy* (London, 1935), *passim*; GS, "Foreign Correspondents in Italy," *NRep*, LXXVI (May 6, 1936), 369–370.

37. GS, *Under the Axe*, x.

38. GS, *Under the Axe*, 1–100. American anti-Fascists subscribed to Fascist publications under pseudonyms as part of the effort to document the regime's policies and propaganda. MC interview, December 1979. Among the sources Salvemini employed were ministerial bulletins, banking reports, statistical abstracts, speeches, parliamentary debates and statutes, internal memoranda, memoirs, and diaries.

39. GS, *Under the Axe*, 144–366.

40. GS, *Under the Axe*, 322–329.

41. GS, *Under the Axe*, 370–376, 390–392.

42. GS, *Under the Axe*, 383–386; NT, "Salvemini storico," 915–917.

43. This theme of the limitations of Mussolini's power is reflected in some of the most important postwar literature on the Fascist regime. See Alberto Aquarone, *L'organizzazione dello stato totalitario* (Turin, 1978) and DeF, *il fas*.

44. GS to AT, November 15, 1934, *TP*; "Mussolini, the Foreign Office and Abyssinia," *The Contemporary Review*, 148 (September 1935), 268–272.

45. GS to AT, September 28, 1935; GS et al., "A Communication" *NRep*, February 12, 1936; GS and George La Piana, *What to Do with Italy* (New York, 1943).

46. CD, *ME*, 143.

47. JB, *IFP*, 145–151.

48. AG, *VCR*, 389ff; CD, *ME*, 150–154; Pugliese, *Rosselli*, 198–211.

49. He published two items in this period on the Spanish Civil War: the preface to CR, *Oggi in Spagna, domani in Italia* (Paris, 1938), and "Britain Wins in Spain," *The Nation*, February 18, 1939, 197–199.

50. GS to AT, October 7, 1936, *AGL*, "Salvemini"; preface to CR, *Oggi in Spagna*, xi-xii; "Italy and the Ethiopian War," *The Gazette* (Montreal), January 27, 1936; "Il Vaticano e la guerra etiopica," I-VII, *Giustizia e Libertà*, September 18–November 20, 1936.

51. See, for example, GS, *Carlo and Nello Rosselli* (London, 1937); "Il mandante" and "Le trovate del mandante," *Giustizia e Libertà*, July 30 and August 20, 1937; "The Rosselli Murders," *NRep*, August 18, 1937; AG, *VCR* II, 505–515; Pugliese, *Rosselli*, 218–226.

52. GS, "Italian Fascist Activities," 18–19.

53. Bicocchi Frezza, "Propaganda fascista," 661–697; JD, *Mfas*, 255–257; GS, *IFAUS*, 169–170; ONI Memo, "Casa Italiana," November 21, 1941, U. S. Department of State, Decimal File, 1930–1944, 865.20211/166.

54. *The Nation*, November 7–21, 1934, 523–524, 550–552, 565, 590; January 30–April 3, 1935, 129–130, 377–378, 388; November 27, 1935, 610.

55. GS letter to M. F. Grilli, December 6, 1934, *The Nation*, January 30, 1935, 129–130.

56. For example, GS letter to *NYT*, November 2, 1940; "The Casa Italiana of Columbia University," *Il Mondo* (NY), May 15, 1941, 5–7; and "The 'Casa Italiana' of Columbia University," *Il Mondo* (NY), July 15, 1941, 11–13.

57. *Congressional Record*, 72, Part 9 (Washington, 1930), May 22, 1930, 9390.

58. Walter Goodman, *The Committee* (New York, 1968), 9–10.

59. Goodman, *The Committee*, 11–14; GS, *IFAUS* (PC introduction), xxx-xxxi.

60. *Investigation of Nazi and Other Propaganda*, House of Representatives, No. 153, 74th Congress, 1st Session, 1935; *Investigation of Communist Propaganda*, House of Representatives, Report 2290, Special Committee on Communist Activities in the United States, January 17, 1931.

61. Annual Reports, U.S. House of Representatives, Committee on Un-American Activities, January 3, 1939; FBI memo, G. C. Burton to Ladd, January 19, 1942; FBI memo, R. R. Roach to Ladd, March 20, 1942, FBI"S" 65–29414; GS, *IFAUS*, (PC introduction), xxxiv.

62. AG, *Sdf*; MS, *The Labour and the Wounds* (London, 1958); MC to PC, November 22, 1965; MC, letter to *NYT*, January 31, 1945.

63. Gaetano Vecchiotti (Italian Consul General, New York) to Ministry of Interior, February 28, 1939, *CPC*, "Bolaffio, Roberto."

64. MC to PC, November 22, 1975; MC interview, December 1979; Renato Poggioli to GS, October 1, 1939 and memo "The Mazzini Society," ISRT, Fondo Mazzini Society.

65. MC, letter to *NYT*, January 31, 1945.

66. "Relazione della prima seduta della Mazzini Society," signed by Lionello Venturi and Renato Poggioli, n.d., *AGL*, "Mazzini Society"; MC to PC, November 22, 1975; MC interview, December 1979; Maddalena Tirabassi, "La Mazzini Society (1940–1946)" in Giorgio Spini et al., *Italia e America*, 141–143. See also JM, *USI*, 25; Ascoli and Arthur Feiler, *Fascism for Whom?* (New York, 1938).

67. GS, G. A. Borgese and Lionello Venturi, "A Statement of the 'Mazzini Society,'" *Il Mondo* (NY), June 15, 1940 from a manuscript dated May 26, 1940.

68. "A.B.C.," Mazzini Society pamphlet (New York: Edizione delle "Mazzini News," n.d. [1940?]); MA, "Salvemini negli Stati Uniti"; Lamberto Mercuri, ed. *Mazzini News* (Foggia, 1990).

69. MA, open letter to Mazzini Society membership, July 18, 1940, *CP*; MC interview, June 1984.

70. GS to AT, October 7, 1936 and December 3, 1938, *TP*; MS, *The Labour*, 134–135.

71. MI to CPC, April 26, 1941; undated memo, "Italian Emergency Rescue Committee," *CPC*"S"; AT to LaP, September 11, 1940, *LaPP*; AG, *Sdf*, 208; MS, *Resistenza ed azione*, 189–191.

72. GS to AT, November 15, 1934, March 17, October 4 and October 29, 1935; AT to GS, November 11, 1935, *TP*. See also "Una lettera di Salvemini ai democratici di Molfetta," *Opere* VII, 549–552.

73. GS to Felix Frankfurter, December 15, 1940, in Max Freedman, ed., *Roosevelt and Frankfurter* (Boston, 1967), 565, and March 19, 1953, *FrP*. "La risposta di Salvemini," *Opere* VII, 550–552; ET, "Nota biografica" in ES, *ACGS*, 269; and BB, entry of January 25, 1956, *Sunset and Twilight*, 421. Frankfurter quoted from the 1940 letter in *Baumgarten v. United States*, 322 U.S. at 674.

74. GS, "Una lettera di Salvemini ai democratici di Molfetta," in *Opere* VII, 551.

75. GS to CPa, July 18, 1942, *PaP*; "The Position of Italian Exiles," *American Mercury*, October 1943, 506; "La risposta di Salvemini," *Opere* VIII, 550–552; GGM, *Problemi*, 97–98; ET, "Nota biografica," 269; MLS, *Sal*, 38; AG, "Salvemini radicale americano," 173; ET, "Interventi," ES, *ACGS*, 187; Randolfo Pacciardi, "Gaetano Salvemini il grande esule," *Archivio Trimestrale*, July–December 1982, 618.

76. GS to ER, November–December 1944, *LdA44*, 46.

77. GS to AT, January 9 and 16, 1941, *TP*; to Armando Borghi, September 13, 1945, *LdA44*, 171; Iris Origo, *A Need to Testify*, 172–175; Donno, "Gli Stati Uniti," 409–410 and GGM, *Problemi*, 98.

78. GS to AT, December 23, 1940, *AGL*, "Salvemini"; Italian Consul, San Francisco, to Italian Embassy, November 25, 1940; Italian Embassy to MAE, February 22,

1941, MI, "Mazzini"; Report, Italian Consul, Boston, to Italian Embassy, January 17, 1941, MI, "Mazzini"; Open letter to "Mazzini Youth," August 6, 1941, ASMAE, *SAP*, 1931–45, Stati Uniti, b. 71 (1941), f. 1, sf. 2; ONI report, February 28, 1941, RG 59, NA, 865.20211, "Mazzini Society"; FBI report, June 3, 1943, RG 59, NA, 865.20211, "Mazzini Society"; Diary of Donald Hall, entry of November 17, 1941, PRO, FO, 33222–02987; *Nazioni Uniti*, July 16, 1942.

79. MI memo, July 15, 1935, *SPD, CR*"S"; MAE to MI, December 12, 1936, March 31, 1938, January 12, 15, and 25, 1939, February 6, 1939, *CPC*"S"; telegram, Italian Embassy, Washington, to MAE, May 17, 1939; MAE to MI, December 16, 1939, *CPC*"S"; telegram, Italian Embassy, Washington, to MAE, March 5, 1940; MI to CPC, March 31, 1941, *CPC*"S"; "Italy's Not Neutral, Says Salvemini," *San Francisco Chronicle*, November 11, 1939; "Les libertés et la dictature," *L'Ordre*, July 17, 1935; Sergio Bucchi, ed., "Le lezioni sulla democrazia di Gaetano Salvemini," *Archivio trimestrale*, July–December 1982, 627–650; "Conferenze Salvemini," *Controcorrente*, January 1944, 4; MC, *Bibliografia*, *passim*.

80. *NYT*, February 17, 1941; *PM*, February 17, 1941. Emphasis added.

81. *Mazzini News*, April 19, 1941; Mercuri, ed., *Mazzini News*, *passim*.

82. "Attività della Mazzini Society," October 7, 1941, *AsP*"M"; report, Italian Consul, Boston, June 9, 1941, *MCP*, b. 121, f. 8, "Associazione antifascista Giuseppe Mazzini."

83. GS, "Italian Fascist Activities," 9–16, 20–24. The pamphlet was published in extended form in 1977 as *Italian Fascist Activities in the United States*, PC, ed.; FBI memos, Burton to Ladd, January 19, 1942; Roach to Ladd, March 20, 1942; Peterson to J. Edgar Hoover, Director, FBI, March 11, 1942; Hoover to Lawrence M. K. Smith, Special War Policies Unit, Department of Justice, November 11, 1942, FBI"S" 65–29414.

84. Telegram, Peterson, SAC, Boston, to A. P. Kitchin, Newark, August 14, 1940, FBI"S" 65–29414.

85. Confidential memo, Sam Klaus, Treasury Department, to H. H. Klegg, FBI, October 18, 1940; Klaus to Hoover, October 18, 1940; Hoover to SAC, Boston, November 1, 1940; SAC, Boston, December 18, 1940, FBI"S" 65–29414.

86. FBI Case Report, C. E. Pelletier, Boston, March 18, 1941; FBI report, W. H. Corrigan, Boston, July 3, 1941; S. K. McKee, SAC, Washington, to Hoover, July 18, 1941; Hoover to SAC, Washington, September 6, 1941; McKee to Hoover, September 11, 1941, FBI"S" 65–29414.

87. Memo, MCP, June 28, 1940, OSS, PWB, Special Report No. 76, "On Documents Found in the MCP, Rome"; AT memo, "The Mazzini Society Influences the Italian Language Press," September 16, 1941, *AGL*, "Mazzini Society," f. 1, sf. 2; PC, "Generoso Pope and the Rise of Italian American Politics, 1925–1936" in Tomasi, ed., *Perspectives*, 264–288; JD, *Mfas*, 84–86; GS, "Italian Fascist Activities," 9.

88. Pope to FDR, September 1, 1936, OF233A, FDRL; John J. Freschi to James A. Farley, May 20, 1937, FDRL, PPF, "Generoso Pope." A record of Fascist awards to American *prominenti* is found in ASMAE, *SAP*, b. 3, f. 6; b. 22, f. 5; b. 31, f. 1.

89. *CPC*, f. 45240, "Giuseppe Lupis"; "Relazione della prima seduta della Mazzini Society," *AGL*, "Mazzini Society"; JD, *Mfas*, 45.

90. GS, *"The New York Times* and Mussolini," January 15, 1940; "Exit Prezzolini," December 15, 1940.

91. GS, "Mr. Churchill Addresses the Italian People" and "Lord Halifax," January 15, 1941; "Pio XII e Roosevelt," January 15, 1940; "Pius XII's Double Fame," July 15, 1940, *Il Mondo* (NY).

92. *NYT*, February 17 and 18, 1941.

93. AT to MA, December 3, 1940, *AGL*, "Mazzini Society," f. 1, s. 1; MA, "Salvemini negli Stati Uniti"; Tirabassi, "Mazzini Society," 145–146; memo, Sforza to Edwin Watson, September 1940; Sforza to Watson, August 27, 1940, *WaP*, Box 13, "Memos to the President"; Sforza to Ickes, July 14, 1941, *AsP* "Sforza" file; MA to Attorney-General R. H. Jackson, FDRL and FBI report, October 3, 1944, FDRL, PPF, "Pope"; Morgenthau Diary, vol. 281, 269–270, *MoP*; Valenti to Dickstein, April 1, 1941, *VaP*; Elena Aga-Rossi, "La politica degli alleati verso l'Italia nel 1943," *Storia contemporanea* III, n. 4 (December 1972), 850.

94. MA to GS, June 24, 1941; GS to MA, n.d. (June 1941?) and August 4, 1941, *AsP*"S"; to MA, July 21, 1941, *AGS* (emphasis added); Lupis to GS, April 17 and August 11, 1941, *AGS*; "The Mazzini Society Influences the Italian Language Press," September 18, 1941, *AGL*, "Mazzini Society," f. 1, s. 1; Ickes, *Secret Diaries* III, 463–467; LAn to GS, July 7, 1941, *AGS*; Montana, *Amarostico*, 100, 130, 190; *Congressional Record*, Vol. 87, part 3, March 25, 1941, 2567–2570; part 5, Appendix, June 17, 1941, 5279 (Washington, D.C., 1941); memo of September 24, 1941, ASMAE, *SAP*, 1931–45, Stati Uniti, b. 71 (1941), f. 1, s. 9.

95. GS to AT, February 19 and 26, 1941, *TP*; to MA, July 21, 1941, *AGS*; to MA, August 4, 1941, *AsP*"S"; to Lupis, August 8, 1941, ISML, *a Prato*, b. 4, f. 1, sf. 3, "Lupis"; AT to MA, December 3, 1940, *AGL*, "Mazzini Society," 145–146.

96. "Free Italians Organize to Oust Duce," *New York Post*, February 17, 1941; AT to GS, February 18 and 20, 1941; GS to AT, February 19 and 26, 1941, *TP*; MA to Enzo Sereni, October 22, 1941, PRO, FO, 371–19938–05909; JM, "Carlo Sforza e l'evoluzione della politica americana verso l'Italia, 1940–1943," *Storia contemporanea*, 7, n. 4 (July 1976), 825–853; Antonio Varsori, *Gli alleati e L'emigrazione democratica antifascista (1940–1943)* (Florence, 1982) and "La politica inglese e il conte Sforza (1940–1943)," *Rivista di studi politici internazionali*, 43, n. 1 (January–March 1976), 31–57; Ennio Di Nolfo, "Perché Sforza non fu premier di un governo all'estero," *CdS*, November 16, 1975; Zeno, *Ritratto di Carlo Sforza*; G. Guglielmo Negri, "Sforza e il consiglio nazionale italiano (1941–1943)," *Nuova Antologia*, October 1976, 195–203; AG, *Sdf*, 221–222; Winston Churchill, *The Second World War: The Gathering Storm* (Boston, 1951); Nancy Hooker, ed., *The Moffat Papers* (Cambridge, 1956), 190, 223; Sforza, *L'Italia dal 1914 al 1944 quale io la vidi* (Rome, 1944), 175 ff.; CD, *ME*, 131–202.

97. Sforza to FDR, December 2, 1941, PSaF, "Italy 1941"; to FDR, April 7, 1942, PPF 6741, FDRL; to GS, April 21, 1941, *TP*; Letters to the Editor, *NYT*, February 12 and July 10, 1941; to Ickes, April 4, 1941 and May 18, 1941, War Files No. 11 and 14, *IP*; Ickes, *Secret Diaries* III, 474; JM, "Sforza," 830 ff.; telegram, Minister of Foreign Affairs to MI, February 19 and 24, 1941; Third Section, AGR Division to MAE, March 5, 1941; Director, Division of Political Police, Leto, to Section 1 AGR Division, April 18, 1941, *CPC*"S."

98. Brailsford to GS, February 8, 1941, *TP*; Carlo Petrone and Antonio Zanelli, letter, London *Times*, February 10, 1941; "Free Italians Organize to Oust Duce," *New York Post*, February 7, 1941; memo, "Free Italy Movement, London," PRO FO, 371–37256–05909, 6; AT to GS, February 18, 1941, *TP*; Britain to Loxley, June 10, 1941, PRO FO 371–29937–05904.

99. GS to MA, August 4, October 26, and November 7, 1941, *AsP*"S"; to AT, January 9, 1941, *TP*.

100. GS, "Nell'imminenza dell'entrata in guerra dell'Italia," *Opere* VII, 18–21; to AT, December 31, 1940, *TP*; *I Am an American*, Robert S. Benjamin, ed. (New York, 1941); *Controcorrente*, December 1940–January 1941; LaP to GS, August 22, 1942, *AGS*; MA to GS, March 10, 1941, *AsP*"S."

101. "Dr. Salvemini Lashes Britain," Boston *Herald*, February 5, 1939, GSS; GS, "Britain Wins in Spain," *The Nation*, February 18, 1939, 197–199; "Mr. Churchill Addresses the Italian People," *Il Mondo* (NY), January 15, 1941; to Isabel Massey, December 30, 1940, PRO FO 371, 29935, Ministry of Information, Postal Censorship.

102. GS to Sforza, July 3, 1941; to MA, July 5, 1941, ISML, *a Prato*, "Mirkovic" file; "Pitfalls of Allied Policy," "Mussolini's Latest Achievements," and telegram to Lord Halifax, *Il Mondo* (NY), July 15, 1941; to Pribichevic, July 24, 1941; to Mirkowich [sic], June 27, 1941, *Il Mondo* (NY), August 15, 1941 and July 24, 1941, ISML, *a Prato*, "Mirkovic" file.

103. Policy Regarding "Free Movements" in the United States (10 December 1941), *Department of State Bulletin*, 5 (129), December 13, 1941, 519–520; GS to Harold B. Hoskins, Department of State, December 26, 1941, RG 59, NA, 865.01/53 1/2; Adolph A. Berle, entry of January 1, 1942, in Berle, *Navigating the Rapids* (New York, 1973), 393; JM, "Sforza"; Alan Cranston to Archibald MacLeish, March 12, 1942, General Correspondence of the Chief, Records of the Foreign Language Section, RG 208, NA.

104. GS, "Government Could Break *Duce*'s Hold on U.S. Italians," *Il Corriere del Popolo* (San Francisco), January 30, 1941; to MA, February 12, 1942, *AGS*; "A Wolf Guardian of the Sheep," *Controcorrente*, March 14, 1942; "Plea to Remove Enemy Stigma from the Italians," *The Boston Globe*, October 11, 1942; JM, "A Question of Loyalty" *The Maryland Historian* 9 (Spring 1978), 60–64.

105. "Italian Aliens," May 25, 1942, Records of the OFF; "Confidential Duplicates of Board Meeting Notes," CWI Meeting, May 18, 1942; board meetings, March 3, March 10, April 28, May 5, May 26, June 9, June 16, July 6, 1942, *MacP*, Miscellaneous Subject File; GS, "Good, But Not Good Enough," *The Nation*, November 7, 1942, 477–478; JM, "A Question of Loyalty," 60–64; PC, "Antonini."

106. FBI memo, Burton to Ladd, January 19, 1942; Peterson to Hoover, March 11, 1941; Hoover to SAC, Boston, February 9, 1942; Roach to Ladd, March 20, 1942; J. T. Madigan to Hoover, June 1, 1942; Hoover to SAC, Philadelphia and New York, August 10, 1942; Buffalo, Albany, Newark, and Cleveland, August 11, 1942; Chicago, August 12, 1942; Hoover to L. Smith, Special War Policies Unit, Department of Justice, November 11, 1942, FBI"S" 65–29414.

107. GS to AT, January 2, 1941, *TP*; "The Staff of *Progresso* and *Corriere*," June 15, 1941 and "Is Mr. Pope a Fascist?" July 15, 1941, *Il Mondo* (NY); "Fascism Without Mussolini," *The Nation*, January 30, 1943, 162–163; "Mussolini Is not Italy," *Pat-*

erson (New Jersey) *Morning Call*, n.d., *CP*; JD, *Mfas*, 346–351; Donno, "Gli Stati Uniti," 408.

108. GS to MA, February 12, 1942, *AGS*; "Wanted: A Policy for Europe's 'Cooling Period,'" *Antioch Review*, December 1942, 522.

109. MA to Berle, December 19, 1941, *AsP*, "Berle" file.

110. GS to MA, February 12, 1942, *AGS*; EG, *Sal*, 185; Adolfo Omodeo, *Libertà e Storia* (Torino, 1960), 411–412 cited in GGM, *Problemi*, 96.

111. MA, "Salvemini negli Stati Uniti"; GGM, *Problemi*, 148–149; Donno, "Gli Stati Uniti," 406; JM, *USI*, 36–42.

112. RB to GS, January 30, 1942, *BoP*, "Salvemini"; GS to MA, February 12, 1942 and April 19, 1942, *AsP*"S"; to RB, April 19, 1942, *AGS,* and May 27, 1942, *AsP*"S"; "La Mazzini," letter to the editor, *Controcorrente*, August–September 1941, IHRC; "Marciare divisi e colpire uniti," and "Per una Concentrazione Repubblicana-Socialista in Italia," *Opere* VII, 416–418 and 616–618; to Henry W. L. Dana, March 31, 1943, Salvemini autograph file, HL; MA, "Notes for the Congress," *Nazioni Unite*, June 11, 1942; *Nazione Unite*, June 18, 1942.

113. Ezio Taddei, "Al congresso della Mazzini," *Il Martello*, June 28, 1942. The opposing view appears in *L'Adunata dei Refrattari*, June 27, 1942.

114. Montana, *Amarostico*, 173–175; MA to GS, March 10, 1941, *AsP*"S"; GS to AT, February 26, 1941 and AT to GS, March 1, 1941, *TP*; RB to GS, April 18, 1941, *AGL*, "Salvemini"; *NYT*, January 11, 1942.

115. GS to MA, February 12, 1942, *AsP*"S."

116. Telegram, MA to GS, n.d. (May 1942?); GS to MA, n.d. (May 1942?), *AGS*.

117. GS to LAn, June 29, 1942, *AnC*, box 17, file 9; JM, *USI*, 30.

118. GS to MA, July 8, 1942, *AGS*; to Cpa, July 13, 1942, *PaP*, box 6; CK telephone interview with MC, February 1985.

119. Hull to American Ambassador, Uruguay, August 11, 1942, RG 59, NA; Sumner Welles, memo of conversation with Sir Ronald Campbell, British Ambassador, Washington, August 14, 1942, RG 59, NA; "Present State of Italian Politics in the United States," *FNB*, n. 162; *AGL*, "Mazzini Society," f. 1, s. 2; Serafino Romauldi, *Presidents and Peons* (New York, 1967); PC, "Antonini," 27; JM, "Sforza," 843ff; Varsori, *Gli alleati*, 159–202.

120. AT to Earl Brennan, OSS, January 7 and November 19, 1943, *TP*; Sforza to MA, June 13, 1943, *AGL*, "Mazzini Society," "Dino Gentili" file; MA to GS, October 20, 1943, *AGS*; to Berle, n.d. 1943 (?), *AsP*, "Berle" file; "The State Department and Free Italy," memo by Marcel Grilli, March 29, 1943, 865.00/6–1543, RG 59, NA; *Department of State Bulletin*, November 7 (177), 925–928; GS, "Intorno a un incidente,"*Opere* VII, 108; "L'affare del Memoriale (Gentili)," *Il Mondo* (NY), March 1943; Varsori, "L'antifascismo e gli alleati," *Storia e politica*, September 1980, 457–507.

121. GS, *IFAUS*, 175–179; 195, 201, 207; "Italian Fascist Activities," 8–9; "Italian Fascist Propaganda Agents on the Radio in New York, Boston and Providence, Rhode Island," manuscript, FBI"S" 62–6442; FBI Case Report, Pelletier, Boston, March 18, 1941, FBI"S" 62–6442, 6, 7, 13; E. B. Hitchcock to Elmer Davis, n.d., OWI, box 1073, "Davis"; Cranston to MacLeish, April 13, 1942, OWI, box 1073, "Davis"; Cranston to Abraham Feller, September 8, 1942, OWI, box 1070; to Paul

Smith, September 8, 1942, OWI, box 1073, "Memos, MacLeish"; Luigi Criscuolo to Lemuel B. Schofield, Chief of U. S. Bureau of Immigration and Naturalization, Philadelphia, December 15, 1942; Earl G. Harrison, Commissioner INS, Philadelphia, to Berle, January 25, 1943, FBI"S" 66–2542; Harrison to Hoover, January 25, 1943, FBI"S" 66–2542; Hoover to Berle, February 25, 1943, FBI"S" 65–29414; "New York Fascists," confidential memo, Office of the Director, Security and Intelligence Division, Headquarters, First Service Command, War Department, March 6, 1944, G-2 Regional File: Italy, Records of the War Department General and Special Staffs, RG 165 NA; SAC, Boston, to Hoover, August 30, 1945, FBI"S" 65–29414; Jeanette Sayre Smith, "Broadcasting for Marginal Americans," *Public Opinion Quarterly*, 6 (1942), 588–603; Nationality Act of 1940, Sec. 335 (a), *U. S. Statutes*, Vol. 54, 1157 and Sec. 338 (b), Vol. 54, 1159.

122. Confidential Memo, USOC, December 4, 1943; Hoover to Berle, July 15, 1944; N. J. L. Peiper, SAC, San Francisco, to Hoover, June 15, 1944, FBI"S" 65–29414; Tom C. Clark, Assistant Attorney General, to Hoover, April 29, 1944, FBI"S" 65–29414; Hoover to Berle, July 15, 1944, FBI"S" 65–29414; SAC, San Francisco, to Hoover, June 15, 1944, FBI"S" 65–29414; Confidential Memo of Postal Censorship, March 15 and May 1, 1945, OC, FBI"S" 62–64427; FBI Case Report, April 26, 1945, Boston; "T-1, Intercepts by National Censorship," SAC, Boston, to Hoover, August 30, 1945; Hoover to Assistant Chief of Staff, G-2, War Department, June 30, 1945; Hoover to Frederick B. Lyon, Chief, Division of Foreign Activities Correlation, State Dept, June 30, 1945, FBI"S" 65–29414.

123. GS, "The King Must Go Out," *The Boston Globe*, September 11, 1943; "L'antifascismo monarchico e conservatore si è suicidato," *Italia Libera* (N. Y.), September 16, 1943; "What Next in Italy," *NRep*, September 16, 1943.

124. GS, "Words and Deeds," *NRep*, August 9, 1943.

125. GS and LaP, *What to Do with Italy*.

126. GS and LaP, *What to Do with Italy*, 32–49.

127. GS, "What Price Badoglio and the King," November 8, 1943, 641–645; "Program for Italy," November 15, 1943, 679–680; "From Moscow to Naples," December 27, 1943, 905–906, *NRep*.

128. GS and LaP, *What to Do with Italy*, 80–89, 160–162.

129. Sturzo, "The Vatican and Fascism as Seen by Salvemini and La Piana," December 17, 1943, and "Beyond Salvemini-La Piana," February 25, 1943, *Commonweal*; *La mia battaglia da New York* (Milan, 1949); to GS, October 6, 1943, 163; "Don Sturzo, the Vatican, Fascism," *Commonweal*, January 28, 1944; GS, "An Answer to Don Sturzo," *The Protestant*, January 1944, 20–27; to Sturzo, November 2, 1943, in Sturzo, *Scritti inediti* (Rome, 1974), 172; GGM, *Problemi*, 106–108.

130. GS and LaP, *What to Do with Italy*, 188–204, 218–243.

131. MA to GS, October 20, 1943, *AGS*.

132. Department of State memo, April 5, 1944, attached to "M. Gaetano Salvemini et la Situation Italienne et Internationale," RG 59, NA, FW 865.00/3–2743.

133. MA to AT, November 30, 1943, *AsP*"T."

134. "Present State of Italian Politics in the United States," December 1, 1943, *FNB*, n. 162; "Free Italian Organizations," memo for Colonel Carter W. Clarke, August 13, 1943, RG 165, NA, Regional files, "Italy 3830"; JD, *Mfas*, 403–407.

135. GS to MA, March 26, 1943, *AsP*"S"; "Present State of Italian Politics in the United States," December 1, 1943, *FNB*, n. 162; MA to AT, November 30, 1943, *AsP*"M"; "The End of Mussolini and the Italian Political Scene in the United States," August 3, 1943, *FNB*, n. B-65; "Gli amici di Generoso Pope provocano la scissione al Congresso della Mazzini," December 4, 1943, newspaper text, *PaP*; "Schism in the Mazzini Society and a New Free Italy Movement," December 21, 1943, *FNB*, n. B-129; PC, "Antonini."

136. "Free Italian Organizations," memo for Colonel Carter W. Clarke; "Schism in the Mazzini Society"; MA to Sturzo, November 29, 1943, *AsP*; MA to AT, November 30, 1943, *AsP*"T"; Tirabassi, "Mazzini Society."

137. MA to AT, November 20, 1943, *AsP*"T."

138. GS to CPa, June 30 and July 18, 1942, *PaP*; "Friends of Italian Freedom Division of the Mazzini Society," July 8, 1942, *PaP*; GS to MC, January 15, 1944, *CP*; to MA, March 26, 1943, *AsP*"S"; Public Meeting Report, January 4, 1944, *FNB*, n. M-126; "An Italian Manifesto," *Life*, 16 (June 19, 1944), 38; "Italian-American Opinion of the Bonomi Government," July 10, 1944, *FNB*, n. B-277; JD, *Mfas*, 419.

139. "Conferenze Salvemini," *Controcorrente*, January 1944, IHRC; "Salvemini's Lecture Tour," February 11, 1944, *FNB*, n. B-156; Rudolph Altrocchi to CPa, October 7, 1943; CPa to GS, October 14, 1943; to Robert G. Sprowl, April 17, 1944; GS to CPa, November 6 and December 23, 1943; "Noted Anti-Fascist to Lecture at UC," press release, October 8, 1943; "Salvemini to fill U.C. Italian Chair," press release, April 20, 1944, *PaP*; GS to LaP, March 15, 1944, *LaPP*.

140. CD, *ME*, 338–339; JM, *USI*, 80–81; DiS, *Italy* (Boulder, 1995), 270–273.

141. "The Badoglio-Togliatti Bloc," *Countercurrent*, April 1944.

142. "Communist Leader Held Man to Watch in Italy," *Los Angeles Times*, April 20, 1944; "Italians Must Choose Ruler, Speaker Says," *Los Angeles Daily News*, April 20, 1944; "Says FDR, Churchill Blunder in Italy," Los Angeles *Herald Express*, April 20, 1944; "Salvemini's speech in Royce Hall," April 19 (n.d.) (1944), *PaP*.

143. Elena Aga-Rossi and Victor Zaslavsky, "L'URSS, il PCI e l'Italia: 1944–1948," *Storia Contemporanea*, December 1994, 929–982. For a different interpretation, see Agosti, *Palmiro Togliatti* (Turin, 1996), 268–282; see also GS, "Il re di maggio nel gennaio 1944," *Opere* VIII, 316–324; MLS, *Sal*, 145.

144. Telegram, Robert Rossen to GS, April 20, 1944; "On the Eve of the Invasion," Writers' Congress promotional flyer; Harry W. Flannery to CPa, April 21 and June 12, 1944, *PaP*; HC to CK, June 1984; "The Stalinists of Hollywood," *Countercurrent*, June 1944, IHRC; "Salvemini and the Comrades," *NRep*, May 1, 1944, 588, *PaP*; *The Nation*, June 3 and 24, 1944, 651–652, 746–747; JD, *Mfas*, 387, 409.

145. Stephen Tanner to GS, September 22, 1944, Tanner Letters.

146. GS to Tanner, July 5, 1944, Tanner Letters.

147. GS to Riccardo Bauer, August 16, 1944, GS, *Ld'A 44*, 19–24; Fulvio Mazza, "Salvemini, il Partito d'azione e il governo di Salerno" in GC, *Sal*, 461–467; GS to Tanner, July 5, 1944, Tanner Letters; "Prigionieri di guerra," *Opere* VII, 533; ET, "Nota biografica," 275; Mina Nassisi, "Salvemini e l'antifascismo democratico" in GC, *Sal*, 419–425.

148. FBI Report, April 26, 1945, "Salvemini," FBI"S" 65–29414, n. 100–101; GS to Lussu, February 27, 1945, GS, *Ld'A 44*, 120. Cardinal Ildefonso Schuster served as a spokesman for the Vatican in the early postwar era.

149. GS to Tanner, September 7, 1944, Tanner Letters.

150. GS, "Per una Concentrazione Repubblicana-Socialista in Italia," *Controcorrente*, November 1944, IHRC; GS to ER (?), February 27, 1945, FBI, Internal Security report, April 26, 1945, FBI"S" 65–29414, 100–801; to Tanner, August 8 and 18 and September 7, 1944, Tanner Letters; to Bauer, August 16, 1944, *Ld'A 44*, 20–21; Mazza, "Salvemini," 464–465.

151. GS to Lussu, February 27, 1945, *Ld'A 44*, 120.

152. On American policy, see JM, *USI*, 24–37.

153. Tanner to GS, September 22, 1944, Tanner Letters; GS to PiC, October 13, 1944, *LdA44*, 25.

154. ER to GS, March 26, 1944; GS to PiC, October 13, 1944; PiC to GS September 17, 1945, *LdA 44*, 17, 25–28, 172.

155. GS to Ada Rossi, June 4, 1945, *LdA 44*, 149–152.

Stipple rendering by Michael J. Coupe.

Chapter 11

Unbroken Circle

The friends that Sforza, Tarchiani and Cianca left behind in New York
found that mine was a "moralist" position, "irascible and quarrelsome,"
and not one of politics.

Gaetano Salvemini, 1945[1]

If to be a political man means to make all the blunders that Lussu has made
lately, I kiss the earth on which I walk that I am not a political man.

Gaetano Salvemini, 1946[2]

Returning in the fall of 1949 to resume his chair of modern history at the University of Florence, Gaetano Salvemini strode purposefully to the rostrum. Many remembered him well. He began, amusing his first Italian audience after more than twenty years in exile: "As we were saying in the last lecture."[3]

Ferruccio Parri had been named president of the Council of Ministers on June 19, 1945, two weeks after Salvemini wrote his emotional letter to Ada Rossi. Salvemini remained in Cambridge, corresponding regularly with Italian friends whose hope was now tempered by the realization that the PdA was making tactical mistakes and, worse, that the spirit of Fascism was alive and well. Calamandrei advised him that, in light of the emergence of neo-Fascism and the monarchist front, he might be better advised to stay in the United States. He agreed, perhaps rationalizing to friends that he did not wish to renounce his U.S. citizenship and could produce infinitely more work at Harvard.[4]

While continuing to publish profusely on contemporary Italian issues, Salvemini also attended to historical scholarship, revising several manuscripts, as well as producing his last important historical interpretation, the long preface to A. William Salomone's *Italian Democracy in the Making*.[5] Clearly influenced by the young historian's judicious assessment of Giolitti, Salvemini now articulated a historical interpretation that he had been developing since the 1920s and that contrasted markedly with the views he had once held during the pre-Fascist era. Explaining Giolitti's unsavory methods of controlling various facets of the political system—especially in the South—he offered this assessment: "Before terming Giolitti a 'parliamentary dictator' one should be careful to qualify those words." If Salvemini had overstated his case against Giolitti before, he now knew better. "A dictator is a man who suppresses freedom of speech, freedom of the press, freedom of association, and sends his opponents to jail or to the next world. Giolitti never did this." Two decades of witnessing the repression of Mussolini, Hitler and Stalin alongside the political machinations of Franklin Roosevelt and American urban "bosses" had helped Salvemini to place Giolitti in better perspective.[6]

   In defense of his previous polemical assaults on Giolitti, Salvemini now explained with remarkable introspection:

While during those years I practised, as well as I could, my profession of historian (which has always been my true profession), I devoted my spare time to a political crusade. . . . Looking back at the work of the crusader after thirty years, I find that I have nothing to regret. I must acknowledge, however, that I would have been wiser had I been more moderate in my criticism of the Giolittian system.[7]

   He granted Salomone his thesis: Italy during the Giolittian era had in fact been a "democracy in the making." Salvemini even admitted some responsibility for the rise of Fascism, because while he and other writers were criticizing Giolitti from the Left, they were also contributing to the political strength of forces from the antidemocratic Right, forces that ultimately prevailed in the Fascist era. If he could relive the decade before World War I, knowing what he now knew, he would be "more indulgent." This was the wise voice of a man who in his seventy-second year could see more clearly not only the errors of his youth but also their impact, and the full range of horrors that the century had unleashed.[8]

   Although Salvemini had for decades recorded his evolving reassessment of Giolitti and the liberal state in various writings, his ideas were now published for the first time in an important book that was destined to reshape American ideas about Italians.[9] Adding his voice to that of Salomone helped to restore the credibility of the Italian people at a key point in wartime decision making. The Fascists had badly damaged America's confidence in the ability of the Italians to govern themselves, in part by their systematic attack on pre-Fascist culture, in part by their autocratic methods. Unless the Allies now believed Italians capable of self-government, they would perpetuate authoritarian traditions, relying on the Vatican and the monarchy, while maintaining outside control for as long as possible. The publication of Salomone's book, including his mentor's preface, amplified Salvemini's call for an immediate return to an autonomous, democratic republic in Italy.

By the time the book appeared at the end of 1945, Franklin Roosevelt's untimely death had handed the reins of American government to the inexperienced Harry Truman, who, lacking his predecessor's links to the Italian-American community, would view Italy's future through the lens of the Cold War. In the midst of economic emergency and sporadic violence, Alcide De Gasperi had replaced Nenni as president of the Council of Ministers, foreclosing the brief governing career of anti-Fascists and launching a series of conservative Christian Democratic (DC) governments that would continue for forty-five years. Although De Gasperi would ultimately earn his personal respect, Salvemini expressed frustration.[10] His production of articles on contemporary politics fell off drastically, partly because he devoted more time to revising historical works for publication in Italy, and partly because of the closing of *Italia Libera*, which he had virtually written and edited since Pacciardi's resignation.[11] It was also in 1945 that Salvemini heard terrible news. A French court had convicted his stepson, Jean Luchaire, of collaboration with the Nazi occupiers in France.

Many years earlier, before the marriage to Fernande, "Giovannino" had won his affection as a surrogate son, but the two had eventually drifted apart over Jean's extremist political associates, one of whom was the young German Otto Abetz. Years later, after France fell to German armies, Jean reunited with Abetz, now Nazi ambassador to the Vichy government, and surfaced as a major propaganda figure in both occupied France and in Germany after the Allied invasion. In 1945, Jean was arrested by the Allies.

In July, Salvemini received a desperate telegram from France, pleading for his intervention with American authorities on Jean's behalf. It was another tortuous ordeal in a life stricken by misfortune, this time cast amid the great drama of war and peace. In a decision that was at the same time personally troubling yet morally clear, he followed principle over sentiment. Having charged American authorities with sheltering Fascists in Italy, he could not ask them now to protect Jean. It was an unavoidable tragedy that he had long feared.[12]

In a letter to Jean's sister, Ghita, also a Nazi collaborator, he tried to explain, "You know the affection that I had for Jean. You can therefore understand how much I grieved his political actions since 1940." If he thought only of Jean and his mother, it would put him in the impossible position of contributing to "the greatest of disasters," Hitler's victory.[13]

On the morning of February 22, 1946, Jean Luchaire was executed. Salvemini flew immediately to Paris to join Fernande. Upon his return, he reluctantly sent her an explanation of Jean's errors which, as difficult as he knew it would be for her to read, serves as a record of his own reasoning. It was not Jean's sympathy for Germany—if that were a capital crime, "half of France would have been condemned to death"—nor was his pacifism after June 1940 inexcusable. His great error was to go to Germany and campaign against the French Resistance. At that point, short of a German victory, he had sealed his own fate. "In the sadness of this hour," Salvemini wrote, "I find two reasons to take comfort. The first is that Jean was spared suffering in prison; death would be for me preferable to prison." The second reason, he concluded, was that Jean knew that he faced death "with dignity, firmness, self respect and kindness to the end."[14]

In the spring of 1946, Salvemini resumed his analysis of Italian politics, disappointed that his advice to Italians had been ignored and his worst fears had materialized: a strong republican-socialist center had failed to develop to fend off the enormous pressure from Right and Left, leaving postwar Italy dominated by communists, clericals, and monarchists. As the Vatican backed the monarchy, both extremes threatened force. Salvemini was better off, he thought, to remain a scholar at Harvard than to pursue his shattered hopes.[15] Still he longed for Italy and began to feel an obligation to return—provided that Italians voted to create a republic. As the referendum neared, his anticipation grew. Believing that an overwhelming endorsement of a republic was necessary, he expected at best a republic with "conservative and clerical tendencies."[16]

On June 2, 1946, in the much awaited institutional referendum, Italians voted narrowly to endorse a republic (with Rome and southern Italy voting for monarchy) and provided the DC a plurality of seats in the Constituent Assembly. In what should have been a moment of great joy, the creation of the republic for which he had worked so tirelessly, Salvemini could not mask his disappointment. "A 54% majority cannot assure the republic a peaceful life," he wrote to historian Leo Valiani. "The English and Americans did not succeed in saving the monarchy, but they succeeded in sabotaging the nascent republic."[17]

In 1947, a postwar Italian state quickly took shape amid economic crisis and against a background of Cold War antagonism. American and Soviet diplomats cautiously monitored the rise of the PCI and Nenni's militant socialist allies.[18] After the Constituent Assembly completed the Constitution, De Gasperi traveled to the United States, where Tarchiani, now Italy's ambassador to Washington, shepherded him among the *prominenti* to Generoso Pope. When De Gasperi returned to form a new government, he named Sforza Minister of Foreign Affairs. Not amused, Salvemini came to believe that historians would one day blame the destruction of anti-Fascism on the "liberators" and on "the complicity of two men: Croce and Sforza."[19]

Salvemini could not have known that Sforza, while promoting his own political ambitions in 1943 meetings with Eden and Churchill, had also strongly opposed the king and Badoglio.[20] However, both the Constitution and the treaty justified aspects of Salvemini's criticism. While the Constitution (effective January 1, 1948) outlawed both Fascism and autocratic rule, it also guaranteed—with the support of the communists—both the permanent position of the Catholic Church in the Italian republic and the Lateran Pacts that Mussolini had signed with the Vatican in 1929. Given the strong position of the American-backed DC, Salvemini's fears that the Fascist government would be replaced by a Vatican-dominated government were realistic. His hopes for a *terza forza* (third force) between communism and Catholicism were sinking.[21]

In the midst of these profound changes in Italian politics, Salvemini remained ambivalent about the prospects of returning to the country of his birth. On the one hand, he saw the promise of a new republic, even a weak one. Urged by Republican Egidio Reale, he considered opening an opposition newspaper. Moreover, the thought of contributing to the intellectual growth of the young generation might inspire him to dedicate his final years to teaching. The Faculty of Letters at the University of Florence had voted to reinstate him in the Chair of Modern History, thereby paving the way for his return.[22]

At the same time, however, he held serious reservations about teaching the generation under forty, tainted by a lifetime of Fascism.[23] "Everyone tells me that the young people are skeptical, indifferent, cynical, fascist," he wrote to Rossi.[24] Accordingly, while offering his Constitutional views and his services to assist Calamandrei in the Constituent Assembly, Salvemini was anything but optimistic about resuming a role in Italy: "I am absolutely convinced that for a man of my ideas there is no possibility of influence in Italy today."[25] He found the idea of returning personally burdensome as well, describing the great dismay that blanketed him each time he anticipated "the most anguished period of [his] life." Embracing old friends again before he died would bring him great joy. However, he wrote:

I am frightened by the idea of everywhere meeting people who fawned over the Fascists down to the last minute, and profited from it, who will throw themselves against me, and kiss me. . . . How will I endure this torture? Will I be able to control my natural impulse to spit on them all?[26]

Salvemini's dream was to slip into Italy using an assumed name, secretly visit his old friends, and leave just as quietly, but this was mere fantasy. After the Ministry of Instruction delayed restoring his position, primarily over the issue of his American citizenship, he decided to accept the offer to give a series of honorary lectures at the university.[27]

In July 1947, amid the debate over the peace treaty, Salvemini returned to Italy after a brief sojourn to London and Paris, where he visited Fernande. Ill now and nearly deaf and blind, she suffered lingering depression from the loss of her son. She pathetically wondered—but did not ask—if he might like her to accompany him to Italy. He continued to write and to send a substantial portion of his paltry salary to pay her bills and provide for her. When he finally left her in her room, he must have doubted that he would see her again. His apprehensions were well founded, for she died in Paris shortly thereafter. [28]

For the next two months he toured northern and central Italy by automobile, avoiding the press while visiting old friends and speaking to as many people as he could.[29] Recording his thoughts in an article entitled "Optimism," he reserved his most effusive praise for the farmers who had already managed to recover from the war's devastation to restore the land to "the most beautiful garden in the world." Railroad recovery was equally impressive, although houses were only slowly being rebuilt. He could not avoid commenting on the stunning presence of the women he saw. They all looked as if they had miraculously escaped from Renaissance paintings to walk the streets, now hatless and more beautiful even than he remembered, queens disguised as ordinary women.

His optimism receded, however, when he saw the lingering spoliation of war. Tuberculosis and rickets afflicted the children of the cities. Hunger persisted, especially in Turin and Milan. Families on fixed incomes were suffering, and many had to sell their furniture for food. Still, he could be hopeful for the next generation, not because of governmental relief efforts but because he believed that individual Italians, whom he had always idealized as "the most humane [people] on earth," would find a way to recover.

Surprisingly, he found himself less pessimistic about Italy's political future than most people he talked to, especially young people. On numerous occasions he delivered variations on a speech in which he offered the same challenge: "It is more difficult to make peace than to make war," he would say. Their history remained to be written. "The malady was long. The convalescence cannot be brief." Their greatest task was ten years of hard work to strengthen the new republic and protect it against the monarchists and the Church. Every time he gave the speech, from Turin to Venice, from Trento to Florence, he saw "eyes sparkling with flashes of conviction and ardor."[30] He remembered discussions lasting into the early morning hours with groups of wide-ranging views, many of them deeply discouraged, "the marvelous enthusiasm of May 1945 [having] vanished."[31]

One night in Turin, as Salvemini spoke to a group of professors, political activists, and Piedmontese partisans, he impressed the young historian Alessandro Galante Garrone, who, ten years later, remembered Salvemini's candor, sense of irony, and irresistible wit:

The old professor turned from one to the other, asked questions, listened eagerly; occasionally laughed, showing his fine row of white teeth, scolded us for what we had not done, or had done wrong, after the Liberation, . . . incited all those who were still hesitant, and outlined a program for the immediate future. . . . Was that the famous old Salvemini? It was we who seemed old, tired, devoured by skepticism.[32]

Salvemini recalled, "It befell me—the methodical pessimist—to give them words of hope."[33] The trip ignited a new enthusiasm to return home.

At the end of November 1947, Salvemini flew to the United States via London to resume his work in the Widener Library and to begin what was to be his final semester of teaching at Harvard. He maintained a cautious optimism, hoping that the moderate Left in Italy would sustain a "nucleus of force" that would provide leadership. At the same time, he was troubled by the portentous image of socialists riding around Rome in automobiles without any apparent understanding that they "must serve the country and not their own vanity." He also hoped that those whose integrity he trusted, such as Calamandrei and Ignazio Silone, could manage to avoid becoming caught up in the immediacy of politics and remain focused on Italy's long-range future.[34] More disturbing was the move by the new Social Democratic Party (PSDI) and Pacciardi's PRI to join the Christian Democrats in the fourth De Gaspari government, a move Salvemini saw as "political suicide" for both. In December, the socialists and communists reaffirmed their Popular Front campaign.[35]

Back in Cambridge, Salvemini did not try to mask his disappointment that Pacciardi, another trusted colleague, had surrendered the high moral ground of his party for short-term political gain.[36] Pacciardi remembered Salvemini's censure: "Men who took power were all equal, that is, contemptible" in Salvemini's eyes.[37] Meanwhile, he continued to publish at a regular pace in both America and Italy and produced occasional historical commentary on such favorite topics as the Risorgimento, the works of Carlo Cattaneo, and the liberal state. With censorship now lifted, Italian publishers presented their first versions of *History and Science*, *Under the Axe of Fascism*, *Il Risorgimento*, and *Mussolini Diplomatico*.

In the spring of 1948, the new Constitution in effect, Italians campaigned ardently for their first post-Fascist parliament. Anti-Fascist fears of a right-wing coup now seemed unrealistic in the face of mounting apprehension that Italian communists would forcefully resist a DC victory. Having articulated the Truman Doctrine and the Marshall Plan, the American president and his new Secretary of State implemented their Cold War strategy for Italy. As the U.S. Congress debated the Marshall Plan, the Truman administration poured almost $60 million of emergency aid to Italy in each of the three months leading up to the election. Concerned that Marshall Plan funds might be derailed for partisan purposes, Salvemini decried the growing American political presence.[38] The U.S. ambassador dispensed funds with strong political implications, American Cardinal Spellman denounced Stalinism, and in March Marshall warned that a communist victory would bring an immediate end to U.S. aid.[39] On April 15, Salvemini's message appeared in *The New York Times* and other American pa-

pers, accompanied by eighty signatures, calling for "an end to all outside interference" and expressing shock at the "participation of the American
Ambassador."[40]

Meanwhile the Socialist (PSI) and Communist (PCI) Parties, outside the DC
coalition for a year, endorsed Soviet foreign policy and condemned De
Gasperi's centrist government before huge Popular Front rallies. In opposition,
Pope Pius XII called on Italian Catholics to do their duty under the threat of
mortal sin, as parish priests endorsed DC candidates. Truman and Marshall
warned that the United States would not tolerate any PCI use of force, while co-
vertly the American government funneled millions of dollars to the political
parties of the center and center left. In New York, Salvemini's old nemesis
Generoso Pope sponsored an anticommunist, pro-DC letter-writing campaign.
De Gasperi recruited the PRI and the PSDI into the DC coalition while the
party's organizers worked feverishly to turn out the vote. On April 18 and 19,
Christian Democrats won a smashing victory: 49 percent of the popular vote
and an absolute majority of seats in the Chamber of Deputies. Neo-Fascist candidates netted a half million votes.[41] On the Left, only the badly beaten PCI remained a force. Salvemini saw an ideological majority under the Vatican's
rod.[42] Venting his acrimony to Rossi, he railed: "I will not die in peace unless I
see Sforza and Croce come to America, exiles after the victory of neo-
Fascism."[43] These were the ruminations of a man who at times seemed to be
still fighting the battle against Fascism, as if he needed that arch-enemy to lend
context and significance to his own political views.

If the election devastated Salvemini's hopes for a *terza forza*, his bitterness
was compounded by the ironic realization that his own American government
had played the role of midwife to the newborn Catholic coalition. "To speak of a
third force in Italy would be vain. For the American government, the third force
is the Vatican," he wrote in disgust.[44] He believed that American foreign correspondents, convinced by the U.S. Embassy of the possibility of a communist
revolution in Italy, had contributed to the victory as well.[45] Although he correctly assessed American support for the DC, Salvemini could not fully appreciate the disappointment shared by many in the American government who,
hoping for a strong showing from moderate parties that could pursue reforms,
were left only with De Gasperi.[46]

The Christian Democrats' victory was the final blow to a life in exile dedicated to replacing Fascism with a secular republic. The reality was that the British and Americans, committed to "stopping the Soviets at the straits of
Messina," had enlisted the DC in their Cold War diplomacy. Although the
Americans had signed a treaty of friendship with Italy in February, Washington
had no clear, positive plan. Salvemini hoped that the De Gasperi government
would bargain for a specific American commitment to protect Italy. "Fortu-

nately," he wrote to Rossi, "Stalin does not yet have the atomic bomb. . . . But how long will that last?"[47]

Two months after the Italian elections, at age seventy-five, Salvemini retired from Harvard with a small pension that he hoped would allow him to split his time between the Harvard libraries and the University of Florence. Italian voters had delivered a political system that would be controlled well beyond the duration of his life by a Christian Democratic establishment, ensuring that any political role he would play upon his return would be clothed in the comfortable, well worn garment of the outsider.[48]

Upon returning to Italy, he would resume the teaching position he had been forced to vacate over two decades earlier, assuming that he could resolve issues of citizenship and pension rights, and that his health could withstand the Florentine winter. Rossi felt that he should dedicate his final years to educating the postwar generation of Italian youth; Salvemini agreed, questioning only the most effective means. A weekly journal could prove useful, they decided, provided they could find investors, but Salvemini remained ambivalent about teaching. Could he not exert greater influence by writing books than by teaching at the university?[49]

With every relapse of bronchial asthma, the prospect of living in an unheated *pensione* and reading manuscripts in a frigid library became increasingly foreboding. "Damn old age!" he wrote to Rossi.[50] In November 1948, Rossi telegramed the long-awaited news that the Education Ministry had at last approved his return to the University of Florence.[51] Tired and demoralized by recurring illness, he nonetheless hoped to recover in time to leave for Europe in the summer so as to teach in the fall of 1949.

The week Salvemini received Rossi's telegram, he cast his ballot for Harry Truman. Ironically, the president's surprising triumph guaranteed that the United States would continue to treat Italian issues in a Cold War context. The United States bolstered Giuseppe Saragat's moderate socialists, and with the help of Antonini's AFL resources, attempted to seize control of the Italian labor unions from the PCI. In the interim, on his return from Moscow, Togliatti committed the PCI against the Marshall Plan. In April 1949, in the face of widespread opposition that included Salvemini's friends Piero Calamandrei and Ugo Guido Mondolfo, Sforza signed the North Atlantic Treaty on behalf of the De Gasperi government, aligning Italy firmly on the side of the West in the Cold War.[52] Salvemini, who had argued against neutrality and pushed for specific NATO guarantees, accepted the signing and moved on to other issues, focusing on wartime history and the new Constitution.[53]

On July 21, Salvemini steamed out of New York accompanied by his close friends Roberto and Maritza Bolaffio. After a brief visit to Paris, they toured Italy, hoping "to see again (before dying) Gubbio, Urbino, and Assisi."[54] In due course, he arrived on a train from Paris, stopping in Turin to visit Galante Garrone, arriving pale and tired in his overcoat and carrying his heavy bag filled with papers. As would be the custom upon his return, a stream of old friends visited. Soon he was writing a spirited response to an article in *La Stampa*, the Turinese daily. He would tire easily, but each morning he would recover, "fresh and laughing like a little boy." Within a few days, he made his long anticipated return to Florence.[55]

On October 16, 1949, before a gathering of friends, students, and faculty at the university where Blackshirts had driven him out of his office and classroom, Salvemini delivered a long speech that is remembered to this day. It was an impassioned tribute to the many professors who had educated him half a century earlier.[56] This exercise, a rare indulgence in sentimentality, indicated a softening of mood that continued to produce a stream of published tributes to old friends and allies: Arturo Toscanini, Lauro De Bosis, Cesare Battisti, the Rosselli brothers, Don Sturzo, and others. In due course, he would resume his history chair but not his strident voice; he would look back more than he had allowed himself to do. No longer would he arouse youth to political action, and although he would refuse to surrender the pen of public commentary, his postwar writing would fail to generate a significant impact.[57]

The emotional speech behind him, he began a course on the Risorgimento. In the now shabby great hall of the faculty of letters, he began without pretense or rhetorical flourish, or even an introduction: "In the middle of the nineteenth century, the northern part of the Italian peninsula was divided among four dynasties and two republics." Old friends who had dropped by to see him after a quarter century recognized the familiar Salveminian *concretismo*. "Mazzini was neither a man of state nor a philosopher. He was a mystic." His lectures, he recalled, were a "volcanic eruption" of improvisation. A new generation of students eagerly leaned forward, taking notes. Galante Garrone, who was in attendance, observed: "[Salvemini] recovered the freshness and enthusiasm of his best years . . . because he had in his blood a passion for teaching."[58]

In leading his students through an exploration of the Italian unification movement, Salvemini attacked the material with youthful ardor.[59] He challenged the ideas of the historian Federico Chabod, a student of Croce, professor at the University of Rome and director of the Crocean institute in Naples, the same man who had assisted Salvemini's escape twenty-five years earlier. In particular, Salvemini contested Chabod's thesis that attributed nationalism to romanticism, citing examples from Dante, Petrarch, and Machiavelli. While giving Chabod his due, Salvemini disagreed with his historical method, accentuating his longstanding rebuttal of Crocean idealism. "According to me," he lectured, "history is made by individuals of blood and bone and not by verbal abstractions." Always the empiricist, Salvemini took issue with Chabod's use of such concepts as a people's "discovery of their soul." Since no people ever possessed any "collective soul," he argued, such metaphors should be left to poets and not be used by historians.[60]

The awful winter of 1949–1950 exceeded Salvemini's worst expectations. He moved into a room at a *pensione* on Via San Gallo, the street where he had lived in the early 1920s. Suffering through the winter with little heat, he battled bronchitis and asthma. His writing efforts diminished to one article per week and, deep into revising several books, he found little time for new historical research. Despite the allure of Harvard's Widener Library, he failed to realize his hope of returning to the United States.[61]

In the academic year 1950–1951, he again taught the course in Italian unification, this time using Adolfo Omodeo's *L'età del Risorgimento italiano*.[62] Meticulously weighing Omodeo's analyses, Salvemini turned the course into a lesson on historical method and interpretation. He implored his young students to remain vigilant in their study, guarding themselves against the dangers of pedantry, ideology, and partisanship. Omodeo's book became the laboratory as he led his class to question each of the author's assumptions. He completed the course with a reconsideration of the French Revolution, once again challenging Omodeo's Crocean interpretations.[63]

In the spring of 1951, ill and looking for relief from the cold streets of Florence, Salvemini accepted the invitation from friends to travel South to Sorrento for Easter. Subsequently, captivated by its serenity, he returned to Sorrento to live his final years.[64]

It is clear that in the 1950s, Salvemini had left behind his best work. It was an impressive legacy that eventually exceeded twenty large volumes of dense material. Some of its distinctive attributes—untiring collection of sources, a hard edge, a dauntless instinct to attack—were now eluding him. He had always written his best work from an adversarial stance—his Mazzinians protecting their Risorgimento from Cavour and the grasping middle class; his southern Italian peasants being exploited by Giolitti and northern industrialists; his Florentine colleagues beaten, repressed, and dehumanized by Blackshirts. His most inspired writing required a villain, but in the Italy of the "economic miracle," the villains were too petty, the battles pale by comparison to world war and Fascist dictatorship. He wrote Galante Garrone in 1955 a kind of historian's testimonial, reaffirming the need for inspiration: "In conducting research, I look always to satisfy a curiosity . . . but this research always originated in moral fixation."[65] Inspiration had led him to interpretations so original and so bold that they are still studied, but there would be no more original works.

Exhausted and sickly though he was, he carried on into his eighties, mustering enough energy to convince some that he had captured a "second youth" and that he "burned with a youthful enthusiasm to the end."[66] His antagonists, especially Croce, may not have observed any diminishing of the Salveminian flame, however. Croce was an intellectual force, a philosopher and historian of international renown who, by avoiding direct criticism of the Fascist regime, had managed to escape Mussolini's repression while continuing to publish his journal, *La Criticà*, in Naples. Croce's willingness to accept such constraints had offended Salvemini's sensibilities for twenty years. His reemergence to play a pivotal role in the immediate postwar era, his accommodation to Allied policies, his conservative political values including advocacy of the monarchy, and his tendency toward intellectual history and philosophical abstraction made him anathema to Salvemini.

Some antagonism had surfaced over the years among these polar opposites in the twentieth-century Italian intellectual and political tradition. Croce's estimate of Salvemini as scholar is part praise of Salvemini's impact, part damnation of his writings. In his classic 1921 book on Italian historiography, Croce had both credited Salvemini with cofounding the "economic-juridical" school of historians and accused the school of improvising history "with audacity of judgment that showed no originality of thought and still fewer scruples about truth."[67] He was more judicious in his appraisal of Salvemini's particular historical works, giving him substantial credit for his *concretismo*. Then in 1928, when Croce published his widely read *History of Italy*, he appraised Salvemini's work with *L'Unità* as "prone to indulge in violent polemics of a moral character, half naive and half unjust, and tinged with utopianism." In the same passage, Croce had underscored his own method by admonishing Italian historians for their insulation from ideals and religious feeling, a rebuke directed in part at Salvemini and his protégés.[68]

Viewing Croce's political influence as a threat to all he had worked for in exile, Salvemini began to criticize his politics even before leaving Cambridge. He was careful to grant the eminent intellectual his place of honor, but he did not refrain from criticizing his political transgressions, such as his "sympathy" for early Fascism. Although acknowledging Italians' "gratitude" for Croce's "silent" resistance to Mussolini's regime, Salvemini attacked fundamental Crocean nineteenth-century liberalism, which lived "in the clouds of abstract ideas."[69]

The differences between the two thus had been well aired by 1949 when Croce published a biting review of Salvemini's *Historian and Scientist*, his major methodological work that had just appeared in Italian translation.[70] Croce argued that "Salvemini remained in 1893," not having matured beyond his early positivism. In fact, as has been pointed out, *Historian and Scientist* bore remarkable similarity to Salvemini's 1902 essay and was consistent with both his approach to history and his Enlightenment-based values.[71] Salvemini responded the next year with his own critique of Crocean idealism,[72] but his final open controversy with Croce came three years later.

Croce touched off the last round with a March 1950 review of Salvemini's preface to the Italian translation of Salomone's *Italian Democracy in the*

Making, published the previous year. In "An Erroneous Preface," Croce chastised Salvemini for inadequate contrition, expecting after forty years that the historian would "correct the mistake" with a complete admission of his error. He softened his criticism with a gracious nod to Salvemini as "personally honest and disinterested and . . . somewhat ingenuous and credulous." Croce proceeded to defend Giolitti as a superb parliamentarian and statesman and courageous reformer and lauded post-Risorgimento Italy as "esteemed and extolled in all of Europe" for its political moderation and for its tolerant government.[73] Salvemini, who must have questioned whether he and Croce had lived in the same country in the first decades of the century, attacked Croce's postwar conservative politics as well as his interpretation of the Giolittian era.[74]

Beyond the polemics with Croce and old adversaries such as Prezzolini, Salvemini carried on in the reviews *Il Ponte*, *Critica Sociale*, and *Il Mondo* a steady campaign of political commentary in support of such causes as electoral reform, a *terza forza*, civil liberties, and European federation. If his attack lacked the rage of his earlier journalistic confrontations with Giolitti and Mussolini, the writing reveals the passion and searing logic that he had never lost. Communist leader Giorgio Amendola remembered Salvemini from these days as a "permanent" heretic and nonconformist.[75] Others found in his last writings a new optimism.[76]

By 1950, Italian politics had settled into a pattern. With the PCI now reduced to a permanent minority, no longer viewed by the United States as an immediate threat to seize power, De Gasperi and his DC successors governed alone or with occasional coalitions, largely committed to the status quo. The reformers of the moderate Left, from which Salvemini's *terza forza* would have come, struggled in feeble disarray. The major electoral questions of the day were no longer grand issues of fundamental justice—the battles for universal suffrage and a republic had been won—but rather institutional issues such as finding a formula for parliamentary representation that would balance Italy's needs for stability with those of fairness. Still, Salvemini found inspiration, as he always had, in the works of Carlo Cattaneo, whose nineteenth century opposition to centralized government was especially pertinent as the new republic took shape a century later.[77]

Salvemini's championing of European federation and electoral reform serve to illustrate his final campaigns. In addressing a Constitutional issue that is still debated, Salvemini surprisingly favored a DC proposal to abandon proportional representation in favor of a majoritarian system that awarded a bonus to the majority. A new law boosting the majority to 65 percent of the seats, later dubbed the *legge truffa* ("fraudulent law"), passed in March 1953.[78]

On the question of European federation, he had argued in 1949 against a disarmed and isolated Italy, in favor of Italian neutrality guaranteed under the Atlantic Pact, similar to the guarantees made to Belgium in the nineteenth century.

He also envisioned an armed, federated Europe, including Italy, that would acquire similar guarantees from the Anglo-Americans against Russian invasion.[79] By 1954, the realities of the Cold War had forced Salvemini to accept Italian membership in NATO.[80]

His commitment to a *terza forza* had never wavered, it had only been disappointed by a series of failures. In the 1950s he discovered a new optimism about the prospects of a combination of secular groups of the democratic Left that would provide an alternative to the doctrinaire forces of the DC and the "totalitarian Stalinism" of the PCI.[81] Even after Pacciardi and Saragat had taken the PRI and the PSDI, respectively, into a DC coalition, Salvemini maintained hope that they could cooperate in forging an opposition movement independent of the PCI.[82] As a major collaborator in the Roman journal *Il Mondo*, he continued to develop the *terza forza* argument.[83] Initially hopeful that the new PSU of Giuseppe Romita could fill the void, he quickly became disillusioned with its leadership.[84]

In May 1953, Salvemini spelled out in *Il Mondo* a specific program of "immediate general interest" that he believed would solidify a *terza forza*. It included commitments to European federation, religious freedom, nationalization of hydroelectricity and telephones, and a massive commitment to school construction. In a call for clarity and simplicity, he applied *concretismo* to the problems of the 1950s.[85] He was, he wrote in 1954, "a democratic socialist of old," with a preference for economic reforms "always less individualistic and more collectivistic." By that summer Salvemini even professed unprecedented hope that Italian communists would eventually adopt democratic methods, although he did not expect to witness such a metamorphosis in his lifetime.[86] Along the lines of Salvemini's *terza forza*, Republican leader Ugo La Malfa, with strong support in the columns of *Il Mondo*, attempted to unify three secular parties (PRI, the Liberal Party or PLI, and PSDI), but was stymied by defeat in the administrative elections of 1951 and 1952. Once again Salvemini saw his hopes for a political alternative dashed.[87]

In championing civil liberties under the new Constitution, Salvemini returned to his Enlightenment roots. He wanted a republic "without adjectives," neither a "social" nor a "clerical" republic, a system that would avoid the ideological rhetoric of Left and Right in its commitment to basic freedoms. He feared for the rights of Italians because the new Constitution was couched in such broad abstractions ("there will be no unemployment"; "labor is sovereign") as to be meaningless. Given the weakness in the traditional commitment to Italian liberties, a body of well-defined laws would bolster protection.[88]

Still, while teaching and trumpeting his long-held values, he seems to have lost in this last decade some of the Salveminian ardor. The gleam remained in his eye, and his logic still cut to the bone, but the political climate had changed, and he simply could not attack an issue like the majoritarian electoral law with the fervor that came so easily in assailing Giolitti's "thugs" thirty years earlier. In one respect, this is unfortunate, because in the last decade of his life, as Italians established critical precedents that would shape the new Constitutional system, he could have contributed; in another sense, it may have been just as well. He had engaged in the modern Italian political dialogue as much as anyone, and a repeat of the *legge truffa* polemic would benefit neither Italian politics nor himself.

If some of the old zeal diminished as he entered his eighth decade, it was displaced by greater contemplation and introspection. In part this was the product of retirement and his return to Italy, a sense that the circle of his life was closing. The poetic moment of his University of Florence speech had taken him back to the professors who had, in that very place, first inspired his study of history. In 1947, he had entered in his diary a passage that succinctly summarized his most profound thoughts, a rare personal, spiritual affirmation from a man who had spent his life criticizing religious dogma, ideology, and abstract philosophy: "I believe only in the *Crito* of Plato and in the 'sermon on the Mount.' "[89]

When Salvemini left Florence for retirement in the warmth of Sorrento in 1951, he continued to publish an average of one article per week through the end of 1955, while ten of his books appeared, six for the first time. It was his great fortune to live out his life at the home of his old friends Donna Titina Ruffini and Giuliana Benzoni (daughter and granddaughter, respectively, of former Foreign Minister Ferdinando Martini) at Villa La Rufola, their home in Sorrento. Salvemini found there animated conversation, a superb library, an ideal ambience for writing and convalescing, and the affection of loving companions. "It was an enchanting place," wrote Iris Origo, who visited him there, "a secluded villa on a little peninsula at Capo di Sorrento, looking down over silvery olive groves to the sea." When he had first fled to England thirty years before, reminiscing with fellow exile Don Sturzo, he had dreamed of once more seeing the Amalfi coast.[90]

Then came the visitors: a steady parade of old friends; young students; political allies; protégés; American, French, and English acquaintances, some with new children; all making pilgrimages to pay their respects. He maintained correspondence with many of them, and news spread among the informal community of Salveminiani that he would be happy to see them in his new home. They remembered spirited exchanges and hearty laughter. Isaiah Berlin recalled from a 1955 visit that, in explaining his poor health, Salvemini remarked: "I can't understand it. Mussolini is dead, Croce is dead. I should be flourishing."[91]

In 1955, Salvemini received two major awards acknowledging his many achievements as a historian: the international prize for history from the Accademia dei Lincei and an honorary degree from Oxford University. Illness prevented one final trip to England, and he thus remained for the duration of his life in the tranquility of Sorrento. In response to queries from the many visitors, he now distilled his political views, returning, he said, to his roots: Mazzini and Cattaneo, his own *concretismo*, a pragmatism equally averse to the dogma of communists and Catholics, and to the simple socialist views he had shared with Turati half a century earlier, believing simply that the poor should have enough to eat. His closest allies were now in the Radical Party, but, maintaining his antipathy towards organized politics, he kept his independence, as he had for more than forty years.[92]

By the summer of 1957, Salvemini's closest friends understood that death now loomed ominously near. Many retained vivid recollections of the old fighter, lying on his deathbed, his spirit and humor indomitable, though his voice weakening, no longer battling, yet embracing death in a veil of calm.

"You have no idea," he said on several occasions, "of how content I am to die this way. To have a peaceful conscience is the only thing that matters. . . . To die smiling."

His hosts were his constant companions until the end, joined by the Bolaffios and a few other close friends. Almost daily, a young priest, Don Rosario Scarpati, stopped at Salvemini's bedside. The two became close friends, but Salvemini maintained his anticlericalism and his religious skepticism to the very end. He emphasized that there would be no deathbed conversion: "Don Rosario, in a few days my young friends will carry me to the cemetery," Salvemini whispered. "You may come too, but dressed like a man [and not as a priest]."[93]

To clarify his stand against a religious funeral, he scratched a note to Don Rosario three days before his death: "I have not changed my mind. I trust you not to allow any mystification." That same day he clarified his religious views in his own "Testament":

If to admire and try to follow the moral teachings of Jesus Christ, without caring whether or not he was the Son of God . . . is being a Christian, I intend to die as a Christian as I tried to live, without success, unfortunately. But I ceased to be a Catholic at the age of eighteen and I intend to die out of the Catholic Church, without any ambiguity.[94]

Still, he was concerned because the maid, Concetta, who nursed him attentively, feared that he would die without the final sacraments. He beckoned Don Rosario to explain, shedding a tear: "She is an angel and does not deserve this grief on my account."

By September, the death watch began. Ernesto Rossi and Enzo Tagliacozzo had joined a few other friends and his sister-in-law, Lidia Minervini. He was ready to die: "This pitiless heart will not give up," he told Rossi. "The doctor is prolonging my agony, not my life."[95] He asked Don Rosario, "Can't you give me a pill? Pray the Almighty to make me die soon."[96]

On September 7, 1957, Salvemini slipped into a coma. As more friends gathered, Don Rosario called to him repeatedly but elicited no response. Finally, the priest thundered: "Professore!"

Gradually Salvemini opened his eyes. "Still alive," he murmured. Then, closing them again, "Goodbye for good." A little later in the morning, he regained his senses and uttered a few phrases that his closest friends recorded.

I have been so happy in my life, so many faithful friends. Thank you for everything. How glad I am to die like this. . . . To pass like this into death, death. I don't understand why people are afraid of death. One should spread the news about this way of coming to an end, so that people would not be afraid. . . . It would interest me to know the precise moment in which I shall be dead. To have a clear conscience is really interesting. . . . I have been fortunate in life and also in death. . . . I should like to embrace you all. . . . How difficult it is to distinguish between life and death. . . . One cannot fix the passage; it is all one. . . . There is no difference between death and life.[97]

The time of death was fixed at 11:30 A.M., two days before his eighty-fourth birthday. Following his instructions, several young friends assisted by Don Rosario carried his casket to its resting place in the Sorrento pauper's cemetery.

NOTES

1. GS to Riccardo Bauer, Emilio Lussu, and Federico Comandini, January 17, 1945, *Ld'A 44*, 76.

2. GS to PiC, May 16, 1946, *Ld'A 44*, 282.

3. Myron P. Gilmore, HSH, LaP, Renato Poggioli, Louis Lyons, "Harvard Commemoration," *Controcorrente*, December 1958, 76.

4. GS to Augusto Torre, February 12, 1946, 213–214; to Reale, March 30 and April 10, 1946, 242, 253–259; Reale to GS, September 24 and 30, 1945, 178 and 183–184; PiC to GS, February 3, 1946, 206–208, *Ld'A 44*.

5. GS, Preface to AWS, *Italian Democracy in the Making* (Philadelphia, 1945), vii-xvi.

6. GS, Introductory Essay, AWS, *IGE*, xiii-xx.

7. GS, Introductory Essay, AWS, *IGE*, xxi.

8. GS, Introductory Essay, AWS, *IGE*, xxi-xxii.

9. See above, chapter 9.

10. GS to Gino Luzzatto, December 3, 1945, 196; to ER, September 8, 1946, 369–374, and June 6, 1949, 289, *Ld'A 47*.

11. Randolfo Pacciardi, "Il grande esule," *Archivio trimestrale*, July–December, 1982, 620; "Pacciardi lascia il giornale," December 16, 1943, *L'Italia Libera*.

12. *Le Procès de Collaboration* (Paris, 1948); HM to GS, June 17, August 9 and 28, September 24, and December 9, 1945, and February 10, 1946; GS to HM, July 3 and October 29, 1945, and February 19, 1946 *AGS*.

13. GS to Ghita Luchaire, July 14, 1945, *AGS*.

14. "Jean Luchaire et de Sable ons été executés ce matin," n.s. (Paris), February 22, 1946; GS to FS, March 18, 1946, *AGS*.

15. GS to V. Fiore, April 2, 1946, quoted in Nassisi, "Gli Stati Uniti," 423.

16. GS to PiC, April 19, 1946, 260–263; to ER, April 22, 1946, 272–275, *Ld'A 44*.

17. GS to Leo Valiani, June 11, 1946, 295–296; to Emilio Lussu, August 7, 1946, 341, *Ld'A 44*.

18. JM, *USI*, 192–193.

19. GS to ER, February 1, 1949, *Ld'A 47*, 263. JM, *USI*, 213–219.

20. JM, *USI*, 57–60.

21. GS, "Discussioni con un cattolico sincero," *Belfagor*, May 1947, 350–355; "Quel povero Gesù Cristo," *Controcorrente*, August 1948, 3–4; "Pacelli e Savoia," *Controcorrente*, May 1949, 1; "La terza via," *Il Mondo* (Rome), March 15, 1952, 1–2.

22. "Salvemini Reappointed to Florence University," OWI press release, February 7, 1945; telegram, Arrigo Bernstein to Salvemini, February 7, 1945; "Statement by Gaetano Salvemini," press release, February 9, 1945; "Salvemini to Resume Post in Italy If Lectures Are Not Restricted," *Christian Science Monitor*, February 9, 1945; PiC to GS, July 2, 1946; GS to the Faculty of Letters, University of Florence, July 22, 1946, *AGS*; Reale to GS, June 10, 1946; GS to ER, July 12 and September 12, 1946, 293–294, 315ff., 378; GS to Franco Venturi, September 17, 1946, 381, GS, *Ld'A 44*.

23. GS to Lionello Venturi, September 17, 1946, *Ld'A 44*, 381.

24. GS to ER, May 7, 1947, *Ld'A 47*, 69.

25. GS to PiC, August 26, 1946, *Ld'A 44*, 365.

26. GS to Reale, September 12, 1946, GS, *Ld'A 44*, 377.

27. AT, Italian Ambassador to the U.S. to GS, March 28, 1945; GS to AT, April 13, 1945, *AGS*; GS to PiC, April 12, 1945, *Ld'A 44*, 139; PiC to GS, July 2, 1946; official memorandum, Faculty of Letters and Philosophy, University of Florence, June 29, 1946, *AGS*; GS to ER, July 27 and September 12, 1946, GS, *Ld'A 44*, 325–326, 376–378.

28. HM to GS, April 14, November 25 and December 23, 1946, *AGS*; Iris Origo, *A Need to Testify*, 182.

29. GS to ER, August 6 and September 14, 1947, *Ld'A 47*, 92 and 106.

30. GS, "Ottimismo," *Opere* VIII, 747–752; GS to ER, September 29, 1947, *Ld'A 47*, 116, and GS to UGM, December 16, 1947, *Ld'A, 47*, 118.

31. GS, diary entry of July 25, 1947, *Lettere dall'esilio* quoted in AGG, *Salvemini e Mazzini*, 330n.

32. AGG, "L'ultimo Salvemini," *Il Ponte*, August-September 1957, quoted in Iris Origo, *A Need to Testify*, 181–182.

33. GS, diary entry of July 25, 1947, *Lettere dall'esilio*.

34. GS to UGM, December 16, 1947, 119–121; to ER, April 23, 1948, 155, *Ld'A 47*.

35. JM, *USI*, 223–230; GS to ER, March 27, 1948, *Ld'A 47*, 142.

36. GS to ER, March 27, 1948, *Ld'A 47*, 142.

37. Pacciardi, "Il grande esule," 620.

38. GS, "Quello che dovrebbe fare il Piano Marshall," *Il Repubblicano* (Turin), February 15, 1948 and "Il Piano Marshall," *Controcorrente*, July, 1948; to ER, Febru-

ary 28, 1948, 128; to Giuliano Benzoni, March 1948, 133–137; GS to Manlio Rossi-Doria, March 14, 1948, 139, *Ld'A 47*.

39. Paul Ginsborg, *A History of Contemporary Italy* (London, 1990), 115–120.

40. *The New York Times*, April 15, 1948; telegram, GS to ER, April 14, 1948, *Ld'A 46*, 146; JM, *USI*, 185–187, 223–235.

41. JM, "Taking Off the Gloves," *Diplomatic History* (Winter 1983), 35–36 and *USI*, 243–249.

42. GS to Mario Vinciguerra, August 6, 1948, *Ld'A 47*, 203.

43. GS to ER, April 12, 1949, *Ld'A 47*, 278.

44. GS to Luigi Morandi, April 24, 1948, *Ld'A 47*, 162. See also GS, "Pacelli e Savoia," *Controcorrente*, May 1949, and "Vatican and Mindszenty," *The Nation*, August 6, 1949.

45. GS to Reale, May 7, 1948, *Ld'A 47*, 171.

46. JM, *USI*, 248–249.

47. GS to ER, September 29 and November 15, 1948, *Ld'A 47*, 220, 241.

48. David W. Bailey, Secretary, President and Fellows of Harvard College, to GS, n.d. 1947; Donald C. McKay to GS, May 22, 1948; Nathan M. Pusey to GS, December 13, 1955; GS to Pusey, January 1, 1956, *AGS*; Myron P. Gilmore, HSH, LaP, Renato Poggioli, Louis Lyons, "Harvard Commemoration," *Controcorrente*, December 1968, 76; MS, "Salvemini esule," *Controcorrente*, December 1968, 61.

49. GS to ER, February 20, April 27, May 13, July 15 and 31, October 17, November 15, 1948, *Ld'A 47*, 127, 168, 177, 194, 200, 228, 242; AGG, *Salvemini e Mazzini*, 332–333; ET, "Nota biografica," 276.

50. GS to ER, May 13, August 31, October 21, November 15, 1948, *Ld'A 47*, 176, 209, 231–232, 242.

51. Telegram, ER to GS, November 5, 1948, *Ld'A 47*, 238.

52. JM, *USI*, 255–271.

53. GS, "Quale neutralità," *L'Italia Socialista* (Rome), January 11, 1949; "Badoglio storico di sé stesso," *Controcorrente*, November 1949, and "Il 'Re di maggio' nel gennaio 1944," *Belfagor*, January 1950; "Federalismo e regionalismo," *Controcorrente*, May 1949.

54. GS to ER, June 6, 1949, *Ld'A 47*, 290.

55. AGG, *Salvemini e Mazzini*, 331–332; MC interview, December 1979.

56. GS, "Una pagina," *Opere* VIII, 48–49; Giovanni Spadolini, "Quattro ricordi di Salvemini," *Archivio Trimestrale*, July–December 1982, 606ff.

57. GS, "Toscanini," *Controcorrente*, September 1948; Preface, Lauro De Bosis, *Storia della mia morte e ultimi scritti* (Turin, 1948); "Marion Rosselli," *Il Ponte*, November 1949; "Ricordando Antonio De Viti de Marco," *Controcorrente*, December 1949; "Ernestina e Cesare Battisti," in *Ernestina Battisti Bittanti* (Milan, 1962), 9–11; "Ricordando i Rosselli," *Controcorrente*, June, 1951; "Saluto a Don Sturzo," *Il Mondo* (Rome), December 1, 1951.

58. GS, "Il Risorgimento (Lezioni universitarie)," *Opere* II, 2, 474; AGG, *Salvemini e Mazzini*, 343; MLS, *Sal*, 40; ET, "Nota biografica," 276; Spadolini, "Quattro ricordi," 607.

59. AGG, *Salvemini e Mazzini*, 344.

60. GS, *Opere* II, 2, 473–663; AGG, *Salvemini e Mazzini*, 297–344; MLS, *Sal*, 254–257.

61. Spadolini, "Quattro ricordi," 603.

62. Omodeo, *L'età del Risorgimento italiano* (Messina, 1932).

63. AGG, *Mazzini e Salvemini*, 344–351; GS, "Sull'illuminismo (dall'ultimo corso del 1950–51)" in AGG, *Mazzini e Salvemini*, 494–505.

64. AGG, *Salvemini e Mazzini* (Firenze, 1981), 328–360; ET, "Nota biografica," 277; Origo, *A Need*, 182.

65. GS to AGG, July 11, 1955 in AGG, *Salvemini e Mazzini*, 340–341.

66. Giuseppe Armani, "Salvemini e Cattaneo (1945–1957)," *Archivio trimestrale*, July–December 1982, 841; AGG, *Salvemini e Mazzini*, 328–329.

67. Croce, *Storia della storiografia italiana nel secolo deimonono* (Bari, 1947), 142–143.

68. Croce, *A History of Italy, 1871–1915* (Oxford, 1929), 250–252.

69. GS, "Che cosa è un 'liberale' italiano nel 1946,"*Opere* VI, 3, 353–386.

70. GS, *Storia e scienza* (Florence, 1948).

71. Croce, review of Salvemini, *Storia e scienza, Quaderni de 'La Critica,'* March 1949, 93–95. See also MLS, *Sal*, 192 ff.

72. GS, "Metodologia crociana," *CS*, August 1950, 219–220.

73. Croce, "Una prefazione sbagliata," *Quaderni della Critica*, n. 16, March 1950, 122–124.

74. GS, "I manutengoli del fascismo," *Il Ponte*, April 1952, 419–428; "Di Croce e dell'equità," *Il Ponte*, July–August, 1954, 1253; "La politica de Benedetto Croce," *Il Ponte*, November 1954, 1728–1743.

75. Giovanni Spadolini, "Quattro ricordi," 612.

76. Giuliano Torlontano, "Salvemini e la lotta politica del secondo dopoguerra" in *Archivio trimestrale*, July–December 1982, 855–874; AGG, *Salvemini e Mazzini*, 353.

77. GS, "Federalismo e regionalismo," *Controcorrente*, May 1949; Armani, "Salvemini e Cattaneo," 852–854.

78. GS, "Proporzionale sproporzionata," *Opere* VIII, 793–802; MLS, *Sal*, 158–159; Giuseppe Mammarella, *Italy After Fascism* (Notre Dame, Indiana, 1966), 249–252; AGG, *Salvemini e Mazzini*, 341; Torlontano, "Salvemini," 855–874.

79. GS, "Quale neutralità," *Opere* VIII, 758–761; to William J. Donovan, October 4, 1948, AGS, "European Federation."

80. GS, "la CED," *Opere* VIII, 871–878; to ER, May 14, July 31, and December 28, 1948, *Ld'A 47*, 178, 201, 252.

81. GS to Vinciguerra, June 28, 1947, *Ld'A 47*, 85.

82. GS to UGM, December 16, 1947, *Ld'A 47*, 119.

83. GS, "Qualche sasso in capponaia (politica socialista)," *Il Mondo* (Rome), December 24, 1949; Torlontano, "Salvemini," 863.

84. GS, "Il mercato delle vacche," *Il Mondo* (Rome), October 4, 1952; "La liquidazione del laicismo," *Critica Sociale*, May 5, 1953.

85. GS, "Un soldo di speranza," *Il Mondo*, May 16, 1953.

86. GS, "La CED," *Il Ponte*, June 1954; Torlontano, "Salvemini," 873; Spadolini, *L'Italia dei laici* (Florence, 1980), 265.

87. Giuseppe Mammarella, *Italy After Fascism*, 241–245; Torlontano, "Salvemini," 864–865.

88. GS, "I coronamenti strutturali," 857–862; "Niente leggi nuove!," 878–879, *Opere* VIII; Torlontano, "Salvemini," 855–874.

89. GS, *Diario*, August 7, 1947.

90. Origo, *A Need*, 183.

91. Origo, *A Need*, 184.

92. ER, "Il non conformista."

93. ER, "Il nonconformista." Translation from Origo, *A Need*, 186.

94. "Dal testamento olografo di GS," *Opere* VIII, 960.

95. ER, "il nonconformista."

96. Origo, *A Need*, 188.

97. "Parole di commiato," *Opere* VIII, 959–960.

Bibliographical Essay

There are so many materials relating directly or indirectly to the life of Gaetano Salvemini as to make it impossible to list them all. The intent of this brief essay is to identify only the most important works used in this study that apply directly to the subject. Consequently, the sources included here represent merely a starting point for further inquiry. Additional references may be found in one of the bibliographies listed below or in the endnotes documenting specific topics in the biography.

There are several indispensable sources for any study of Salvemini, including his own published works and correspondence. Most important are his *Opere*, 19 vols. (Milan, 1961–1974); *Carteggio, 1894–1902, 1912–1914* and *1921–1926*, ed. Enzo Tagliacozzo (Bari, 1988, 1984, 1985); *Lettere dall'America 1944/1946* and *1947/1949*, ed. Alberto Merola (Bari, 1967, 1968); and his many books, published primarily in Italian and English language editions and noted appropriately in the text. The introductory essays to the various volumes of this *Opere* include worthwhile contributions by Gaetano Arfe, Lamberto Borghi, Sergio Bucchi, Alessandro Galante Garrone, Elvira Gencarelli, Ernesto Sestan, Roberto Vivarelli, Franco Venturi, and others. Additional Salvemini correspondence has been published, including "Carteggio Salvemini-Rossi," Umberto Morra, ed., *Il Mondo*, January 26 and February 2, 9, and 16, 1960, 11–12; and *Lettere inedite di Gaetano Salvemini a Bernard e Mary Berenson*, Iris Origo, ed., *Nuova Antologia* (Rome-Florence), July 1982, 162–215.

The definitive catalogue of works by and about Salvemini, *Bibliografia salveminiana, 1892–1984* (Rome, 1986), was assembled and published with the greatest care by his longtime colleague Michele Cantarella.

Manuscript materials relating to Salvemini's life and career are abundant and scattered. Among the collections holding the most important manuscripts for this study (see the Abbreviations section for complete citation) are the following: the *Archivio Gaetano Salvemini*, the Roberto Bolaffio Papers, the Alberto Tarchiani Papers, and the *Archivio Giustizia e Libertà*, all housed at the ISRT (Florence); the Luigi Antonini Collection (Cornell University); the Max Ascoli Papers (Boston University); the Lauro de Bosis Collection (Harvard University); the Felix Frankfurter Papers (Library of Congress, Washington); the Papers of Fiorello LaGuardia (Municipal Archives, New York); the Giorgio La Piana Papers (Andover-Harvard Theological Library, Cambridge); the Mazzini Society Papers (ACS, Rome); the Constantine Panunzio Papers (Stanford); and three Harvard University collections: the Salvemini scrapbooks (Houghton Library), the Salvemini publications (Widener Library), and the Salvemini files (Harvard University Archives).

Official documents for the study of Salvemini are available on both sides of the Atlantic. In the Italian state archives, the most useful Salvemini materials are found in the following collections (again, see the Abbreviations section): the Ministero degli Affari Esteri; the Ministero della Cultura Popolare; and the Ministero dall'Interno. In the official American archives, materials can be found in various Record Groups (see RG in the Abbreviations), including the Allied Control Commission (Italy); the Combined Chiefs of Staff; the Foreign Nationalities Branch, the Office of Strategic Services; and the Office of Naval Intelligence. The Federal Bureau of Investigation (Department of Justice) and the Franklin D. Roosevelt Library are among other official United States archives that house Salvemini materials.

Numerous colleagues, students, and friends of Salvemini published accounts, both scholarly and personal, that can be considered primary sources as well. Of these materials, the point of departure is the work of A. William Salomone, including "Momenti di storia, frammenti di ricordi con Salvemini tra Stati Uniti e Italia," *Archivio Trimestrale*, 8 (July–December 1982) and "Salvemini e Giolitti," *Rassegna Storica Toscana*, April–June 1958, 121–151. Among other important published primary sources are Max Ascoli, "Salvemini negli Stati Uniti," *La Voce Repubblicana*, December 20–21, 1967, 16, 24; Norman Kogan, "Salvemini in America," *Il Mondo* (Rome), October 8, 1957, 9–10; Gino Luzzatto, "L'Eredità di Salvemini," *Rassegna Storica Toscana*, April–June 1958, 81–83 and "Il merito di Salvemini," *Il Mondo* (Rome), June 28, 1955, 9; Iris Origo, *A Need to Testify* (New York, 1984); Randolfo Pacciardi, "Gaetano Salvemini il grande esule," *Archivio Trimestrale*, July–December 1982, 614–619; Ernesto Rossi, "Il non conformista," *Il Mondo* (Rome), September 17, 1957; 1794–1795; Max Salvadori, *Resistenza ed azione* (Bari, 1961) and "Antifascisti italiani negli Stati Uniti" in *Atti del congresso internazionale di storia americana* (Genoa, 1978); Giovanni

Spadolini, "Quattro ricordi di Salvemini," *Archivio Trimestrale*, July–December 1982, 606ff.; and Enzo Tagliacozzo, "L'Opera di Gaetano Salvemini negli Stati Uniti d'America," *Rassegna Storica Toscana* 20 (January–June, 1974), 19–36, and "Ricordo di Salvemini," *Rassegna Storia Toscana* 4 (April–June 1958), 179–196.

The secondary literature on Salvemini is vast and varied. Again, only the most important of those works are listed here. Several booklength biographical studies exist: Massimo L. Salvadori's *Gaetano Salvemini* (Turin, 1963), which presents a careful analysis of his life and ideas; *Gaetano Salvemini nel cinquantennio liberale* (Florence, 1959) and *Gaetano Salvemini: Un profilo biografico* (Rome, 1963), published by Salvemini's former assistant and friend Enzo Tagliacozzo; and a Marxist indictment by Gaspare De Caro, *Gaetano Salvemini* (Turin, 1970).

In addition, a number of excellent topical studies of Salvemini exist. Analyses of Salvemini's basic political principles include Giuseppe Armani, "Salvemini e Cattaneo (1945–1957)," *Archivio trimestrale*, July–December 1982, 841; Lelio Basso, *Gaetano Salvemini, socialista e meridionalista* (Manduria, 1959); Sergio Bucchi, ed., "Le lezioni sulla democrazia di Gaetano Salvemini," *Archivio Trimestrale*, July–December 1982, 627–650; Alessandro Galante Garrone, *Salvemini e Mazzini* (Messina, 1981); and Leo Valiani, "Salvemini e il socialismo," *La Voce Repubblicana*, December 20–21, 1967, 14–20. Beniamino Finocchiaro, ed., *L'Unità di Gaetano Salvemini* (Venice, 1958) provides a means to understand Salvemini's published views in the pre–World War I era as does Raffaele Colapietra, ed., *Gaetano Salvemini e Molfetta* (Bari, n.d.), on the subject of Salvemini's hometown political socialization.

Several works prove particularly useful in providing understanding of Salvemini as teacher and scholar. They include Giampiero Carocci, "Salvemini e la politica estera del fascismo," *Studi Storici*, 11 (1968), 218–224; Giuseppe Galasso, "Un maestro di moralità,"*La Voce Repubblicana*, December 20–21, 1967; Lamberto Naldini, "Salvemini Maestro a Pisa," *Belfagor* XII (1957), 697– 700; Piero Pieri, "Gaetano Salvemini, Storico dell'età moderna e contemporanea," *Rassegna Storica Toscana* IV (1958), 115–120; Dante Puzzo, "Gaetano Salvemini: A Historiographical Essay," *Journal of the History of Ideas*, 20 (1959), 217–235; Rosario Romeo, "Salvemini storico," *Il Mondo* (Rome), September 24, 1957; Carlo Schiffrer, "Salvemini Maestro," *Trieste Rivista politica giuliana*, 4 (1957), 34–35; and Franco Venturi, "Salvemini storico," *Il Ponte* XIII (1957).

Important studies of Salvemini as anti-Fascist exile include Gaetano Arfe, "Salvemini nella concentrazione antifascista," *Il Ponte* 13 (1957), 1168–1171; Piero Calamandrei, "Il Manganello, la cultura e la giustizia" in Salvemini, Rossi, and Calamandrei, *Non Mollare* (Florence, 1955); Philip Cannistraro, "Understanding America" and Spencer Di Scala, "Salvemini in the United

States" in Di Scala, ed. *Italian Socialism* (Amherst, Mass., 1996), 177–182 and 167–176; Aldo Garosci, *Storia dei fuorusciti* (Bari, 1953); Gian Giacomo Migone, "A proposito de *L'Italia vista dall'America* di Gaetano Salvemini," in his *Problemi di Storia nei rapporti tra l'Italia e Stati Uniti* (Turin, 1971).

Various anthologies and proceedings of conventions provide additional secondary resources. Among them are Alberto Aquarone et al., *Gaetano Salvemini nella cultura e nella politica italiana* (Rome, 1967); Norberto Bobbio et al., *Salvemini: Una vita per la libertà* (Rome, 1971); Roberto Brandi et al., *Atti del Convegno su Gaetano Salvemini* (Milan, 1977); Gaetano Cingari, ed., *Gaetano Salvemini tra politica e storia* (Bari, 1986); Ernesto Sestan, Eugenio Garin, et al., *Gaetano Salvemini* (Bari, 1959); and *Salvemini: Alcuni significanti tributi*, special Salvemini edition of *Controcorrente* (Boston), 1958.

Finally, several good bibliographies exist that facilitate any study of modern Italian history such as this and provide, at the same time, the means to further inquiry into the many historical topics relating indirectly to Salvemini's life. Among the best are Frank Coppa and William Roberts, *Modern Italian History: An Annotated Bibliography* (New York, 1990); Charles Delzell, *Italy in the Twentieth Century* (Washington, DC, 1980); Clara Lovett, *Contemporary Italy: A Selective Bibliography* (Washington, DC, 1985); and the excellent bibliography included in Spencer Di Scala's *Italy From Revolution to Republic*, 2nd. ed. (Boulder, 1998).

Index

About the Author

CHARLES KILLINGER is a professor of history at Valencia Community College.